Find the Beat
Check us o

D0009617

www.shojobeat.com!

Tell us what you think about Shojo Beat Manga!

Our survey is now available online. Go to:

shojobeat.com/mangasurvey

Help us make our product offerings better!

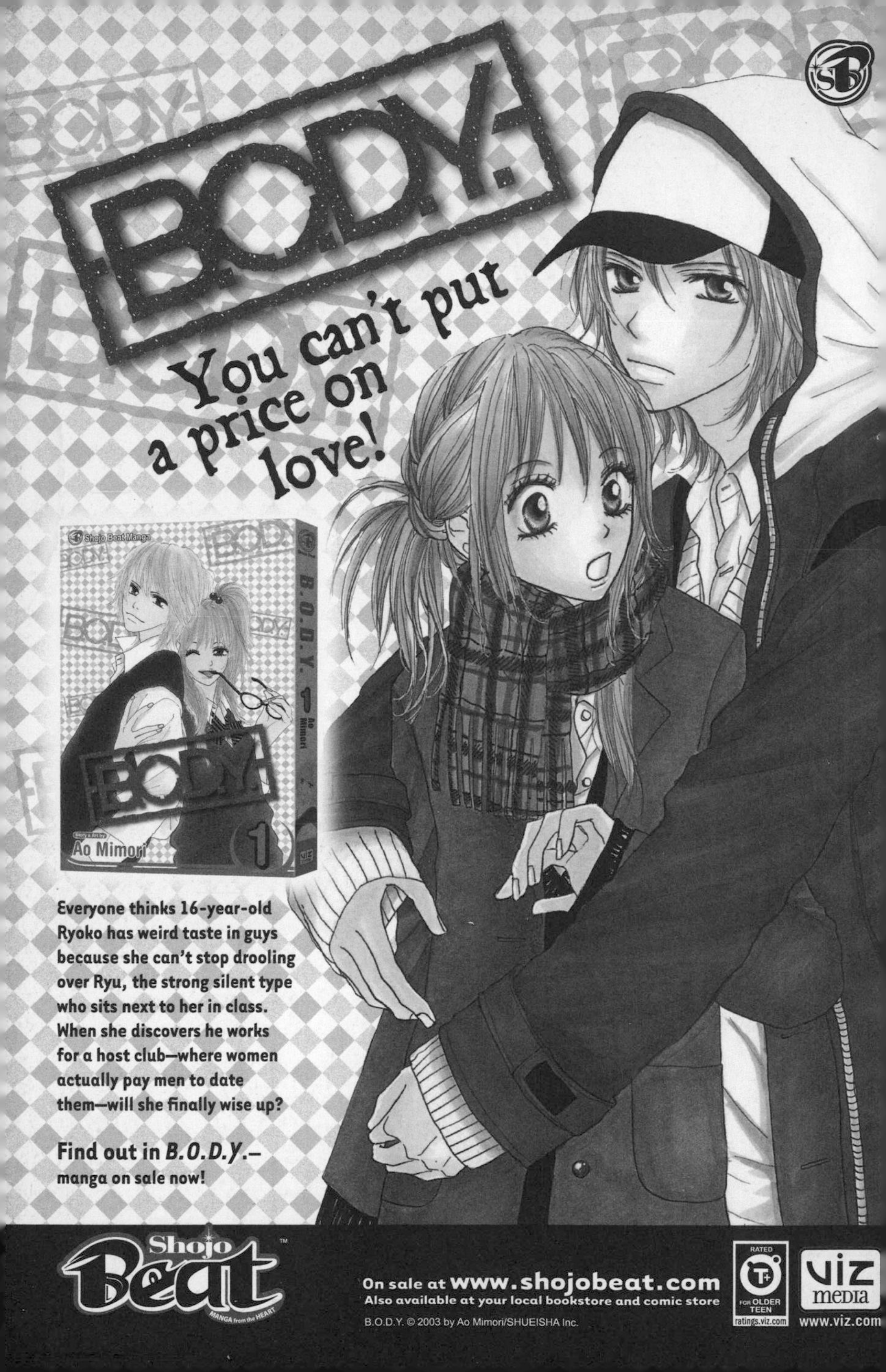
B.O.D.Y.
You can't put a price on love!
Shojo Beat Manga
B.O.D.Y.
1
Ao Mimori
Story & Art by
Ao Mimori
Everyone thinks 16-year-old Ryoko has weird taste in guys because she can't stop drooling over Ryu, the strong silent type who sits next to her in class. When she discovers he works for a host club—where women actually pay men to date them—will she finally wise up?
Find out in B.O.D.Y.—manga on sale now!
Shojo Beat
MANGA from the HEART
On sale at www.shojobeat.com
Also available at your local bookstore and comic store
B.O.D.Y. © 2003 by Ao Mimori/SHUEISHA Inc.
RATED T+ FOR OLDER TEEN
ratings.viz.com
VIZ media
www.viz.com

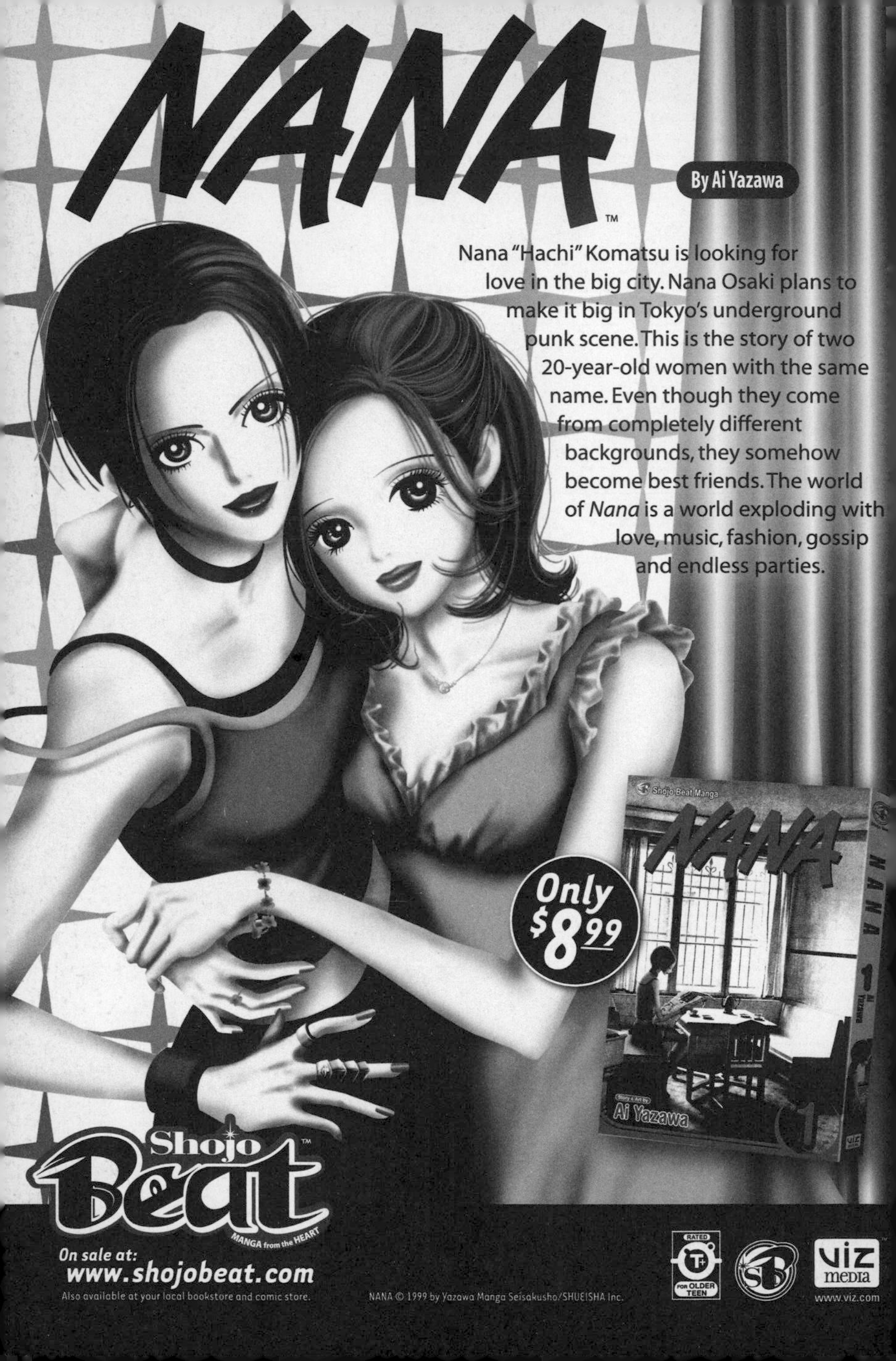
NANA™
By Ai Yazawa
Nana "Hachi" Komatsu is looking for love in the big city. Nana Osaki plans to make it big in Tokyo's underground punk scene. This is the story of two 20-year-old women with the same name. Even though they come from completely different backgrounds, they somehow become best friends. The world of *Nana* is a world exploding with love, music, fashion, gossip and endless parties.
Shojo Beat Manga
NANA
Story & Art by
Ai Yazawa
1
Only $8.99
Shojo Beat™
MANGA from the HEART
On sale at:
www.shojobeat.com
Also available at your local bookstore and comic store.
NANA © 1999 by Yazawa Manga Seisakusho/SHUEISHA Inc.
RATED T+ FOR OLDER TEEN
viz media
www.viz.com

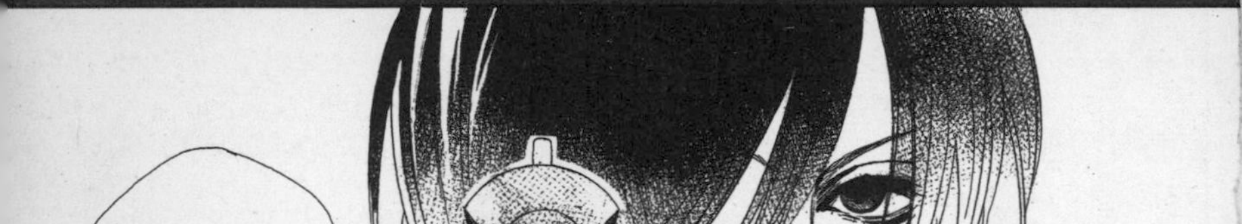
UNLESS YOU WANT TO DIE.

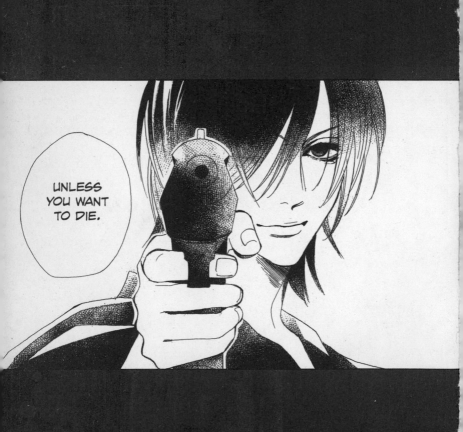

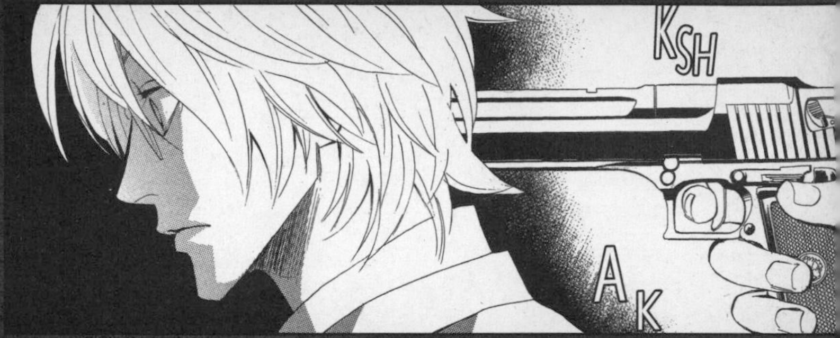
KSH
AK

Shojo Beat

BLANK SLATE

Vol. 1

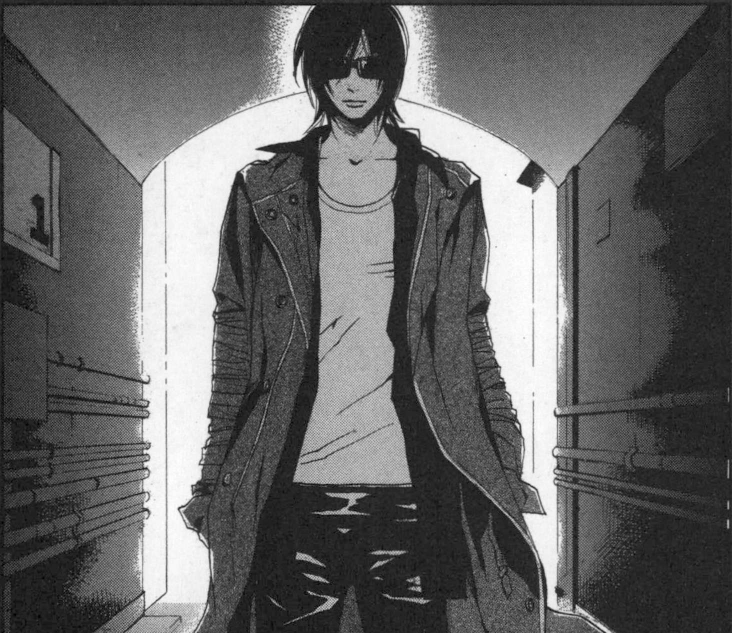

Story & Art by Aya Kanno

Vol. 1

Contents

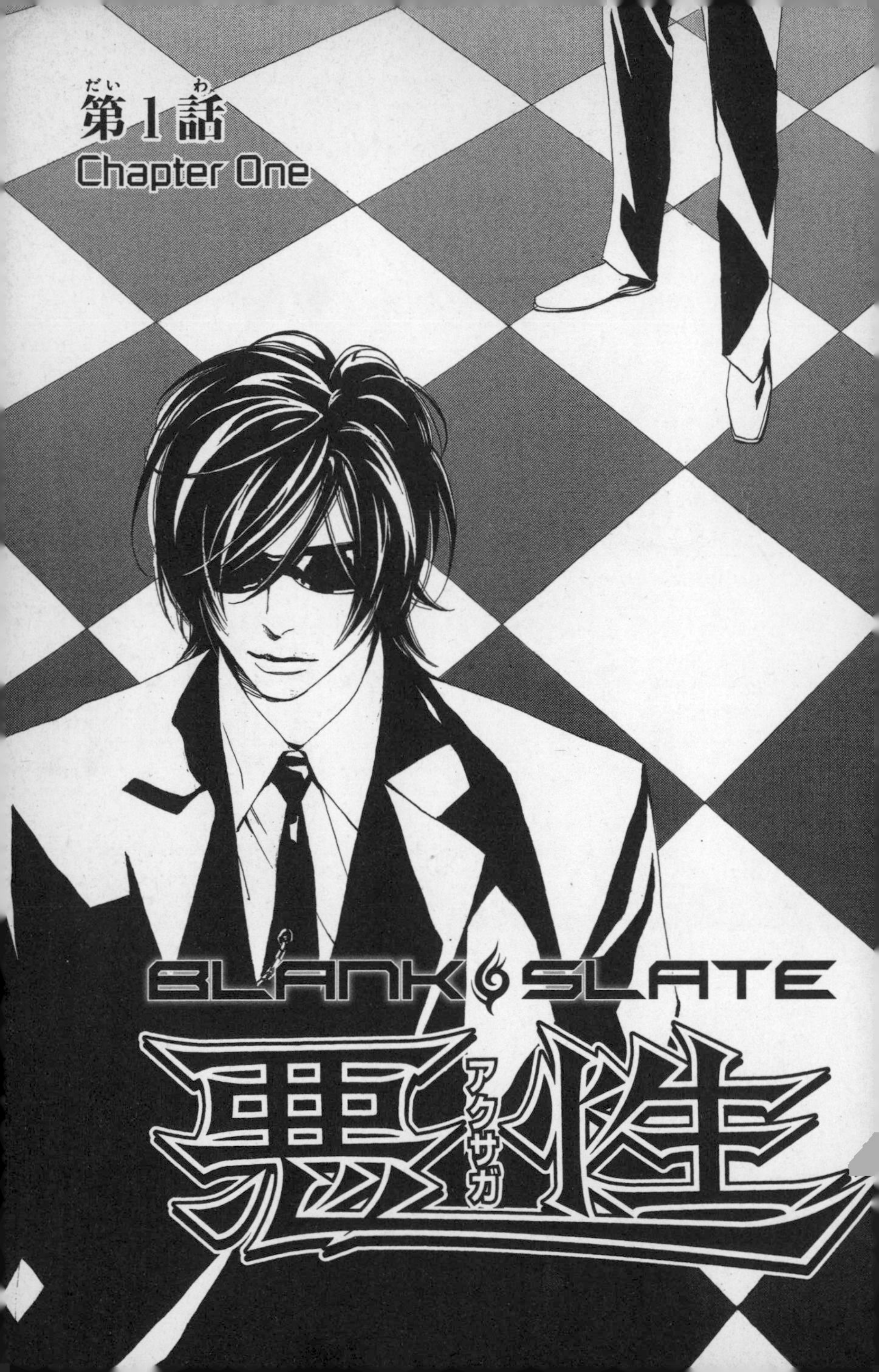
第1話
Chapter One
BLANK SLATE
悪性
アクサガ

Another time, another world...

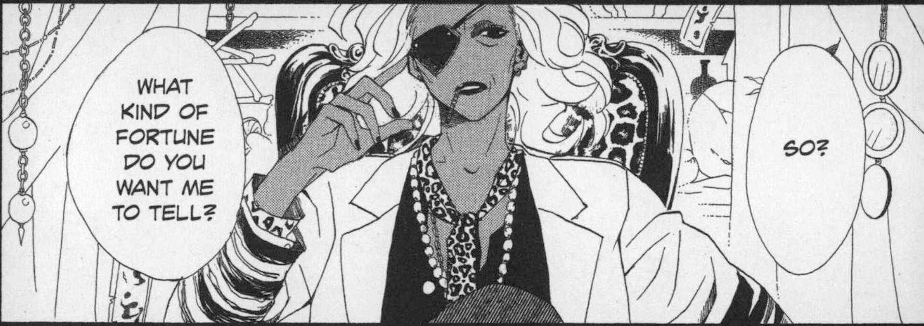
SO?
WHAT KIND OF FORTUNE DO YOU WANT ME TO TELL?

The story of a man...

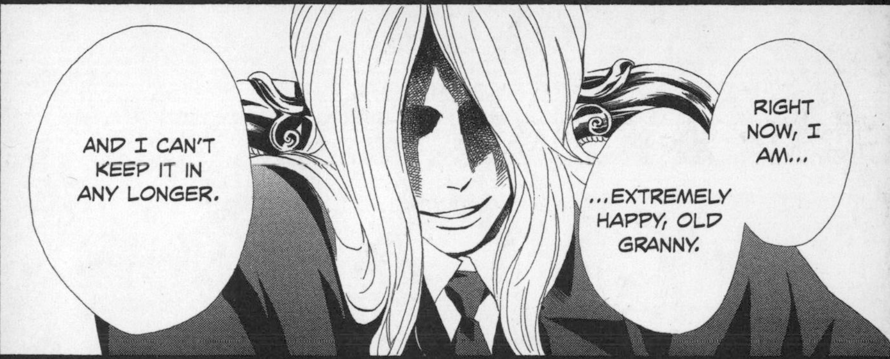
RIGHT NOW, I AM...
...EXTREMELY HAPPY, OLD GRANNY.
AND I CAN'T KEEP IT IN ANY LONGER.

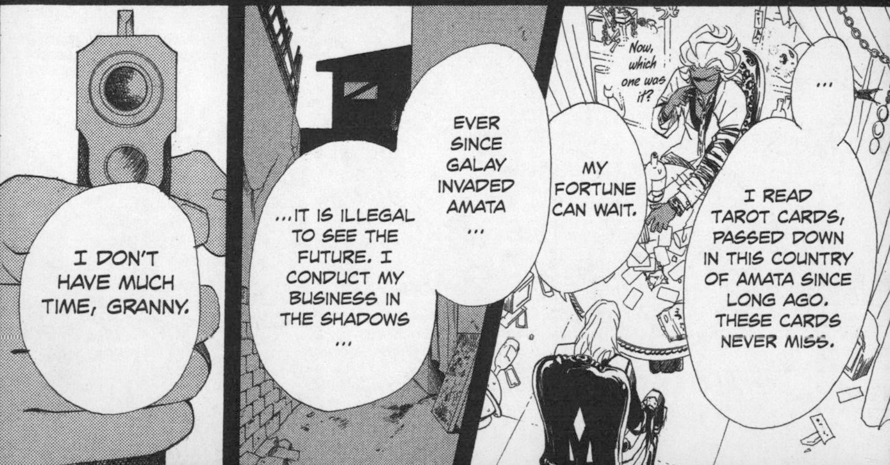
...
Now, which one was it?
I READ TAROT CARDS, PASSED DOWN IN THIS COUNTRY OF AMATA SINCE LONG AGO. THESE CARDS NEVER MISS.
MY FORTUNE CAN WAIT.
EVER SINCE GALAY INVADED AMATA ...
...IT IS ILLEGAL TO SEE THE FUTURE. I CONDUCT MY BUSINESS IN THE SHADOWS ...
I DON'T HAVE MUCH TIME, GRANNY.

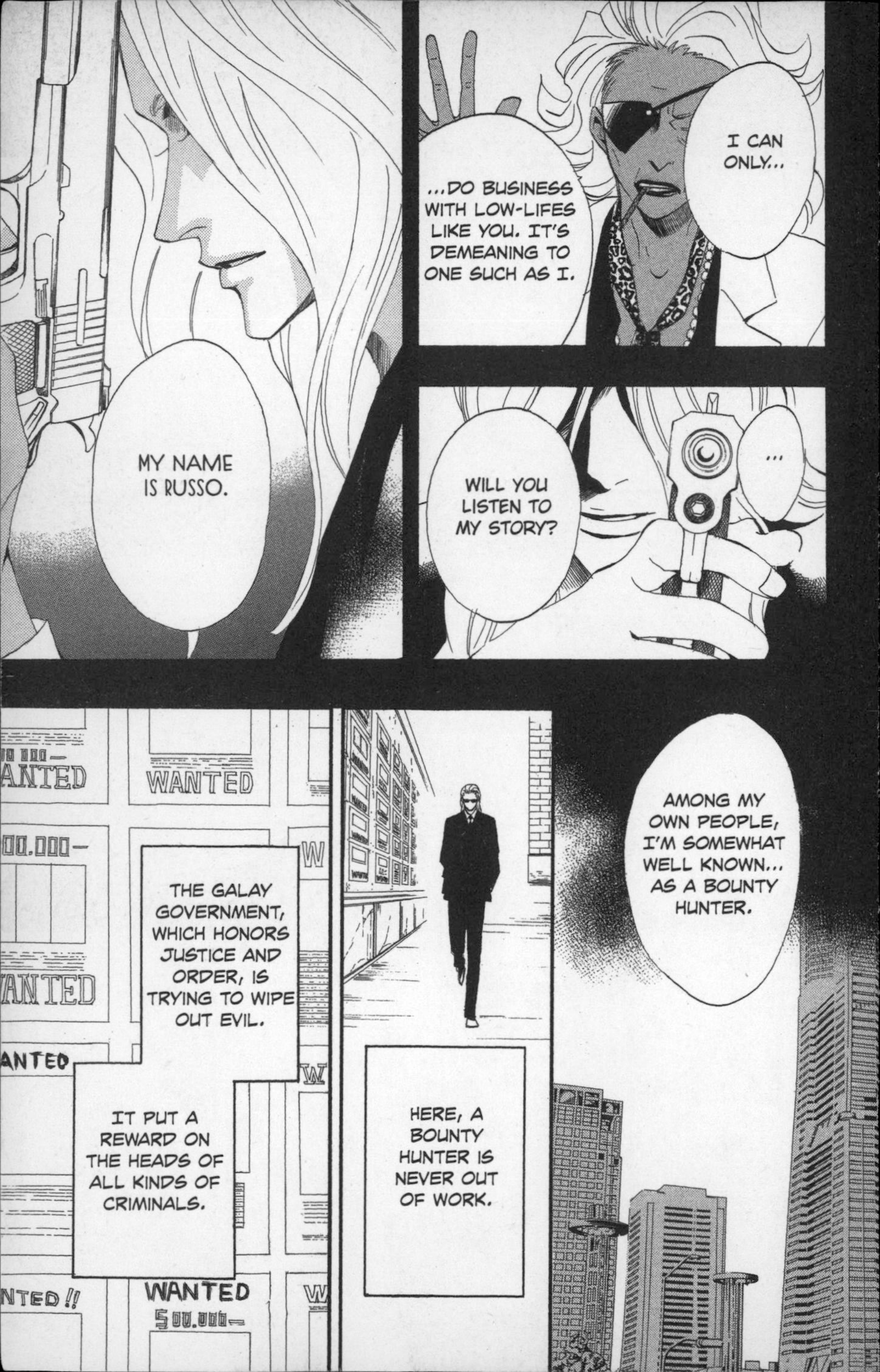
I CAN ONLY...
...DO BUSINESS WITH LOW-LIFES LIKE YOU. IT'S DEMEANING TO ONE SUCH AS I.
...
WILL YOU LISTEN TO MY STORY?
MY NAME IS RUSSO.
AMONG MY OWN PEOPLE, I'M SOMEWHAT WELL KNOWN... AS A BOUNTY HUNTER.
HERE, A BOUNTY HUNTER IS NEVER OUT OF WORK.
THE GALAY GOVERNMENT, WHICH HONORS JUSTICE AND ORDER, IS TRYING TO WIPE OUT EVIL.
IT PUT A REWARD ON THE HEADS OF ALL KINDS OF CRIMINALS.

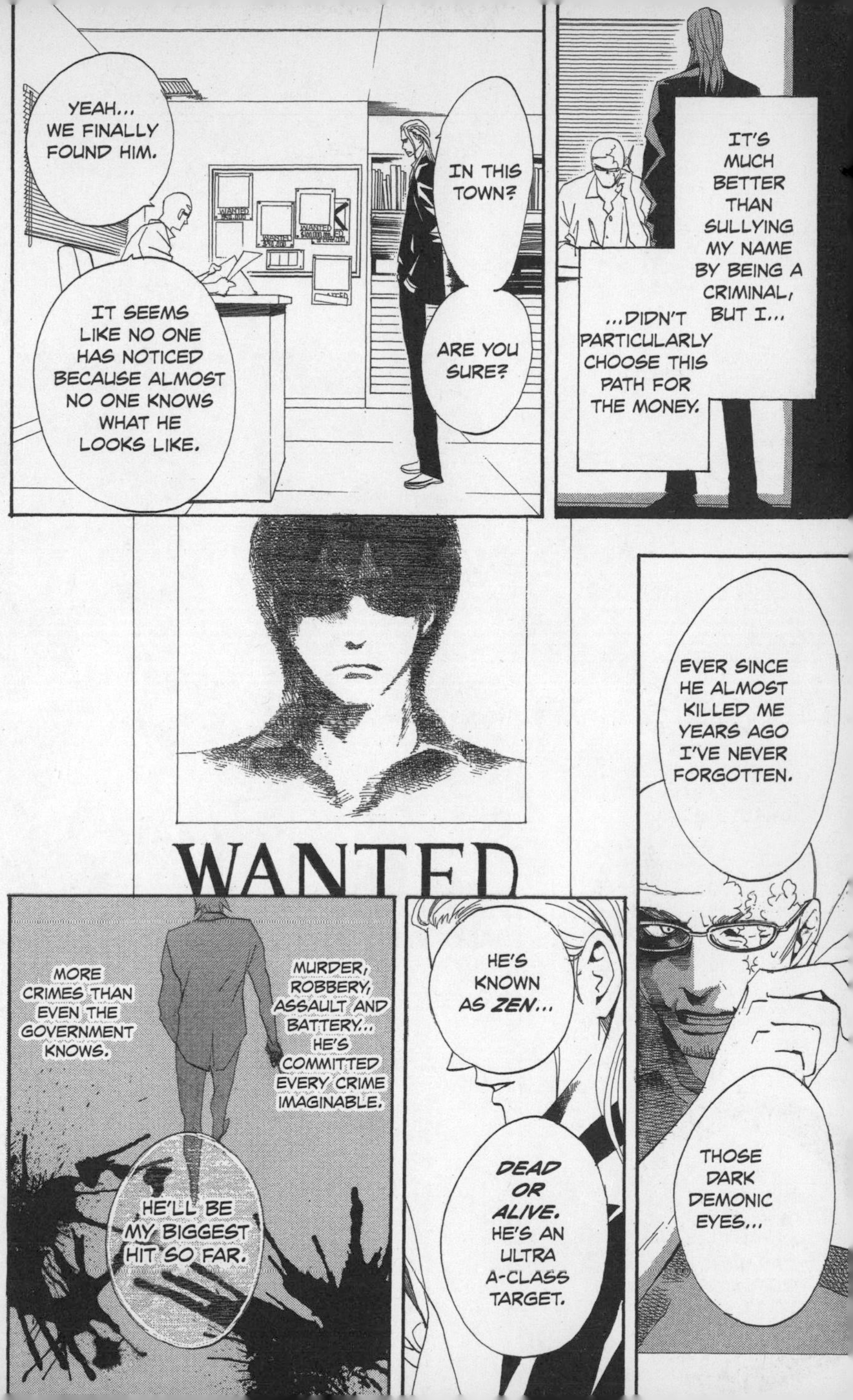
IT'S MUCH BETTER THAN SULLYING MY NAME BY BEING A CRIMINAL, BUT I...
...DIDN'T PARTICULARLY CHOOSE THIS PATH FOR THE MONEY.
IN THIS TOWN?
ARE YOU SURE?
YEAH... WE FINALLY FOUND HIM.
IT SEEMS LIKE NO ONE HAS NOTICED BECAUSE ALMOST NO ONE KNOWS WHAT HE LOOKS LIKE.
EVER SINCE HE ALMOST KILLED ME YEARS AGO I'VE NEVER FORGOTTEN.
THOSE DARK DEMONIC EYES...
WANTED
HE'S KNOWN AS *ZEN*...
DEAD OR ALIVE. HE'S AN ULTRA A-CLASS TARGET.
MURDER, ROBBERY, ASSAULT AND BATTERY... HE'S COMMITTED EVERY CRIME IMAGINABLE.
MORE CRIMES THAN EVEN THE GOVERNMENT KNOWS.
HE'LL BE MY BIGGEST HIT SO FAR.

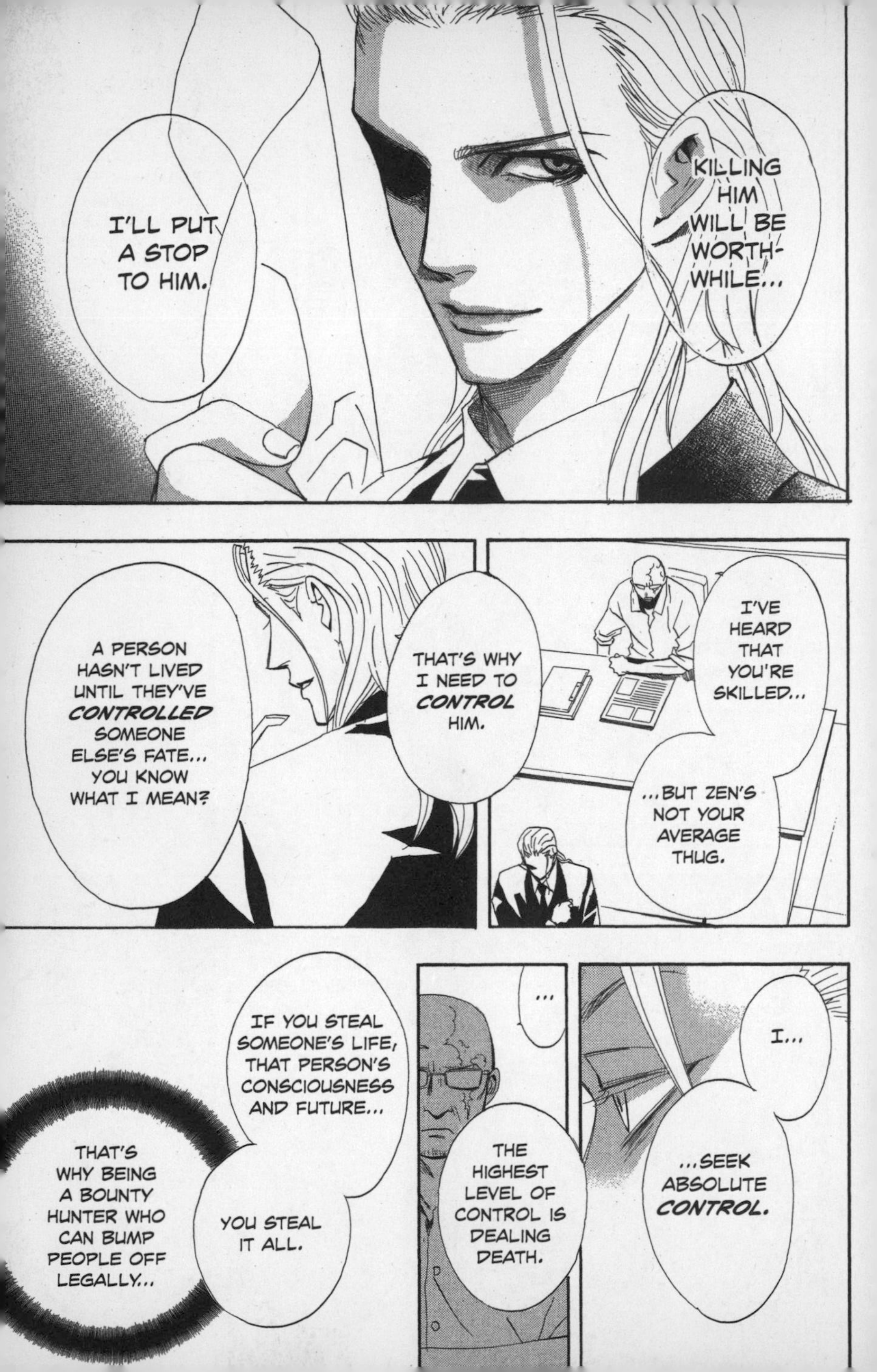
KILLING HIM WILL BE WORTH-WHILE...
I'LL PUT A STOP TO HIM.
I'VE HEARD THAT YOU'RE SKILLED...
...BUT ZEN'S NOT YOUR AVERAGE THUG.
THAT'S WHY I NEED TO *CONTROL* HIM.
A PERSON HASN'T LIVED UNTIL THEY'VE *CONTROLLED* SOMEONE ELSE'S FATE... YOU KNOW WHAT I MEAN?
I...
...SEEK ABSOLUTE *CONTROL.*
...
THE HIGHEST LEVEL OF CONTROL IS DEALING DEATH.
IF YOU STEAL SOMEONE'S LIFE, THAT PERSON'S CONSCIOUSNESS AND FUTURE...
YOU STEAL IT ALL.
THAT'S WHY BEING A BOUNTY HUNTER WHO CAN BUMP PEOPLE OFF LEGALLY...

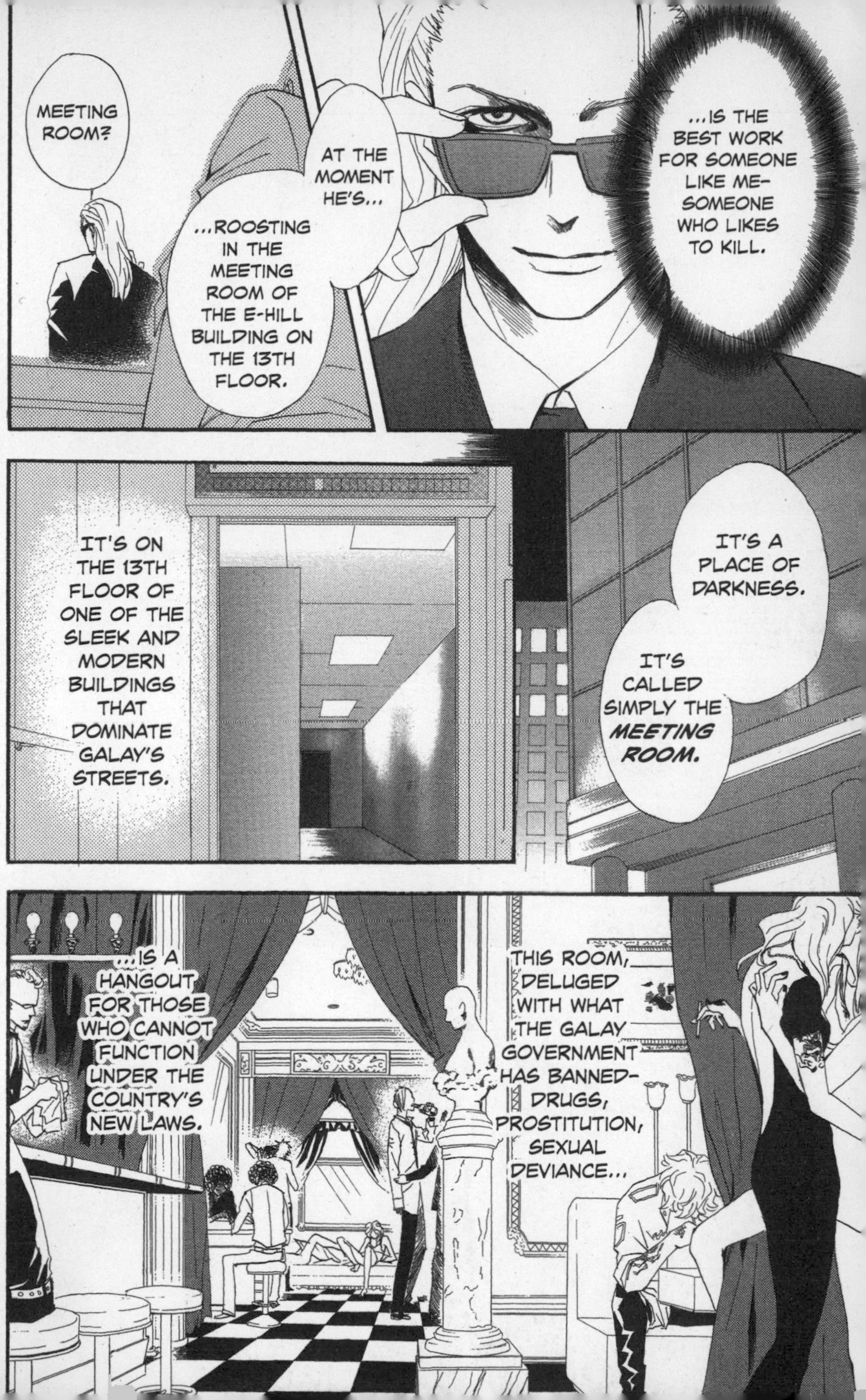
...IS THE BEST WORK FOR SOMEONE LIKE ME- SOMEONE WHO LIKES TO KILL.
AT THE MOMENT HE'S...
...ROOSTING IN THE MEETING ROOM OF THE E-HILL BUILDING ON THE 13TH FLOOR.
MEETING ROOM?
IT'S A PLACE OF DARKNESS.
IT'S CALLED SIMPLY THE *MEETING ROOM.*
IT'S ON THE 13TH FLOOR OF ONE OF THE SLEEK AND MODERN BUILDINGS THAT DOMINATE GALAY'S STREETS.
THIS ROOM, DELUGED WITH WHAT THE GALAY GOVERNMENT HAS BANNED- DRUGS, PROSTITUTION, SEXUAL DEVIANCE...
...IS A HANGOUT FOR THOSE WHO CANNOT FUNCTION UNDER THE COUNTRY'S NEW LAWS.

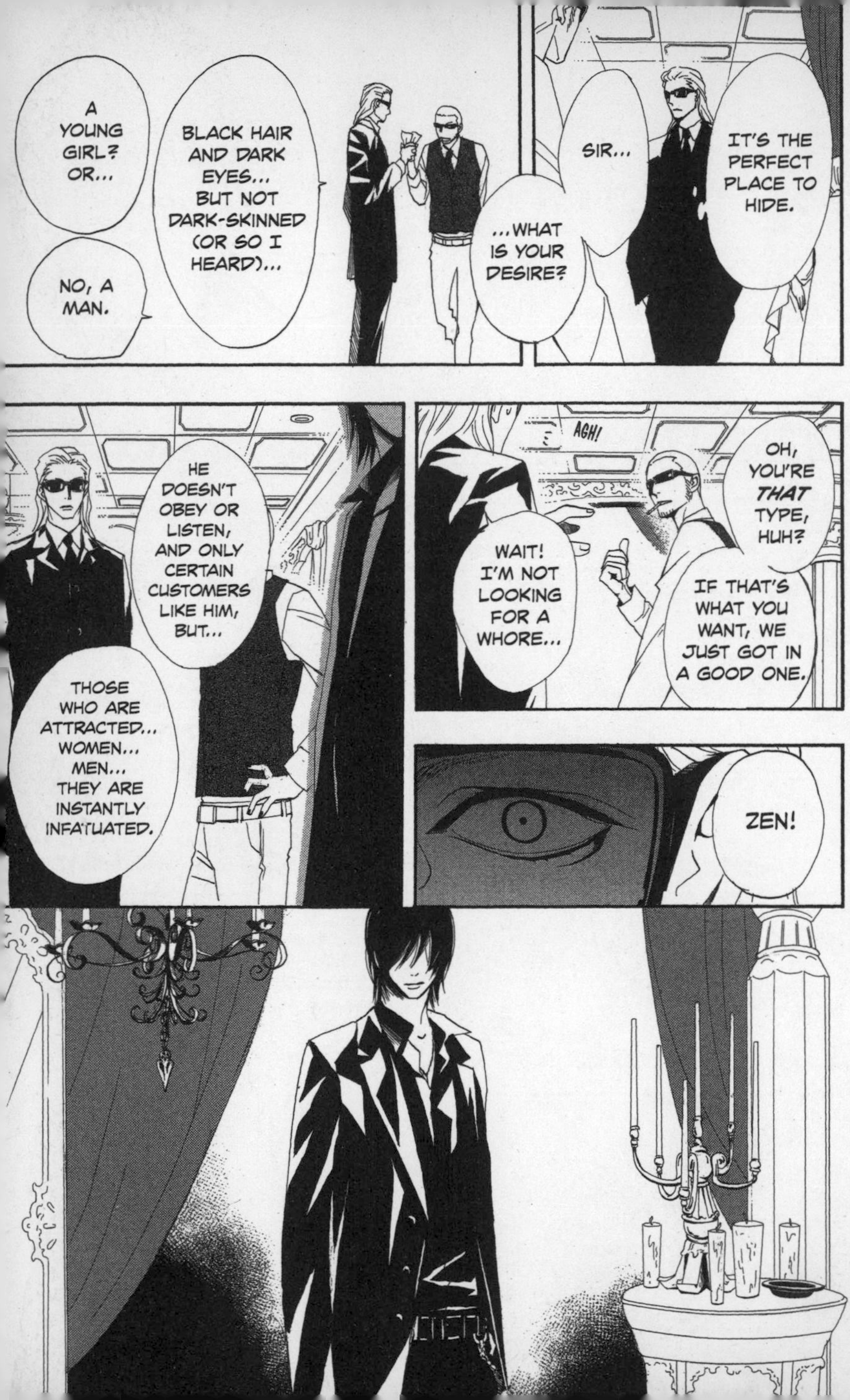
IT'S THE PERFECT PLACE TO HIDE.
SIR...
...WHAT IS YOUR DESIRE?
BLACK HAIR AND DARK EYES... BUT NOT DARK-SKINNED (OR SO I HEARD)...
A YOUNG GIRL? OR...
NO, A MAN.
OH, YOU'RE *THAT* TYPE, HUH?
AGH!
IF THAT'S WHAT YOU WANT, WE JUST GOT IN A GOOD ONE.
WAIT! I'M NOT LOOKING FOR A WHORE...
ZEN!
HE DOESN'T OBEY OR LISTEN, AND ONLY CERTAIN CUSTOMERS LIKE HIM, BUT...
THOSE WHO ARE ATTRACTED... WOMEN... MEN... THEY ARE INSTANTLY INFATUATED.

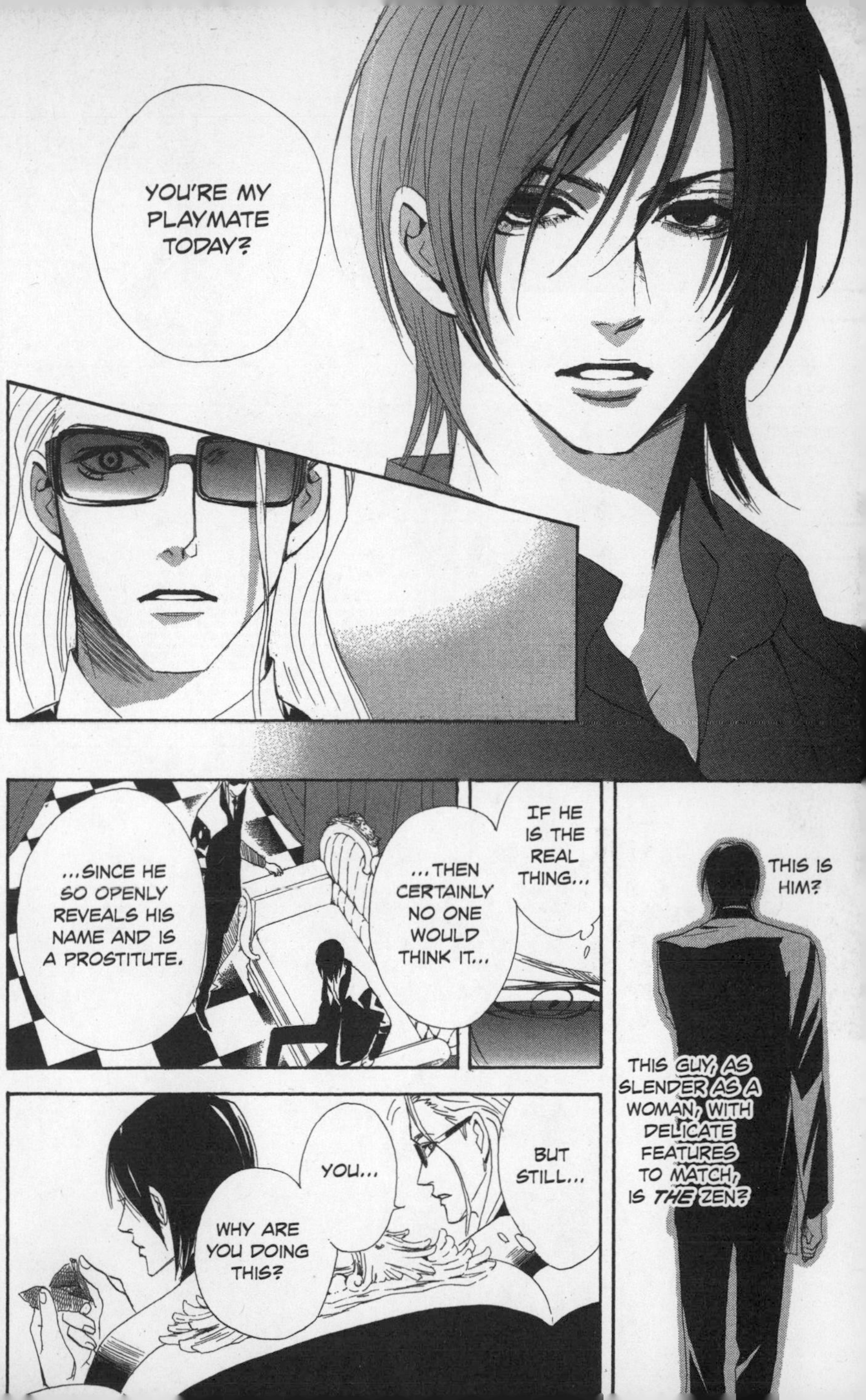
YOU'RE MY PLAYMATE TODAY?
THIS IS HIM?
THIS GUY, AS SLENDER AS A WOMAN, WITH DELICATE FEATURES TO MATCH, IS *THE* ZEN?
IF HE IS THE REAL THING...
...THEN CERTAINLY NO ONE WOULD THINK IT...
...SINCE HE SO OPENLY REVEALS HIS NAME AND IS A PROSTITUTE.
BUT STILL...
YOU...
WHY ARE YOU DOING THIS?

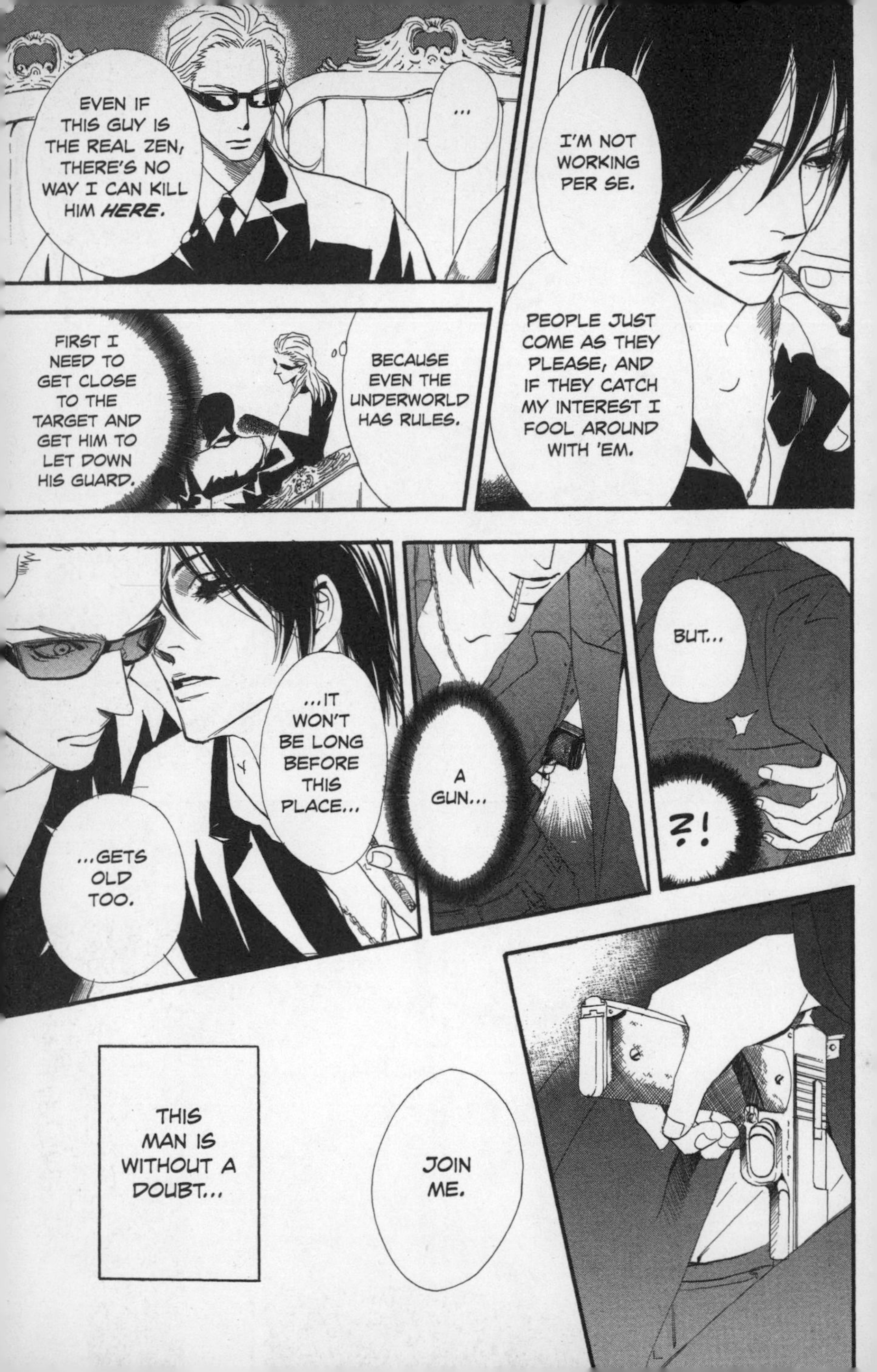
I'M NOT WORKING PER SE.
PEOPLE JUST COME AS THEY PLEASE, AND IF THEY CATCH MY INTEREST I FOOL AROUND WITH 'EM.
...
EVEN IF THIS GUY IS THE REAL ZEN, THERE'S NO WAY I CAN KILL HIM *HERE.*
BECAUSE EVEN THE UNDERWORLD HAS RULES.
FIRST I NEED TO GET CLOSE TO THE TARGET AND GET HIM TO LET DOWN HIS GUARD.
BUT...
?!
A GUN...
...IT WON'T BE LONG BEFORE THIS PLACE...
...GETS OLD TOO.
JOIN ME.
THIS MAN IS WITHOUT A DOUBT...

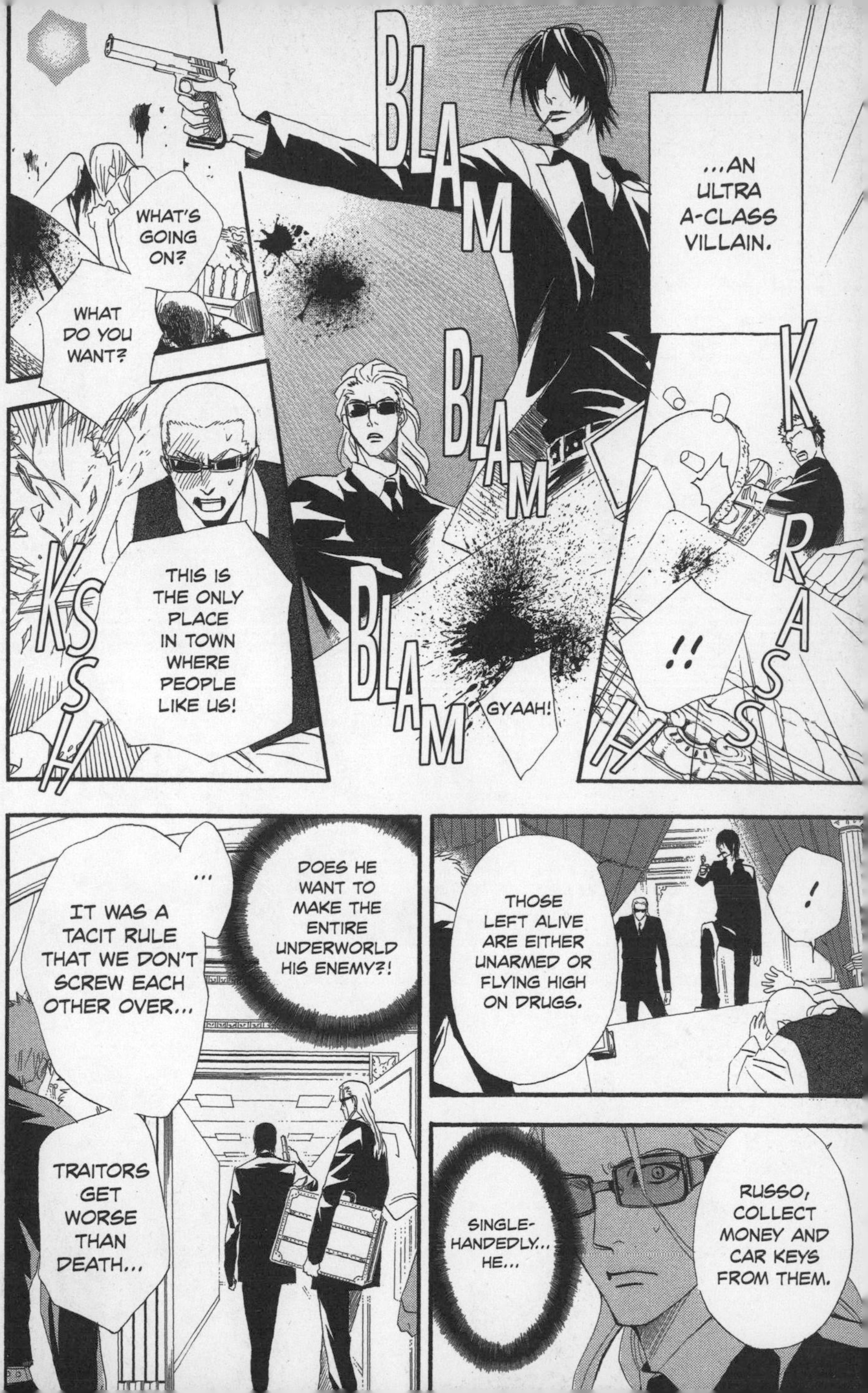
...AN ULTRA A-CLASS VILLAIN.
BLAM
BLAM
WHAT'S GOING ON?
WHAT DO YOU WANT?
KRASSH
!!
BLAM
GYAAH!
KSSH
THIS IS THE ONLY PLACE IN TOWN WHERE PEOPLE LIKE US!
!
THOSE LEFT ALIVE ARE EITHER UNARMED OR FLYING HIGH ON DRUGS.
RUSSO, COLLECT MONEY AND CAR KEYS FROM THEM.
SINGLE-HANDEDLY... HE...
DOES HE WANT TO MAKE THE ENTIRE UNDERWORLD HIS ENEMY?!
...
IT WAS A TACIT RULE THAT WE DON'T SCREW EACH OTHER OVER...
TRAITORS GET WORSE THAN DEATH...

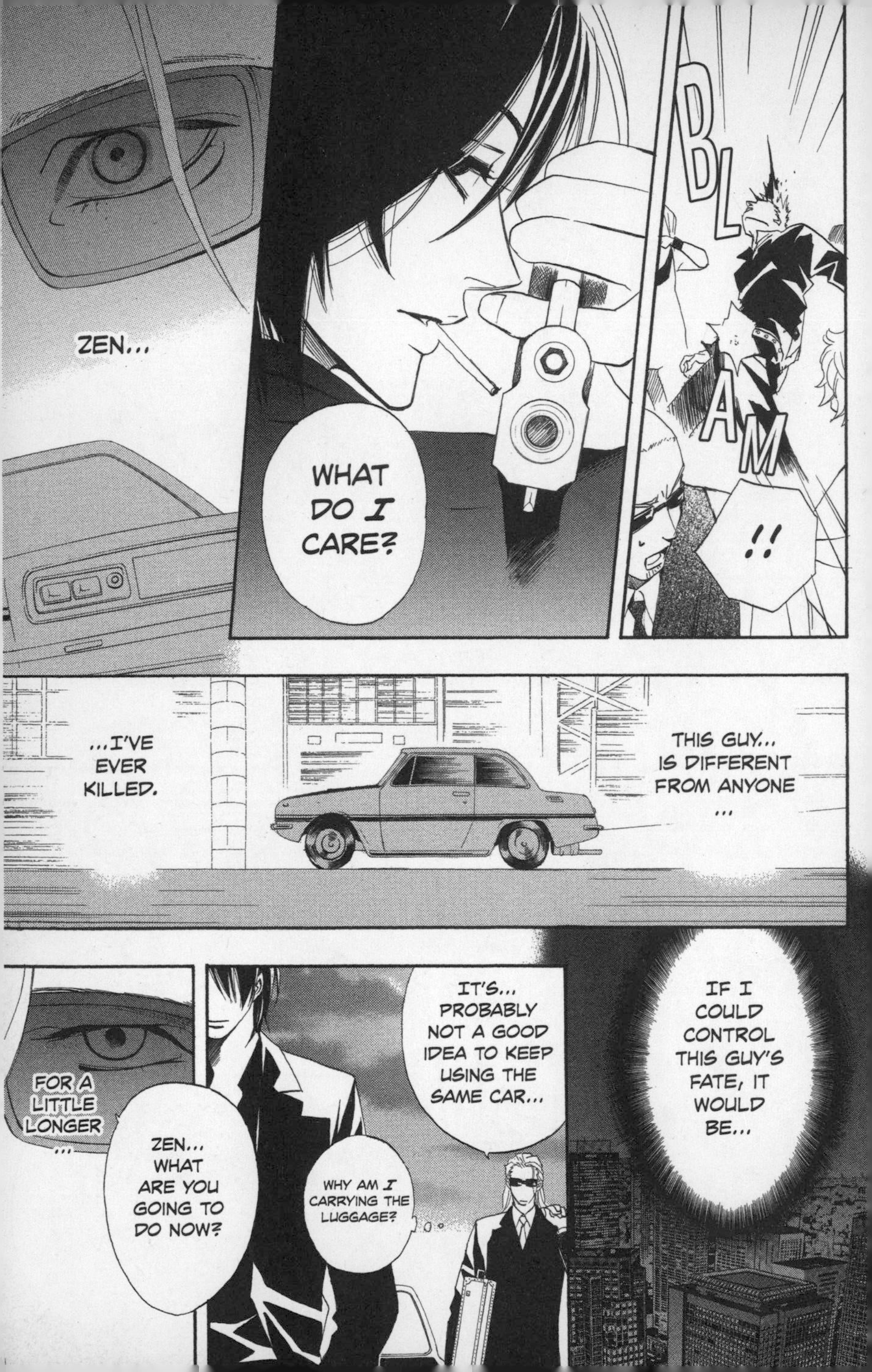
BLAM
!!
WHAT DO I CARE?
ZEN...
THIS GUY... IS DIFFERENT FROM ANYONE ...
...I'VE EVER KILLED.
IF I COULD CONTROL THIS GUY'S FATE, IT WOULD BE...
IT'S... PROBABLY NOT A GOOD IDEA TO KEEP USING THE SAME CAR...
ZEN... WHAT ARE YOU GOING TO DO NOW?
WHY AM I CARRYING THE LUGGAGE?
FOR A LITTLE LONGER ...

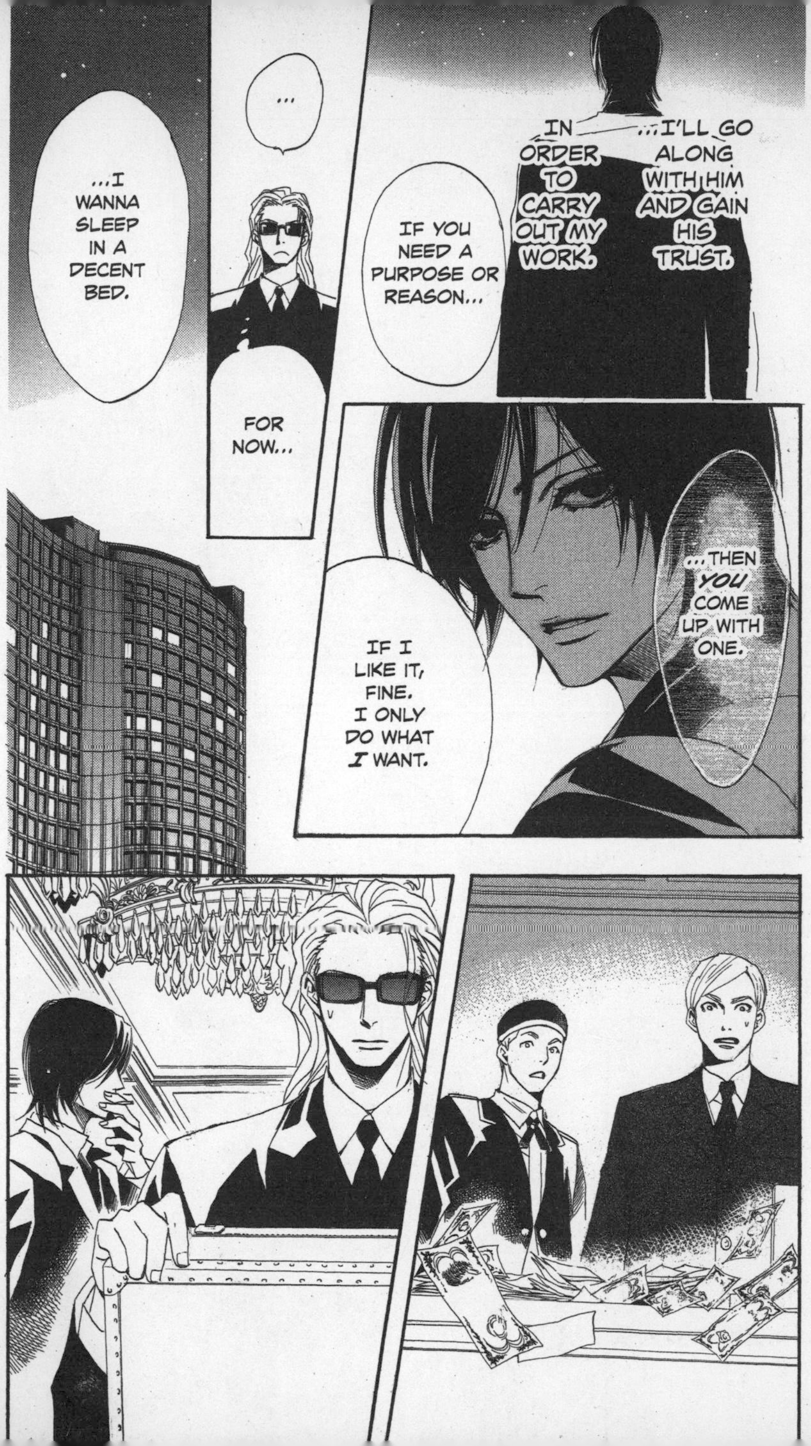

...I'LL GO ALONG WITH HIM AND GAIN HIS TRUST.
IN ORDER TO CARRY OUT MY WORK.
IF YOU NEED A PURPOSE OR REASON...
...THEN *YOU* COME UP WITH ONE.
IF I LIKE IT, FINE. I ONLY DO WHAT *I* WANT.
...
FOR NOW...
...I WANNA SLEEP IN A DECENT BED.

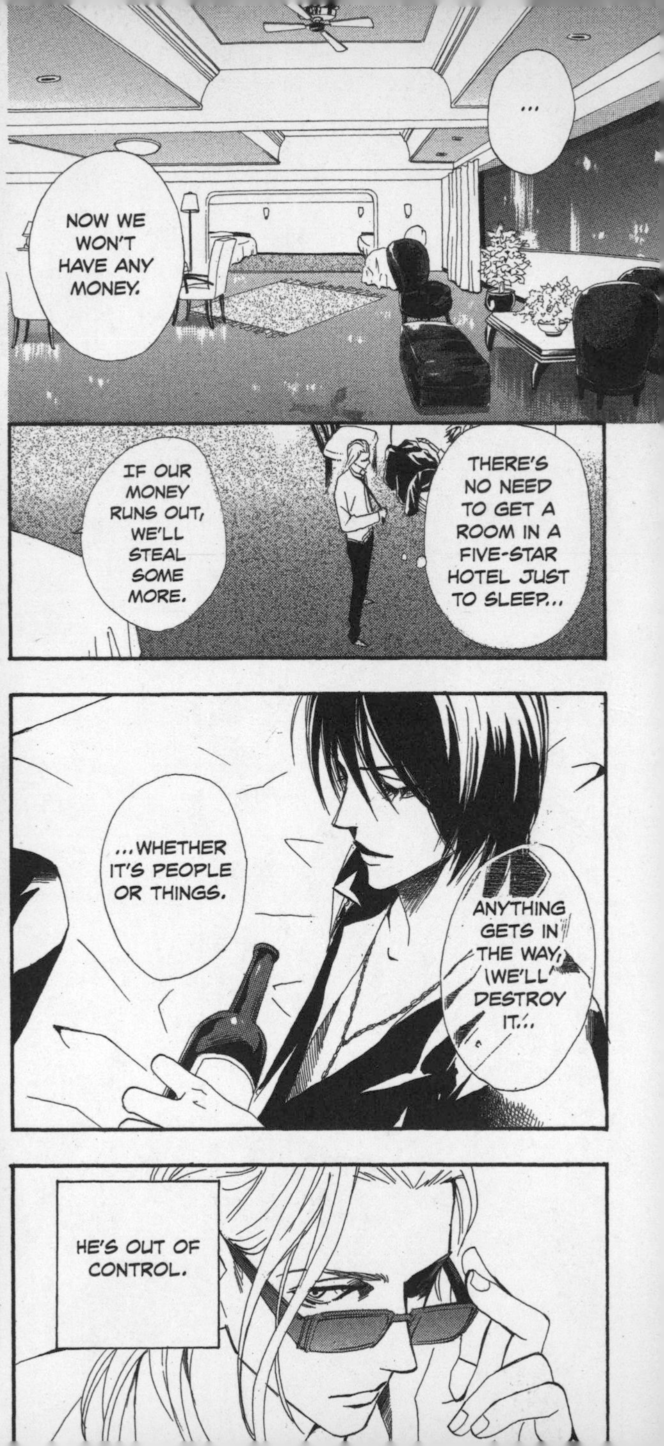
...
NOW WE WON'T HAVE ANY MONEY.
THERE'S NO NEED TO GET A ROOM IN A FIVE-STAR HOTEL JUST TO SLEEP...
IF OUR MONEY RUNS OUT, WE'LL STEAL SOME MORE.
ANYTHING GETS IN THE WAY, WE'LL DESTROY IT...
...WHETHER IT'S PEOPLE OR THINGS.
HE'S OUT OF CONTROL.

1

It's nice to meet you...

Or...hello.

This is Aya Kanno.

First of all, I need to apologize for something. Those of you who read *Blank Slate* when it was running in the magazine may have already noticed, but the Chapter 1 from that time has not been included in this graphic novel. Instead, Chapter 4 of the bonus episodes has been included as Chapter 1. This isn't a mistake, it was something I wanted. I'm terribly sorry to those of you who read the magazine, but I hope you will understand... I'll talk about why I did this in the next sidebar.

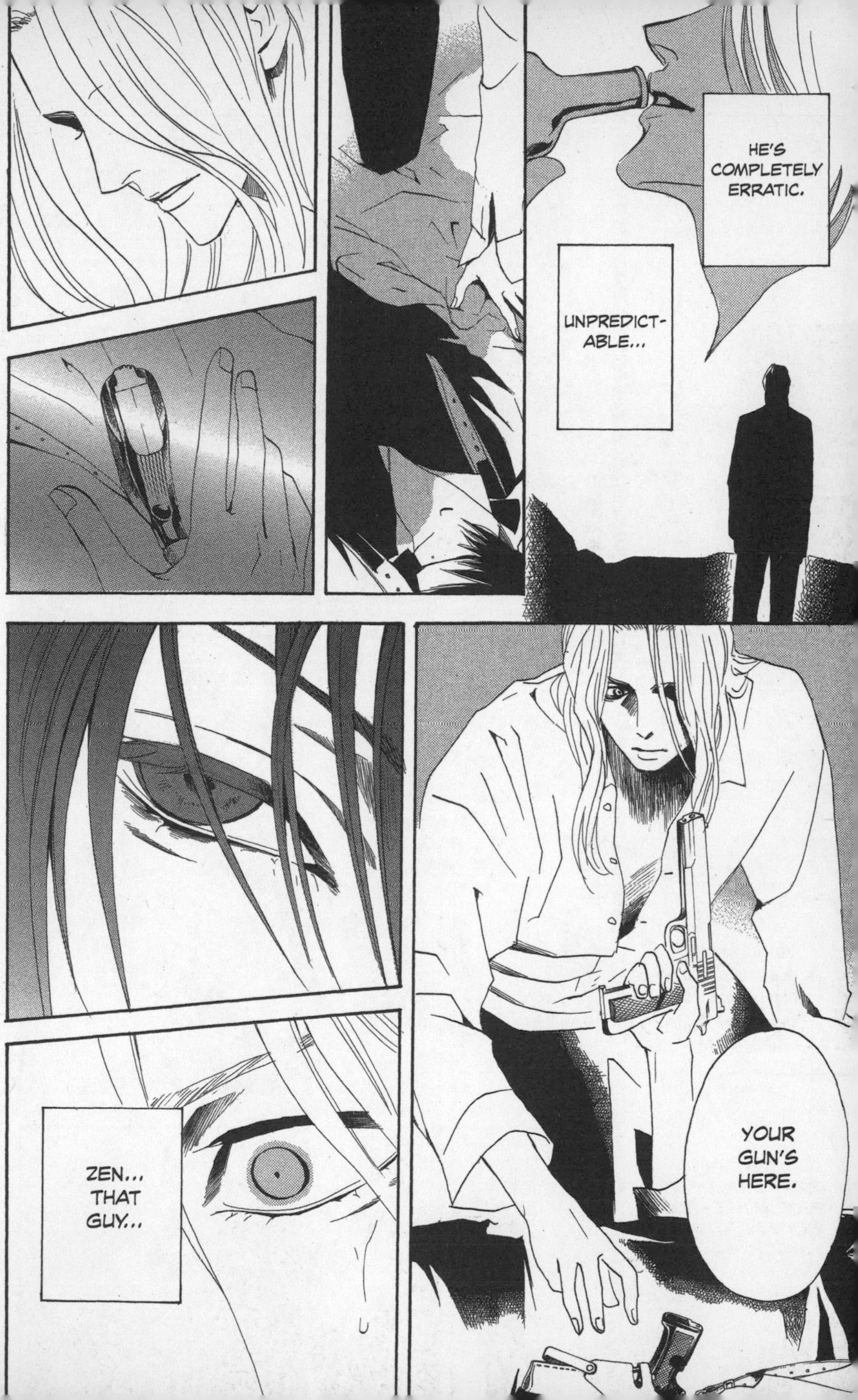
HE'S COMPLETELY ERRATIC.
UNPREDICT-ABLE...
YOUR GUN'S HERE.
ZEN... THAT GUY...

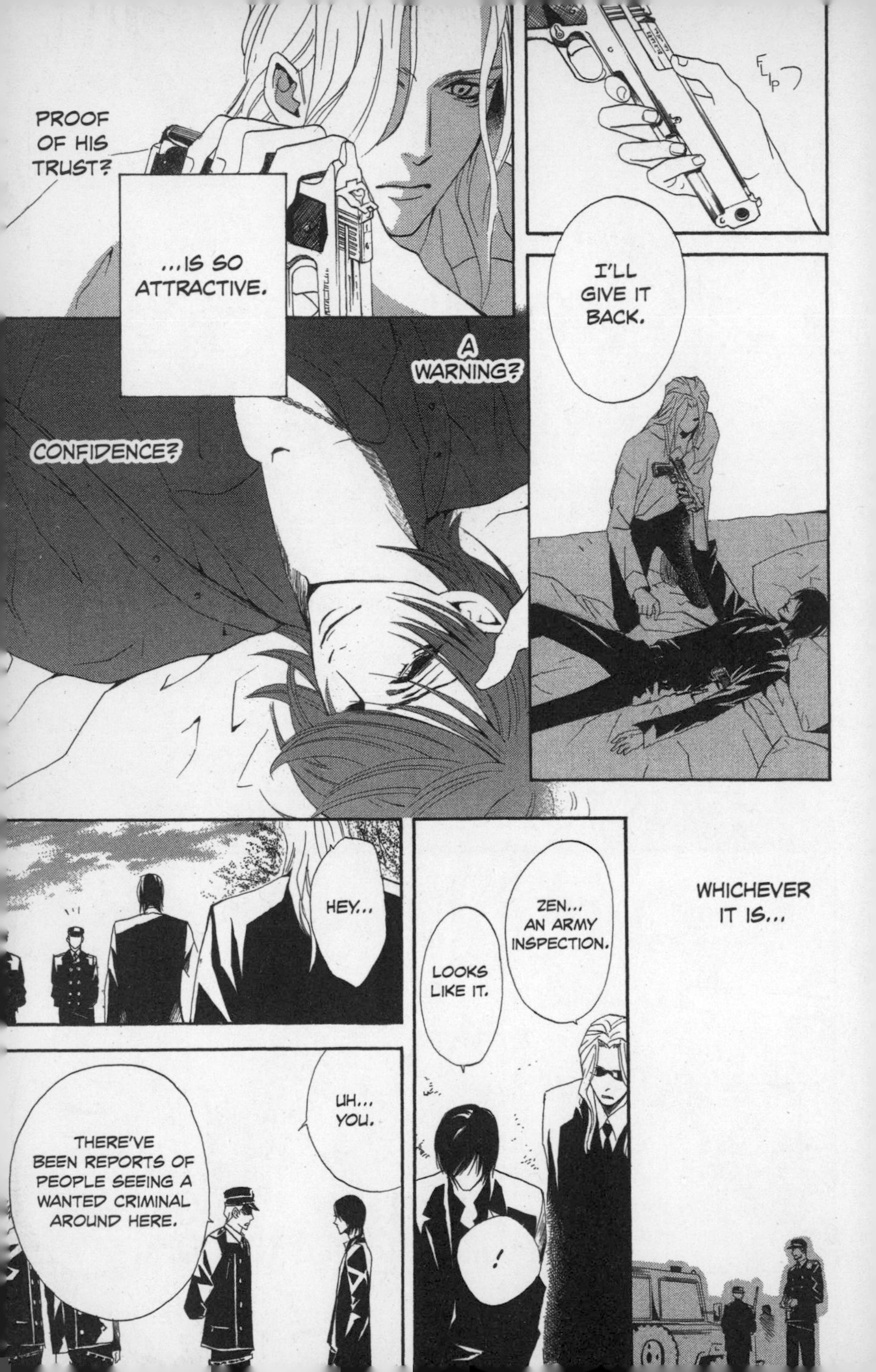
FLIP
I'LL GIVE IT BACK.
PROOF OF HIS TRUST?
A WARNING?
CONFIDENCE?
...IS SO ATTRACTIVE.
WHICHEVER IT IS...
ZEN... AN ARMY INSPECTION.
LOOKS LIKE IT.
!
HEY...
UH... YOU.
THERE'VE BEEN REPORTS OF PEOPLE SEEING A WANTED CRIMINAL AROUND HERE.

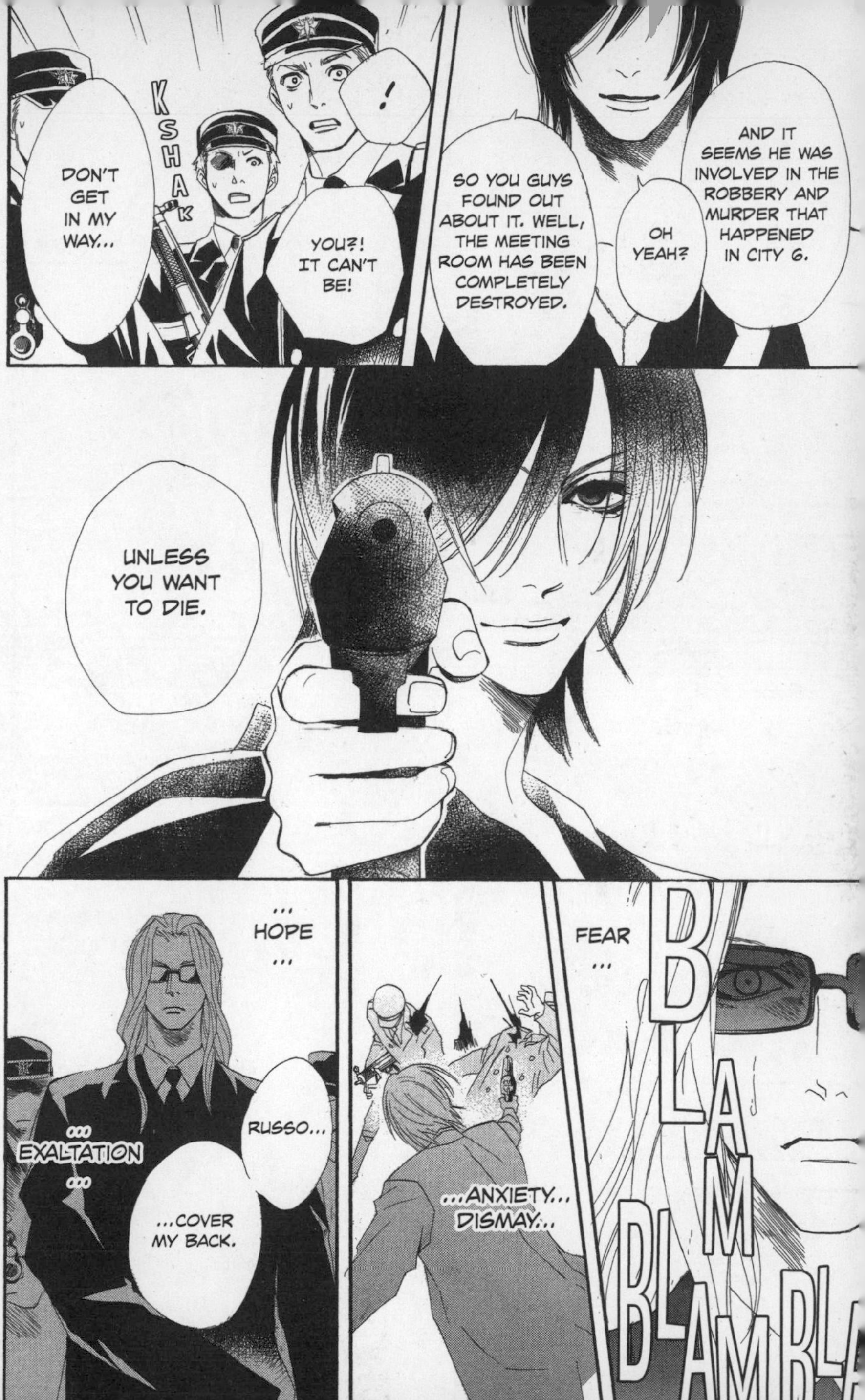
AND IT SEEMS HE WAS INVOLVED IN THE ROBBERY AND MURDER THAT HAPPENED IN CITY 6.
OH YEAH?
SO YOU GUYS FOUND OUT ABOUT IT. WELL, THE MEETING ROOM HAS BEEN COMPLETELY DESTROYED.
!
YOU?! IT CAN'T BE!
KSHAK
DON'T GET IN MY WAY...
UNLESS YOU WANT TO DIE.
BLAM
BLAM BLAM BLA
FEAR...
...ANXIETY... DISMAY...
...HOPE...
RUSSO...
...EXALTATION...
...COVER MY BACK.

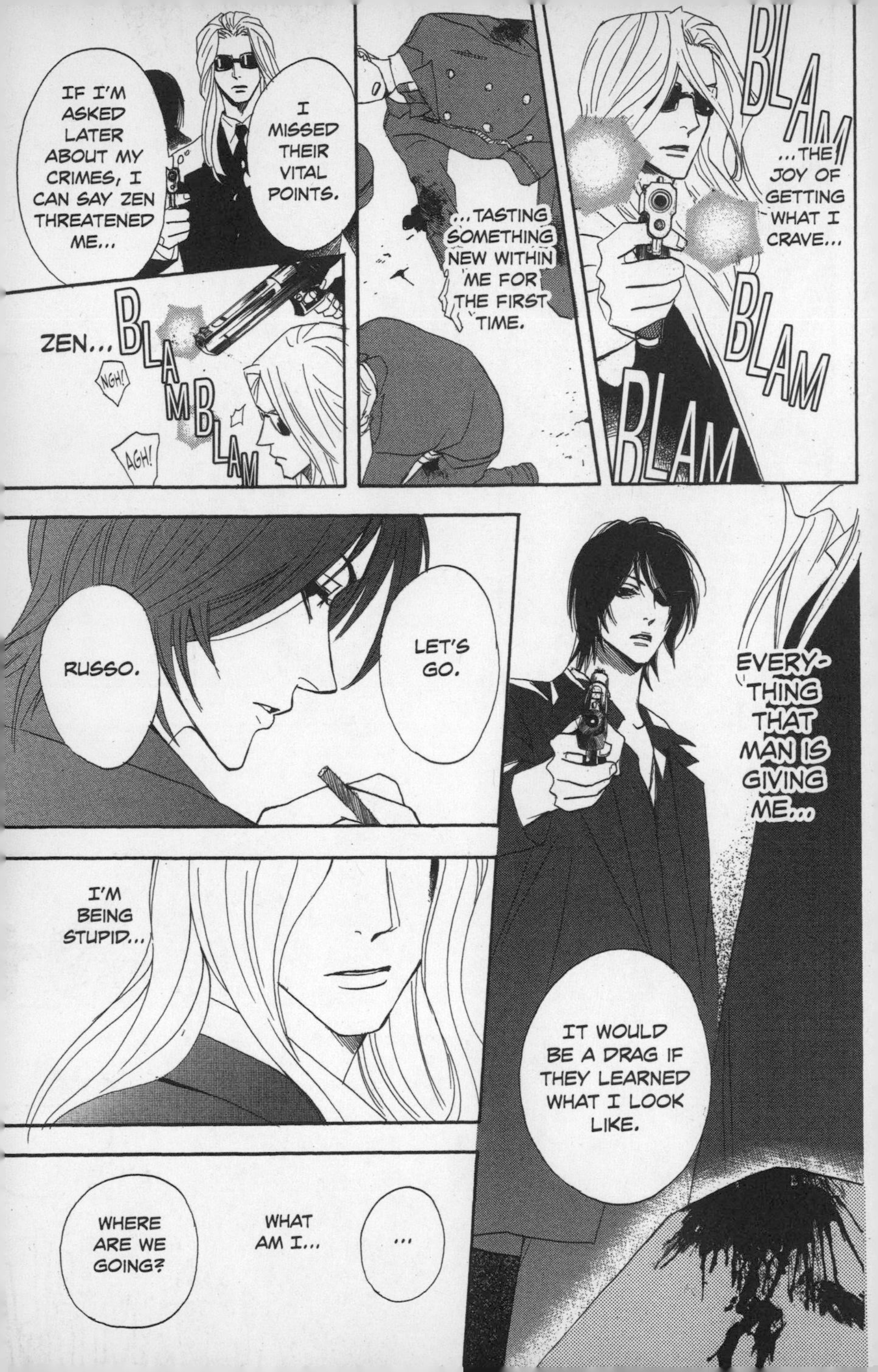
BLAM
...THE JOY OF GETTING WHAT I CRAVE...
BLAM
BLAM
...TASTING SOMETHING NEW WITHIN ME FOR THE FIRST TIME.
I MISSED THEIR VITAL POINTS.
IF I'M ASKED LATER ABOUT MY CRIMES, I CAN SAY ZEN THREATENED ME...
ZEN...
BLAM
NGH!
BLAM
AGH!
EVERY-THING THAT MAN IS GIVING ME...
IT WOULD BE A DRAG IF THEY LEARNED WHAT I LOOK LIKE.
LET'S GO.
RUSSO.
I'M BEING STUPID...
...
WHAT AM I...
WHERE ARE WE GOING?

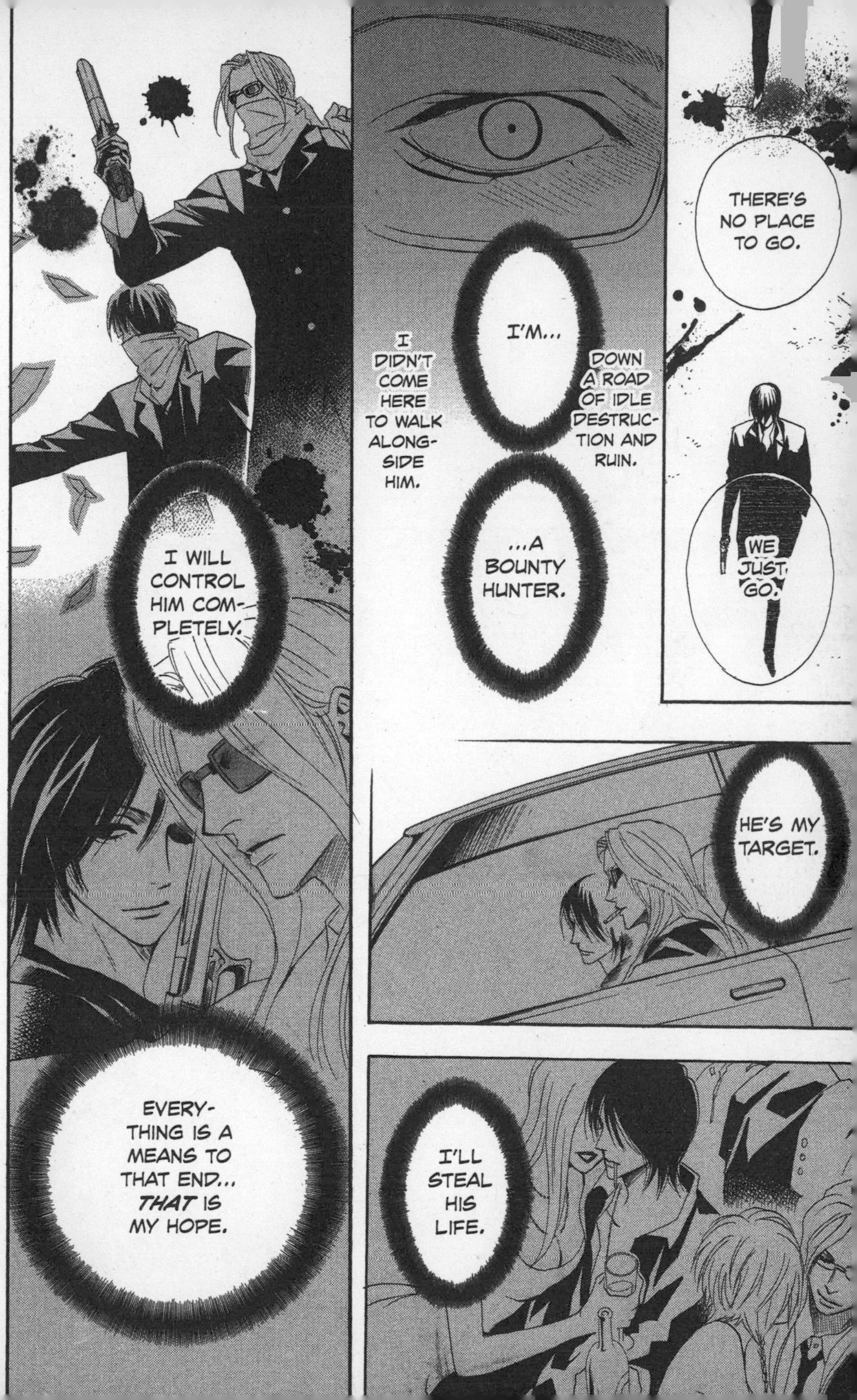
THERE'S NO PLACE TO GO.
WE JUST GO.
I'M...
DOWN A ROAD OF IDLE DESTRUCTION AND RUIN.
I DIDN'T COME HERE TO WALK ALONGSIDE HIM.
...A BOUNTY HUNTER.
HE'S MY TARGET.
I'LL STEAL HIS LIFE.
I WILL CONTROL HIM COMPLETELY.
EVERYTHING IS A MEANS TO THAT END... *THAT* IS MY HOPE.

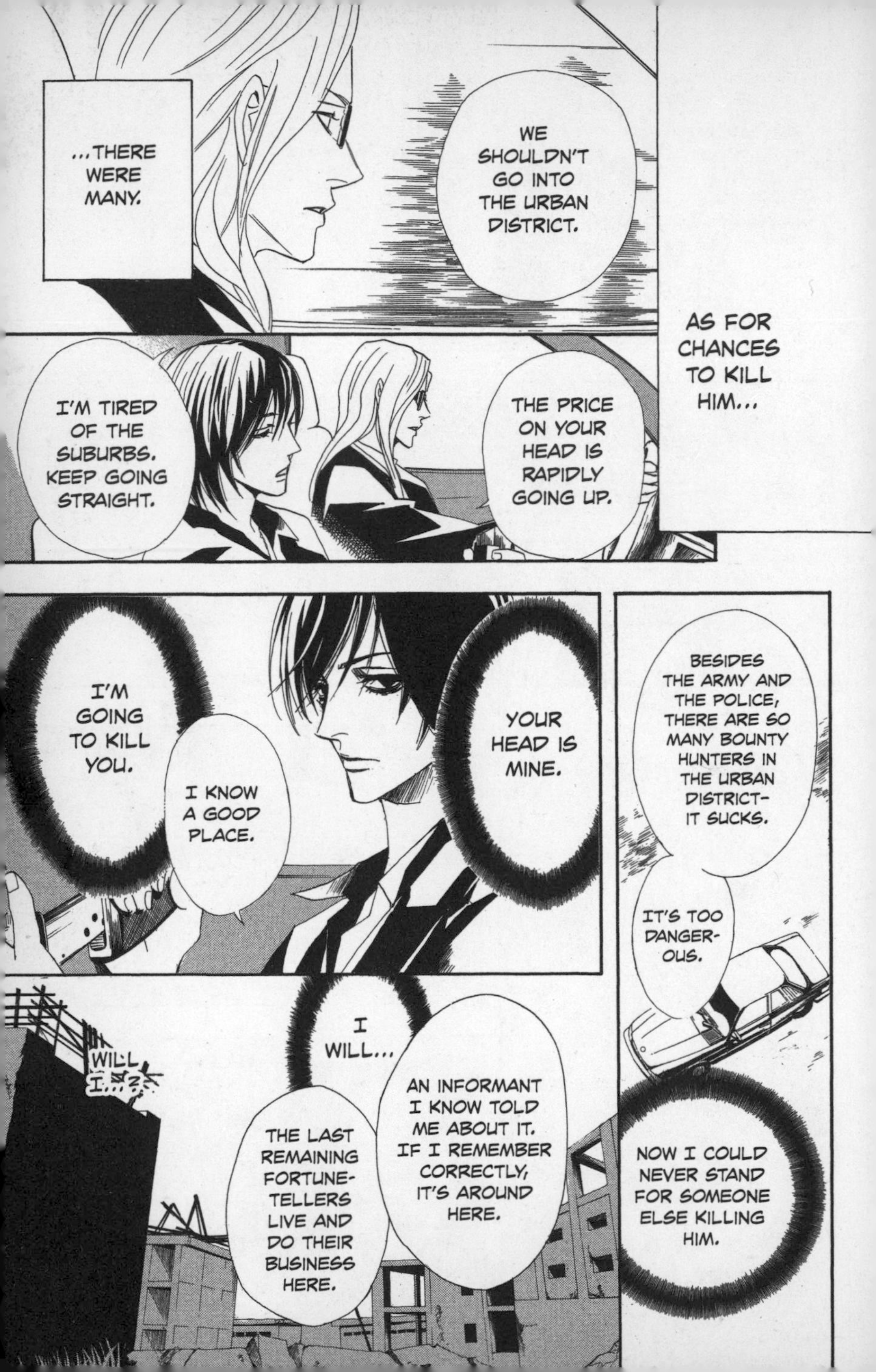
AS FOR CHANCES TO KILL HIM...
...THERE WERE MANY.
WE SHOULDN'T GO INTO THE URBAN DISTRICT.
THE PRICE ON YOUR HEAD IS RAPIDLY GOING UP.
I'M TIRED OF THE SUBURBS. KEEP GOING STRAIGHT.
BESIDES THE ARMY AND THE POLICE, THERE ARE SO MANY BOUNTY HUNTERS IN THE URBAN DISTRICT- IT SUCKS.
IT'S TOO DANGER-OUS.
NOW I COULD NEVER STAND FOR SOMEONE ELSE KILLING HIM.
YOUR HEAD IS MINE.
I'M GOING TO KILL YOU.
I KNOW A GOOD PLACE.
I WILL...
AN INFORMANT I KNOW TOLD ME ABOUT IT. IF I REMEMBER CORRECTLY, IT'S AROUND HERE.
THE LAST REMAINING FORTUNE-TELLERS LIVE AND DO THEIR BUSINESS HERE.
WILL I...?

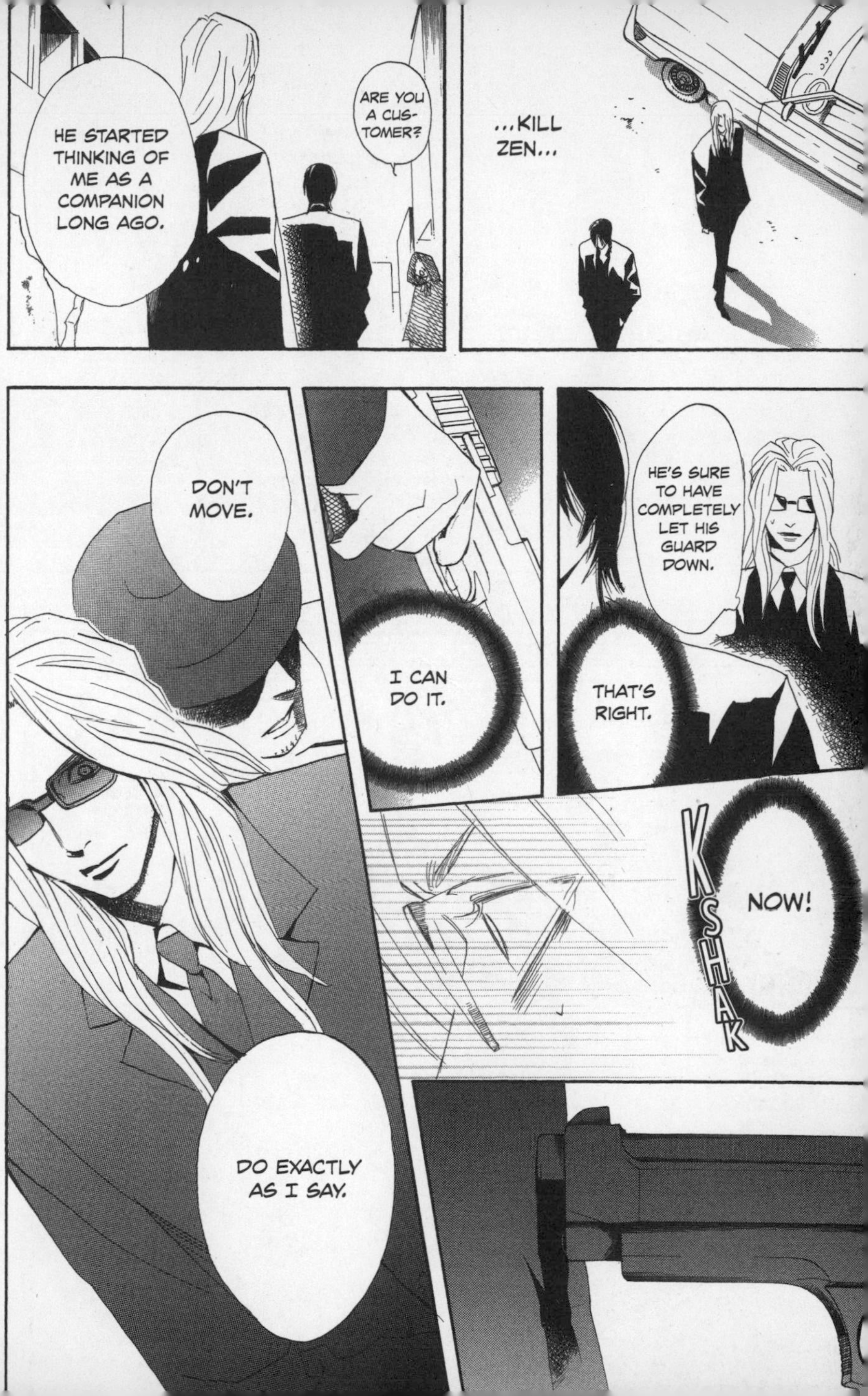
...KILL ZEN...
ARE YOU A CUS-TOMER?
HE STARTED THINKING OF ME AS A COMPANION LONG AGO.
HE'S SURE TO HAVE COMPLETELY LET HIS GUARD DOWN.
THAT'S RIGHT.
I CAN DO IT.
KSHAK
NOW!
DON'T MOVE.
DO EXACTLY AS I SAY.

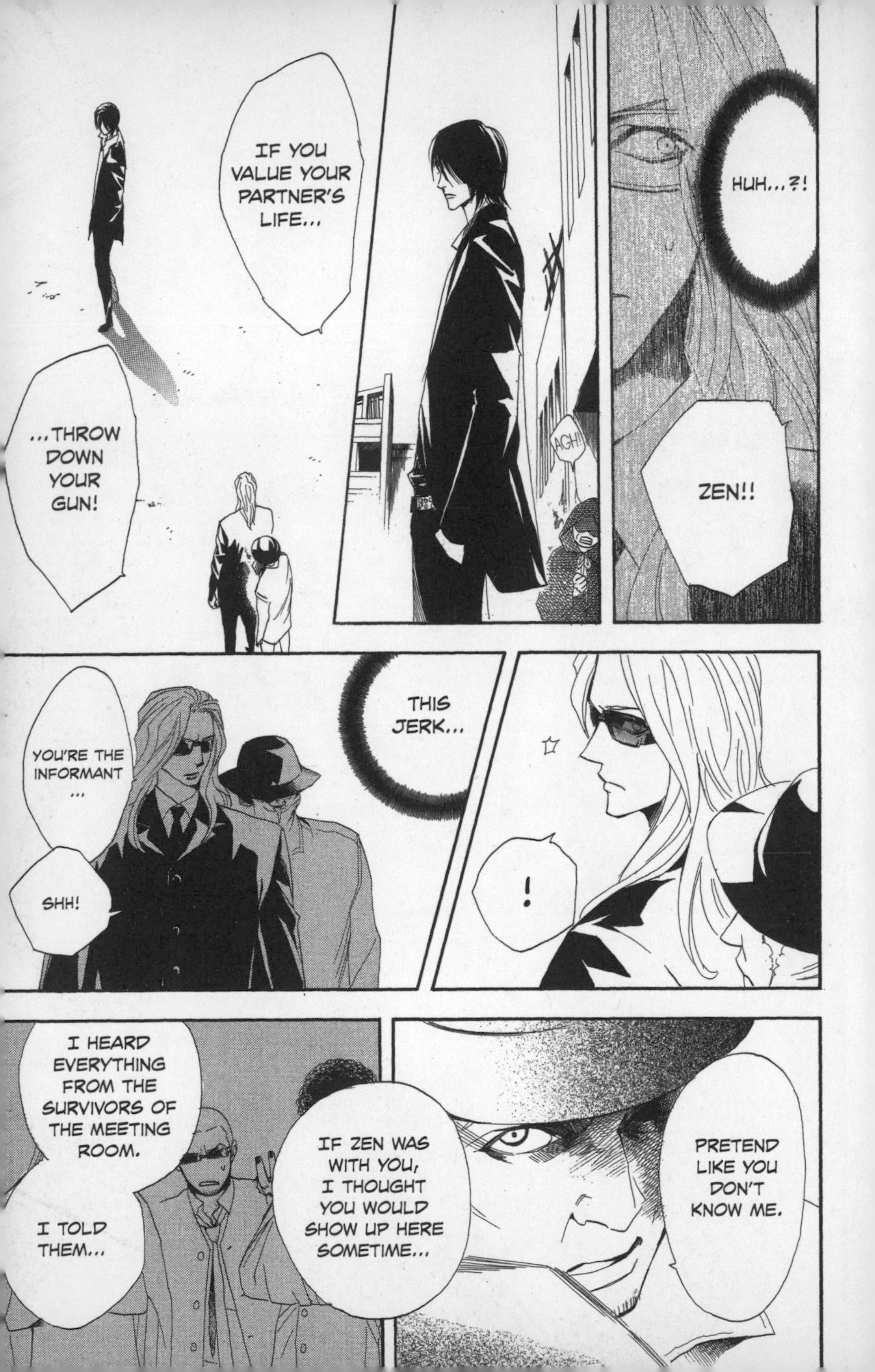
HUH...?!
ZEN!!
AGH!
IF YOU VALUE YOUR PARTNER'S LIFE...
...THROW DOWN YOUR GUN!
!
THIS JERK...
YOU'RE THE INFORMANT ...
SHH!
PRETEND LIKE YOU DON'T KNOW ME.
IF ZEN WAS WITH YOU, I THOUGHT YOU WOULD SHOW UP HERE SOMETIME...
I HEARD EVERYTHING FROM THE SURVIVORS OF THE MEETING ROOM.
I TOLD THEM...

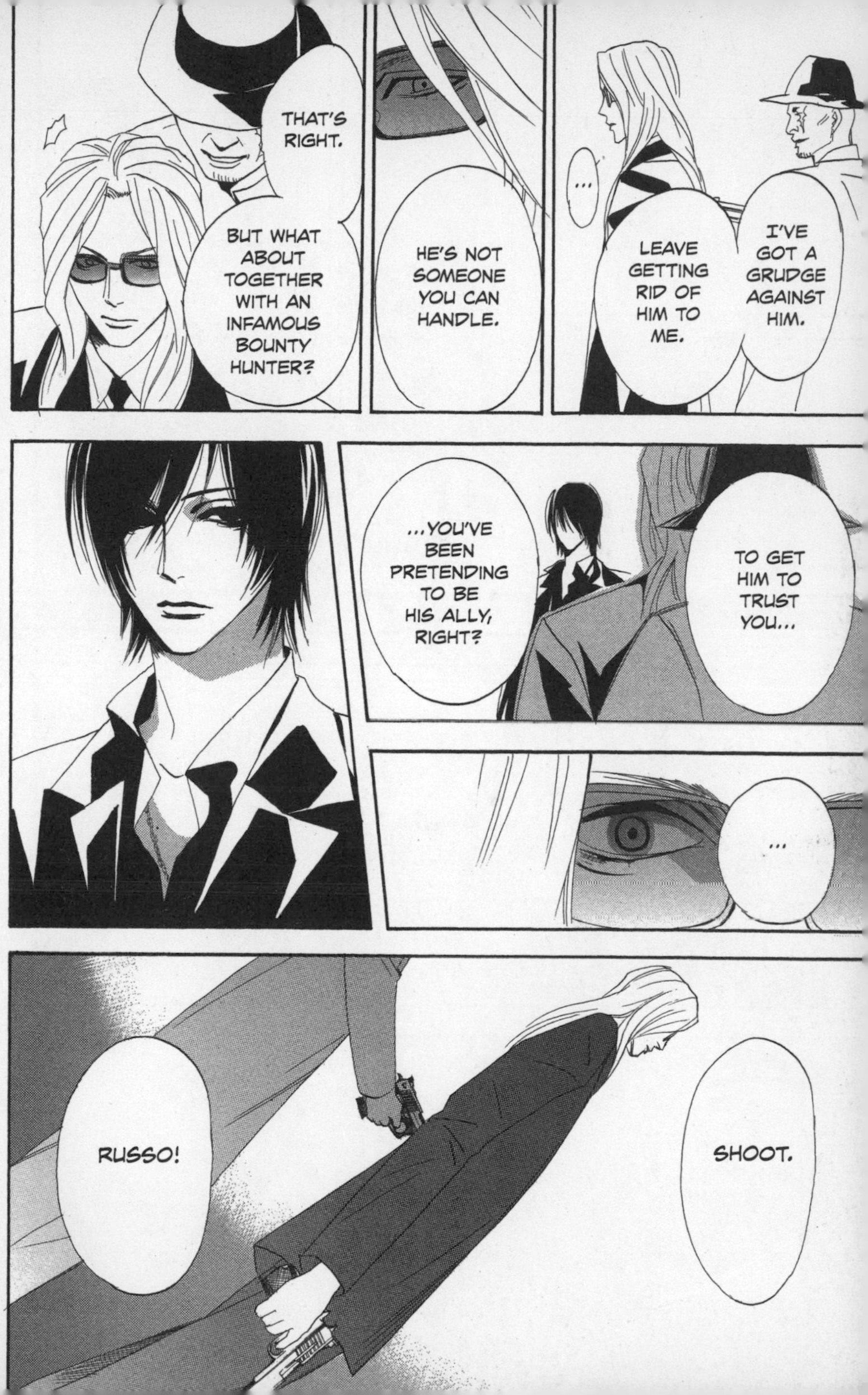
I'VE GOT A GRUDGE AGAINST HIM.
LEAVE GETTING RID OF HIM TO ME.
...
HE'S NOT SOMEONE YOU CAN HANDLE.
THAT'S RIGHT.
BUT WHAT ABOUT TOGETHER WITH AN INFAMOUS BOUNTY HUNTER?
TO GET HIM TO TRUST YOU...
...YOU'VE BEEN PRETENDING TO BE HIS ALLY, RIGHT?
...
SHOOT.
RUSSO!

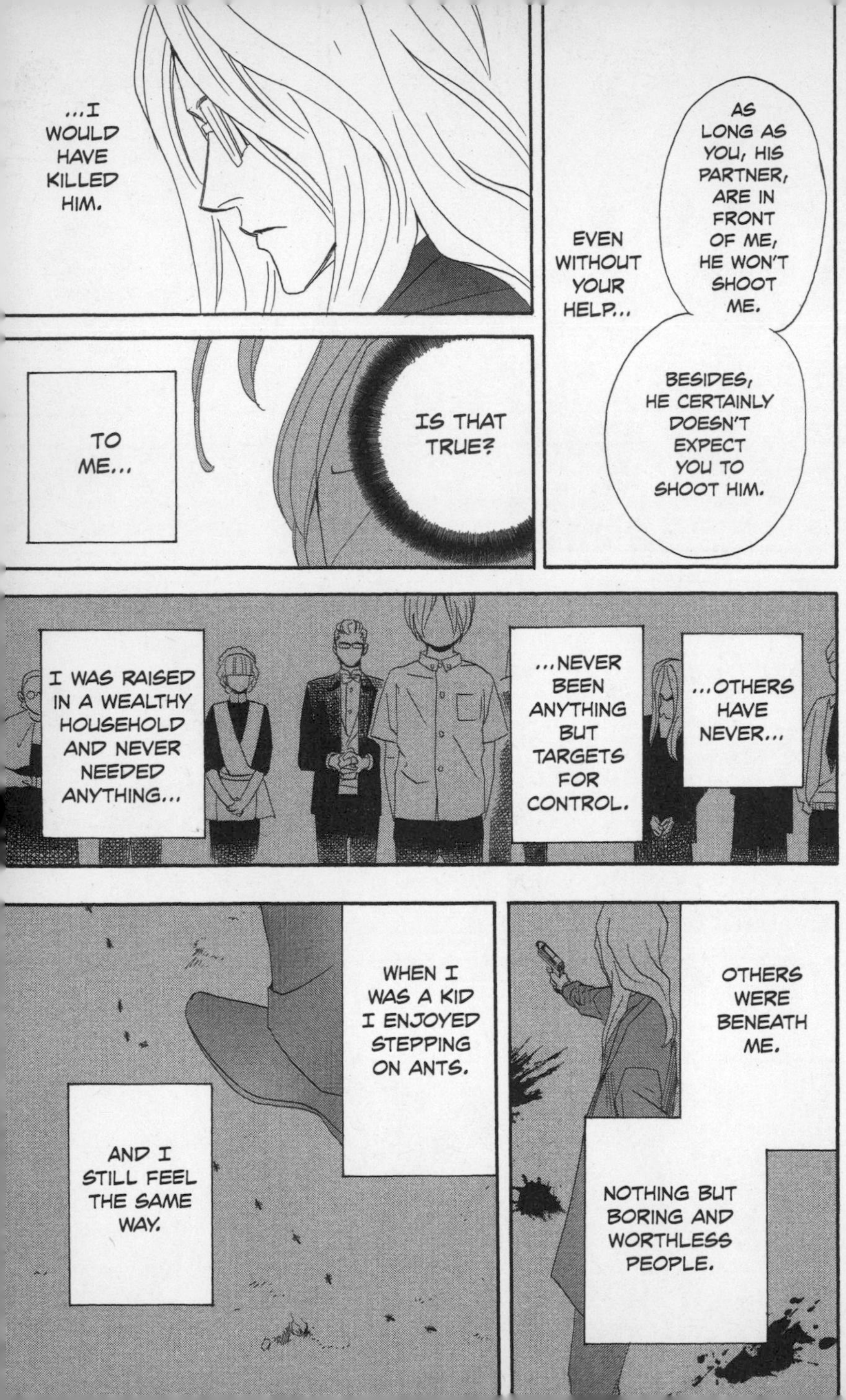
AS LONG AS YOU, HIS PARTNER, ARE IN FRONT OF ME, HE WON'T SHOOT ME.
EVEN WITHOUT YOUR HELP...
BESIDES, HE CERTAINLY DOESN'T EXPECT YOU TO SHOOT HIM.
...I WOULD HAVE KILLED HIM.
IS THAT TRUE?
TO ME...
...OTHERS HAVE NEVER...
...NEVER BEEN ANYTHING BUT TARGETS FOR CONTROL.
I WAS RAISED IN A WEALTHY HOUSEHOLD AND NEVER NEEDED ANYTHING...
OTHERS WERE BENEATH ME.
NOTHING BUT BORING AND WORTHLESS PEOPLE.
WHEN I WAS A KID I ENJOYED STEPPING ON ANTS.
AND I STILL FEEL THE SAME WAY.

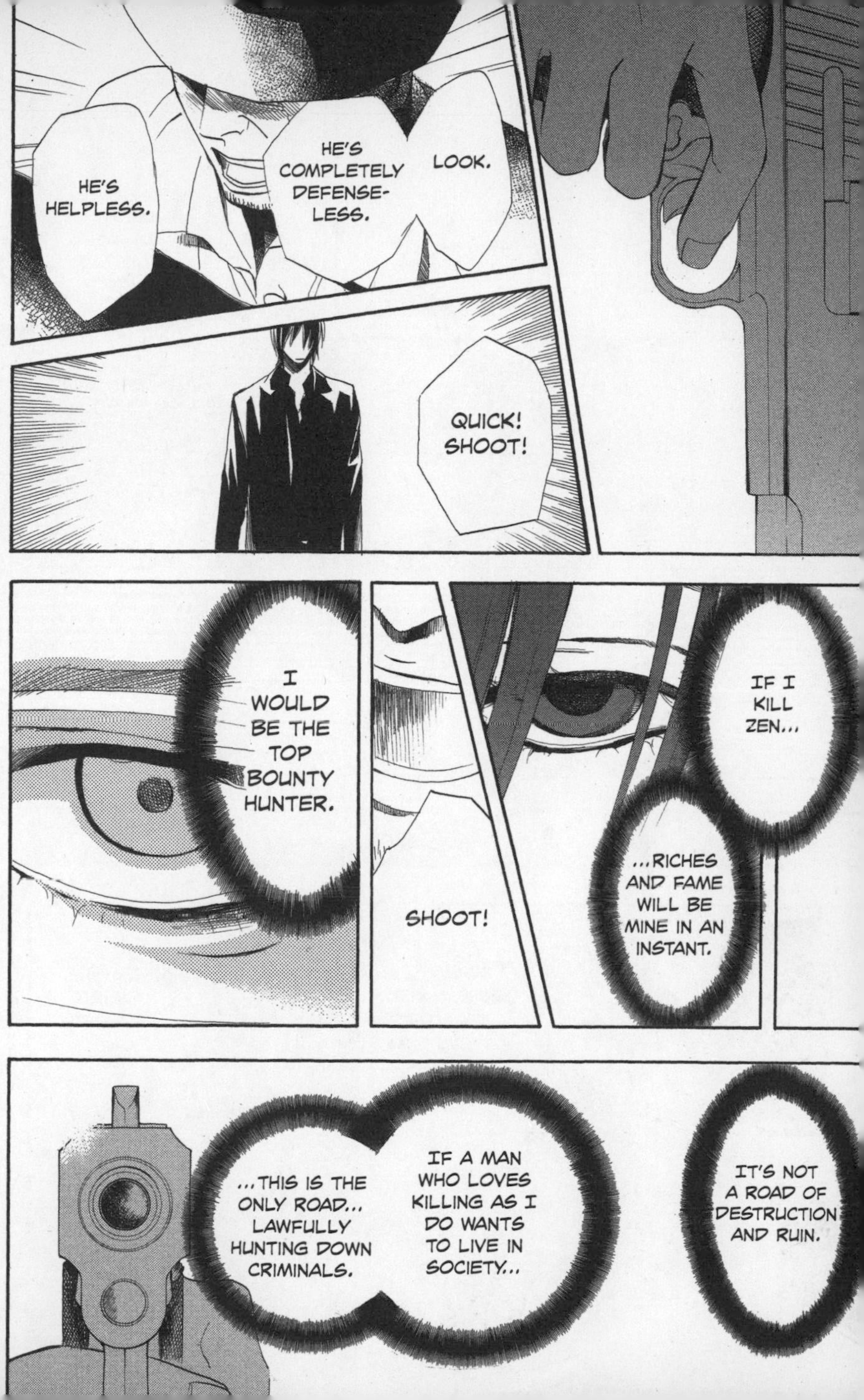
LOOK.
HE'S COMPLETELY DEFENSE-LESS.
HE'S HELPLESS.
QUICK! SHOOT!
IF I KILL ZEN...
...RICHES AND FAME WILL BE MINE IN AN INSTANT.
SHOOT!
I WOULD BE THE TOP BOUNTY HUNTER.
IT'S NOT A ROAD OF DESTRUCTION AND RUIN.
IF A MAN WHO LOVES KILLING AS I DO WANTS TO LIVE IN SOCIETY...
...THIS IS THE ONLY ROAD... LAWFULLY HUNTING DOWN CRIMINALS.

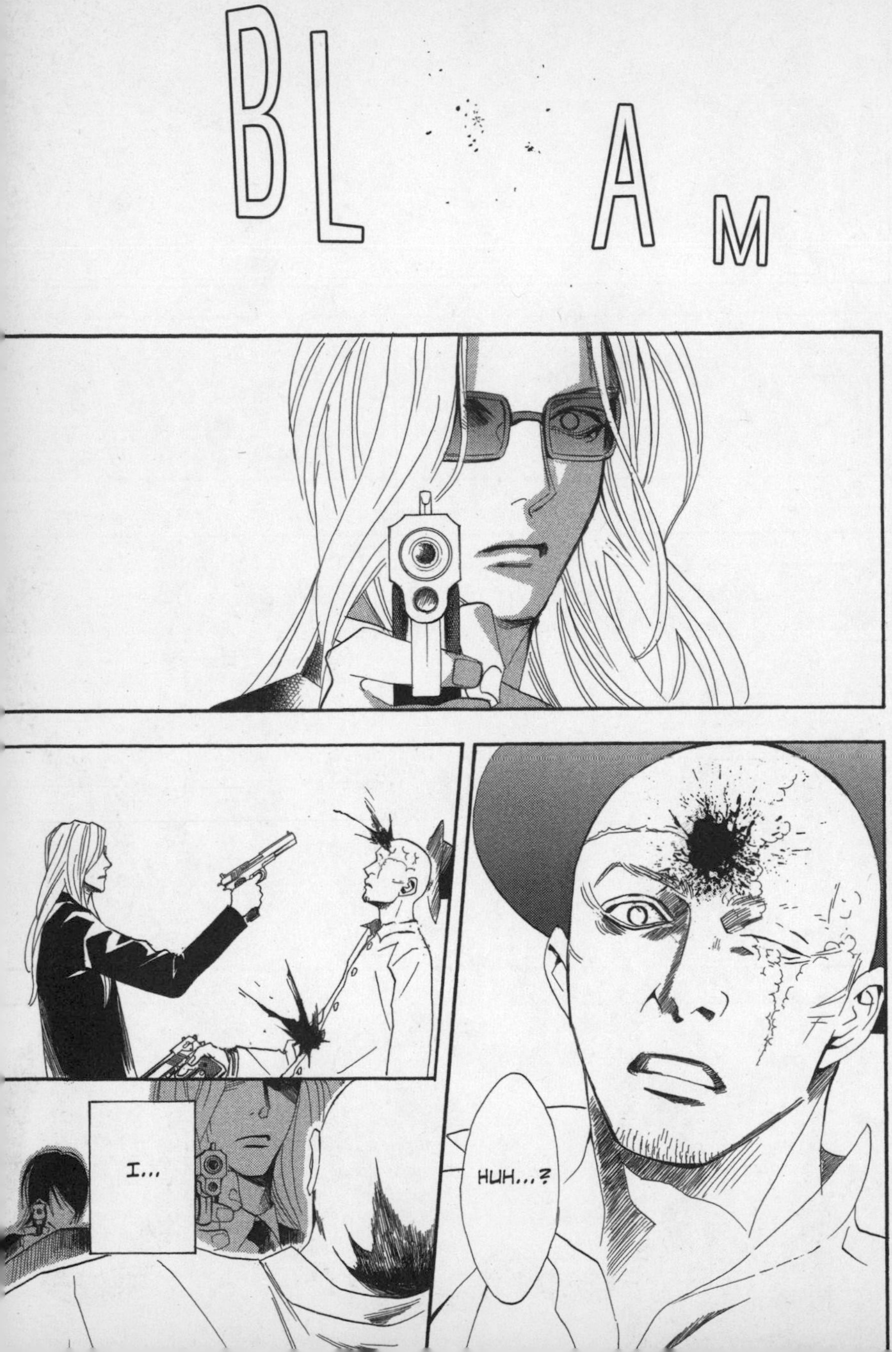
BLAM
HUH...?
I...

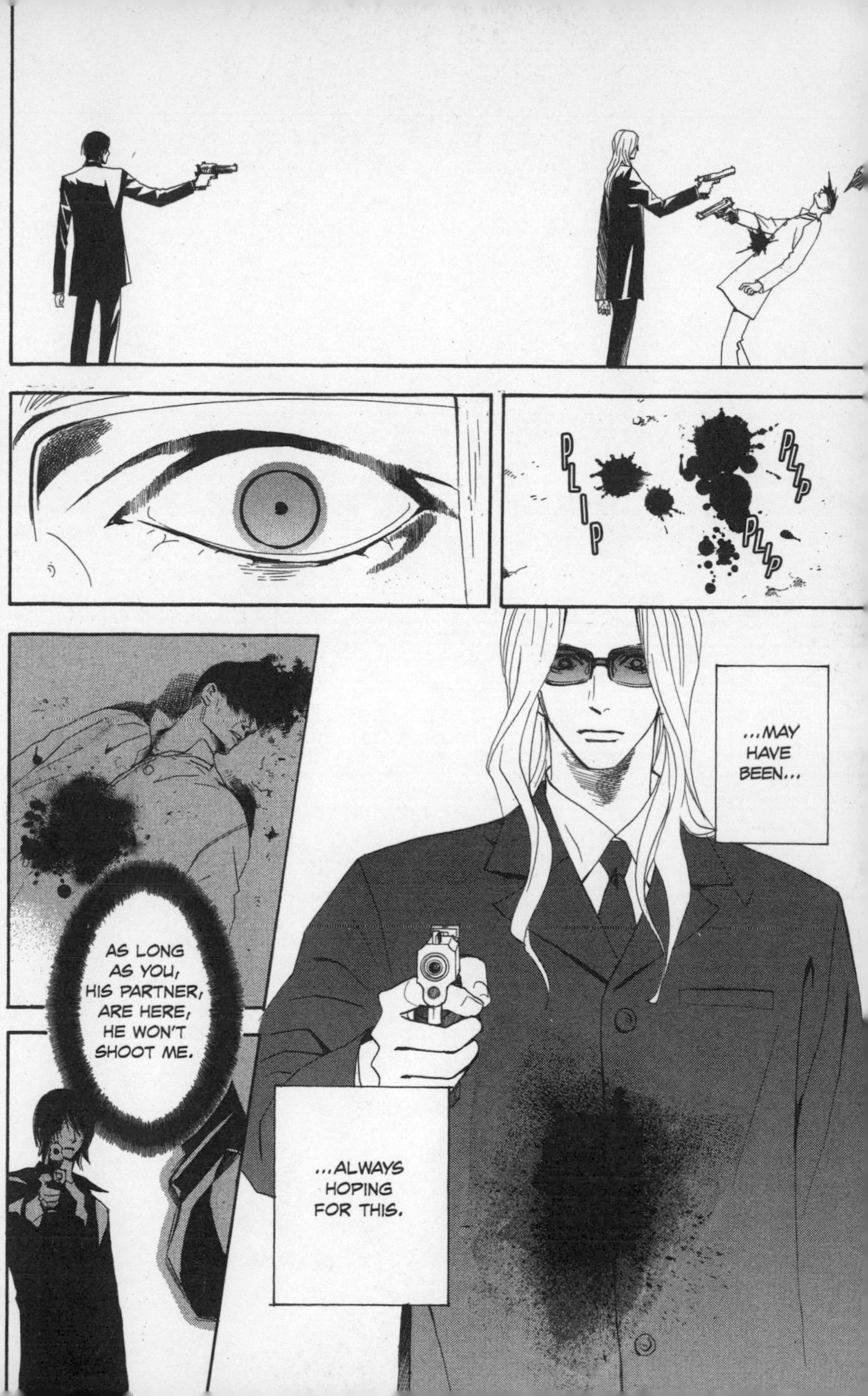
PLIP
PLIP
PLIP
...MAY HAVE BEEN...
...ALWAYS HOPING FOR THIS.
AS LONG AS YOU, HIS PARTNER, ARE HERE, HE WON'T SHOOT ME.

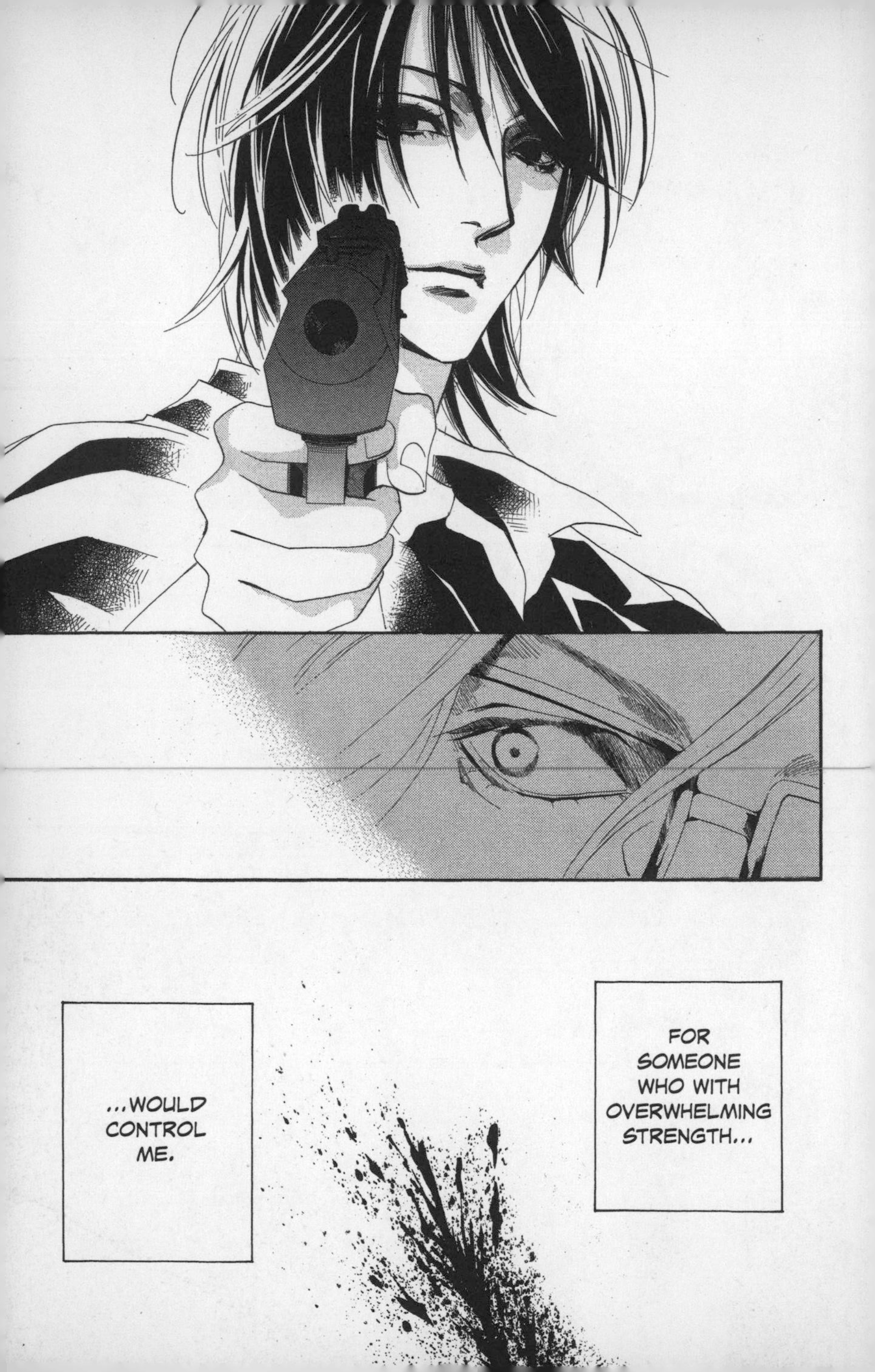
FOR SOMEONE WHO WITH OVERWHELMING STRENGTH...
...WOULD CONTROL ME.

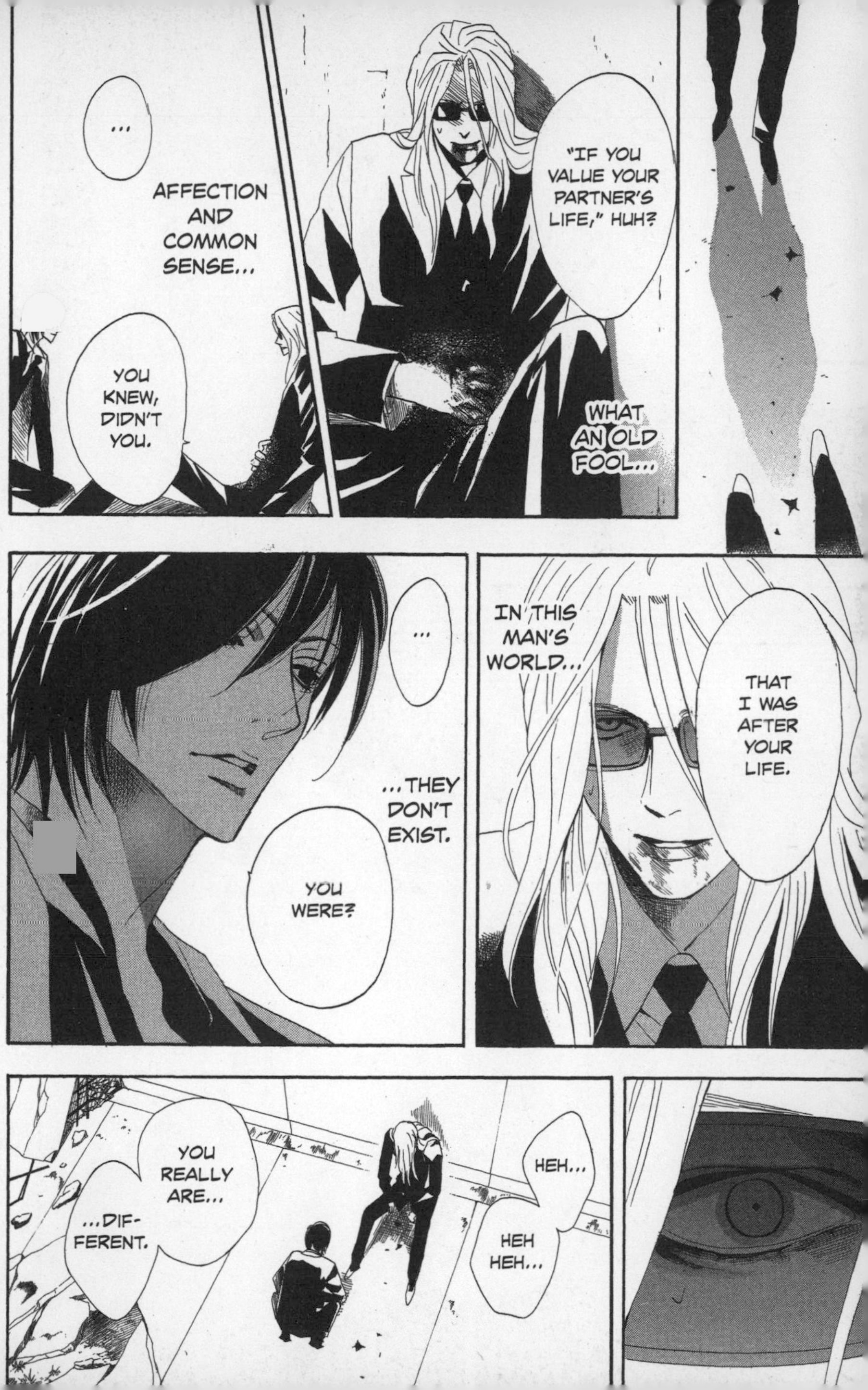
"IF YOU VALUE YOUR PARTNER'S LIFE," HUH?
WHAT AN OLD FOOL...
...
AFFECTION AND COMMON SENSE...
YOU KNEW, DIDN'T YOU.
THAT I WAS AFTER YOUR LIFE.
IN THIS MAN'S WORLD...
...
...THEY DON'T EXIST.
YOU WERE?
HEH...
HEH HEH...
YOU REALLY ARE...
...DIF-FERENT.

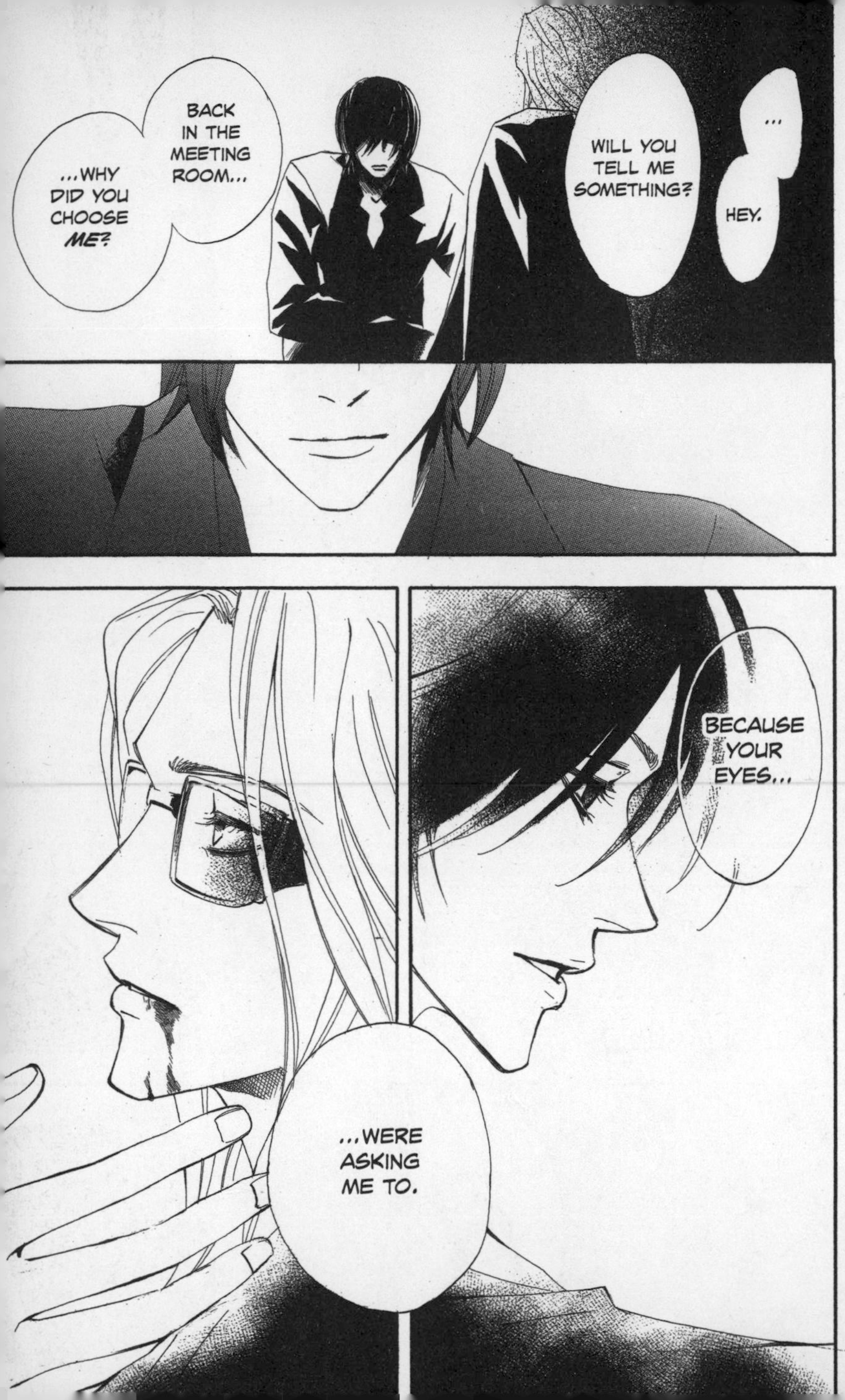
...
HEY.
WILL YOU TELL ME SOMETHING?
BACK IN THE MEETING ROOM...
...WHY DID YOU CHOOSE *ME*?
BECAUSE YOUR EYES...
...WERE ASKING ME TO.

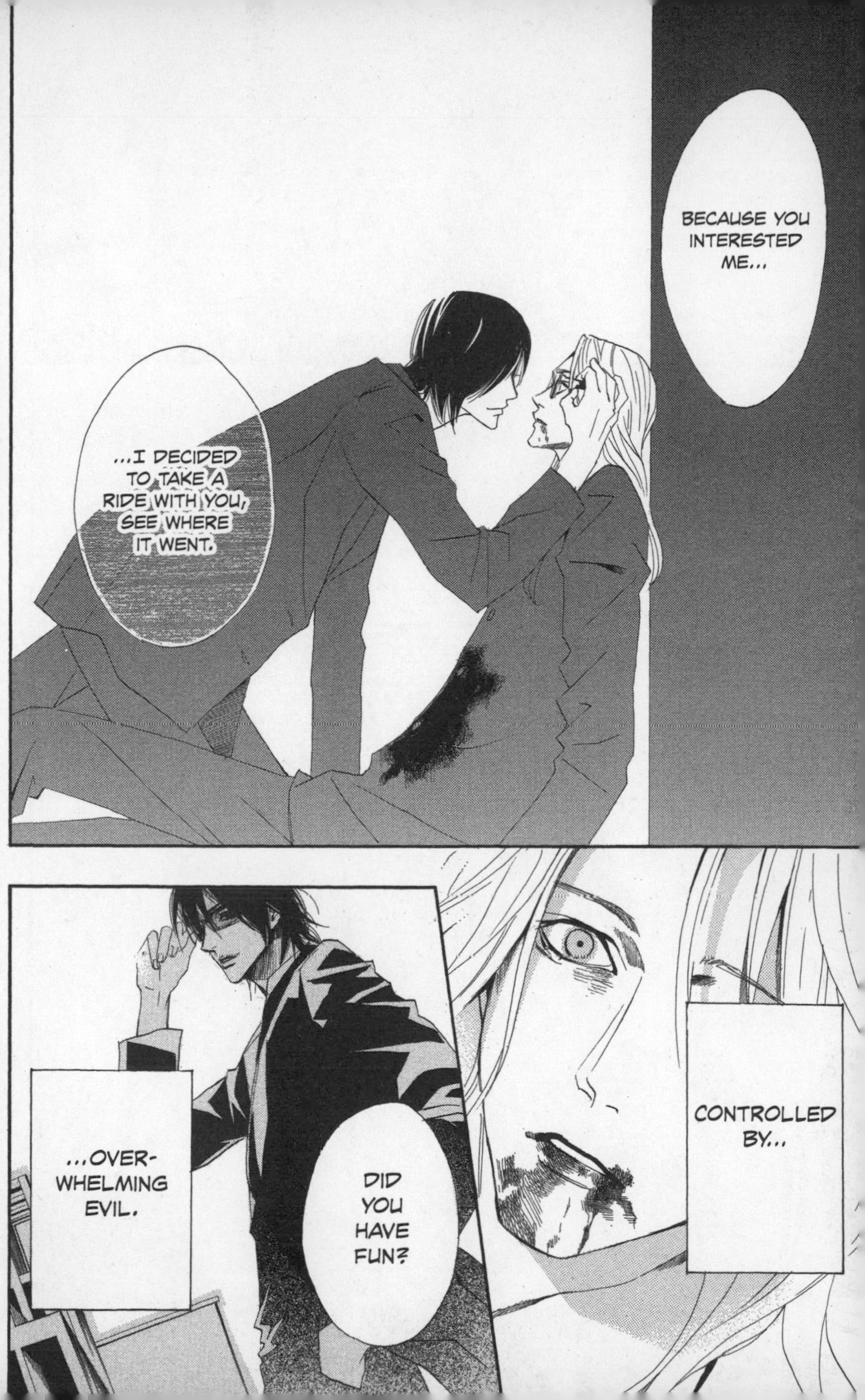
BECAUSE YOU INTERESTED ME...
...I DECIDED TO TAKE A RIDE WITH YOU, SEE WHERE IT WENT.
CONTROLLED BY...
DID YOU HAVE FUN?
...OVER-WHELMING EVIL.

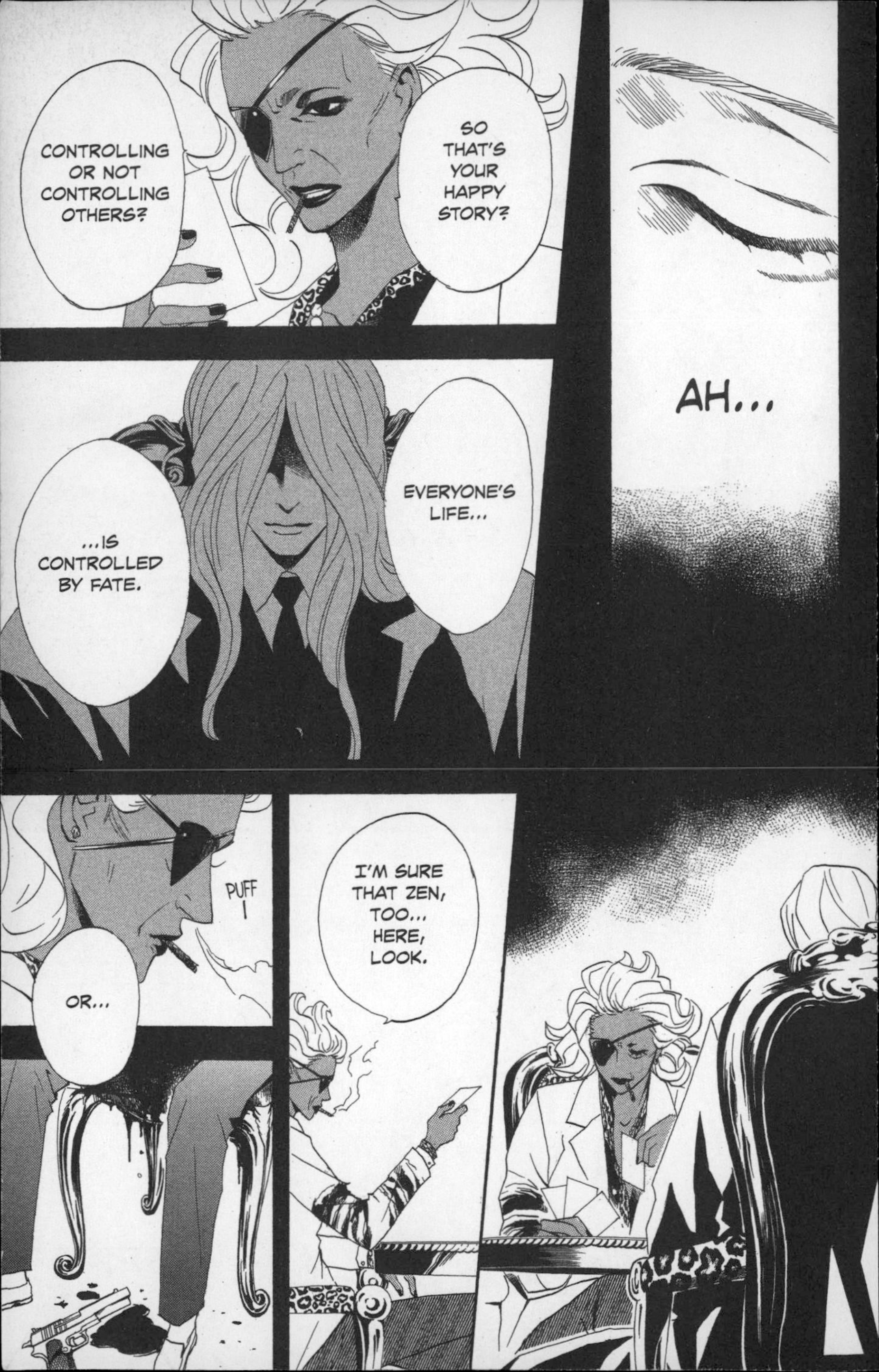
AH...
SO THAT'S YOUR HAPPY STORY?
CONTROLLING OR NOT CONTROLLING OTHERS?
EVERYONE'S LIFE...
...IS CONTROLLED BY FATE.
I'M SURE THAT ZEN, TOO... HERE, LOOK.
PUFF
OR...

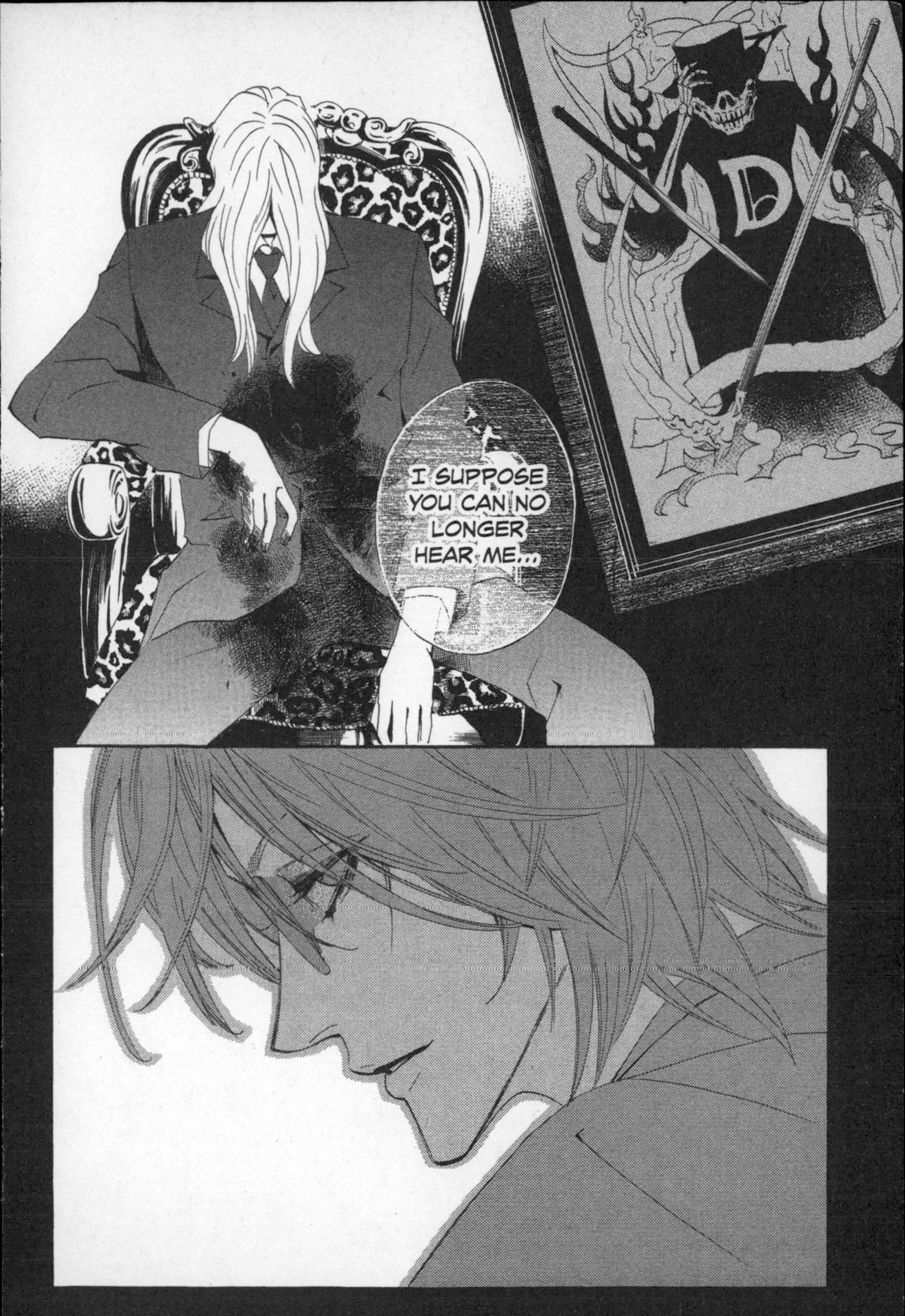
I SUPPOSE YOU CAN NO LONGER HEAR ME...

Blank Slate Chapter 1 / The End

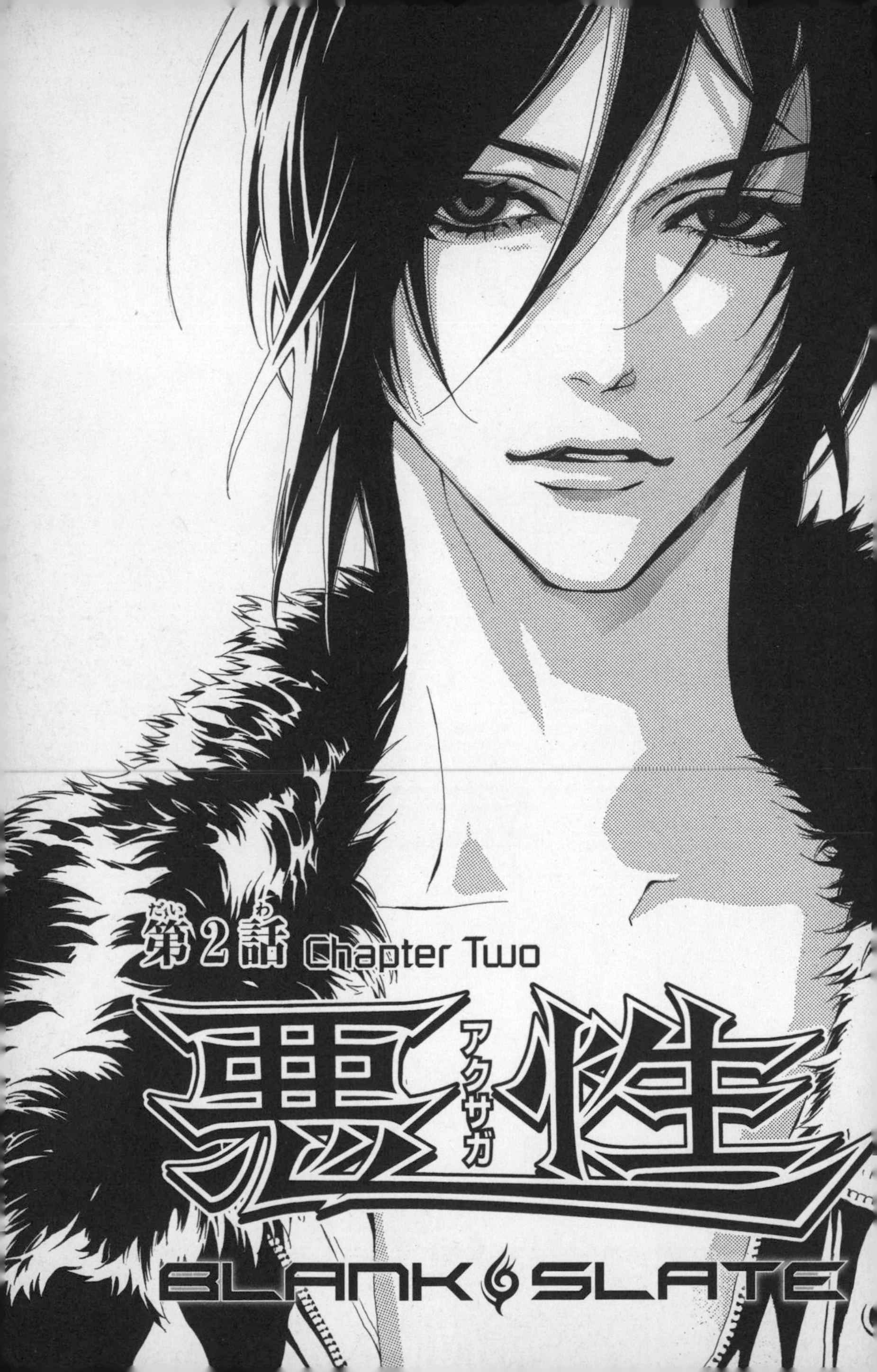
第2話 Chapter Two
悪性
アクサガ
BLANK SLATE

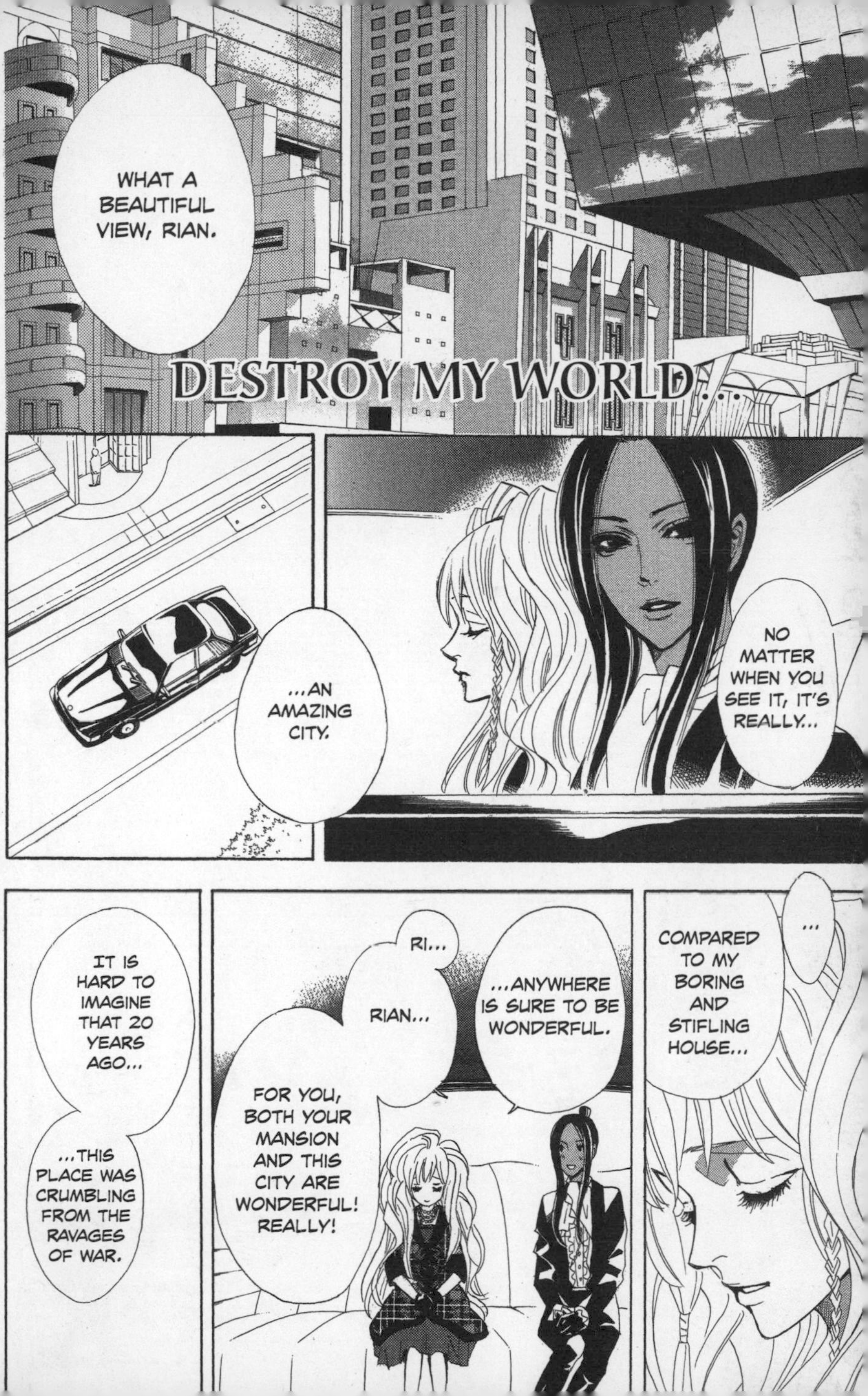
WHAT A BEAUTIFUL VIEW, RIAN.
DESTROY MY WORLD...
NO MATTER WHEN YOU SEE IT, IT'S REALLY...
...AN AMAZING CITY.
...
COMPARED TO MY BORING AND STIFLING HOUSE...
...ANYWHERE IS SURE TO BE WONDERFUL.
RI...
RIAN...
FOR YOU, BOTH YOUR MANSION AND THIS CITY ARE WONDERFUL! REALLY!
IT IS HARD TO IMAGINE THAT 20 YEARS AGO...
...THIS PLACE WAS CRUMBLING FROM THE RAVAGES OF WAR.

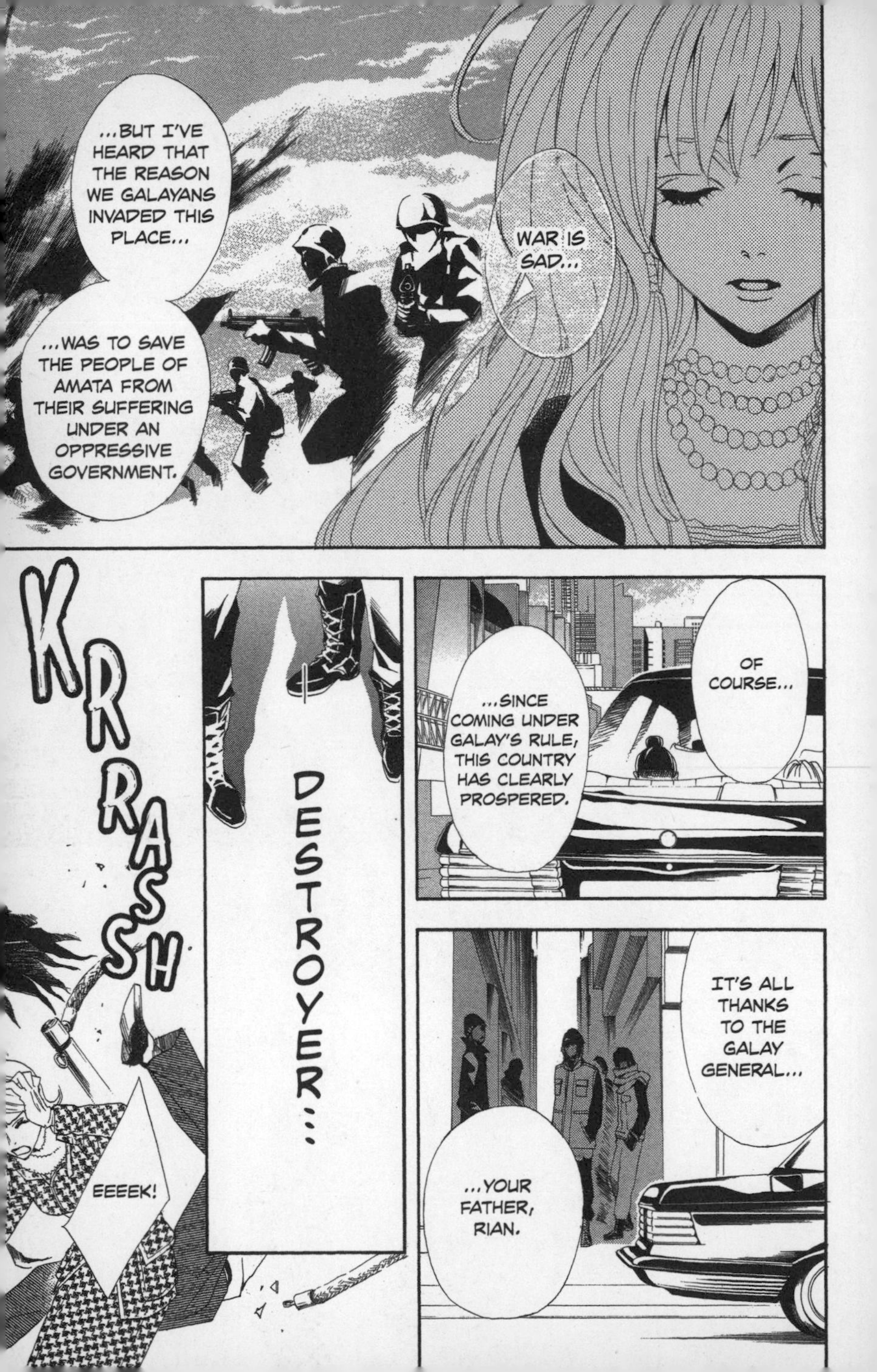
WAR IS SAD...
...BUT I'VE HEARD THAT THE REASON WE GALAYANS INVADED THIS PLACE...
...WAS TO SAVE THE PEOPLE OF AMATA FROM THEIR SUFFERING UNDER AN OPPRESSIVE GOVERNMENT.
OF COURSE...
...SINCE COMING UNDER GALAY'S RULE, THIS COUNTRY HAS CLEARLY PROSPERED.
IT'S ALL THANKS TO THE GALAY GENERAL...
...YOUR FATHER, RIAN.
DESTROYER...
KRRASH
EEEEK!

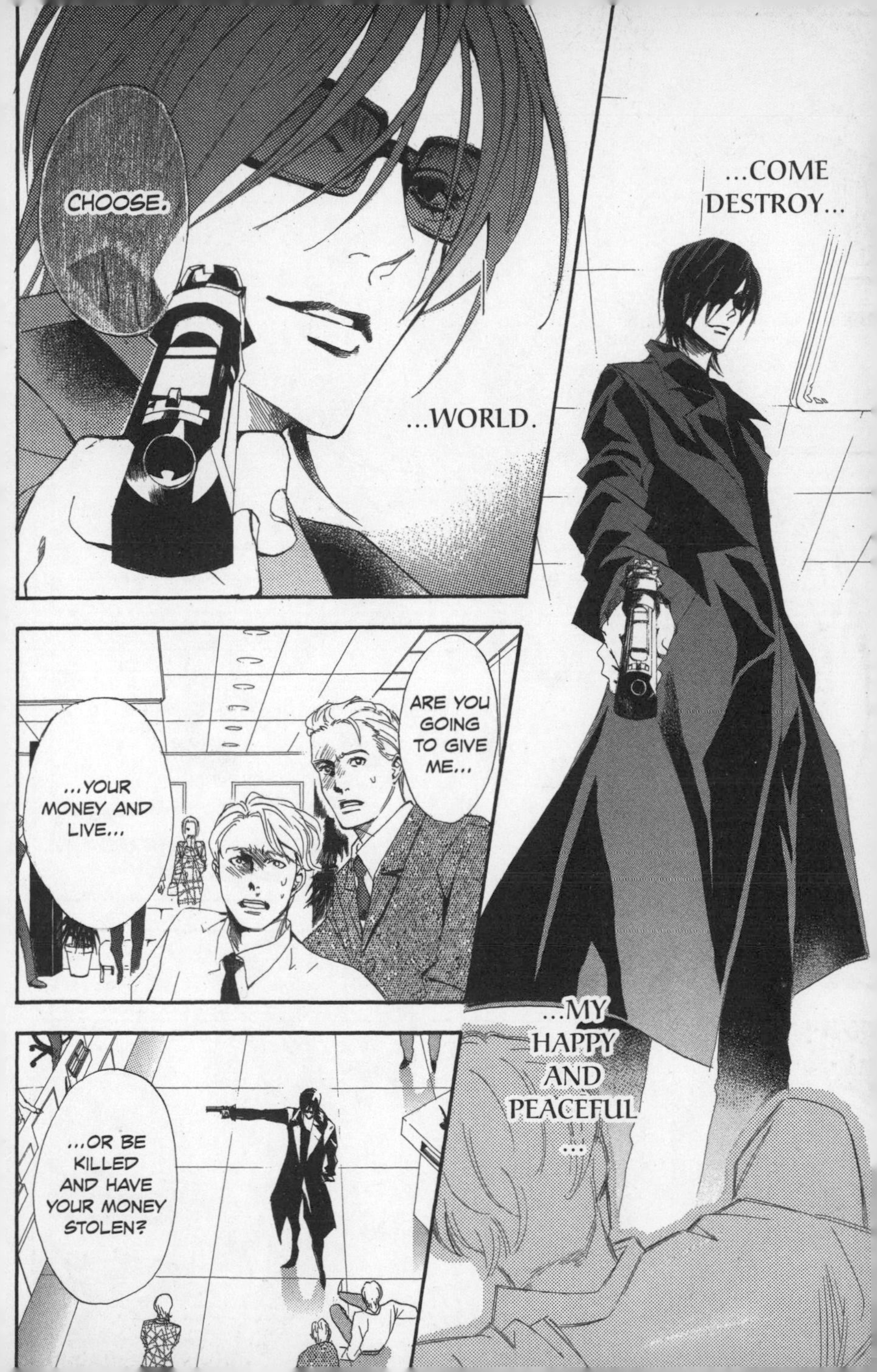
...COME DESTROY...
...MY HAPPY AND PEACEFUL ...
...WORLD.
CHOOSE.
ARE YOU GOING TO GIVE ME...
...YOUR MONEY AND LIVE...
...OR BE KILLED AND HAVE YOUR MONEY STOLEN?

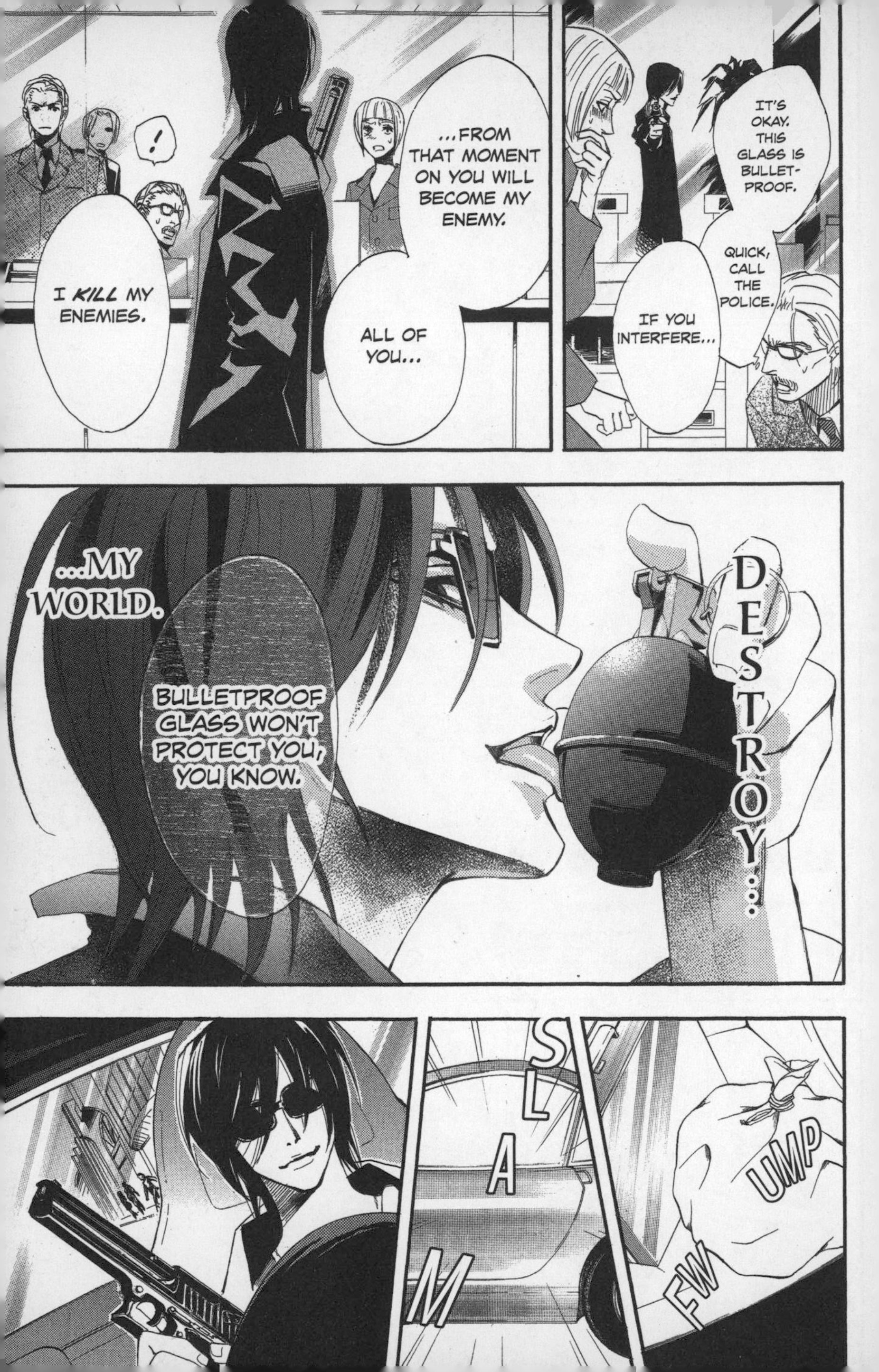
IT'S OKAY. THIS GLASS IS BULLET-PROOF.
QUICK, CALL THE POLICE.
IF YOU INTERFERE...
...FROM THAT MOMENT ON YOU WILL BECOME MY ENEMY.
ALL OF YOU...
!
I *KILL* MY ENEMIES.
DESTROY...
BULLETPROOF GLASS WON'T PROTECT YOU, YOU KNOW.
...MY WORLD.
FWUMP
SLAM

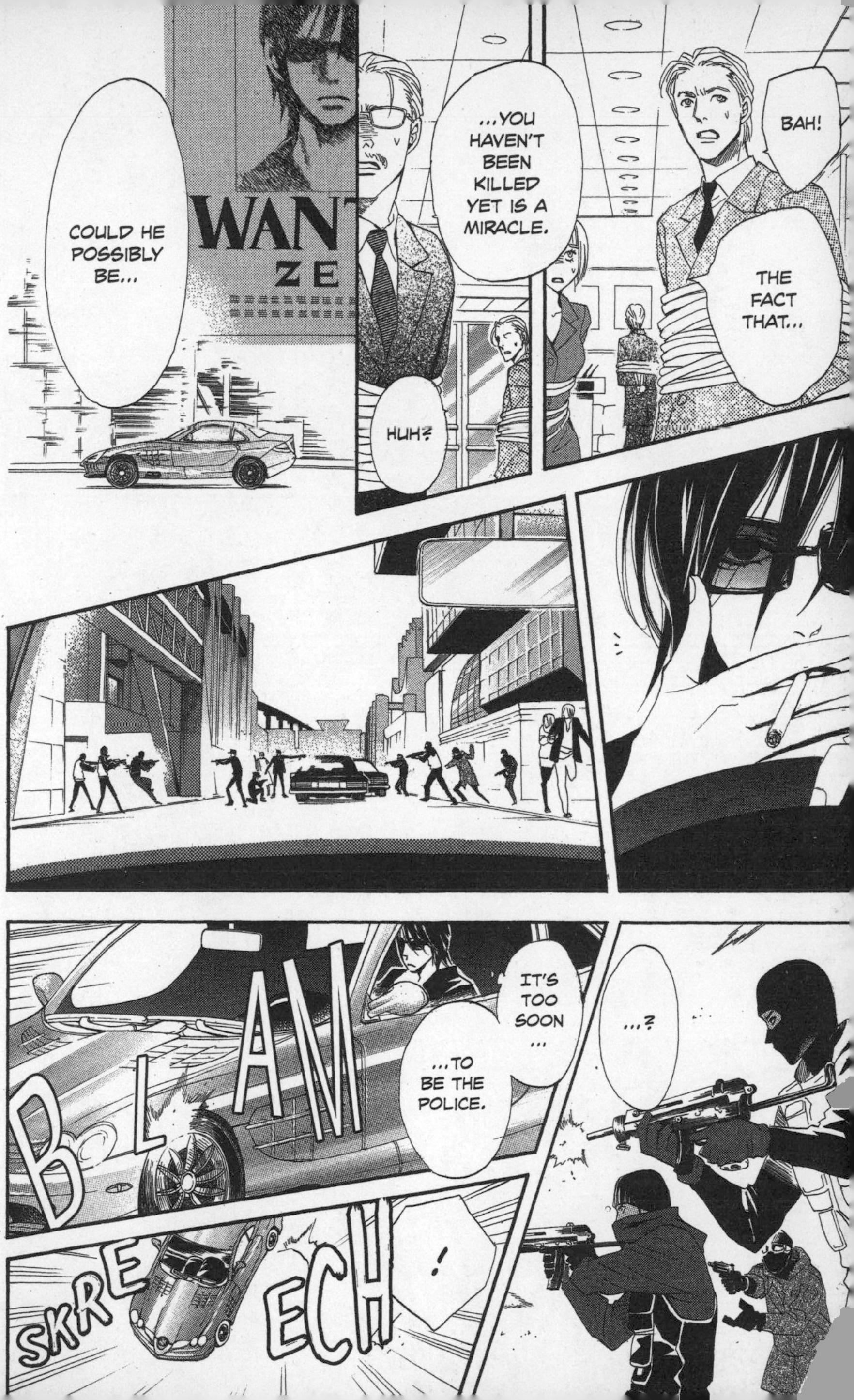
BAH!
THE FACT THAT...
...YOU HAVEN'T BEEN KILLED YET IS A MIRACLE.
HUH?
WANT
ZE
COULD HE POSSIBLY BE...
...?
IT'S TOO SOON...
...TO BE THE POLICE.
BLAM
!
SKREECH

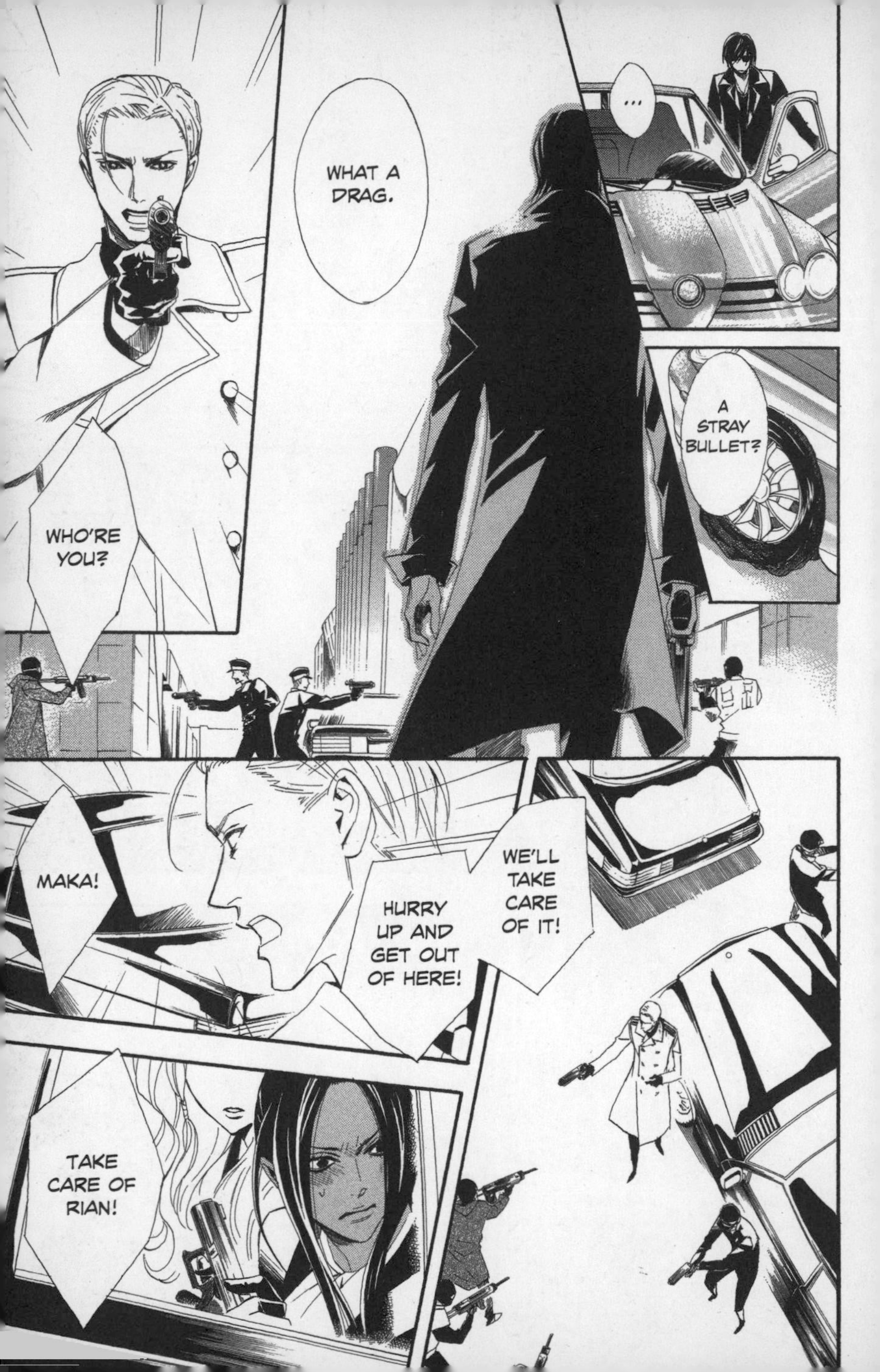
...
A STRAY BULLET?
WHAT A DRAG.
WHO'RE YOU?
WE'LL TAKE CARE OF IT!
HURRY UP AND GET OUT OF HERE!
MAKA!
TAKE CARE OF RIAN!

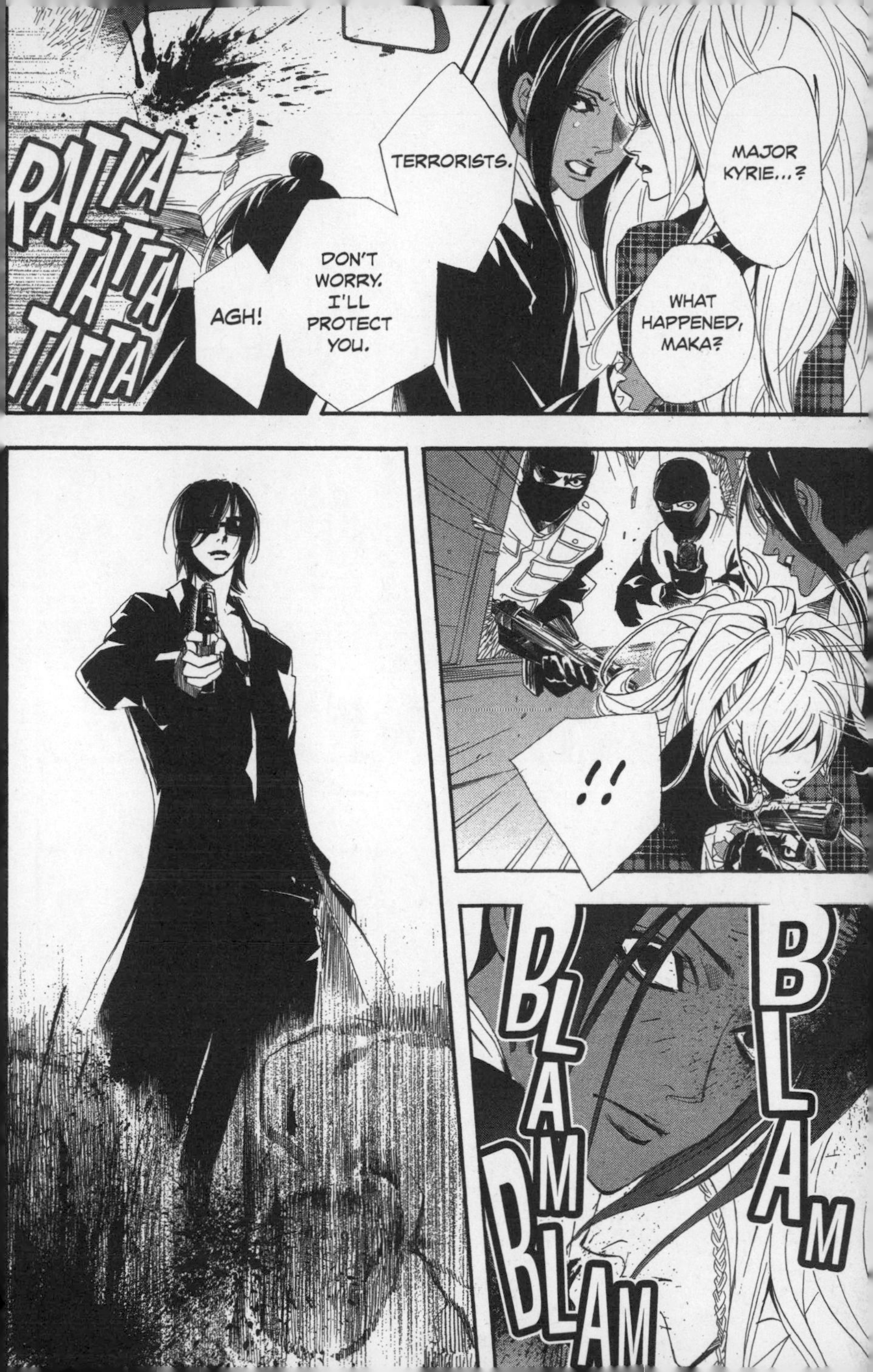
MAJOR KYRIE...?
WHAT HAPPENED, MAKA?
TERRORISTS.
DON'T WORRY. I'LL PROTECT YOU.
AGH!
RATTA TATTA TATTA
!!
BLAM
BLAM
BLAM

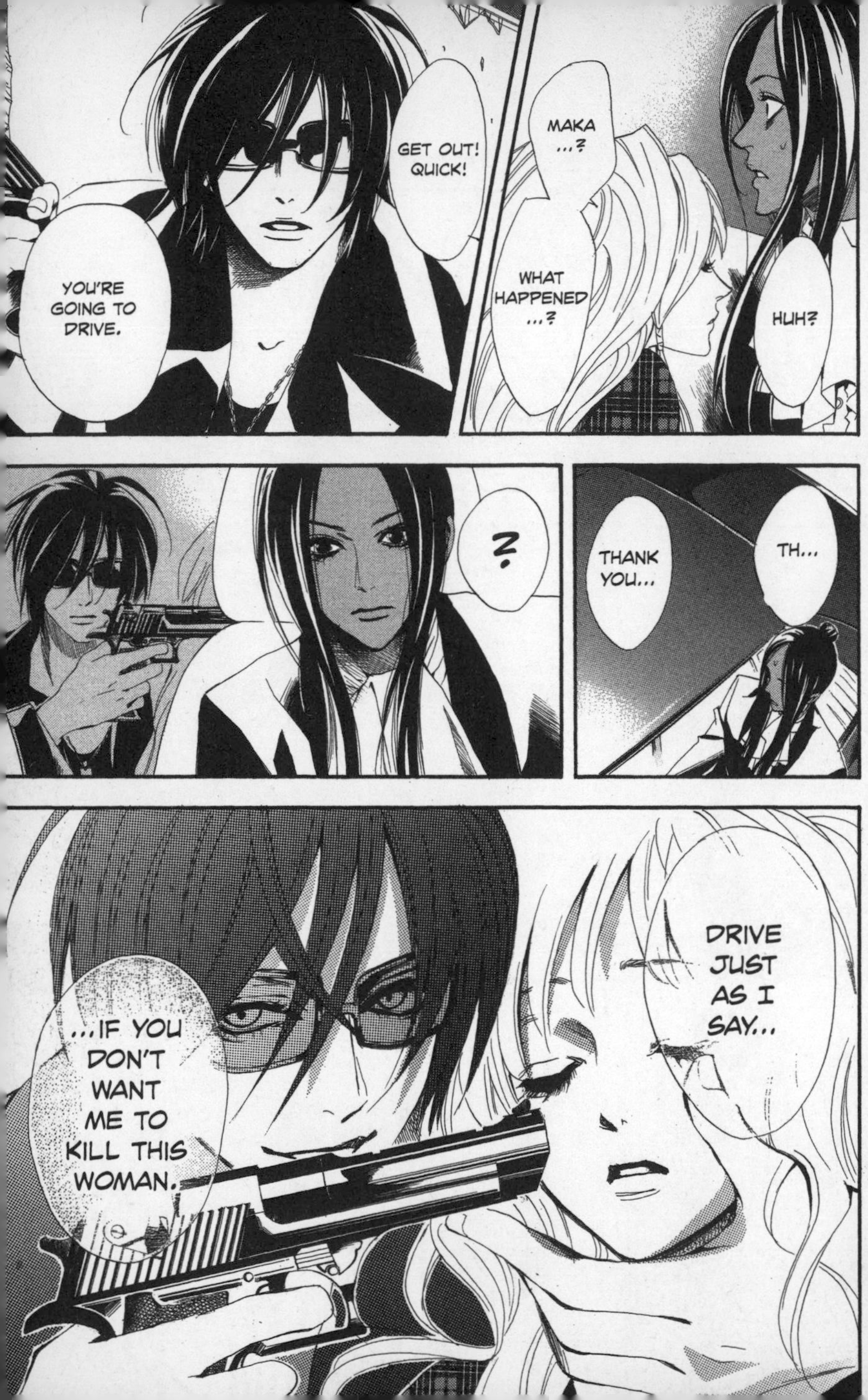
MAKA ...?
WHAT HAPPENED ...?
HUH?
GET OUT! QUICK!
YOU'RE GOING TO DRIVE.
TH...
THANK YOU...
?
DRIVE JUST AS I SAY...
...IF YOU DON'T WANT ME TO KILL THIS WOMAN.

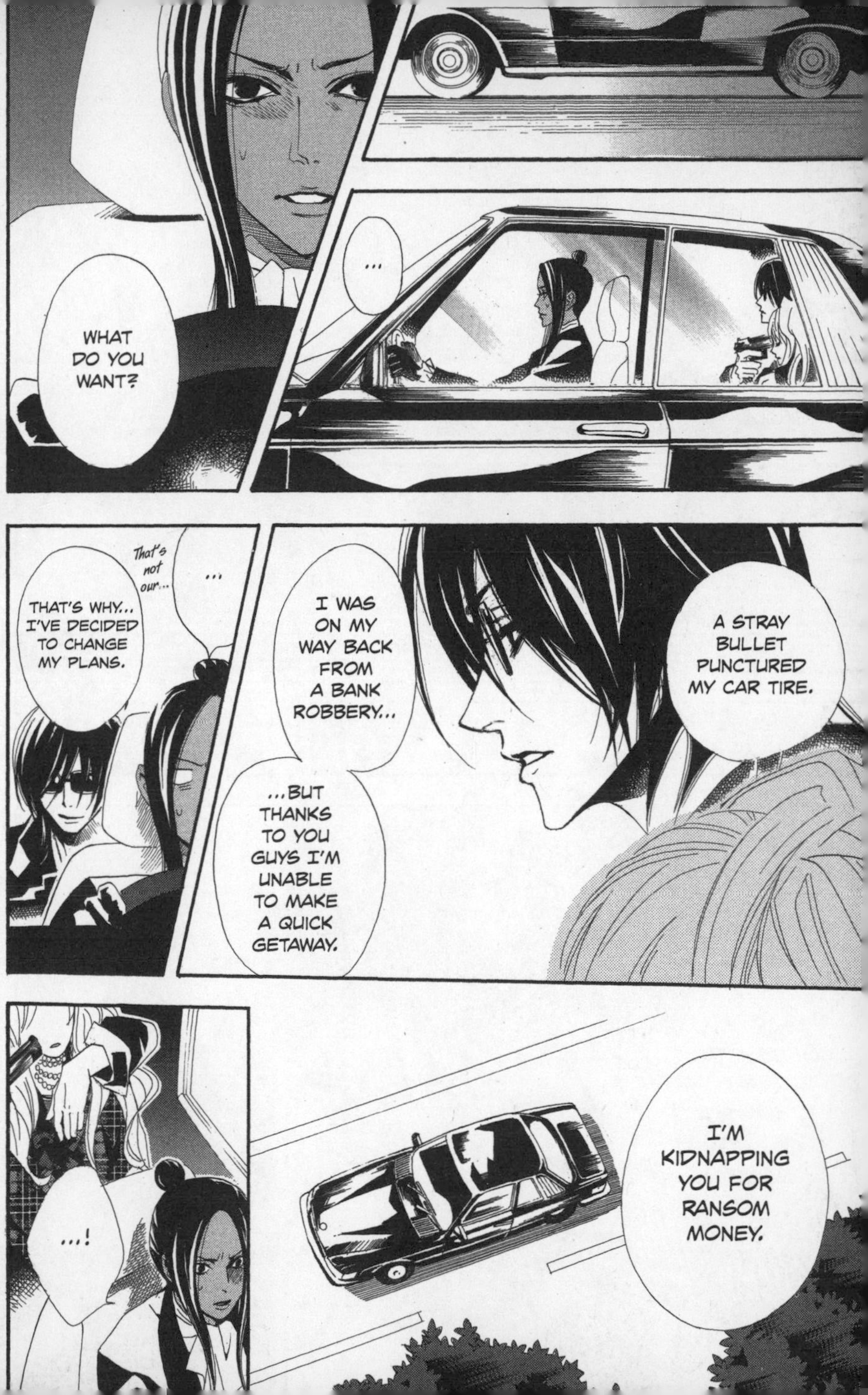
...
WHAT DO YOU WANT?
A STRAY BULLET PUNCTURED MY CAR TIRE.
I WAS ON MY WAY BACK FROM A BANK ROBBERY...
...BUT THANKS TO YOU GUYS I'M UNABLE TO MAKE A QUICK GETAWAY.
...
That's not our...
THAT'S WHY... I'VE DECIDED TO CHANGE MY PLANS.
I'M KIDNAPPING YOU FOR RANSOM MONEY.
...!

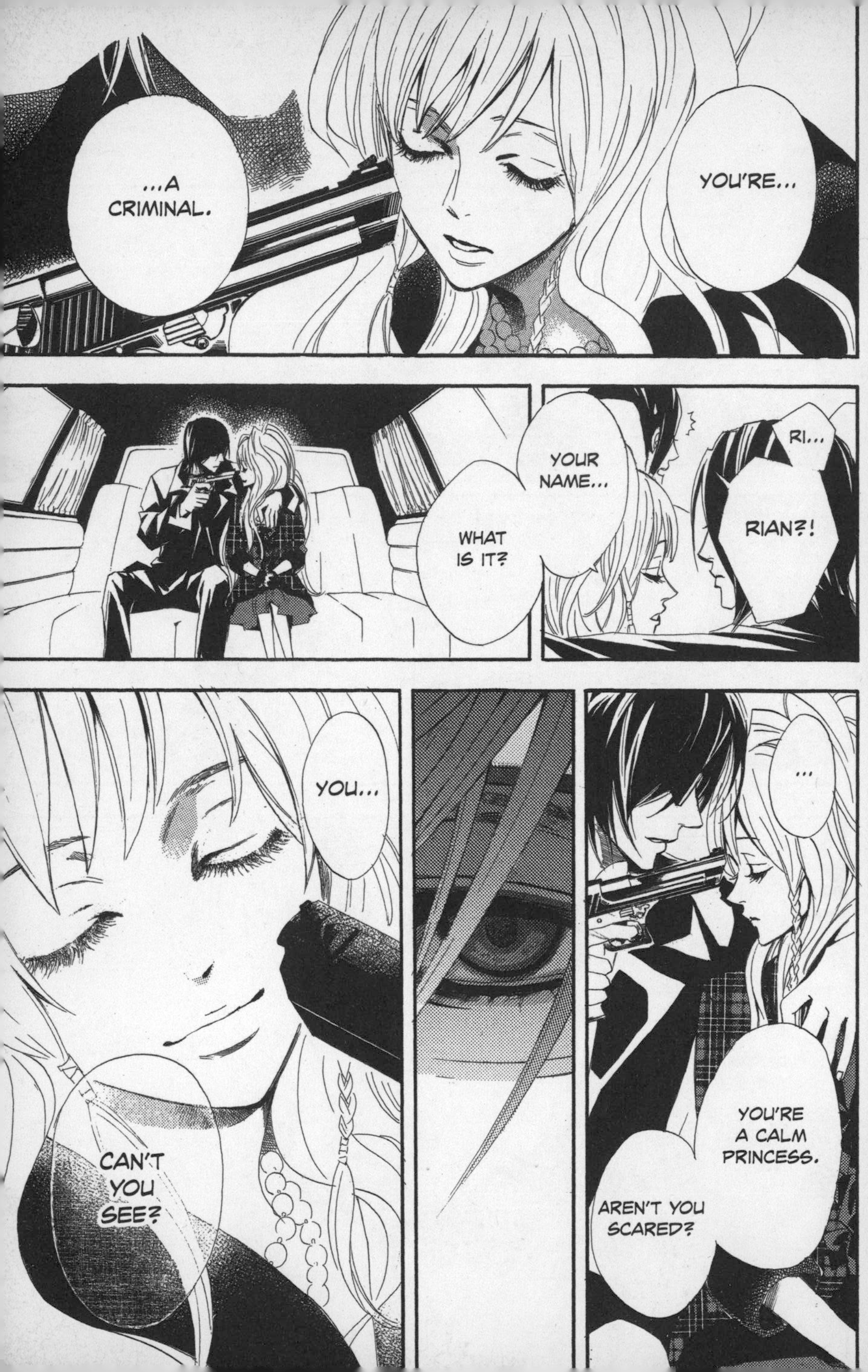
YOU'RE...
...A CRIMINAL.
RI...
RIAN?!
YOUR NAME...
WHAT IS IT?
...
YOU'RE A CALM PRINCESS.
AREN'T YOU SCARED?
YOU...
CAN'T YOU SEE?

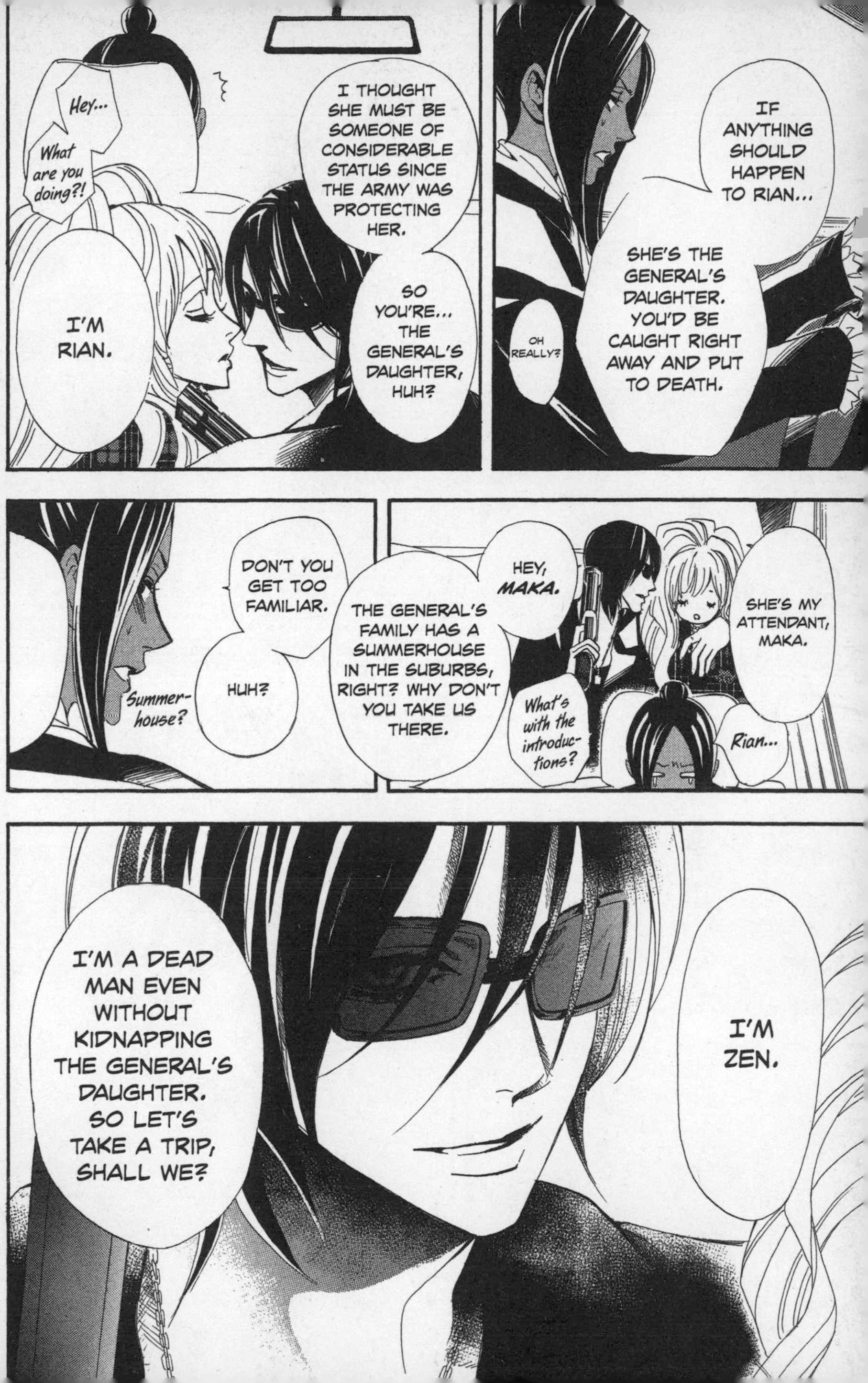
IF ANYTHING SHOULD HAPPEN TO RIAN...
SHE'S THE GENERAL'S DAUGHTER. YOU'D BE CAUGHT RIGHT AWAY AND PUT TO DEATH.
OH REALLY?
I THOUGHT SHE MUST BE SOMEONE OF CONSIDERABLE STATUS SINCE THE ARMY WAS PROTECTING HER.
Hey...
What are you doing?!
SO YOU'RE... THE GENERAL'S DAUGHTER, HUH?
I'M RIAN.
SHE'S MY ATTENDANT, MAKA.
HEY, *MAKA.*
Rian...
What's with the introductions?
THE GENERAL'S FAMILY HAS A SUMMERHOUSE IN THE SUBURBS, RIGHT? WHY DON'T YOU TAKE US THERE.
DON'T YOU GET TOO FAMILIAR.
HUH?
Summer-house?
I'M ZEN.
I'M A DEAD MAN EVEN WITHOUT KIDNAPPING THE GENERAL'S DAUGHTER. SO LET'S TAKE A TRIP, SHALL WE?

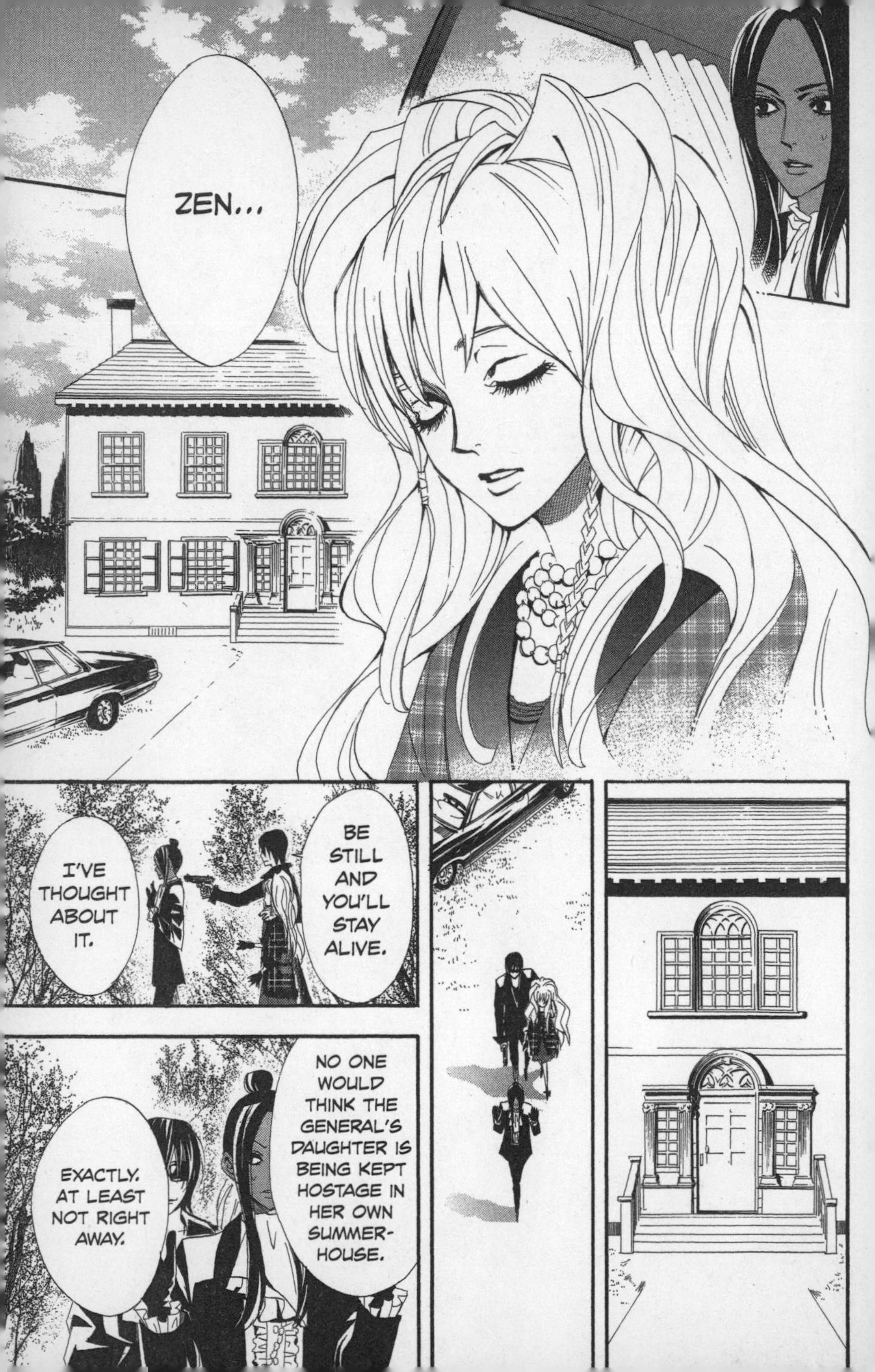
ZEN...
BE STILL AND YOU'LL STAY ALIVE.
I'VE THOUGHT ABOUT IT.
NO ONE WOULD THINK THE GENERAL'S DAUGHTER IS BEING KEPT HOSTAGE IN HER OWN SUMMER-HOUSE.
EXACTLY. AT LEAST NOT RIGHT AWAY.

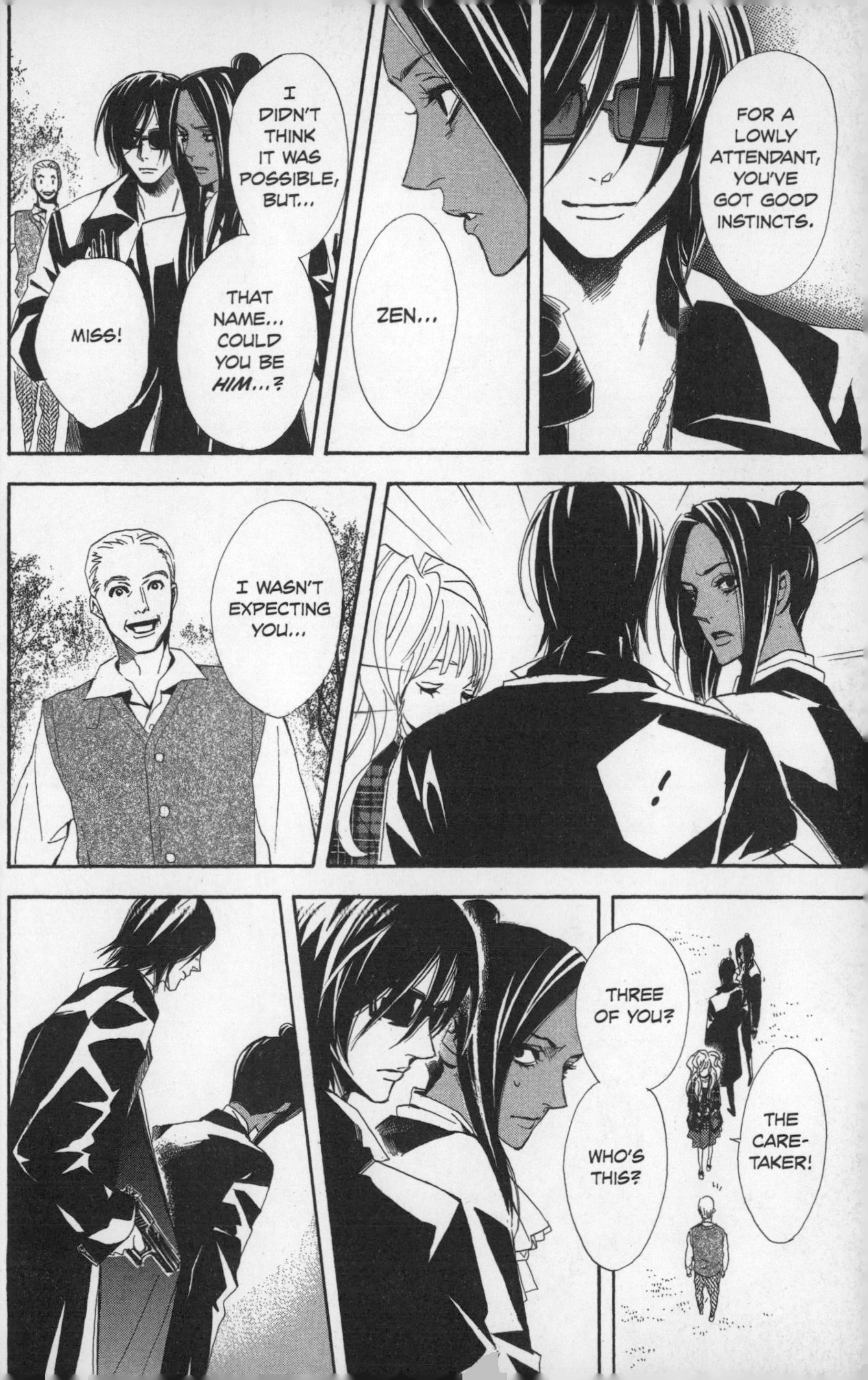
FOR A LOWLY ATTENDANT, YOU'VE GOT GOOD INSTINCTS.
ZEN...
I DIDN'T THINK IT WAS POSSIBLE, BUT...
THAT NAME... COULD YOU BE *HIM*...?
MISS!
!
I WASN'T EXPECTING YOU...
THREE OF YOU?
THE CARE-TAKER!
WHO'S THIS?

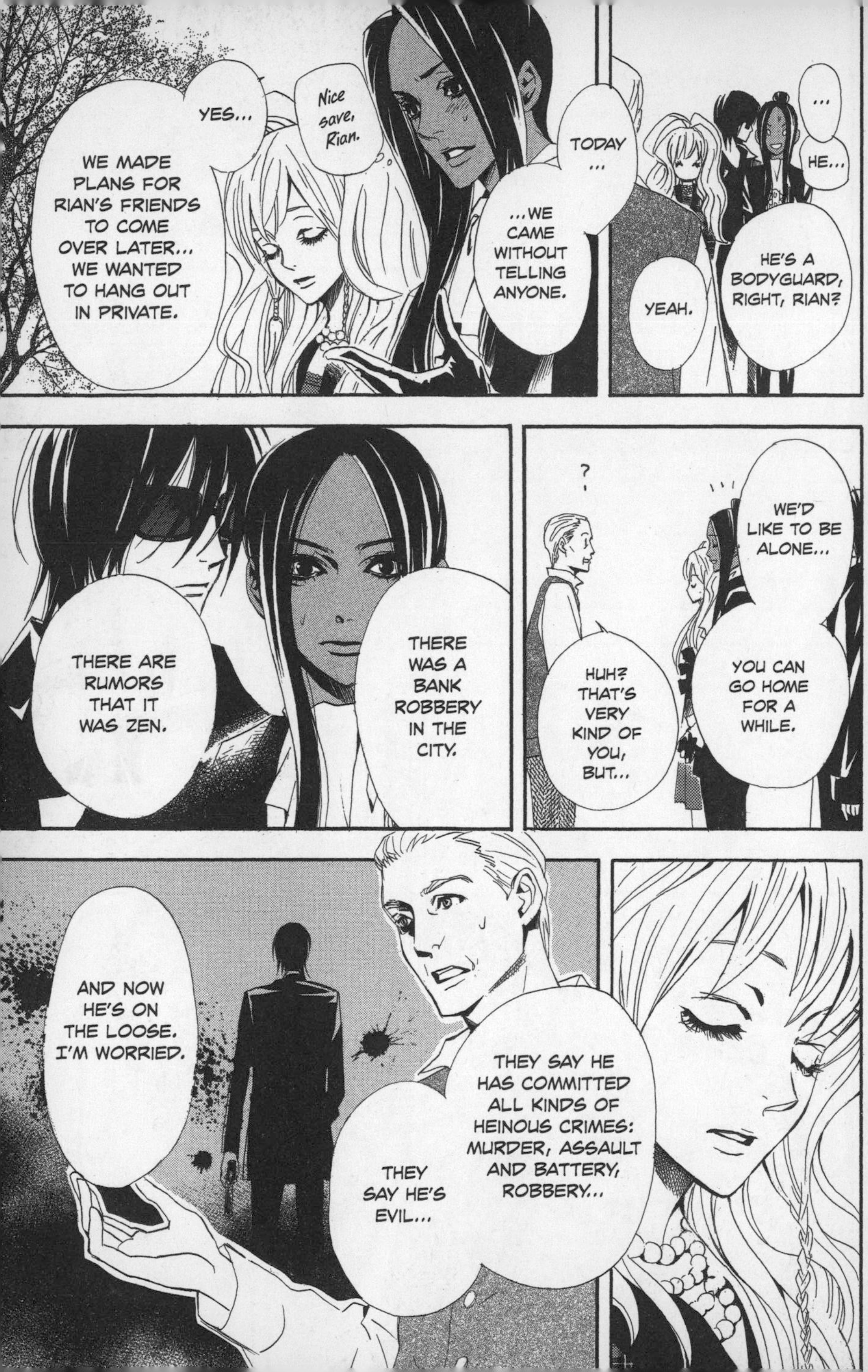
...
HE...
HE'S A BODYGUARD, RIGHT, RIAN?
YEAH.
TODAY ...
...WE CAME WITHOUT TELLING ANYONE.
Nice save, Rian.
YES...
WE MADE PLANS FOR RIAN'S FRIENDS TO COME OVER LATER... WE WANTED TO HANG OUT IN PRIVATE.
?
WE'D LIKE TO BE ALONE...
YOU CAN GO HOME FOR A WHILE.
HUH? THAT'S VERY KIND OF YOU, BUT...
THERE WAS A BANK ROBBERY IN THE CITY.
THERE ARE RUMORS THAT IT WAS ZEN.
THEY SAY HE HAS COMMITTED ALL KINDS OF HEINOUS CRIMES: MURDER, ASSAULT AND BATTERY, ROBBERY...
THEY SAY HE'S EVIL...
AND NOW HE'S ON THE LOOSE. I'M WORRIED.

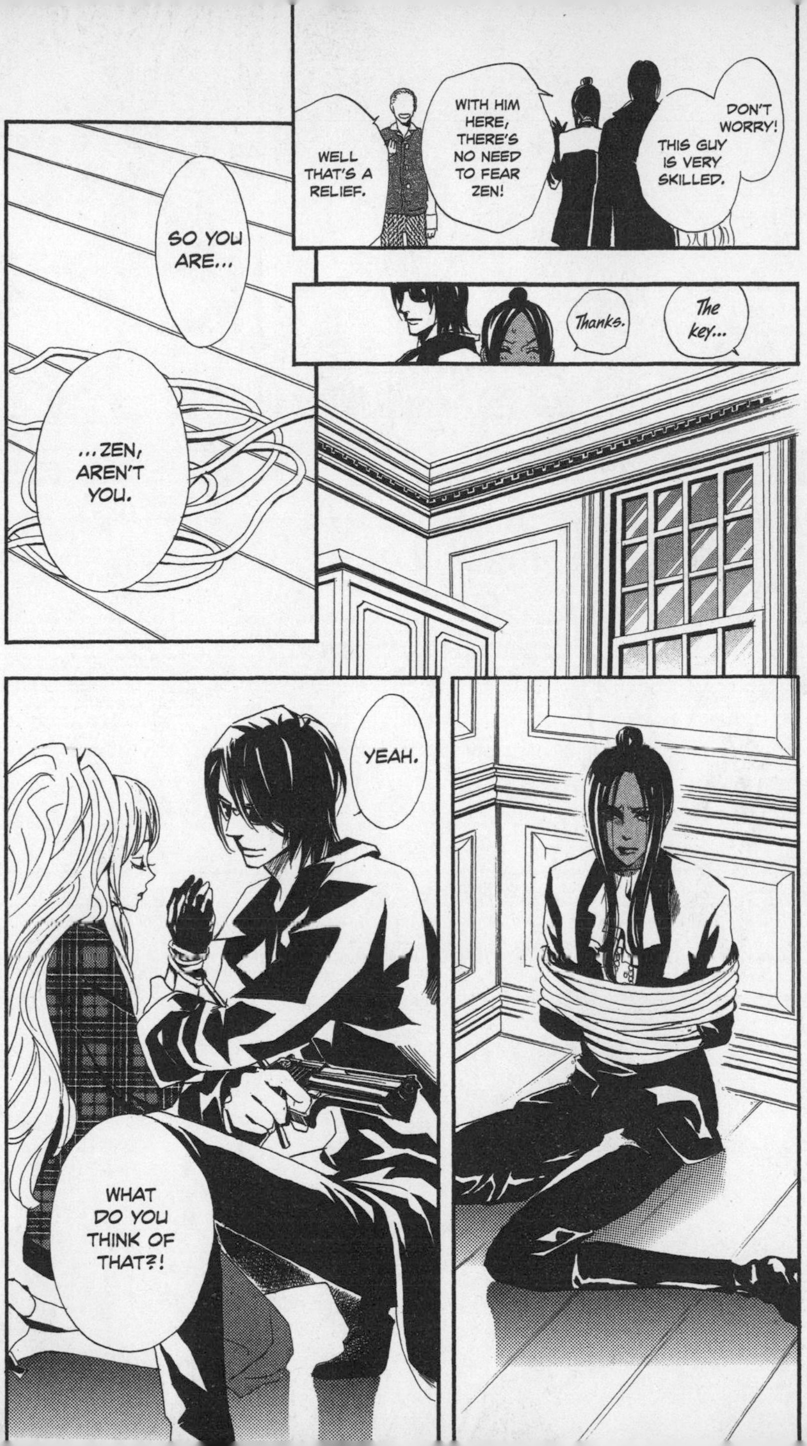
DON'T WORRY! THIS GUY IS VERY SKILLED.
WITH HIM HERE, THERE'S NO NEED TO FEAR ZEN!
WELL THAT'S A RELIEF.
The key...
Thanks.
SO YOU ARE...
...ZEN, AREN'T YOU.
YEAH.
WHAT DO YOU THINK OF THAT?!

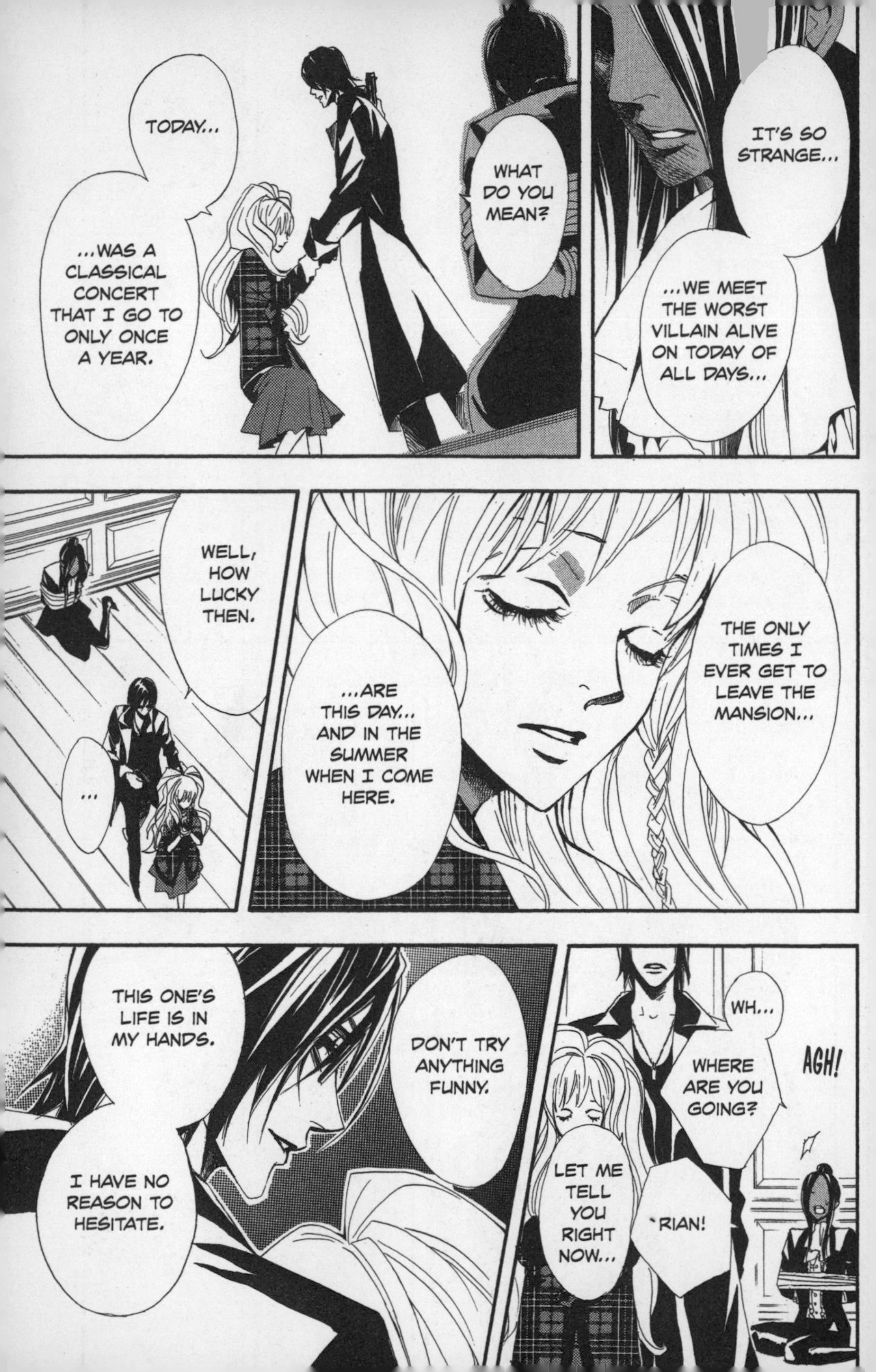
IT'S SO STRANGE...
...WE MEET THE WORST VILLAIN ALIVE ON TODAY OF ALL DAYS...
WHAT DO YOU MEAN?
TODAY...
...WAS A CLASSICAL CONCERT THAT I GO TO ONLY ONCE A YEAR.
THE ONLY TIMES I EVER GET TO LEAVE THE MANSION...
...ARE THIS DAY... AND IN THE SUMMER WHEN I COME HERE.
WELL, HOW LUCKY THEN.
...
WH...
WHERE ARE YOU GOING?
AGH!
'RIAN!
LET ME TELL YOU RIGHT NOW...
DON'T TRY ANYTHING FUNNY.
THIS ONE'S LIFE IS IN MY HANDS.
I HAVE NO REASON TO HESITATE.

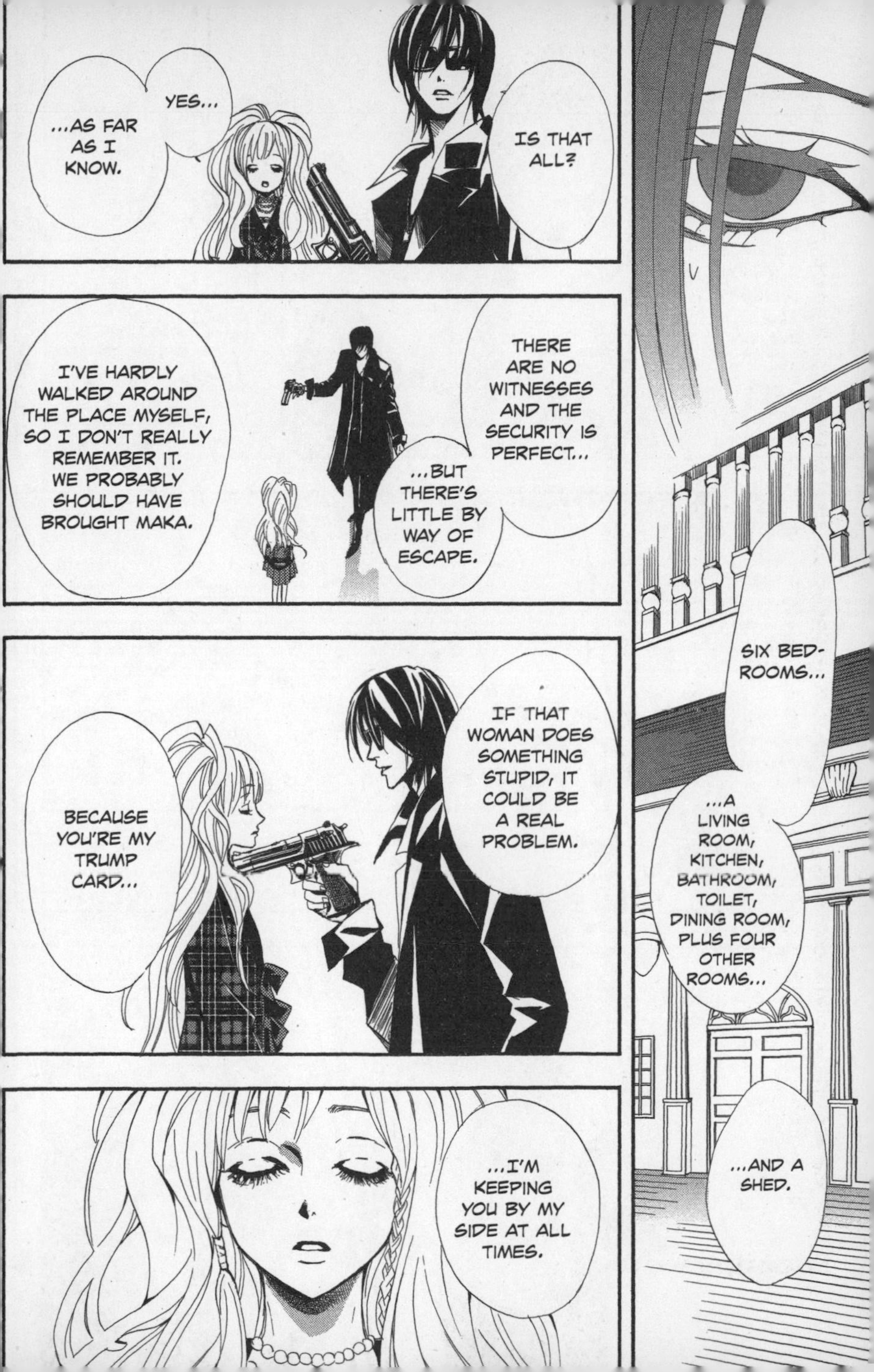
SIX BEDROOMS...
...A LIVING ROOM, KITCHEN, BATHROOM, TOILET, DINING ROOM, PLUS FOUR OTHER ROOMS...
...AND A SHED.
IS THAT ALL?
YES... ...AS FAR AS I KNOW.
THERE ARE NO WITNESSES AND THE SECURITY IS PERFECT...
...BUT THERE'S LITTLE BY WAY OF ESCAPE.
I'VE HARDLY WALKED AROUND THE PLACE MYSELF, SO I DON'T REALLY REMEMBER IT. WE PROBABLY SHOULD HAVE BROUGHT MAKA.
IF THAT WOMAN DOES SOMETHING STUPID, IT COULD BE A REAL PROBLEM.
BECAUSE YOU'RE MY TRUMP CARD...
...I'M KEEPING YOU BY MY SIDE AT ALL TIMES.

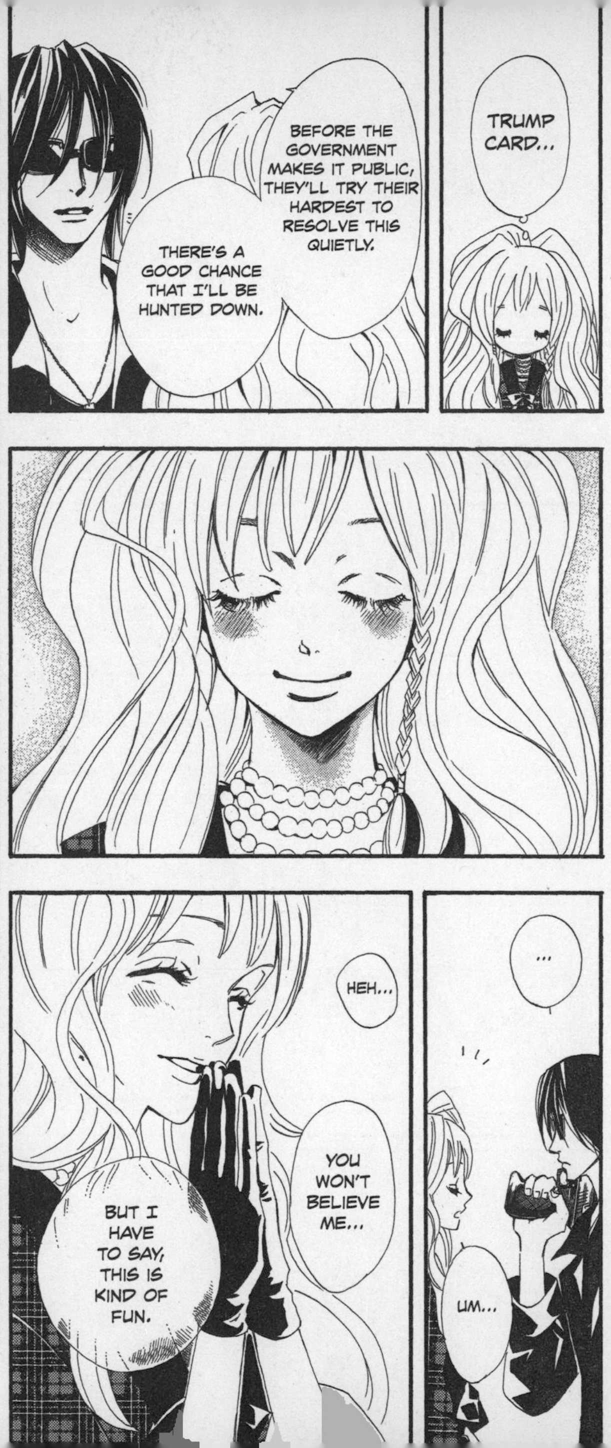
TRUMP CARD...
BEFORE THE GOVERNMENT MAKES IT PUBLIC, THEY'LL TRY THEIR HARDEST TO RESOLVE THIS QUIETLY.
THERE'S A GOOD CHANCE THAT I'LL BE HUNTED DOWN.
...
UM...
HEH...
YOU WON'T BELIEVE ME...
BUT I HAVE TO SAY, THIS IS KIND OF FUN.

2

It's completely my fault, but when I wrote the first episode of *Blank Slate*, I didn't think it would be serialized just like that, and I wrote the first episode completely viewing it as a standalone. Even should it be serialized, I thought I would be able to make a fresh start at it, so I was surprised when I saw it in the magazine as "Chapter 1"... Because of that, a lack of consistency arose between the serialized *Blank Slate* and the "Chapter 1" in the magazine, so I decided to change Chapter 1 in order to make the story easier to understand when we put out the graphic novel.
(To be continued...)

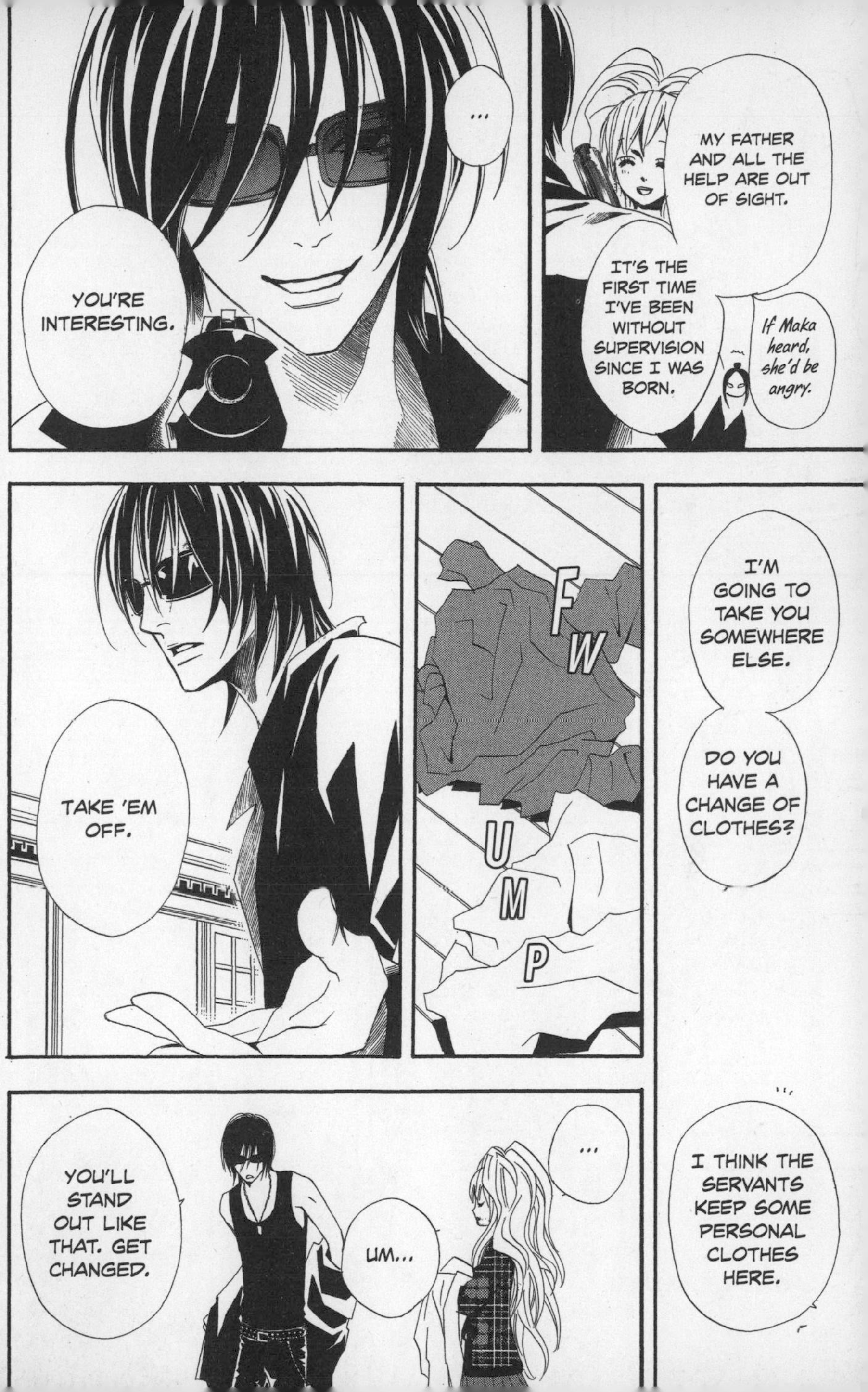
MY FATHER AND ALL THE HELP ARE OUT OF SIGHT.
IT'S THE FIRST TIME I'VE BEEN WITHOUT SUPERVISION SINCE I WAS BORN.
If Maka heard, she'd be angry.
...
YOU'RE INTERESTING.
I'M GOING TO TAKE YOU SOMEWHERE ELSE.
DO YOU HAVE A CHANGE OF CLOTHES?
FWUMP
TAKE 'EM OFF.
I THINK THE SERVANTS KEEP SOME PERSONAL CLOTHES HERE.
...
UM...
YOU'LL STAND OUT LIKE THAT. GET CHANGED.

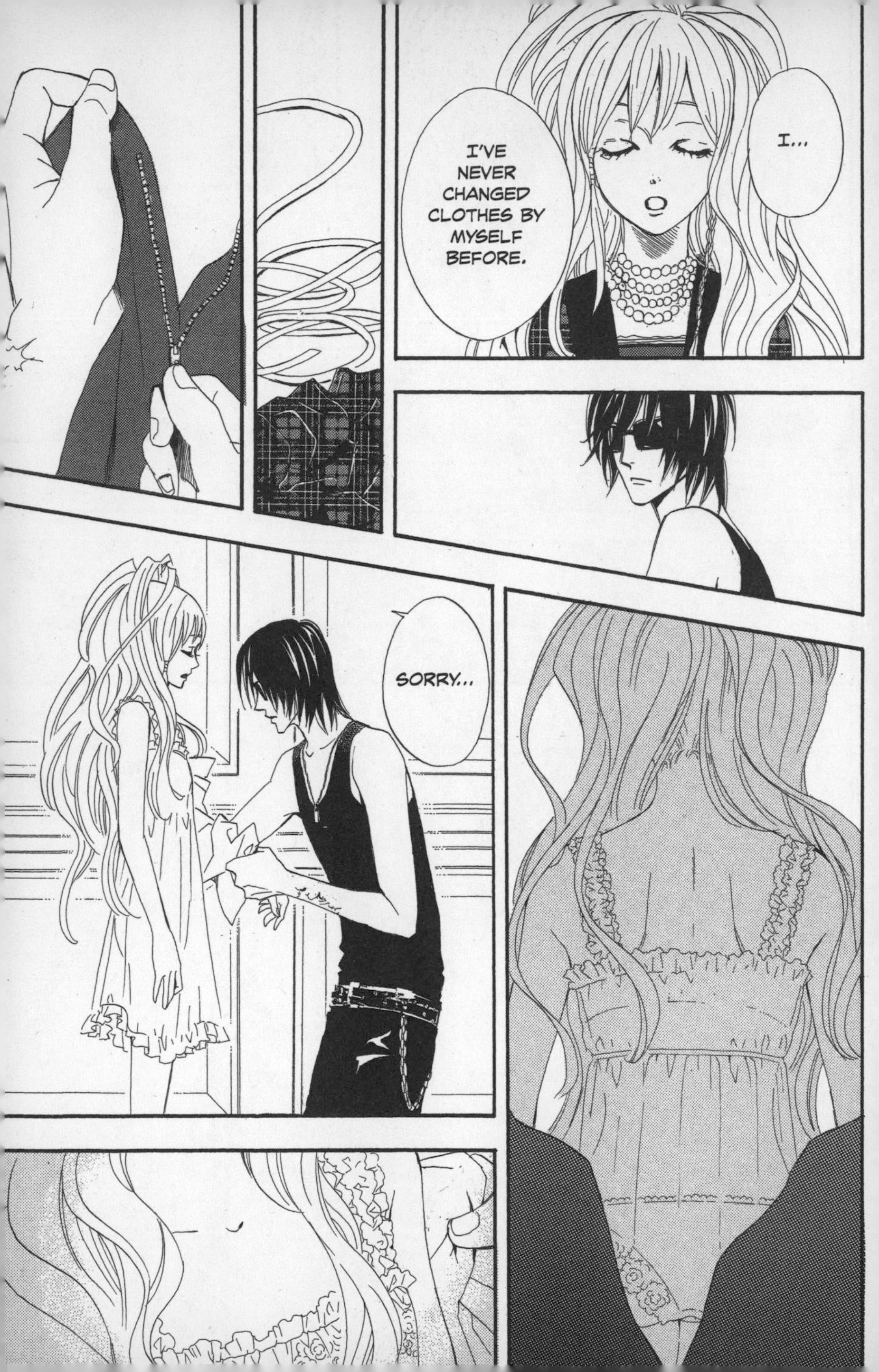
I...
I'VE NEVER CHANGED CLOTHES BY MYSELF BEFORE.
SORRY...

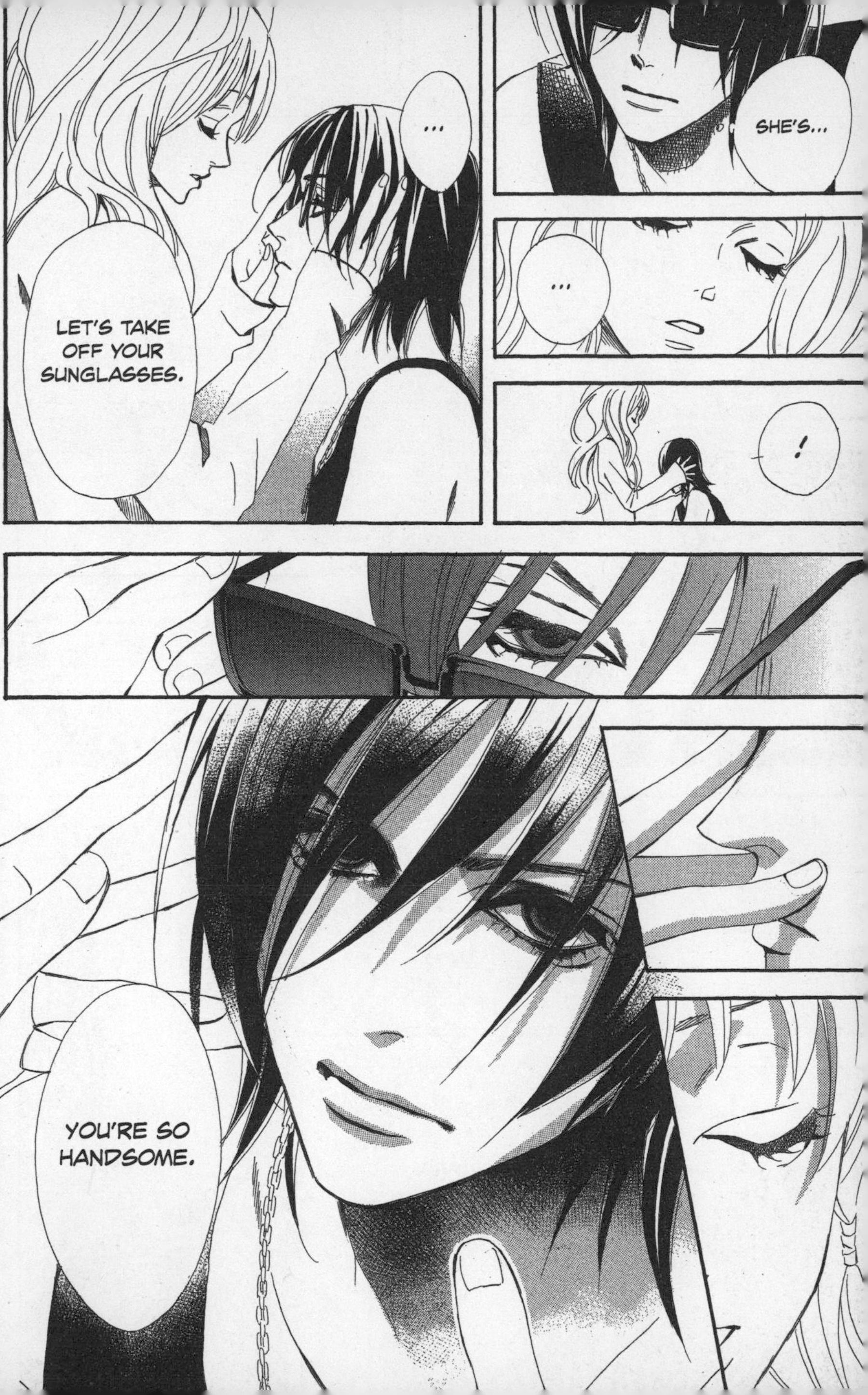
SHE'S...
...
!
...
LET'S TAKE OFF YOUR SUNGLASSES.
YOU'RE SO HANDSOME.

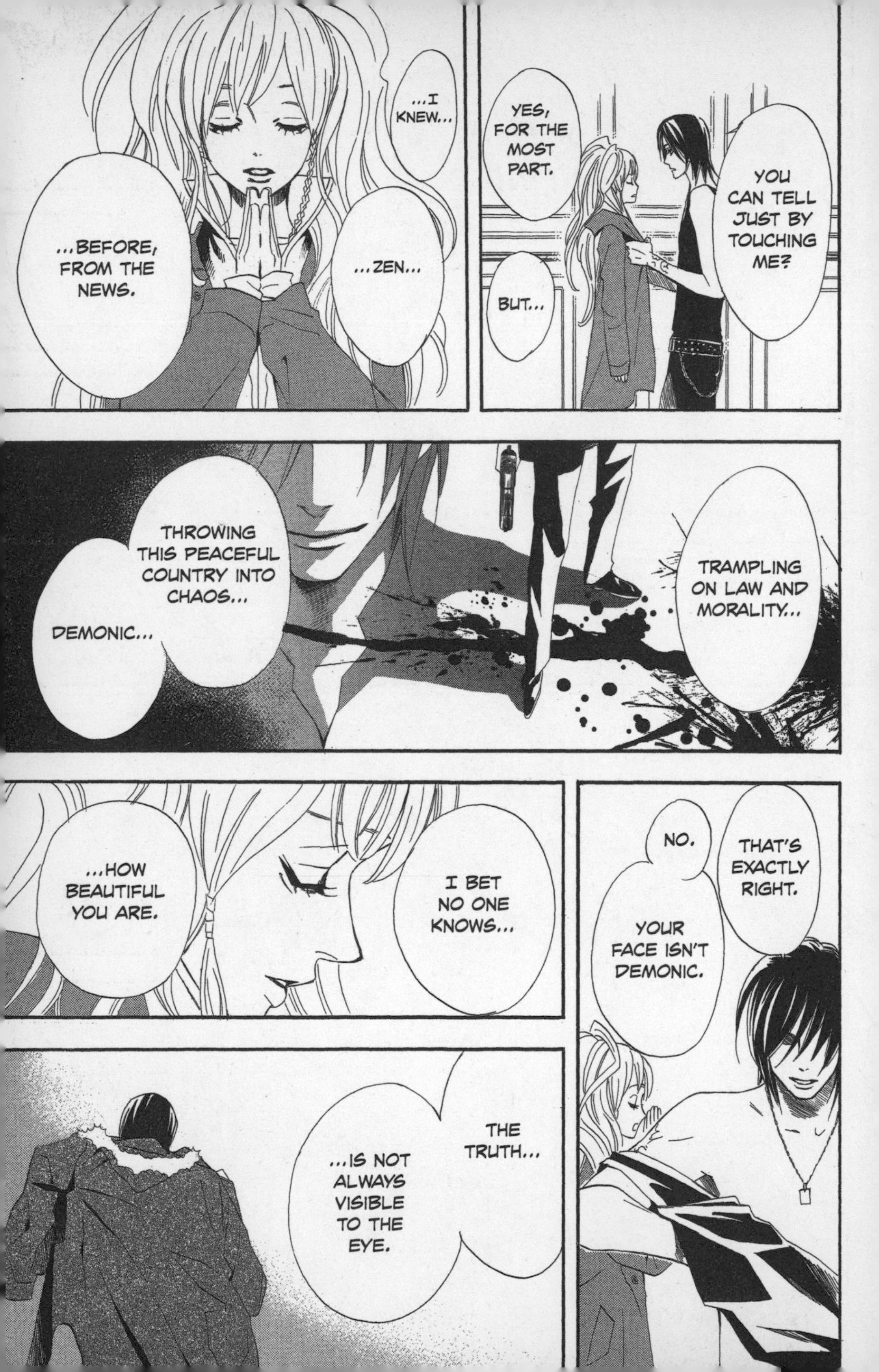
YOU CAN TELL JUST BY TOUCHING ME?
YES, FOR THE MOST PART.
BUT...
...I KNEW...
...ZEN...
...BEFORE, FROM THE NEWS.
TRAMPLING ON LAW AND MORALITY...
THROWING THIS PEACEFUL COUNTRY INTO CHAOS...
DEMONIC...
THAT'S EXACTLY RIGHT.
NO.
YOUR FACE ISN'T DEMONIC.
I BET NO ONE KNOWS...
...HOW BEAUTIFUL YOU ARE.
THE TRUTH...
...IS NOT ALWAYS VISIBLE TO THE EYE.

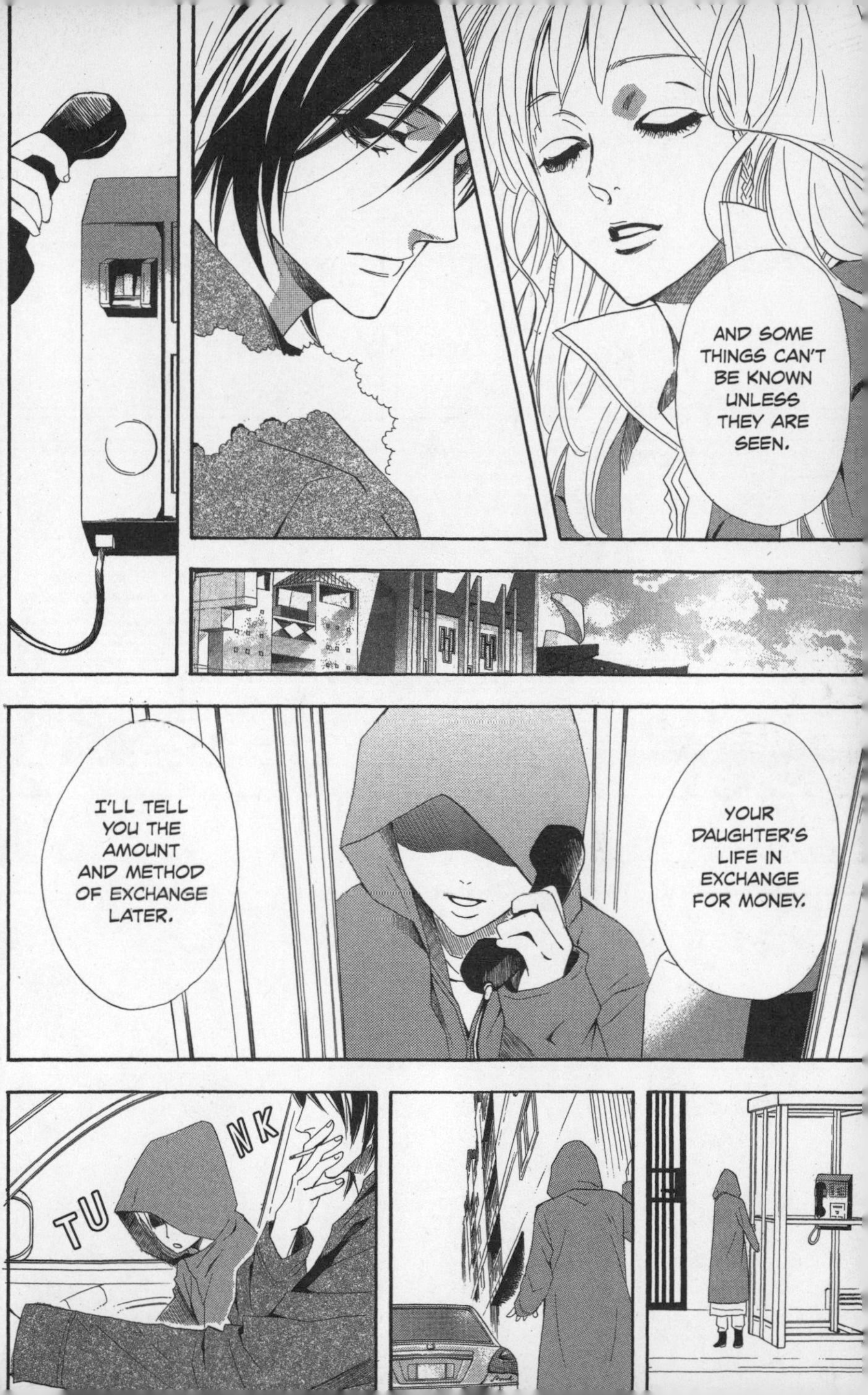
AND SOME THINGS CAN'T BE KNOWN UNLESS THEY ARE SEEN.
YOUR DAUGHTER'S LIFE IN EXCHANGE FOR MONEY.
I'LL TELL YOU THE AMOUNT AND METHOD OF EXCHANGE LATER.
TU
NK

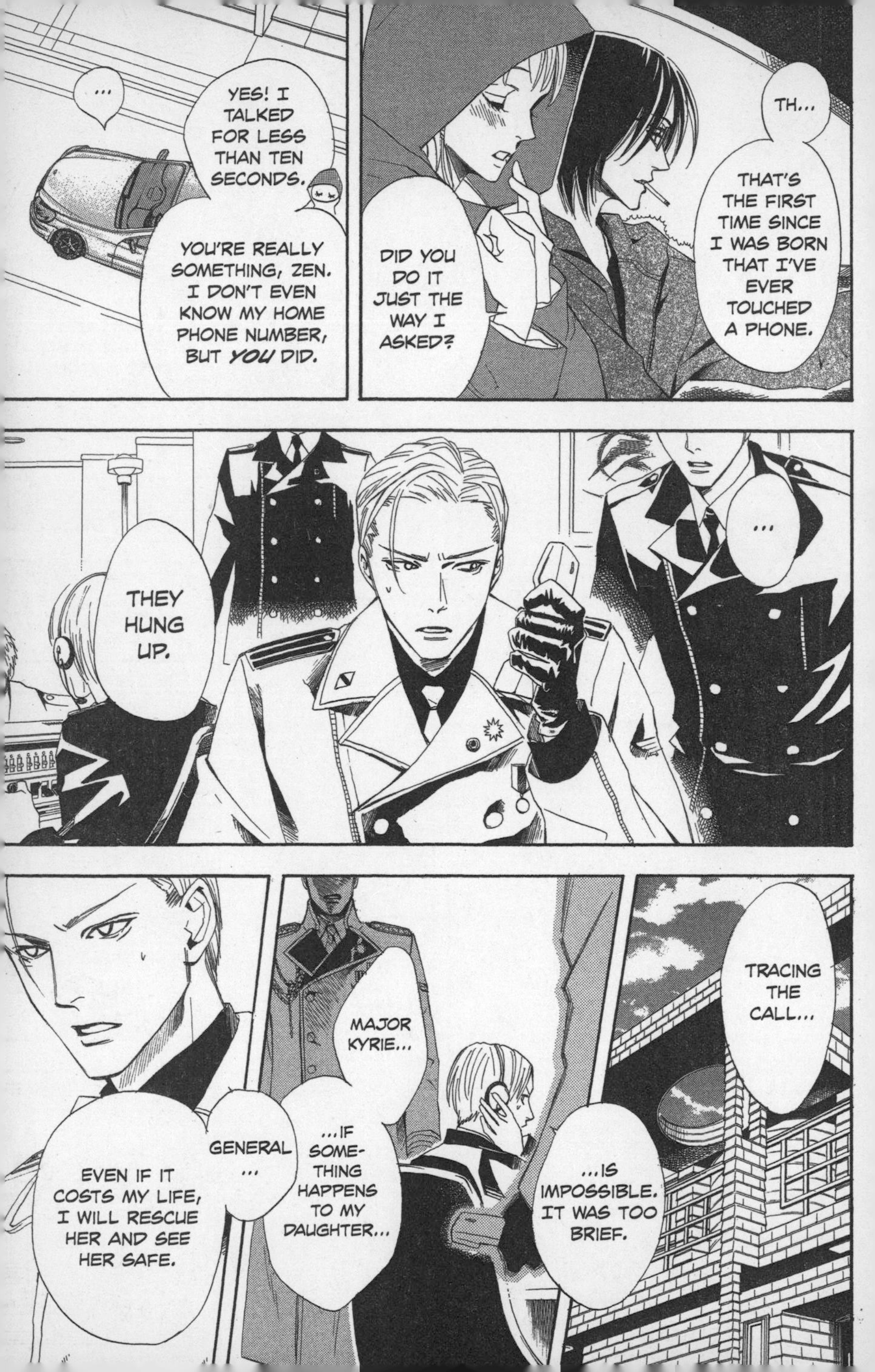
TH...
THAT'S THE FIRST TIME SINCE I WAS BORN THAT I'VE EVER TOUCHED A PHONE.
DID YOU DO IT JUST THE WAY I ASKED?
YES! I TALKED FOR LESS THAN TEN SECONDS.
...
YOU'RE REALLY SOMETHING, ZEN. I DON'T EVEN KNOW MY HOME PHONE NUMBER, BUT *YOU* DID.
...
THEY HUNG UP.
TRACING THE CALL...
...IS IMPOSSIBLE. IT WAS TOO BRIEF.
MAJOR KYRIE...
...IF SOMETHING HAPPENS TO MY DAUGHTER...
GENERAL...
EVEN IF IT COSTS MY LIFE, I WILL RESCUE HER AND SEE HER SAFE.

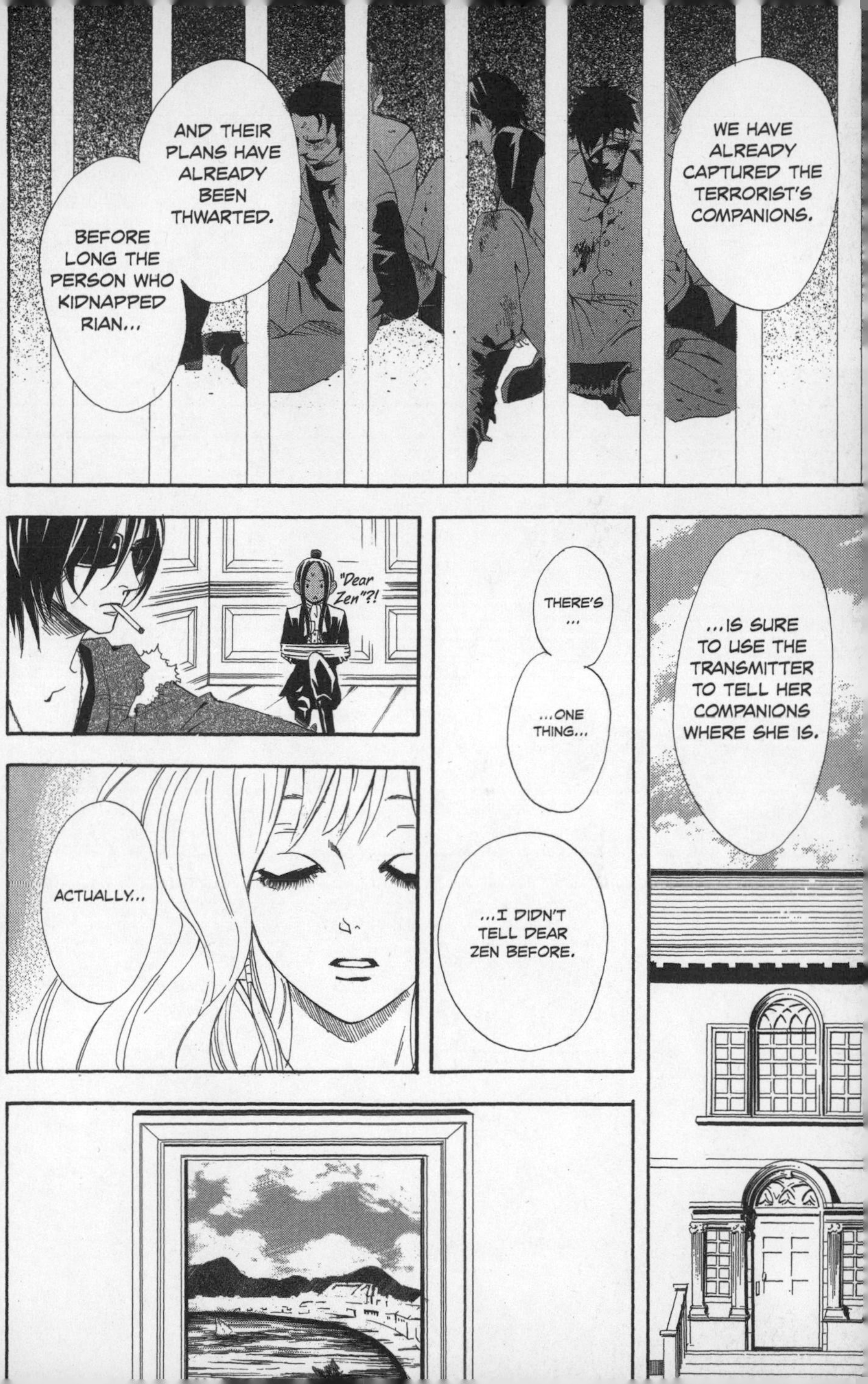
WE HAVE ALREADY CAPTURED THE TERRORIST'S COMPANIONS.
AND THEIR PLANS HAVE ALREADY BEEN THWARTED.
BEFORE LONG THE PERSON WHO KIDNAPPED RIAN...
...IS SURE TO USE THE TRANSMITTER TO TELL HER COMPANIONS WHERE SHE IS.
THERE'S...
...ONE THING...
...I DIDN'T TELL DEAR ZEN BEFORE.
"Dear Zen"?!
ACTUALLY...

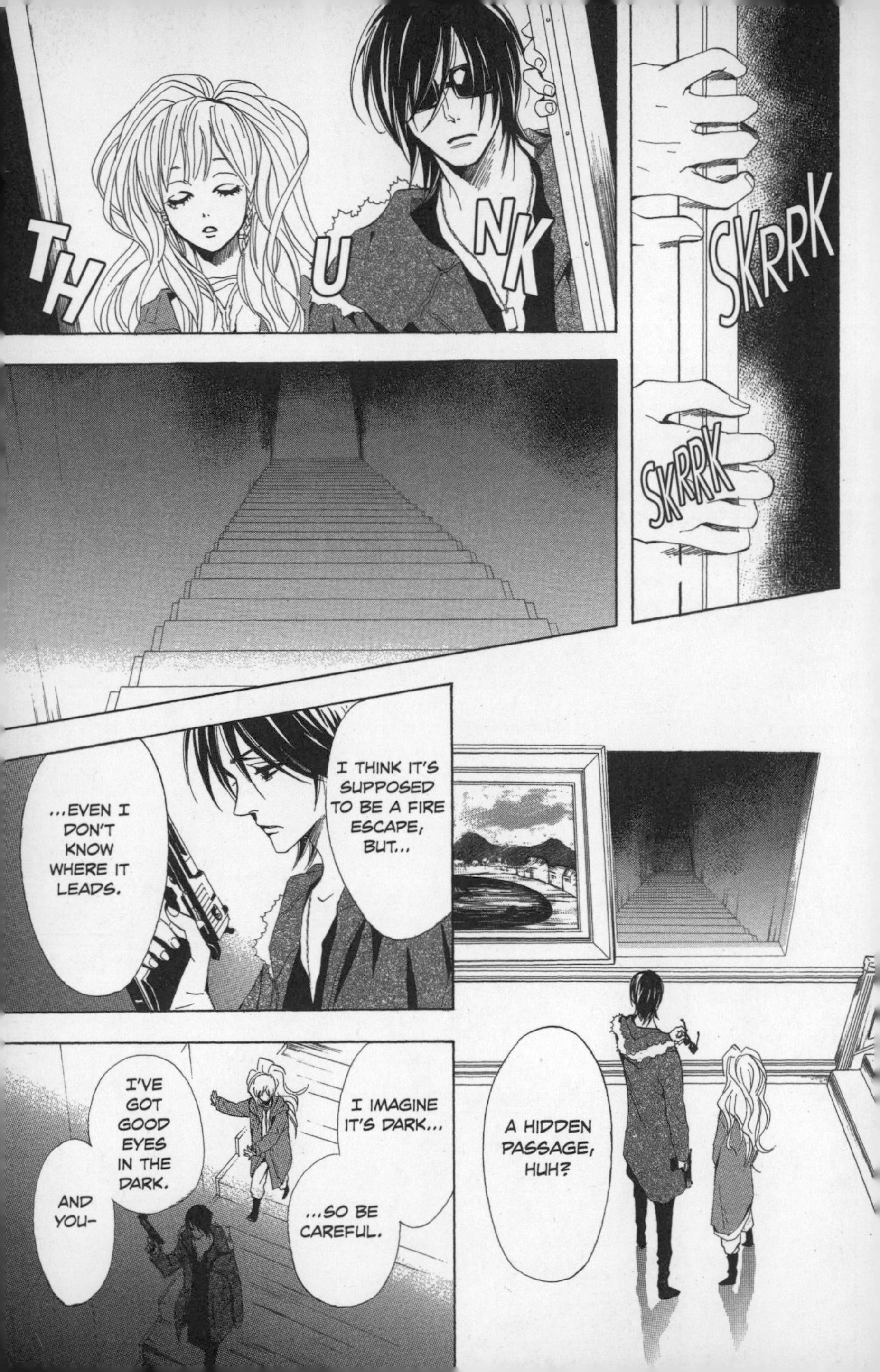
SKRRK
SKRRK
THUNK
A HIDDEN PASSAGE, HUH?
I THINK IT'S SUPPOSED TO BE A FIRE ESCAPE, BUT...
...EVEN I DON'T KNOW WHERE IT LEADS.
I IMAGINE IT'S DARK...
...SO BE CAREFUL.
I'VE GOT GOOD EYES IN THE DARK.
AND YOU-

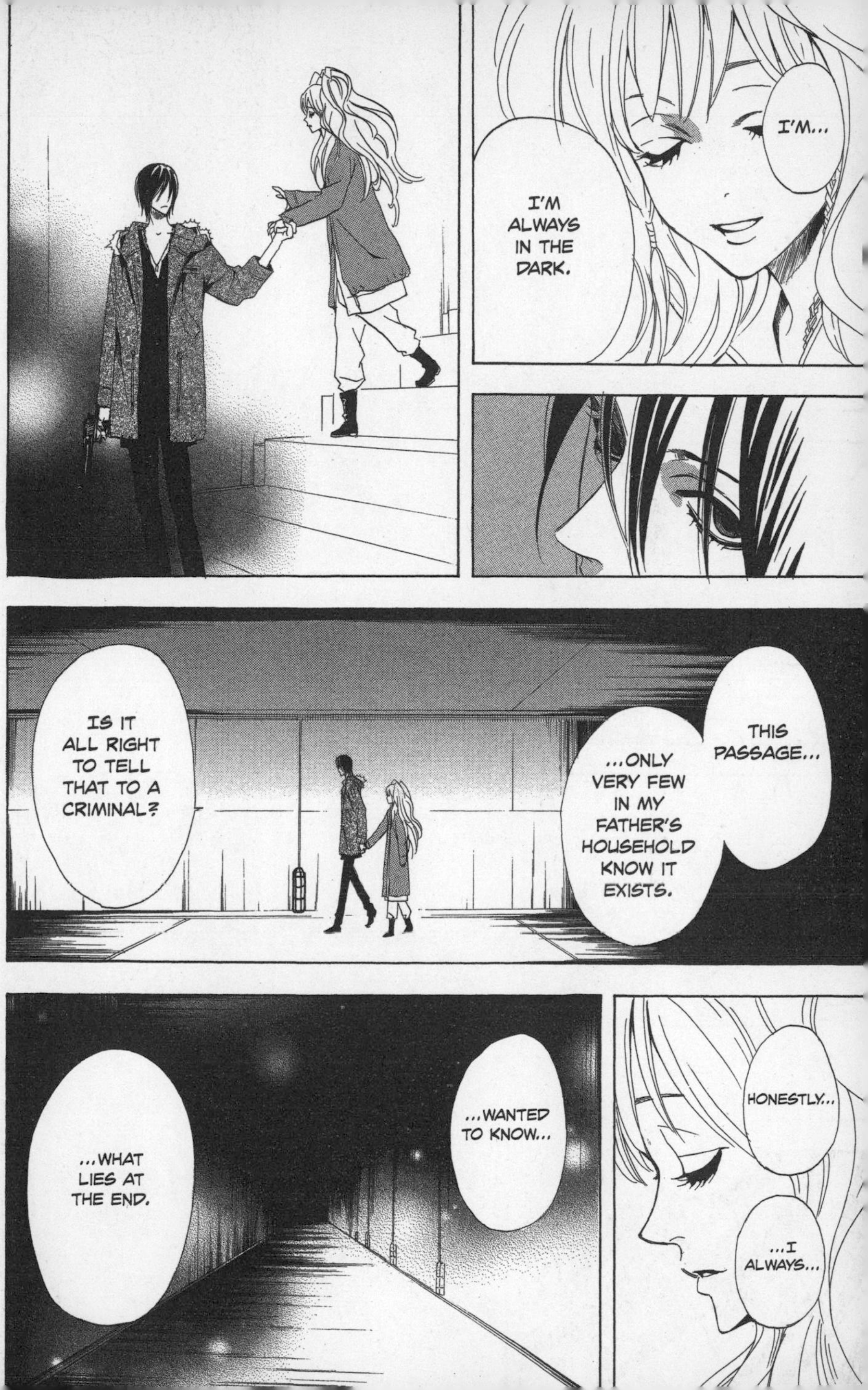
I'M...
I'M ALWAYS IN THE DARK.
THIS PASSAGE...
...ONLY VERY FEW IN MY FATHER'S HOUSEHOLD KNOW IT EXISTS.
IS IT ALL RIGHT TO TELL THAT TO A CRIMINAL?
HONESTLY...
...I ALWAYS...
...WANTED TO KNOW...
...WHAT LIES AT THE END.

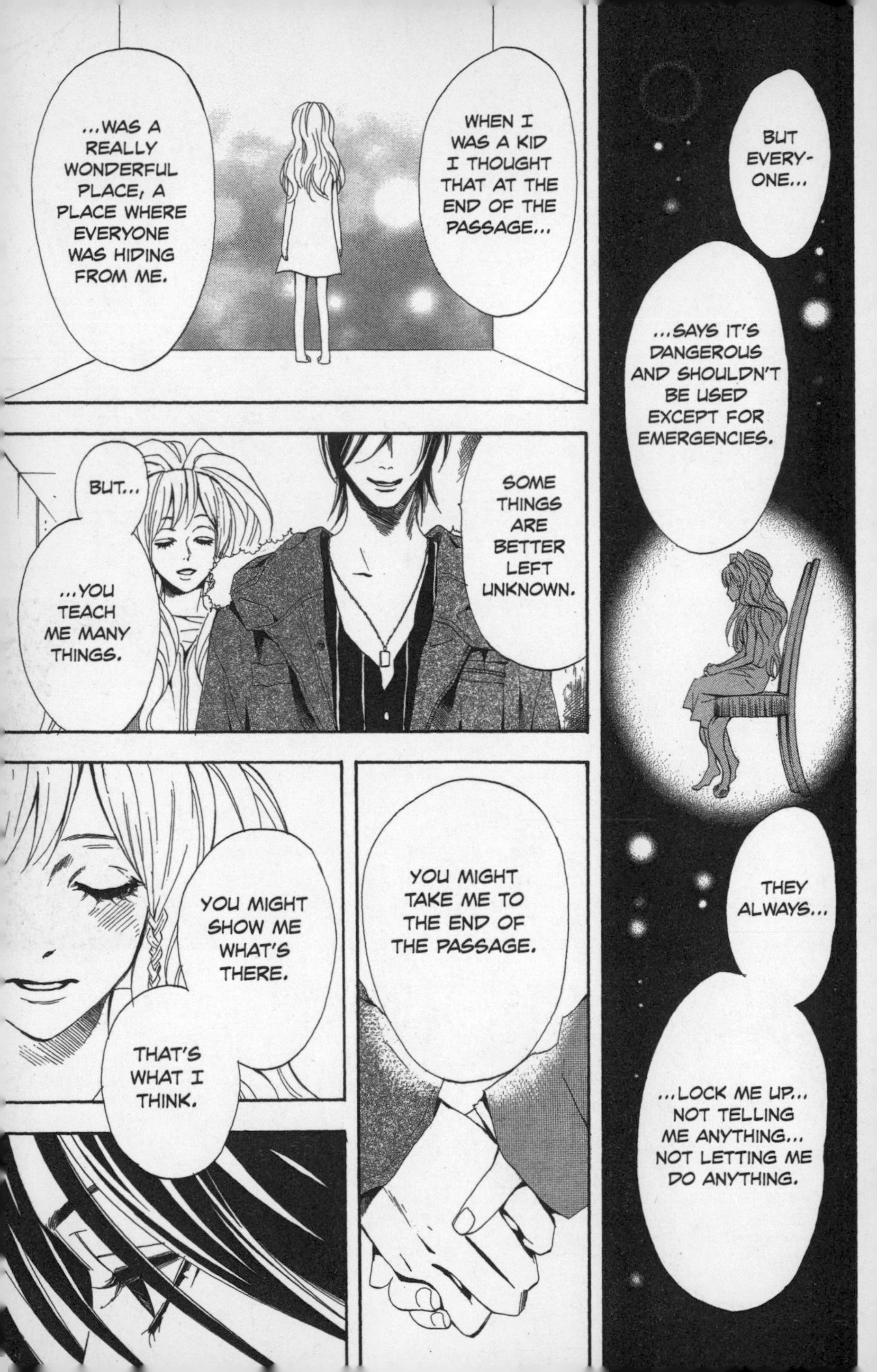
BUT EVERY-ONE...
...SAYS IT'S DANGEROUS AND SHOULDN'T BE USED EXCEPT FOR EMERGENCIES.
THEY ALWAYS...
...LOCK ME UP... NOT TELLING ME ANYTHING... NOT LETTING ME DO ANYTHING.
WHEN I WAS A KID I THOUGHT THAT AT THE END OF THE PASSAGE...
...WAS A REALLY WONDERFUL PLACE, A PLACE WHERE EVERYONE WAS HIDING FROM ME.
SOME THINGS ARE BETTER LEFT UNKNOWN.
BUT...
...YOU TEACH ME MANY THINGS.
YOU MIGHT TAKE ME TO THE END OF THE PASSAGE.
YOU MIGHT SHOW ME WHAT'S THERE.
THAT'S WHAT I THINK.

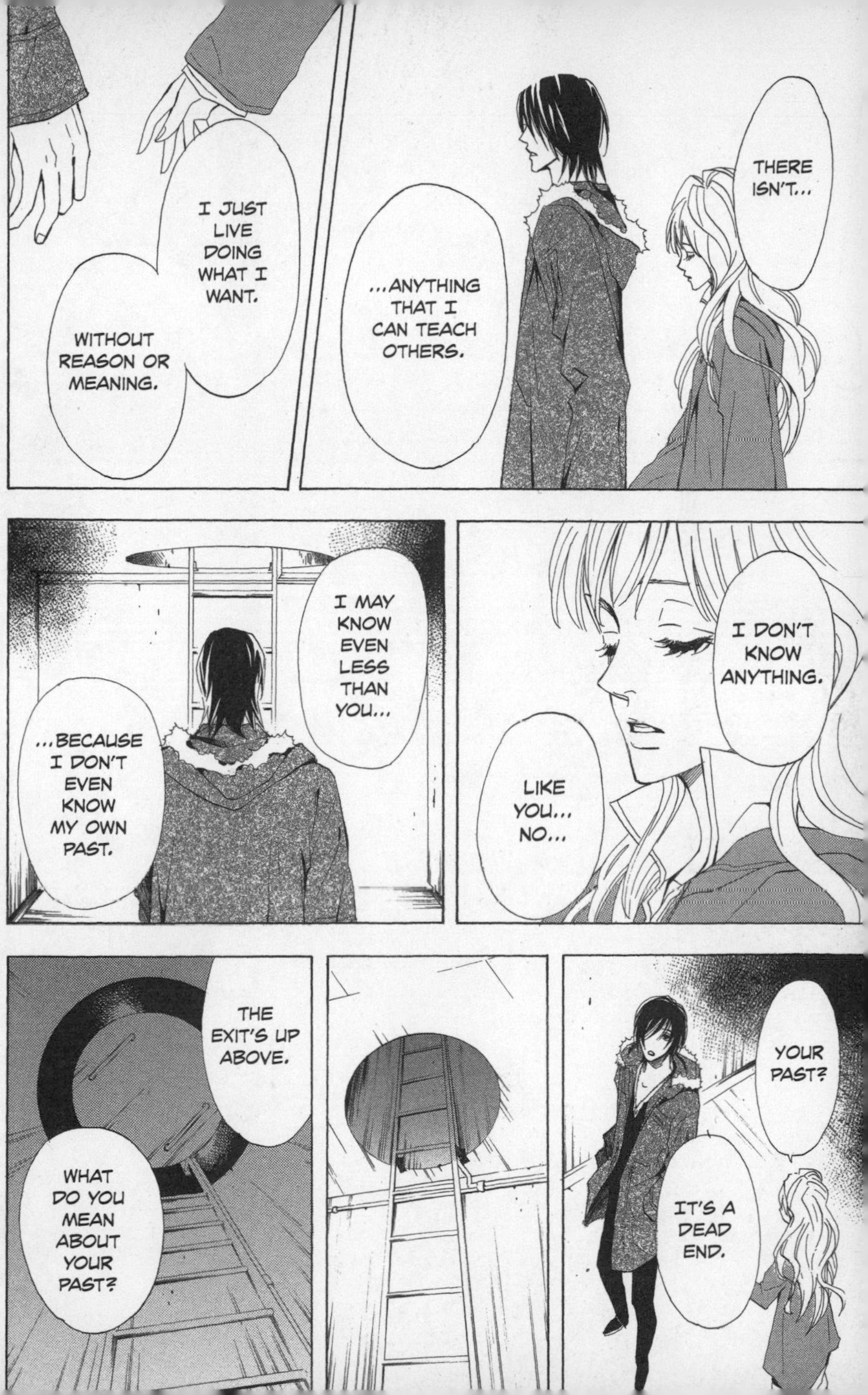
THERE ISN'T...
...ANYTHING THAT I CAN TEACH OTHERS.
I JUST LIVE DOING WHAT I WANT.
WITHOUT REASON OR MEANING.
I DON'T KNOW ANYTHING.
LIKE YOU... NO...
I MAY KNOW EVEN LESS THAN YOU...
...BECAUSE I DON'T EVEN KNOW MY OWN PAST.
YOUR PAST?
IT'S A DEAD END.
THE EXIT'S UP ABOVE.
WHAT DO YOU MEAN ABOUT YOUR PAST?

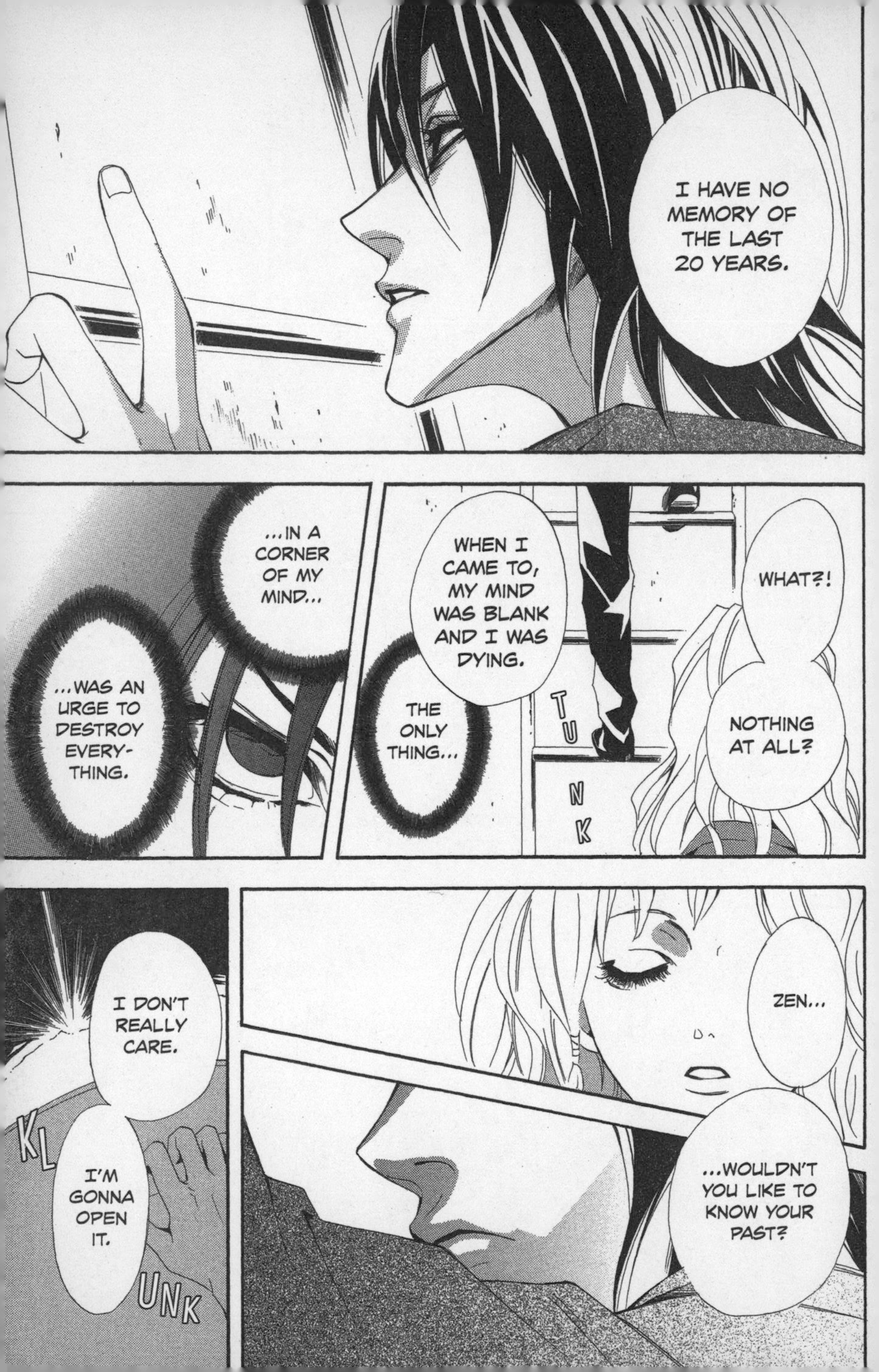
I HAVE NO MEMORY OF THE LAST 20 YEARS.
WHAT?!
NOTHING AT ALL?
WHEN I CAME TO, MY MIND WAS BLANK AND I WAS DYING.
TUNK
THE ONLY THING...
...IN A CORNER OF MY MIND...
...WAS AN URGE TO DESTROY EVERY-THING.
ZEN...
...WOULDN'T YOU LIKE TO KNOW YOUR PAST?
I DON'T REALLY CARE.
I'M GONNA OPEN IT.
KLUNK

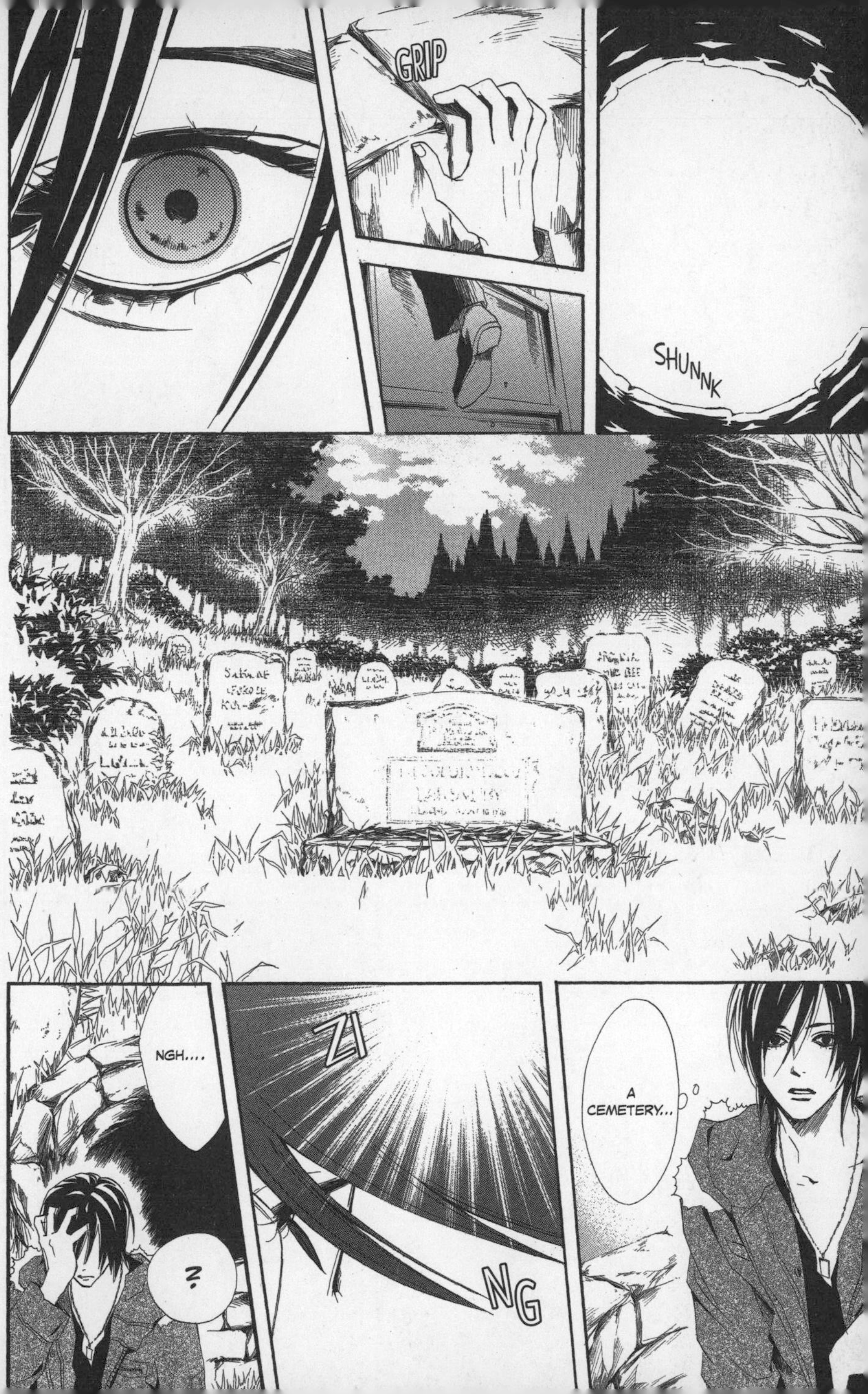
SHUNNK
GRIP
A CEMETERY...
ZI
NG
NGH....
?

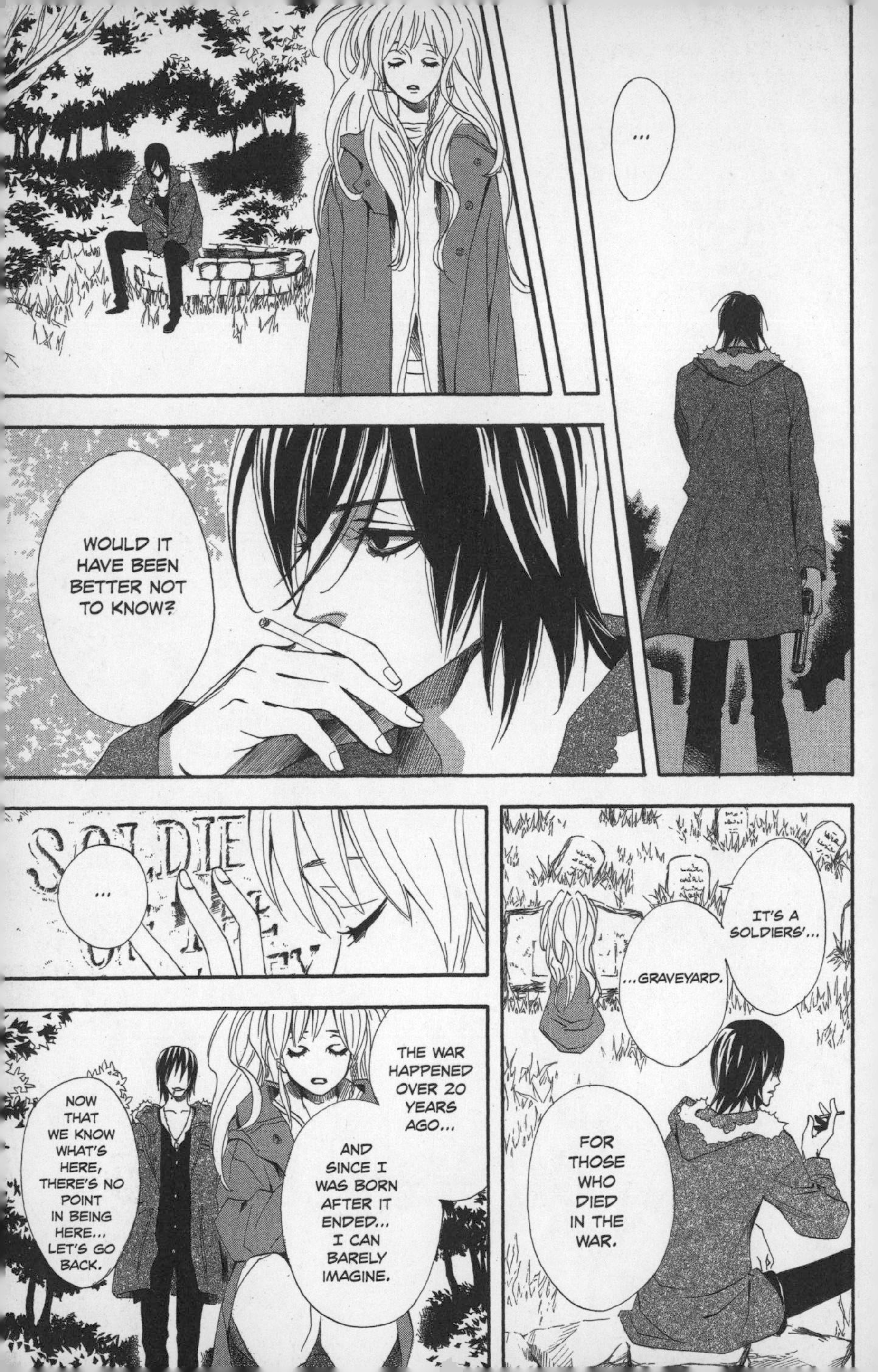
...
WOULD IT HAVE BEEN BETTER NOT TO KNOW?
IT'S A SOLDIERS'...
...GRAVEYARD.
FOR THOSE WHO DIED IN THE WAR.
SOLDIE
...
THE WAR HAPPENED OVER 20 YEARS AGO...
AND SINCE I WAS BORN AFTER IT ENDED... I CAN BARELY IMAGINE.
NOW THAT WE KNOW WHAT'S HERE, THERE'S NO POINT IN BEING HERE... LET'S GO BACK.

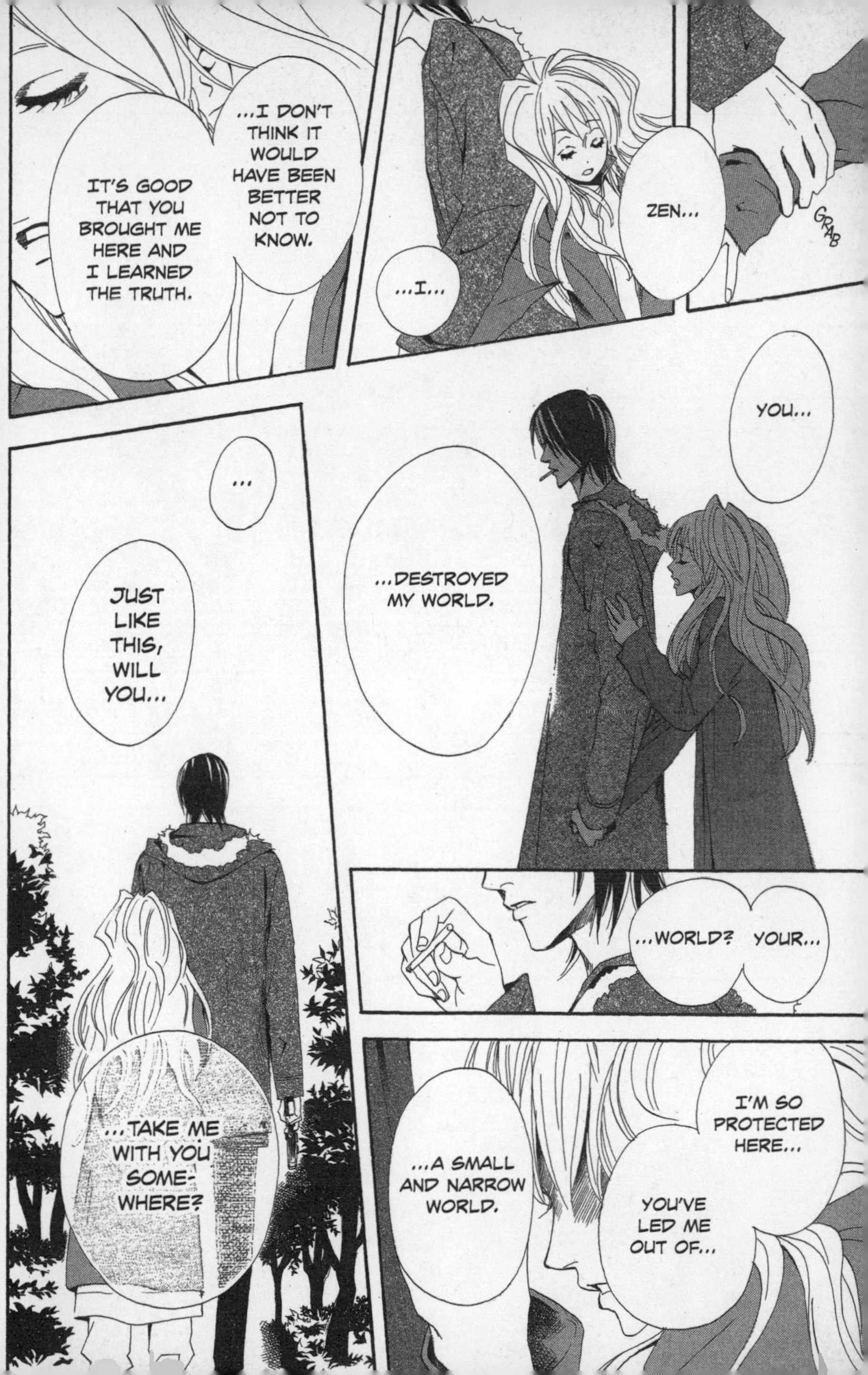
GRAB
ZEN...
...I...
...I DON'T THINK IT WOULD HAVE BEEN BETTER NOT TO KNOW.
IT'S GOOD THAT YOU BROUGHT ME HERE AND I LEARNED THE TRUTH.
YOU...
...DESTROYED MY WORLD.
YOUR...
...WORLD?
I'M SO PROTECTED HERE...
YOU'VE LED ME OUT OF...
...A SMALL AND NARROW WORLD.
...
JUST LIKE THIS, WILL YOU...
...TAKE ME WITH YOU SOME-WHERE?

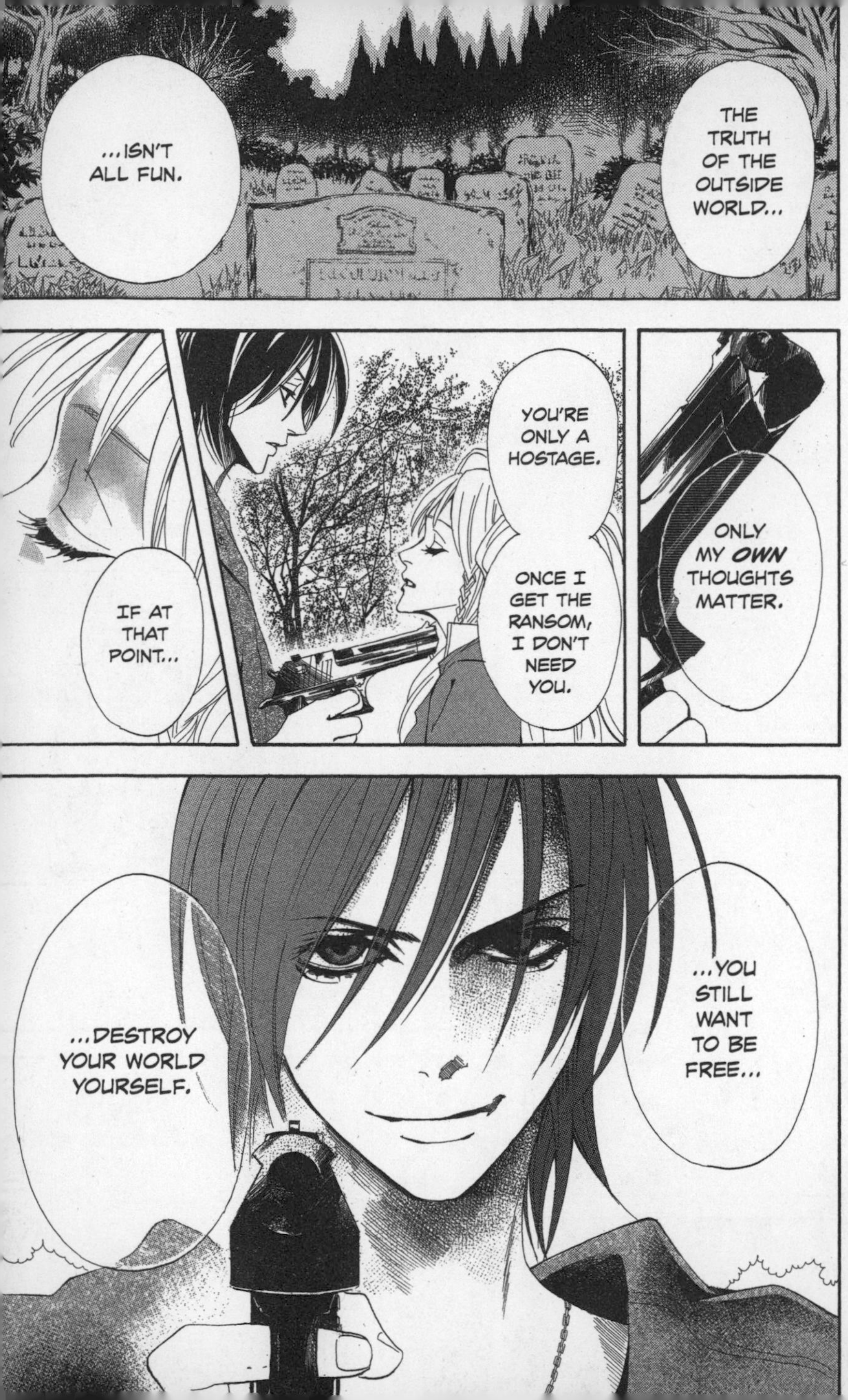
THE TRUTH OF THE OUTSIDE WORLD...
...ISN'T ALL FUN.
ONLY MY *OWN* THOUGHTS MATTER.
YOU'RE ONLY A HOSTAGE.
ONCE I GET THE RANSOM, I DON'T NEED YOU.
IF AT THAT POINT...
...YOU STILL WANT TO BE FREE...
...DESTROY YOUR WORLD YOURSELF.

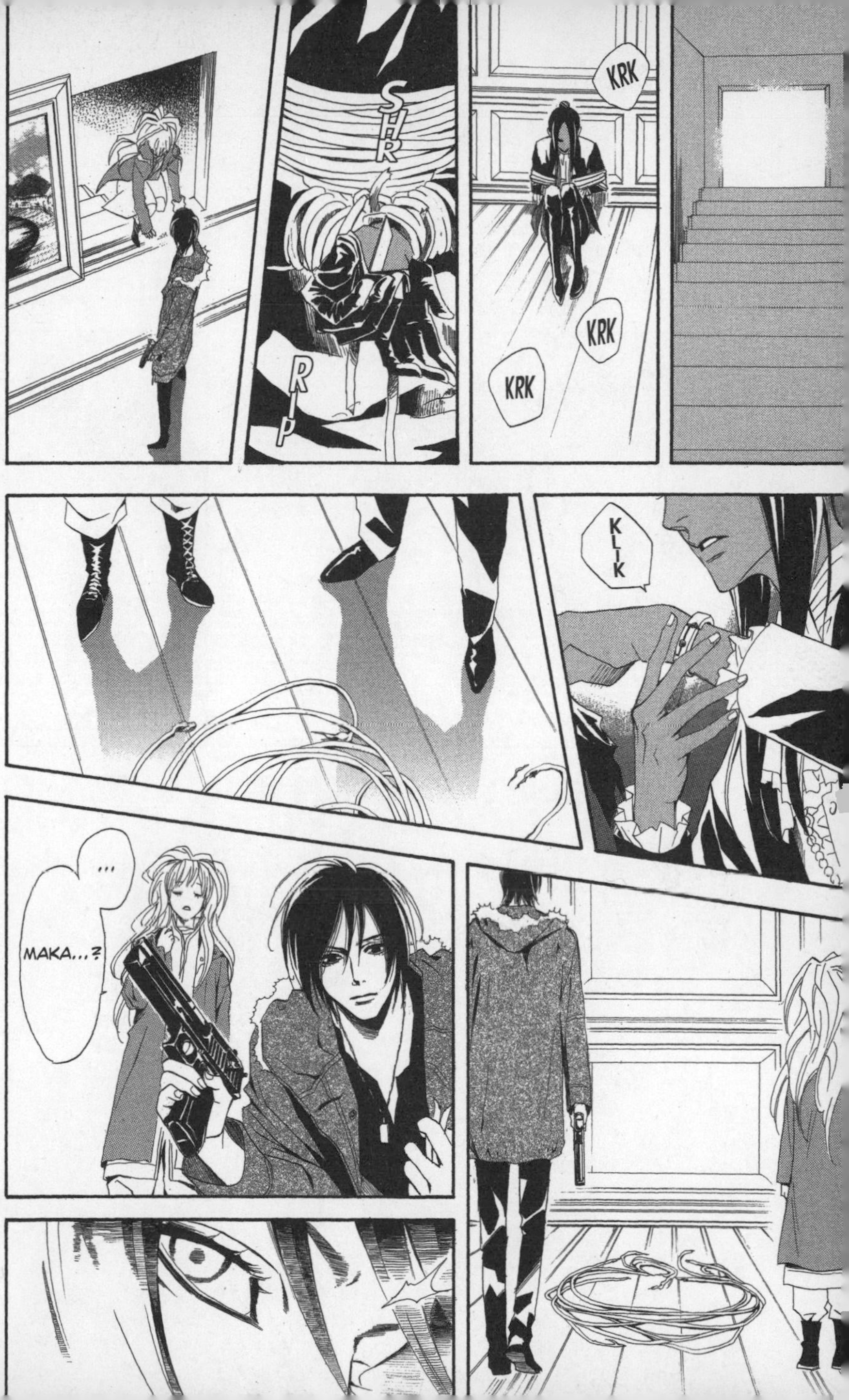
KRK
KRK
KRK
SHR
RIP
KLIK
...
MAKA...?

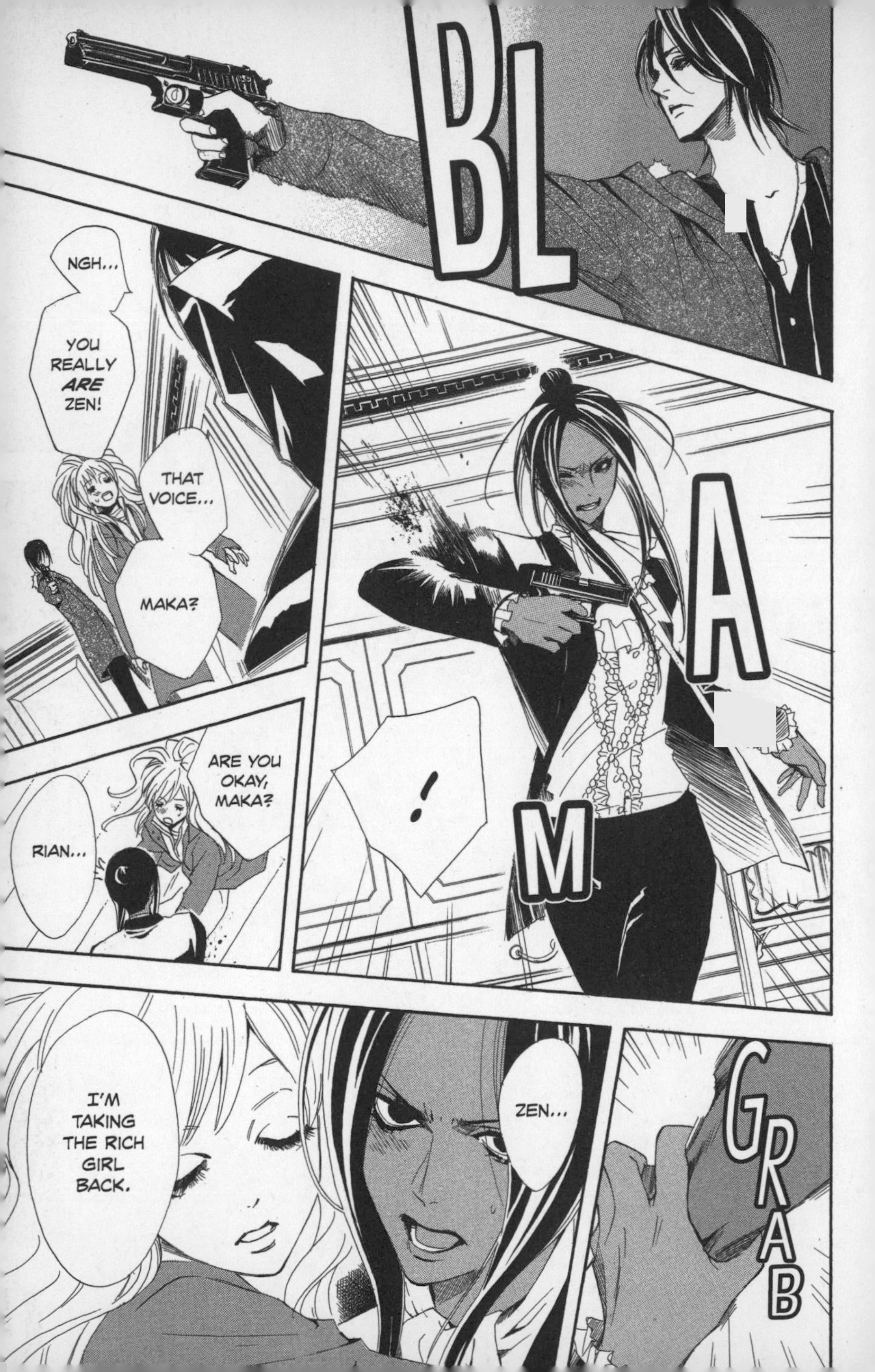
BL
A
M
!
NGH...
YOU REALLY *ARE* ZEN!
THAT VOICE...
MAKA?
ARE YOU OKAY, MAKA?
RIAN...
GRAB
ZEN...
I'M TAKING THE RICH GIRL BACK.

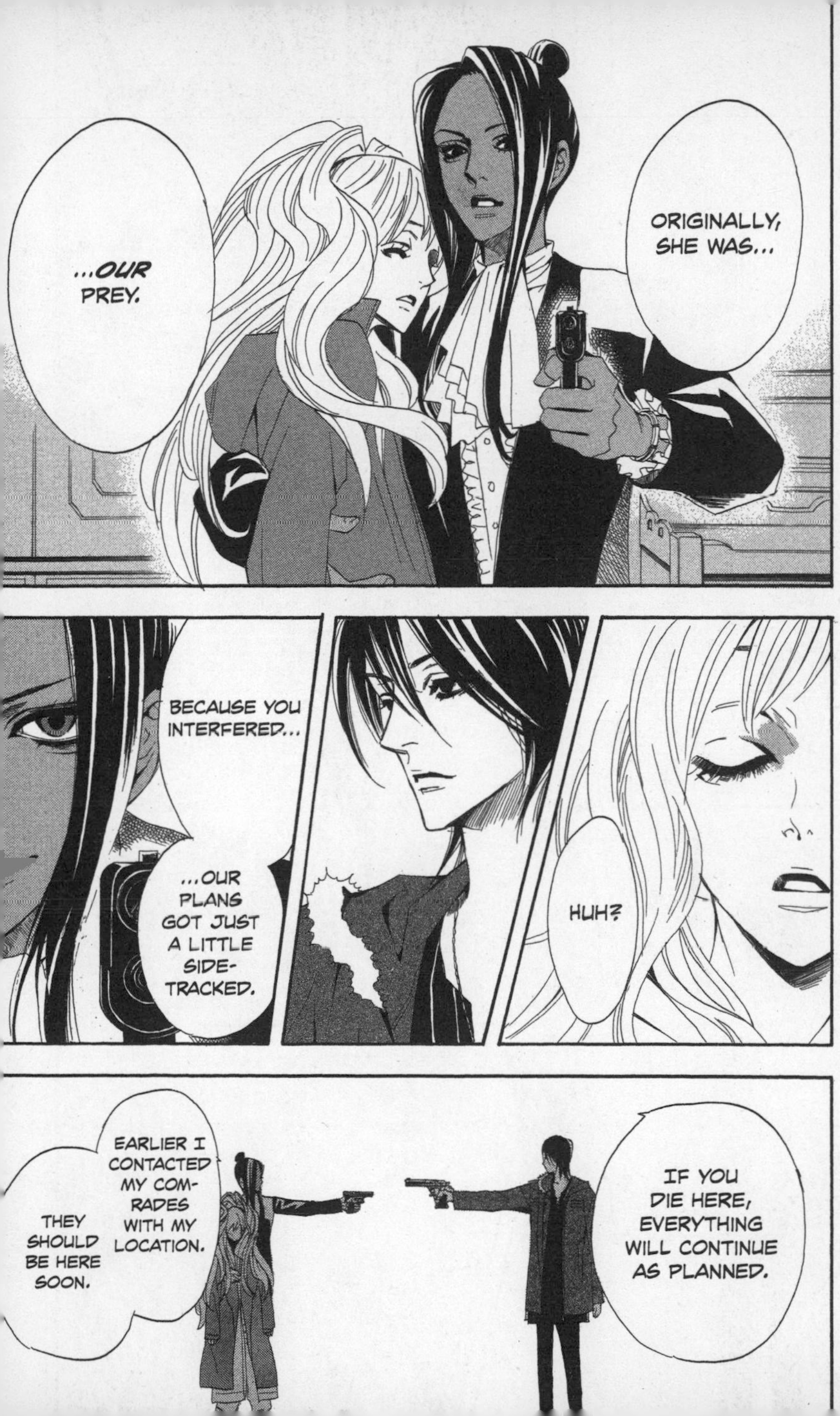
ORIGINALLY, SHE WAS...
...OUR PREY.
HUH?
BECAUSE YOU INTERFERED...
...OUR PLANS GOT JUST A LITTLE SIDE-TRACKED.
IF YOU DIE HERE, EVERYTHING WILL CONTINUE AS PLANNED.
EARLIER I CONTACTED MY COM-RADES WITH MY LOCATION.
THEY SHOULD BE HERE SOON.

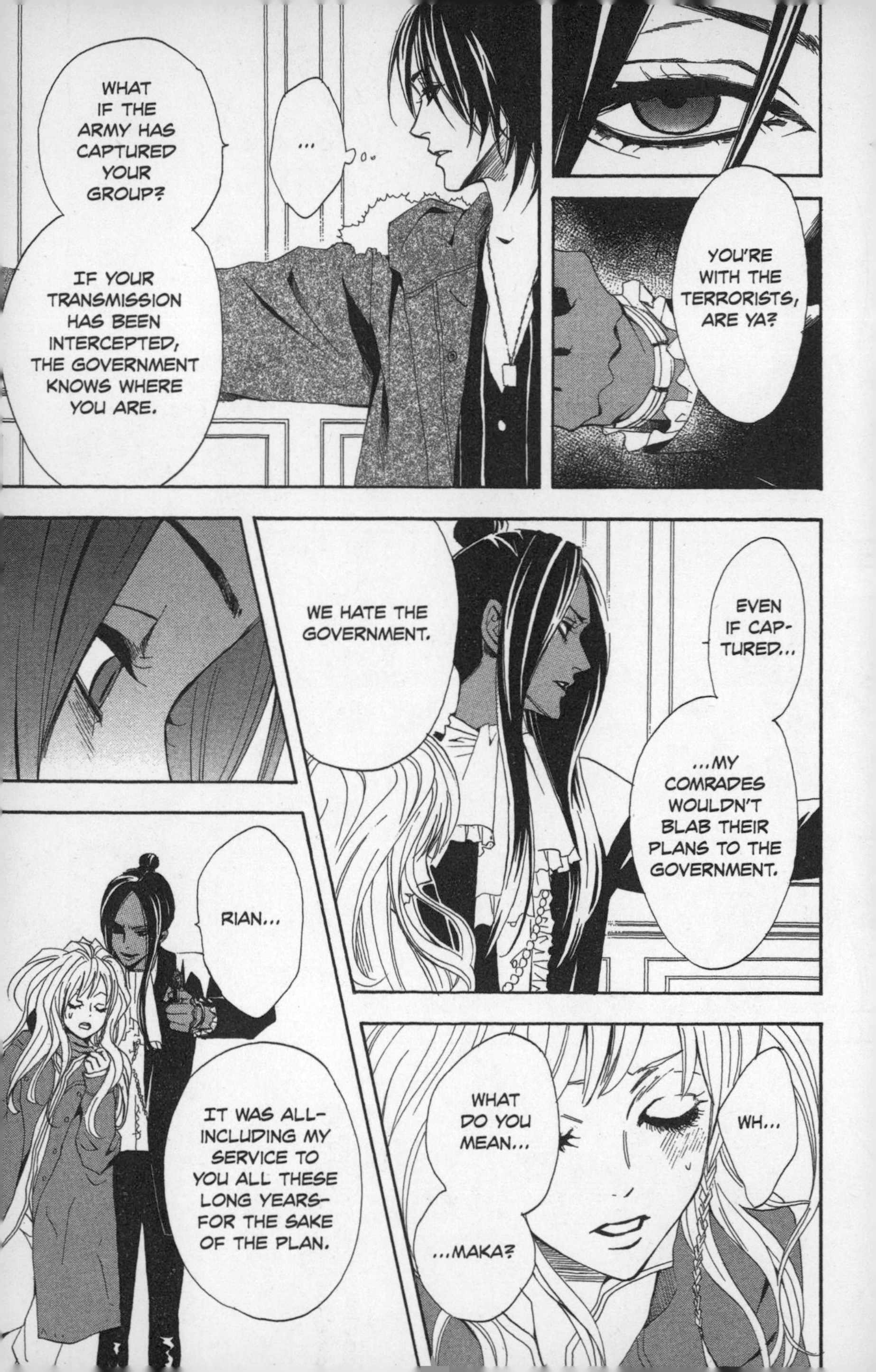
YOU'RE WITH THE TERRORISTS, ARE YA?
...
WHAT IF THE ARMY HAS CAPTURED YOUR GROUP?
IF YOUR TRANSMISSION HAS BEEN INTERCEPTED, THE GOVERNMENT KNOWS WHERE YOU ARE.
EVEN IF CAP-TURED...
...MY COMRADES WOULDN'T BLAB THEIR PLANS TO THE GOVERNMENT.
WE HATE THE GOVERNMENT.
WH...
WHAT DO YOU MEAN...
...MAKA?
RIAN...
IT WAS ALL-INCLUDING MY SERVICE TO YOU ALL THESE LONG YEARS-FOR THE SAKE OF THE PLAN.

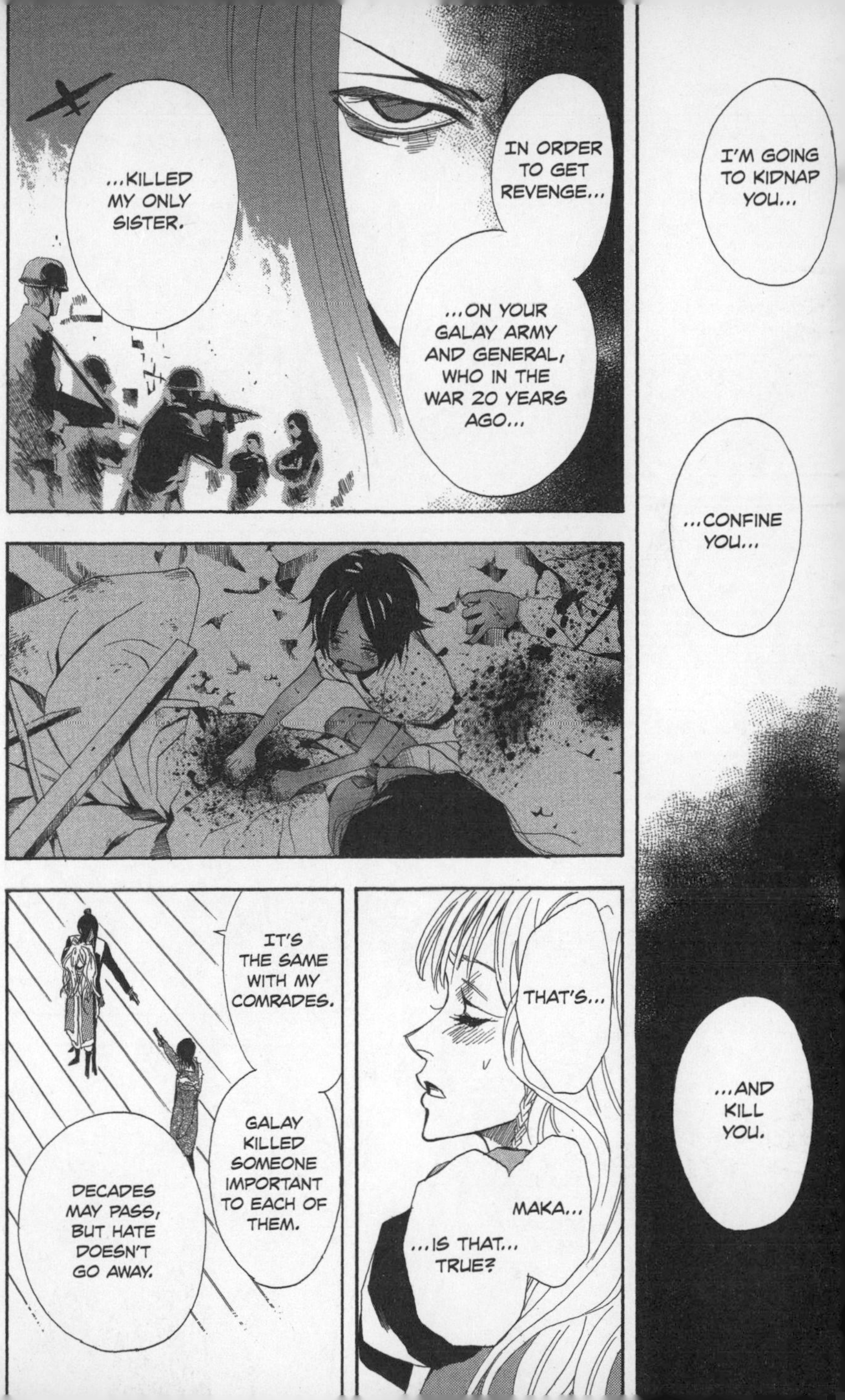
I'M GOING TO KIDNAP YOU...
...CONFINE YOU...
...AND KILL YOU.
IN ORDER TO GET REVENGE...
...ON YOUR GALAY ARMY AND GENERAL, WHO IN THE WAR 20 YEARS AGO...
...KILLED MY ONLY SISTER.
THAT'S...
MAKA...
...IS THAT... TRUE?
IT'S THE SAME WITH MY COMRADES.
GALAY KILLED SOMEONE IMPORTANT TO EACH OF THEM.
DECADES MAY PASS, BUT HATE DOESN'T GO AWAY.

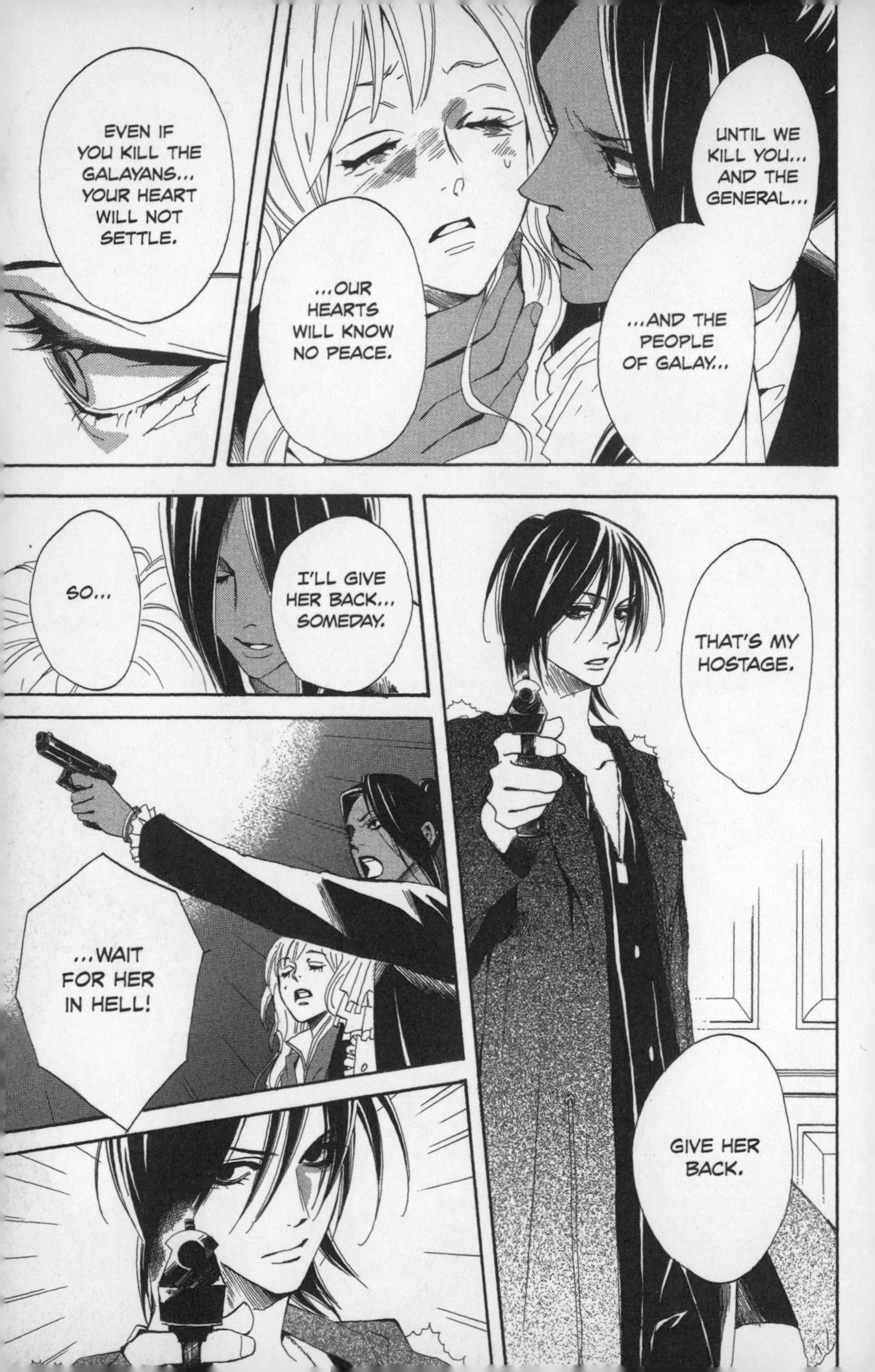
UNTIL WE KILL YOU... AND THE GENERAL...
...AND THE PEOPLE OF GALAY...
...OUR HEARTS WILL KNOW NO PEACE.
EVEN IF YOU KILL THE GALAYANS... YOUR HEART WILL NOT SETTLE.
THAT'S MY HOSTAGE.
GIVE HER BACK.
I'LL GIVE HER BACK... SOMEDAY.
SO...
...WAIT FOR HER IN HELL!

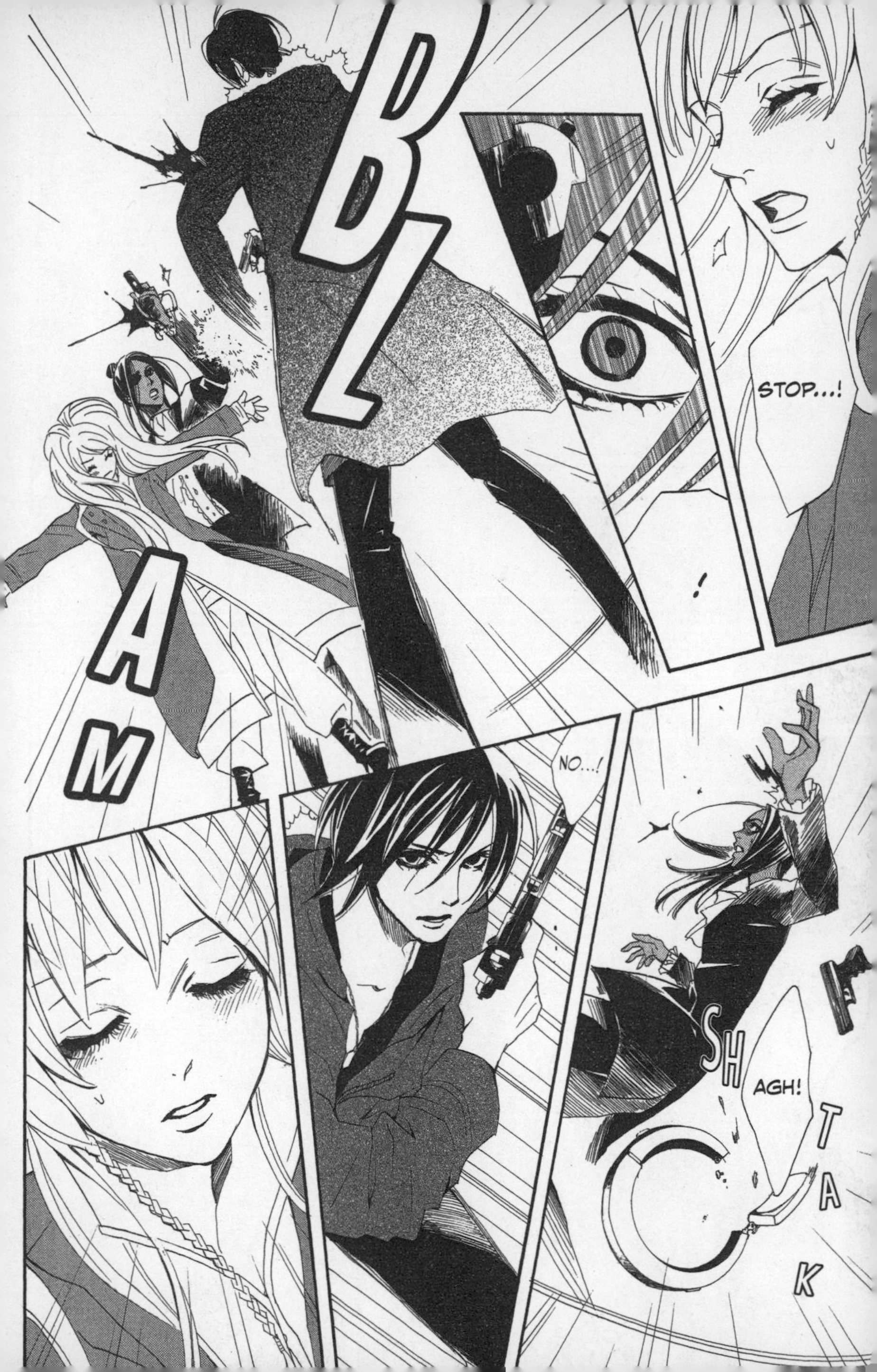
STOP...!
!
BDLAM
SHTAK
AGH!
NO...!

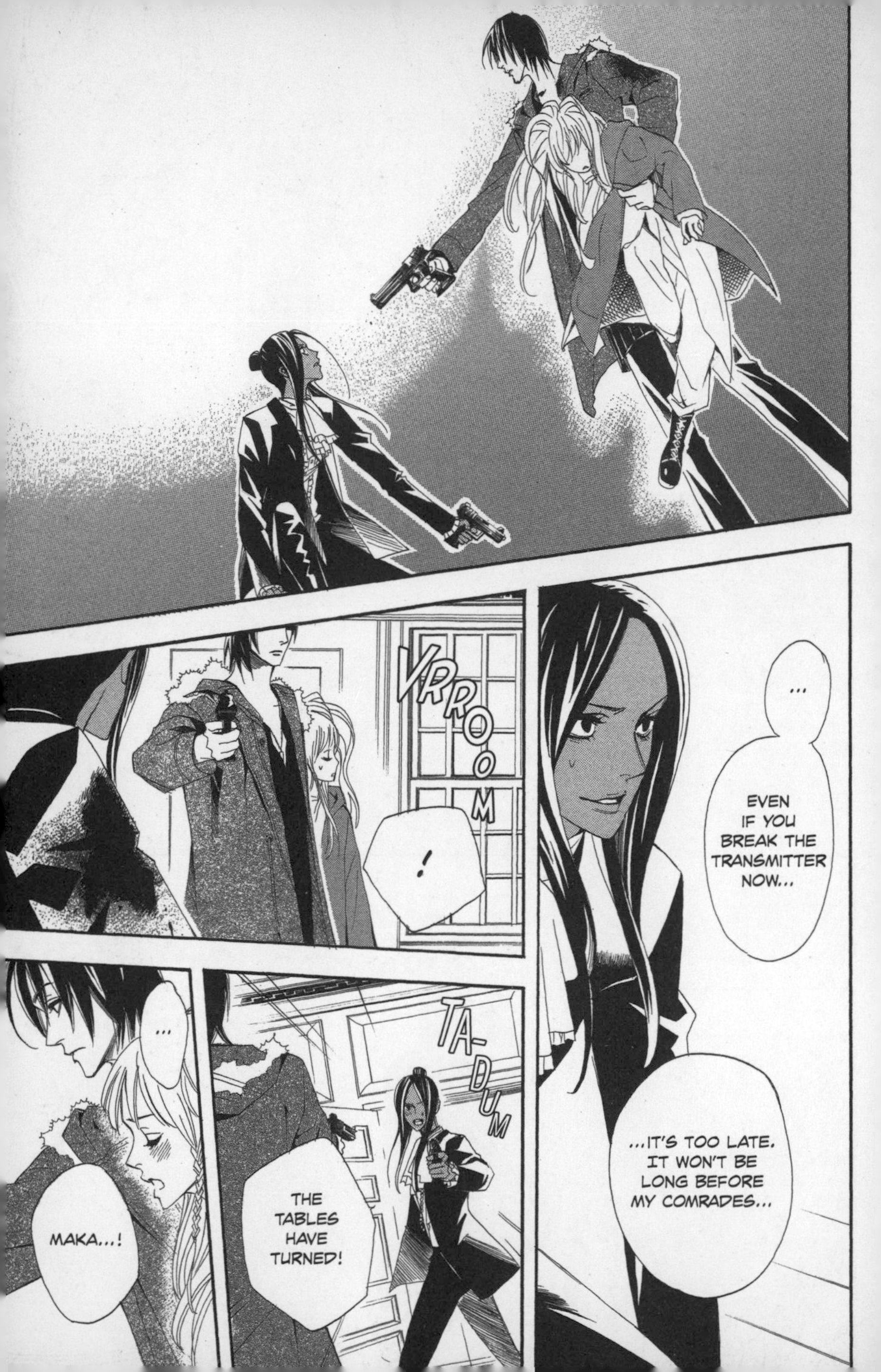
...
EVEN IF YOU BREAK THE TRANSMITTER NOW...
...IT'S TOO LATE. IT WON'T BE LONG BEFORE MY COMRADES...
VRROOM
!
TA-DUM
THE TABLES HAVE TURNED!
...
MAKA...!

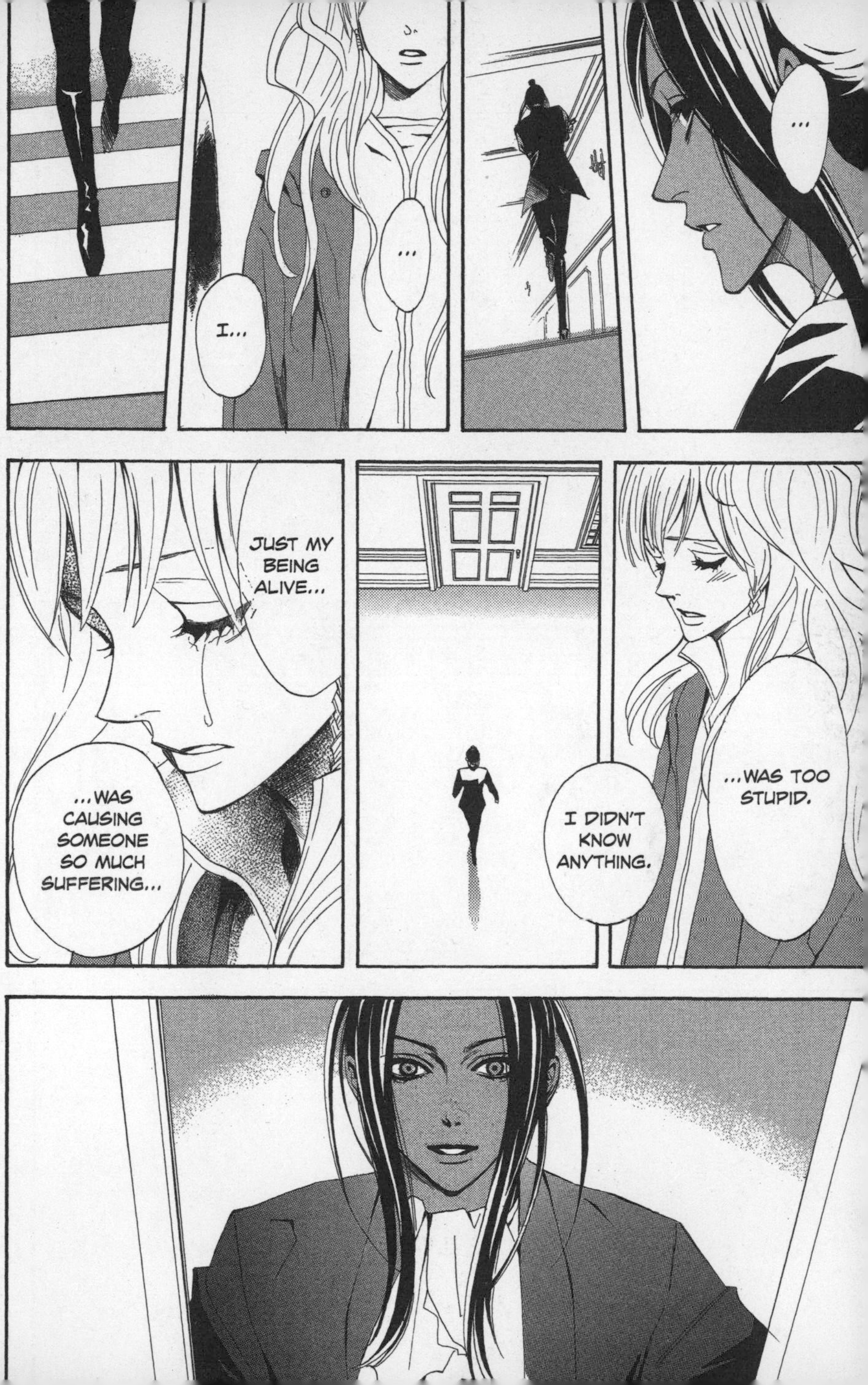
...
...
I...
...WAS TOO STUPID.
I DIDN'T KNOW ANYTHING.
JUST MY BEING ALIVE...
...WAS CAUSING SOMEONE SO MUCH SUFFERING...

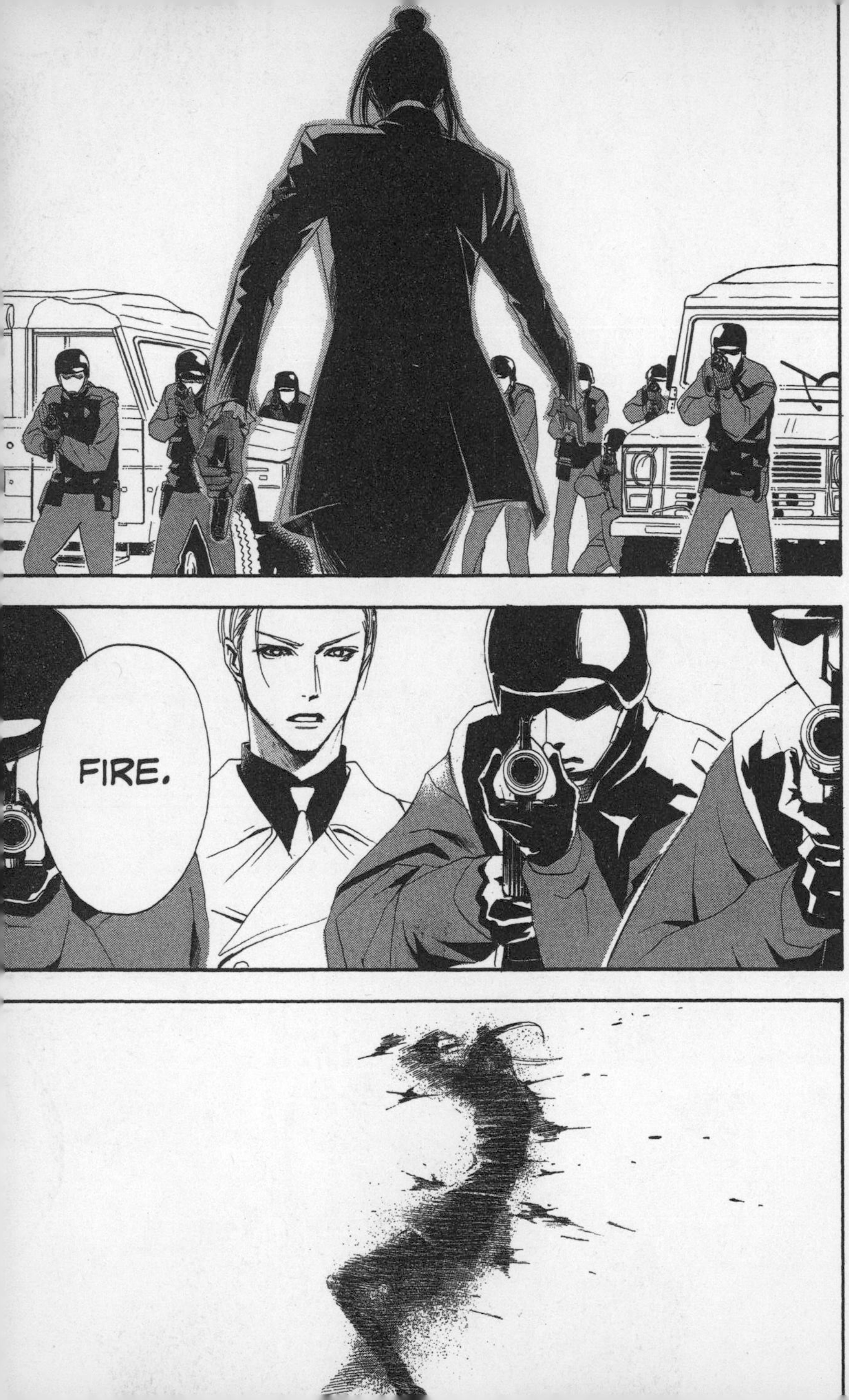
FIRE.

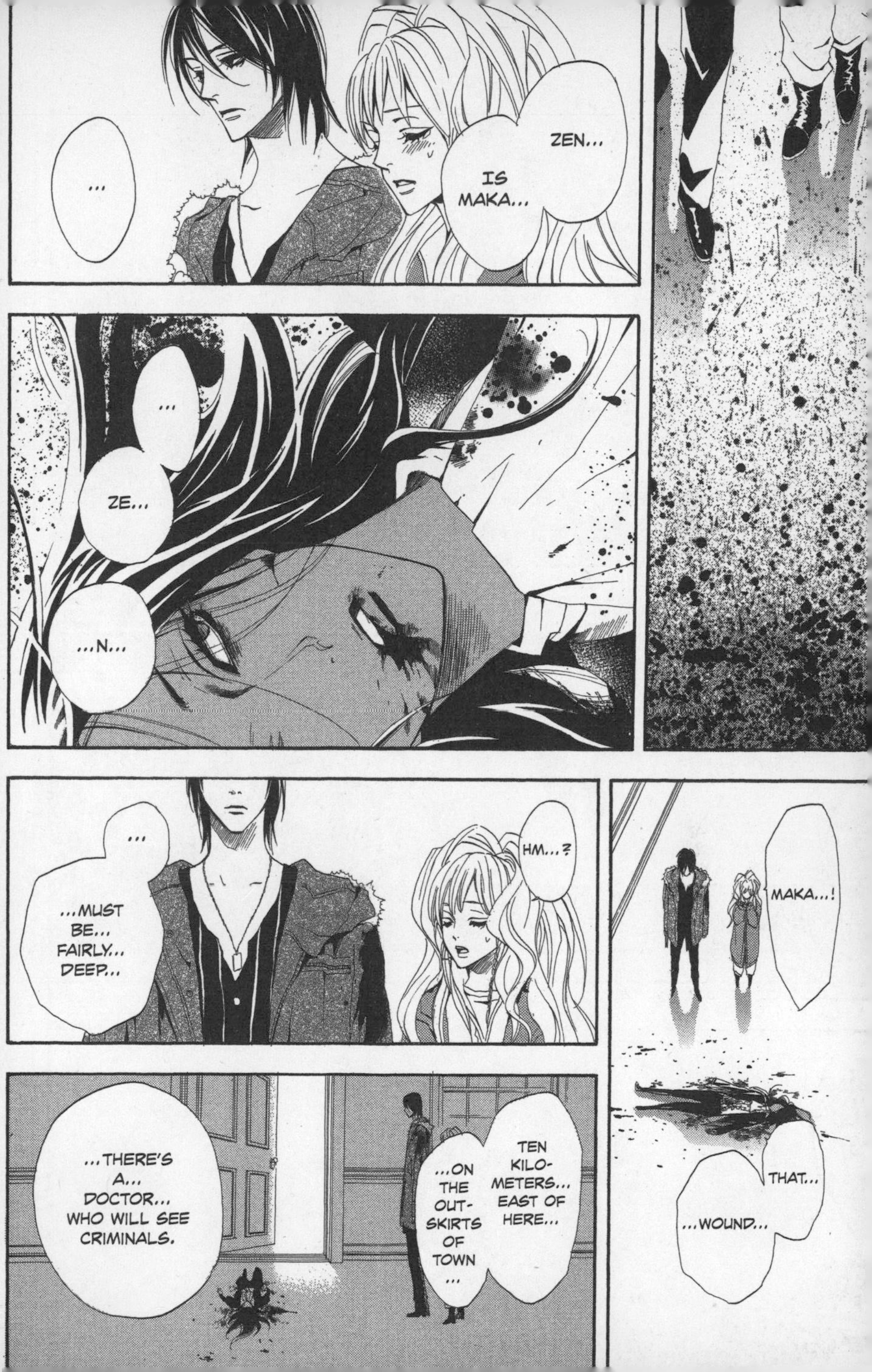
ZEN... IS MAKA...
...
...
ZE...
...N...
MAKA...!
THAT...
...WOUND...
HM...?
...
...MUST BE... FAIRLY... DEEP...
TEN KILO-METERS... EAST OF HERE...
...ON THE OUT-SKIRTS OF TOWN...
...THERE'S A... DOCTOR... WHO WILL SEE CRIMINALS.

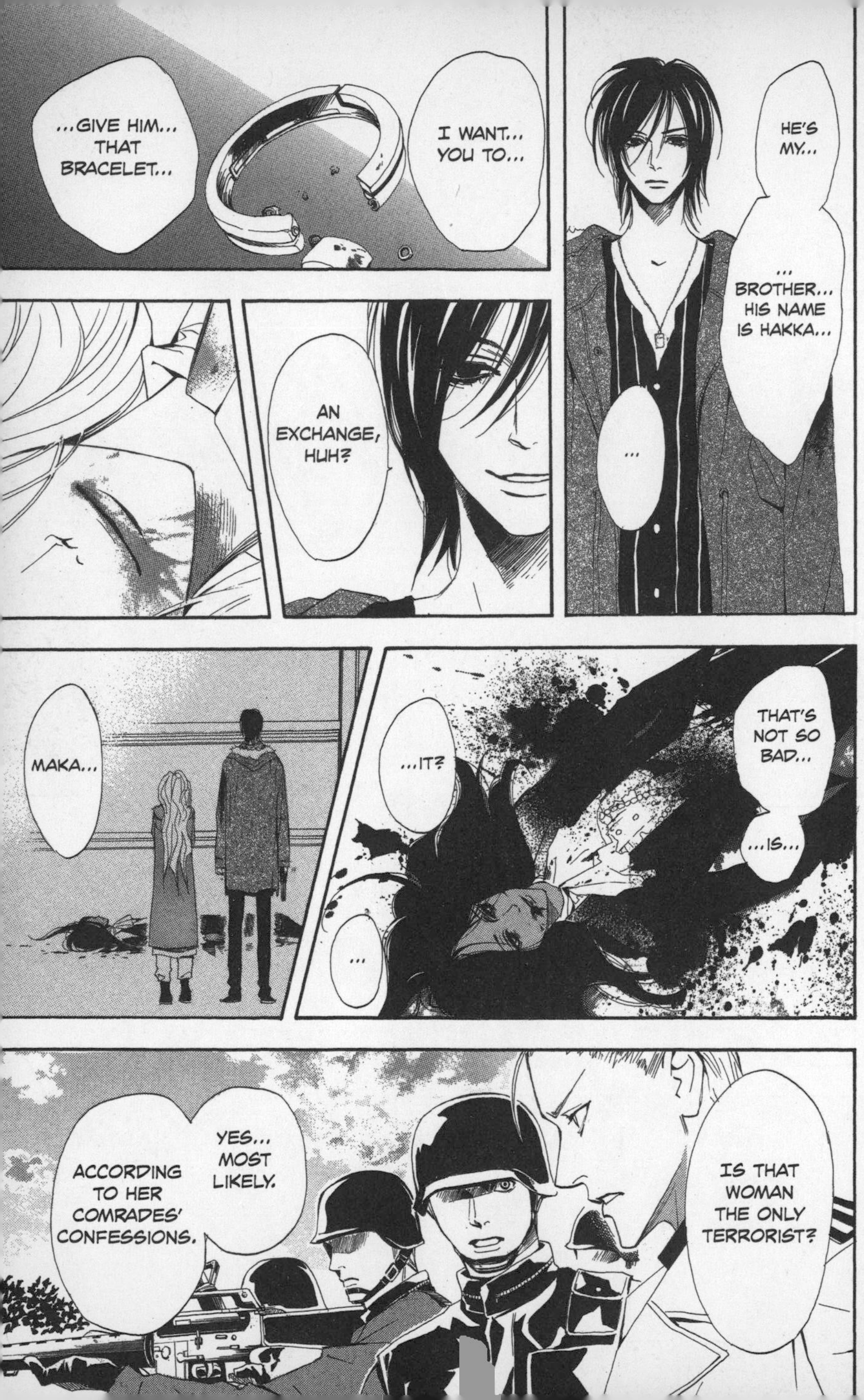
HE'S MY...
...BROTHER... HIS NAME IS HAKKA...
...
I WANT... YOU TO...
...GIVE HIM... THAT BRACELET...
AN EXCHANGE, HUH?
THAT'S NOT SO BAD...
...IS...
...IT?
...
MAKA...
IS THAT WOMAN THE ONLY TERRORIST?
YES... MOST LIKELY.
ACCORDING TO HER COMRADES' CONFESSIONS.

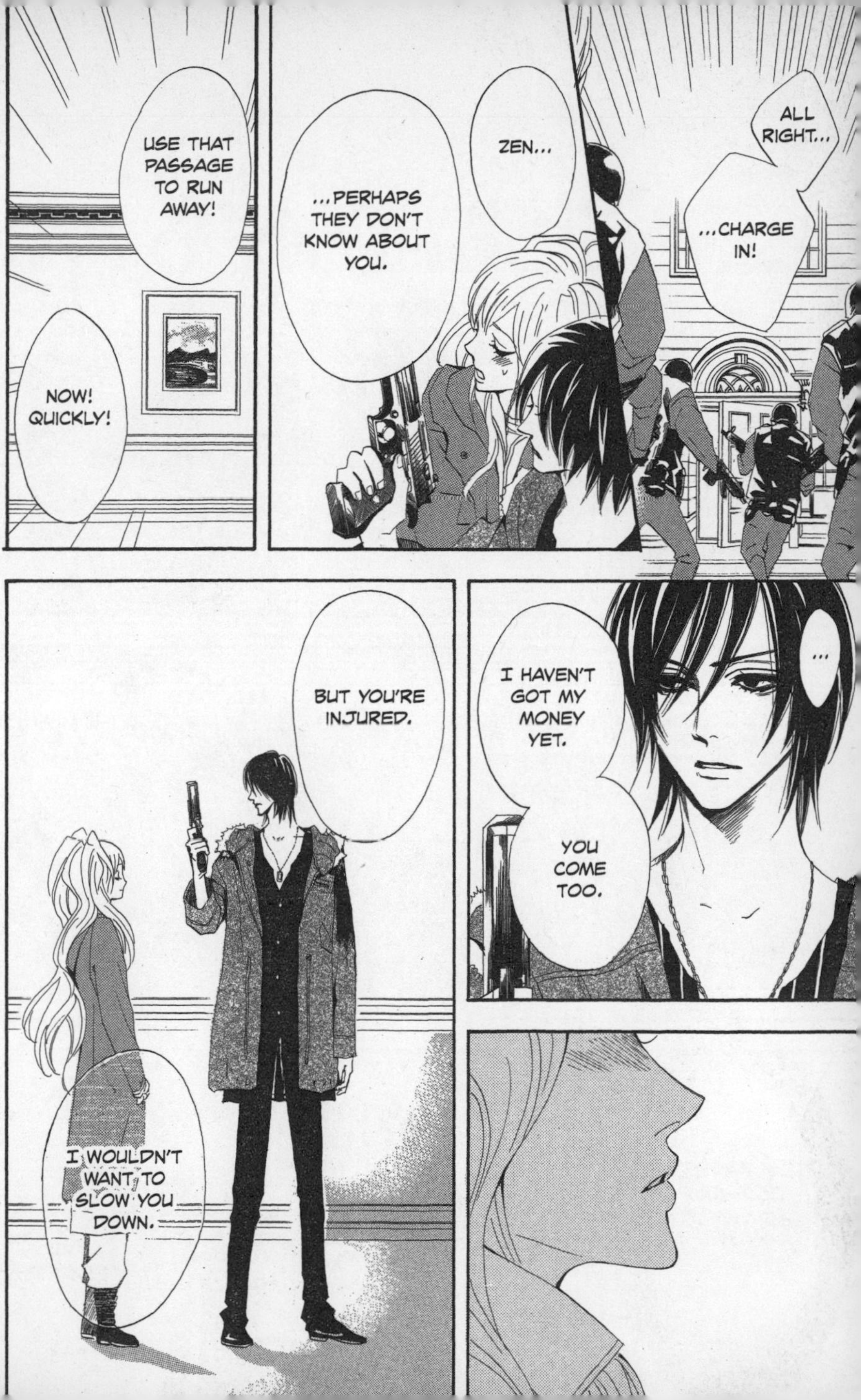
ALL RIGHT...
...CHARGE IN!
ZEN...
...PERHAPS THEY DON'T KNOW ABOUT YOU.
USE THAT PASSAGE TO RUN AWAY!
NOW! QUICKLY!
...
I HAVEN'T GOT MY MONEY YET.
YOU COME TOO.
BUT YOU'RE INJURED.
I WOULDN'T WANT TO SLOW YOU DOWN.

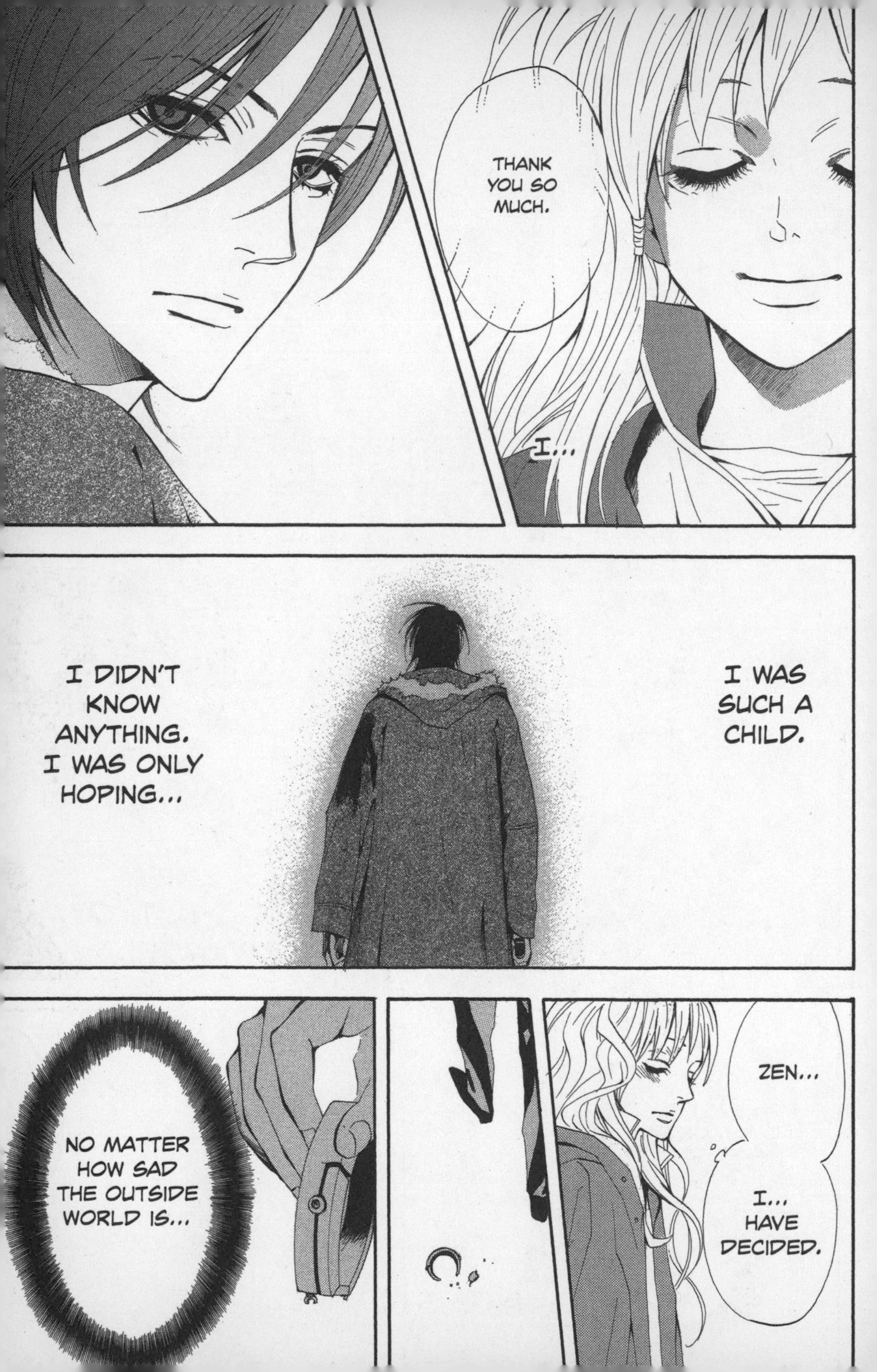
THANK YOU SO MUCH.
I...
I WAS SUCH A CHILD.
I DIDN'T KNOW ANYTHING. I WAS ONLY HOPING...
ZEN...
I... HAVE DECIDED.
NO MATTER HOW SAD THE OUTSIDE WORLD IS...

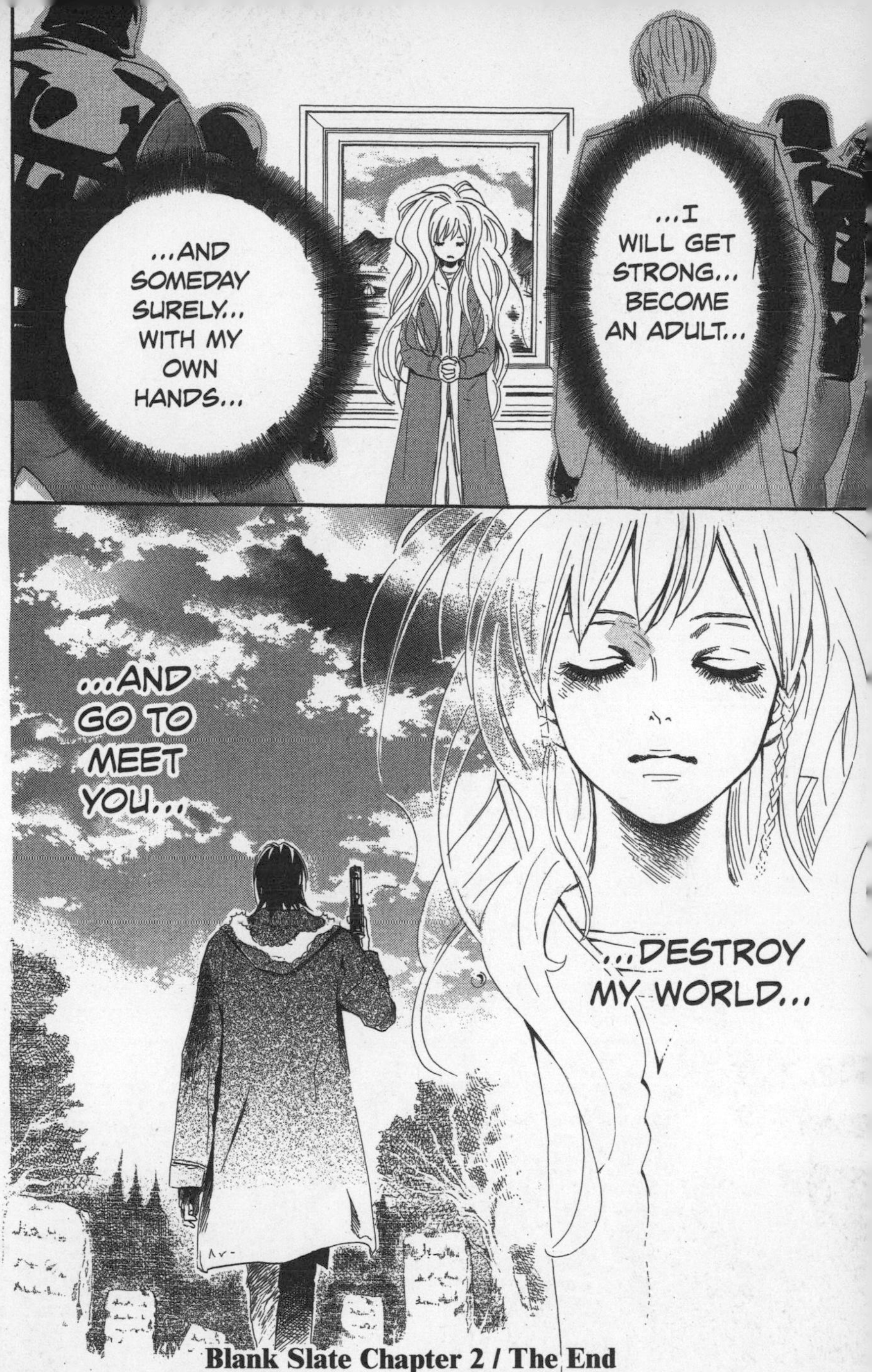
...I WILL GET STRONG... BECOME AN ADULT...
...AND SOMEDAY SURELY... WITH MY OWN HANDS...
...DESTROY MY WORLD...
...AND GO TO MEET YOU...

Blank Slate Chapter 2 / The End

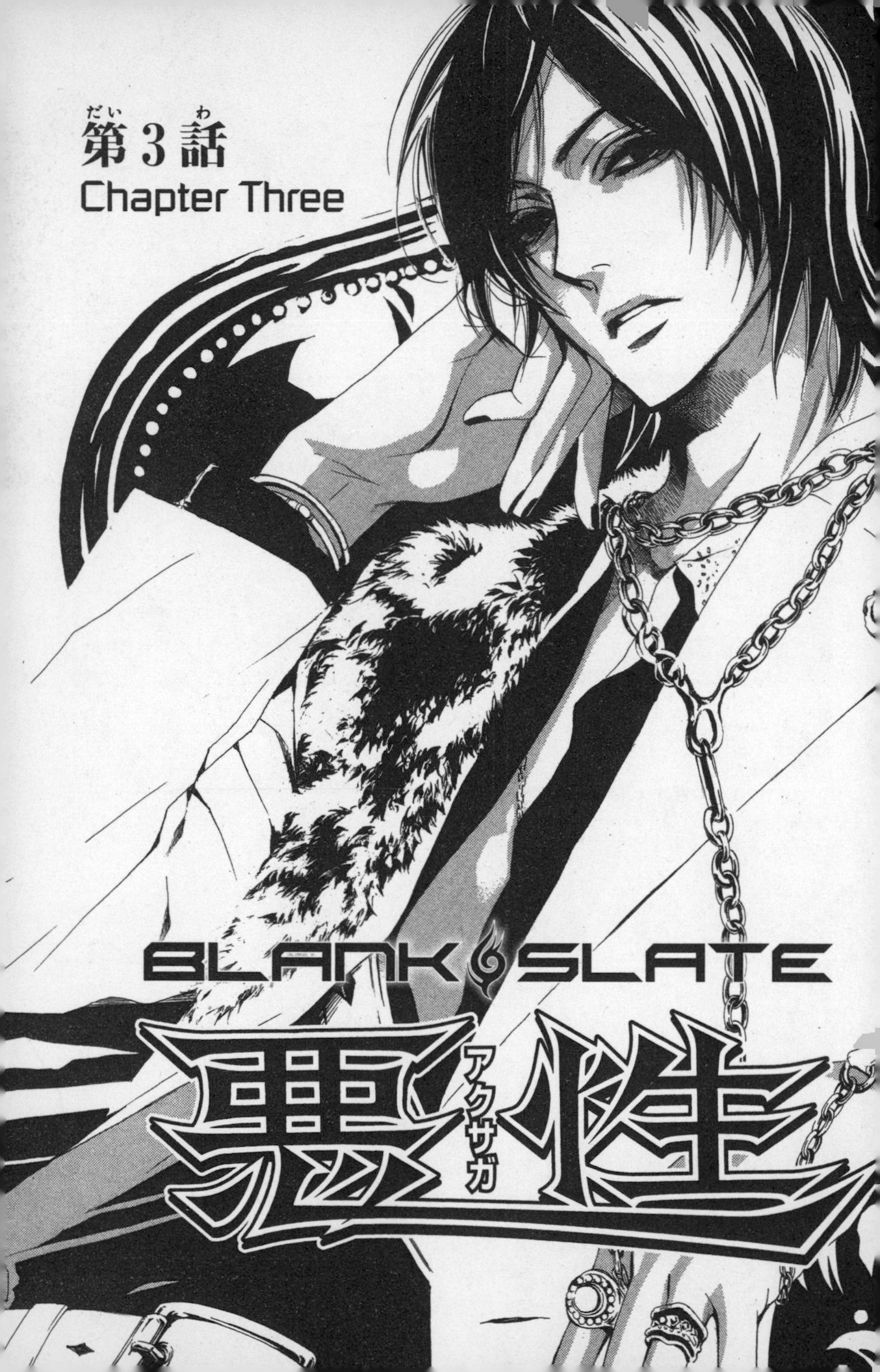
第3話
Chapter Three
BLANK SLATE
悪性
アクサガ

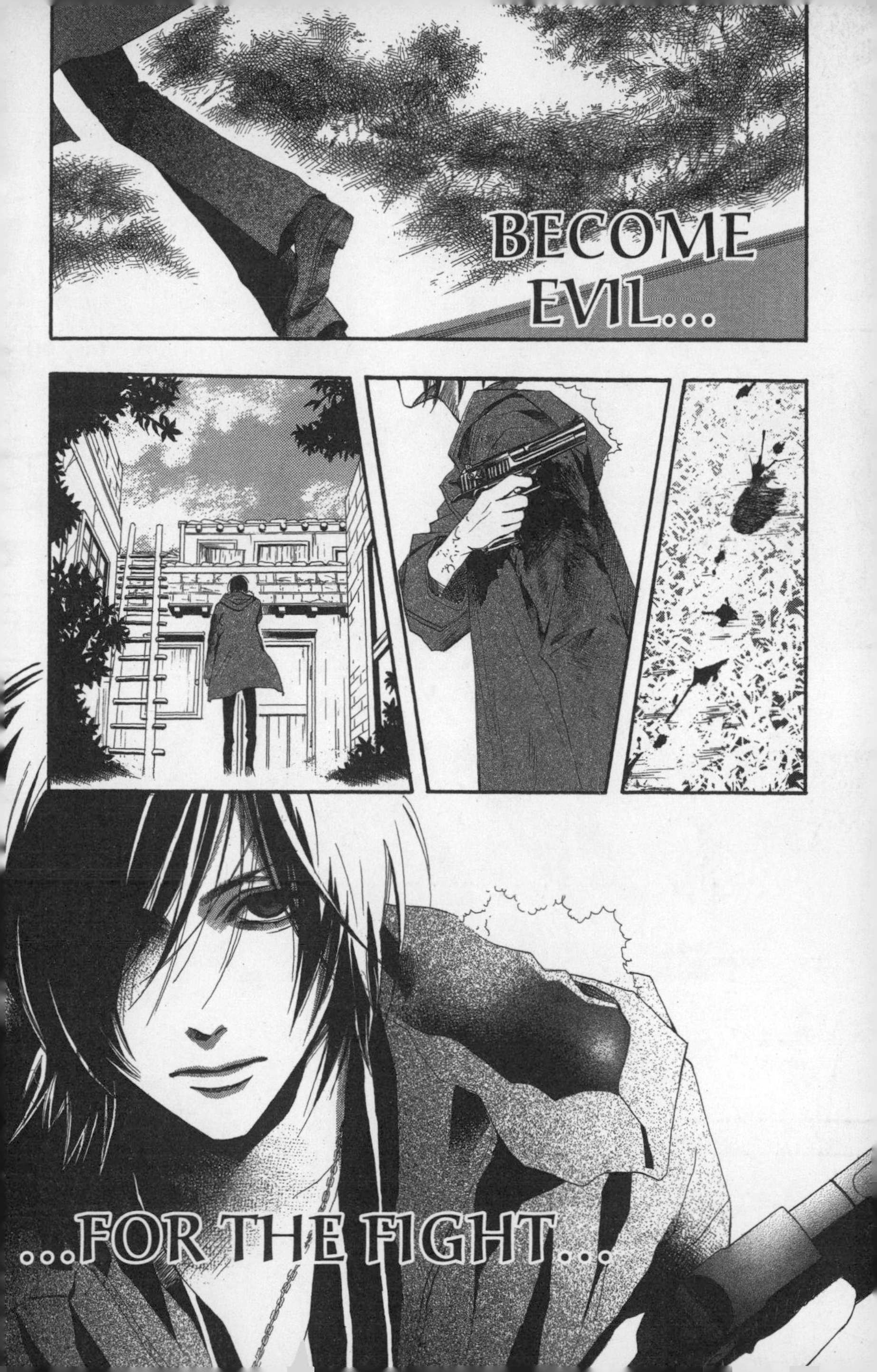
BECOME EVIL...
...FOR THE FIGHT...

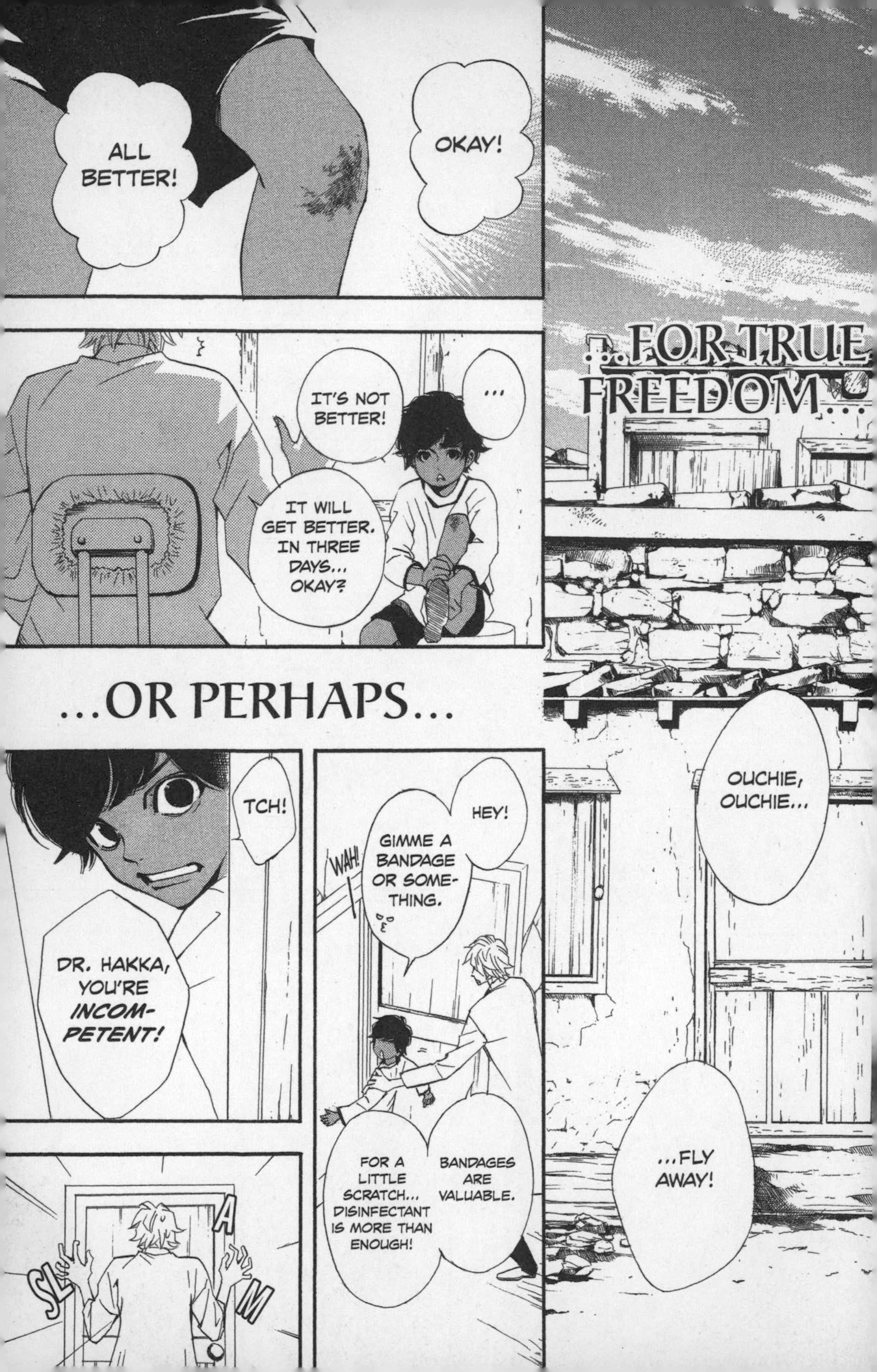

...FOR TRUE FREEDOM...
OUCHIE, OUCHIE...
...FLY AWAY!
OKAY!
ALL BETTER!
...
IT'S NOT BETTER!
IT WILL GET BETTER. IN THREE DAYS... OKAY?
...OR PERHAPS...
HEY!
GIMME A BANDAGE OR SOMETHING.
WAH!
BANDAGES ARE VALUABLE.
FOR A LITTLE SCRATCH... DISINFECTANT IS MORE THAN ENOUGH!
TCH!
DR. HAKKA, YOU'RE *INCOMPETENT!*
SLAM

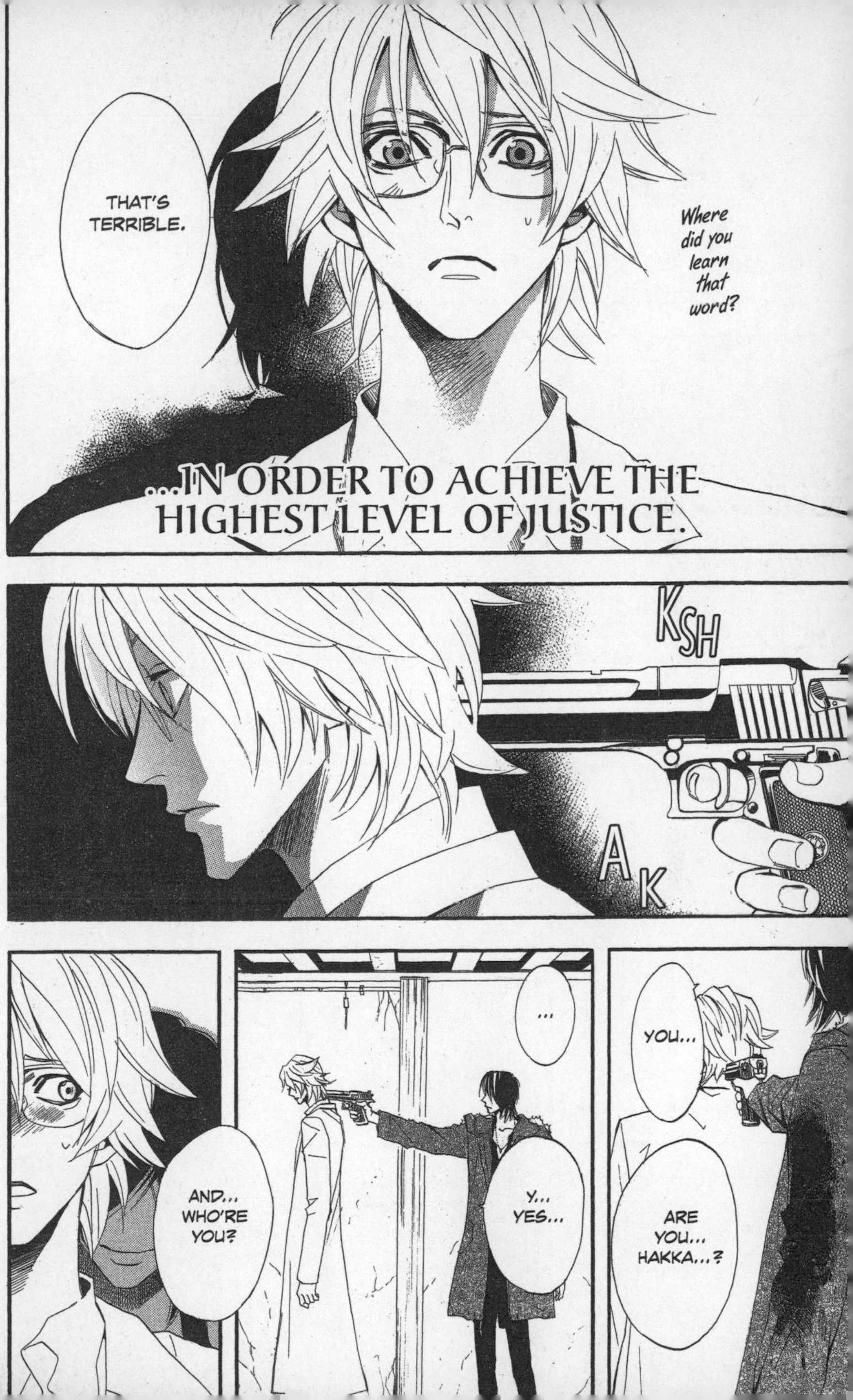
Where did you learn that word?
THAT'S TERRIBLE.
...IN ORDER TO ACHIEVE THE HIGHEST LEVEL OF JUSTICE.
KSH
AK
YOU...
ARE YOU... HAKKA...?
...
Y... YES...
AND... WHO'RE YOU?

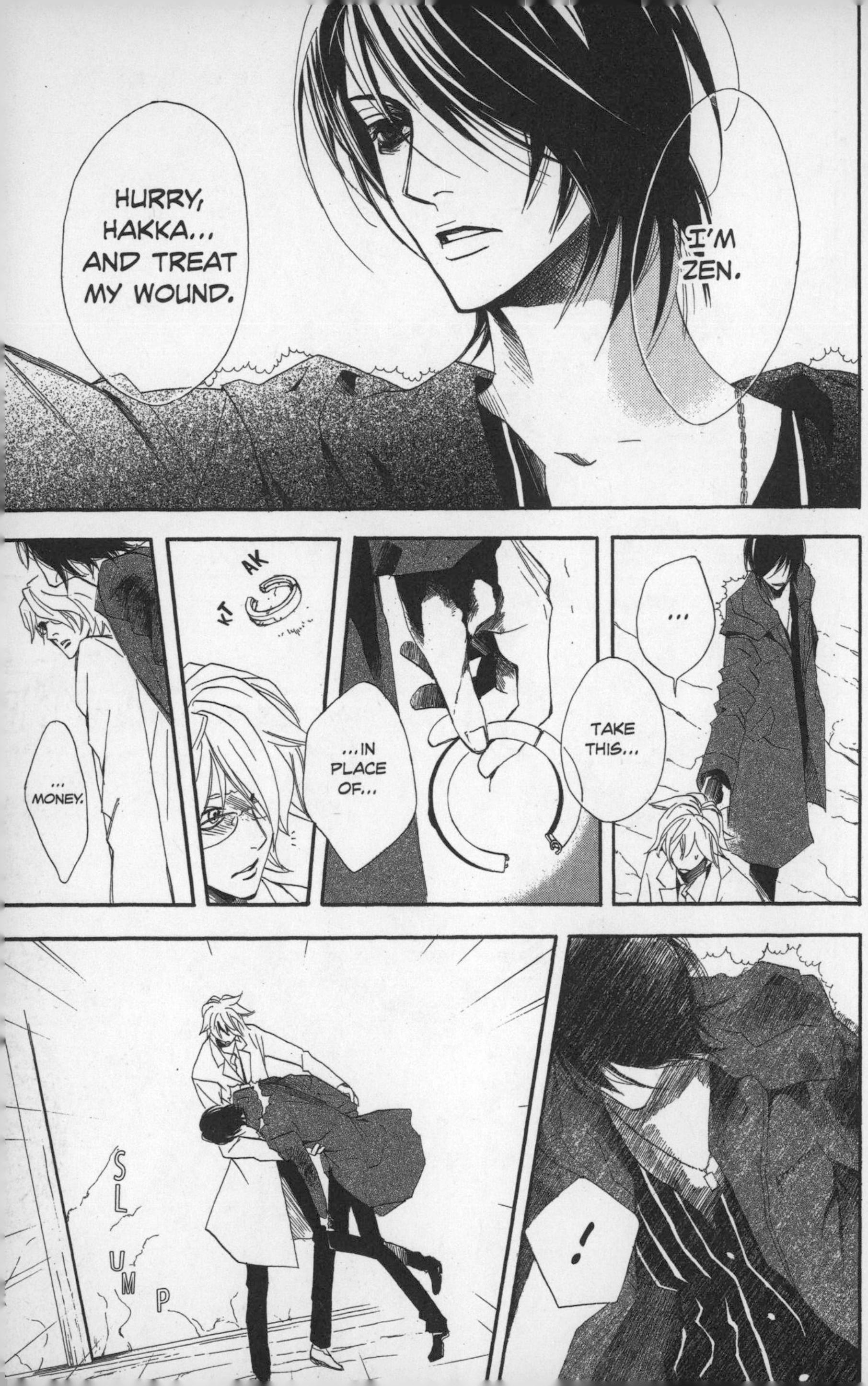
I'M ZEN.
HURRY, HAKKA... AND TREAT MY WOUND.
...
TAKE THIS...
...IN PLACE OF...
KTAK
... MONEY.
!
SLUMP

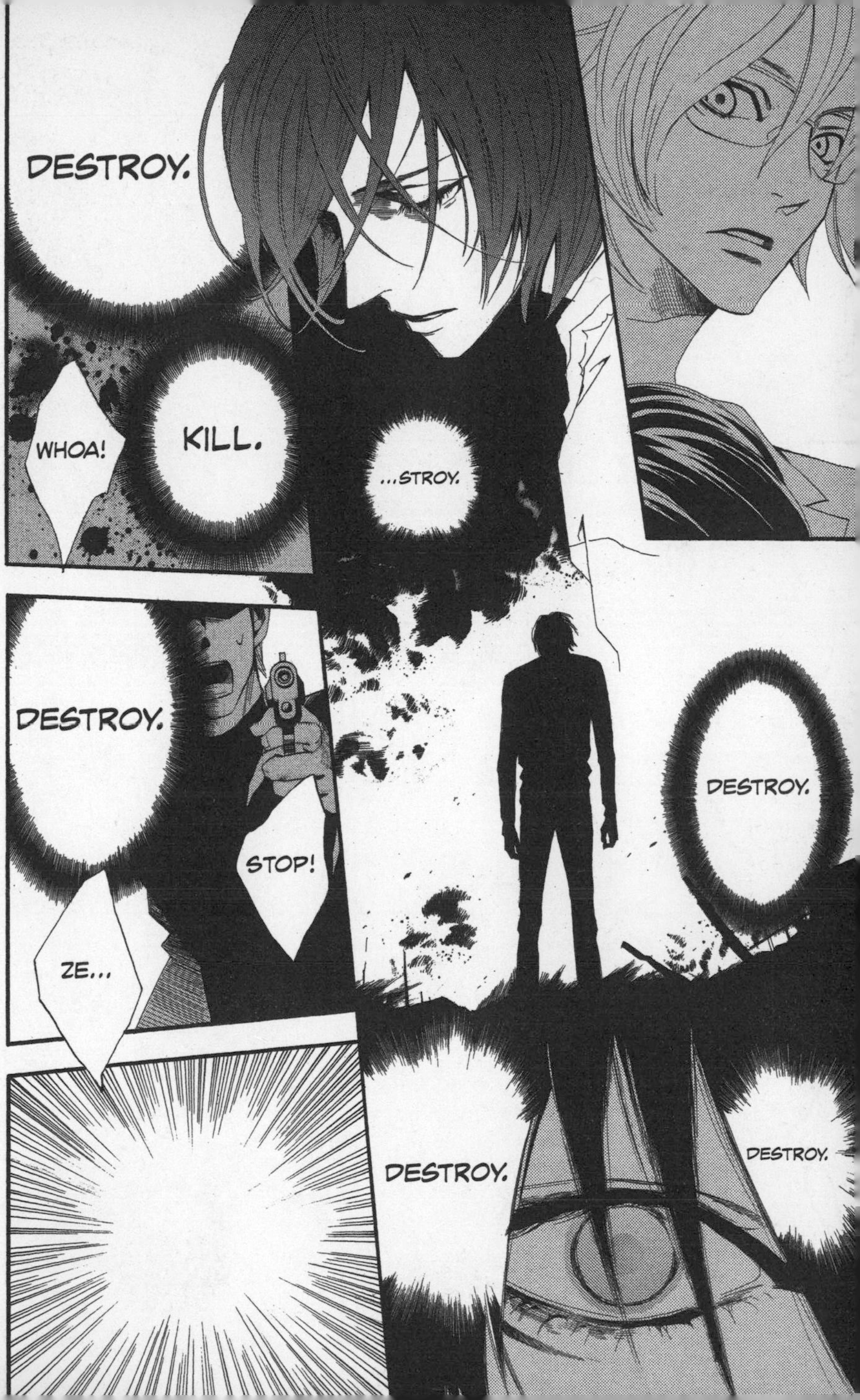
...STROY.
DESTROY.
KILL.
WHOA!
DESTROY.
DESTROY.
STOP!
ZE...
DESTROY.
DESTROY.

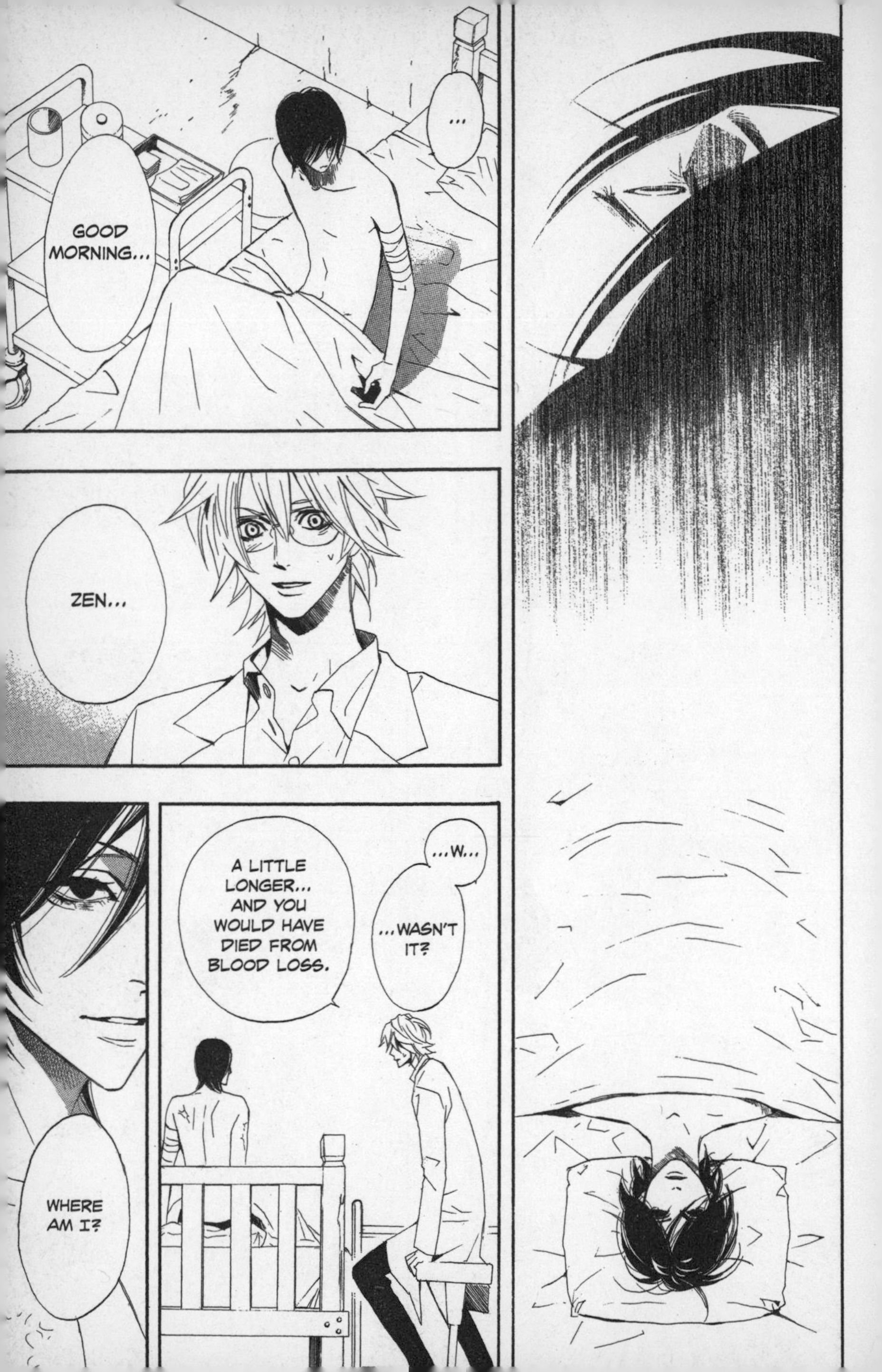
...
GOOD MORNING...
ZEN...
...W...
...WASN'T IT?
A LITTLE LONGER... AND YOU WOULD HAVE DIED FROM BLOOD LOSS.
WHERE AM I?

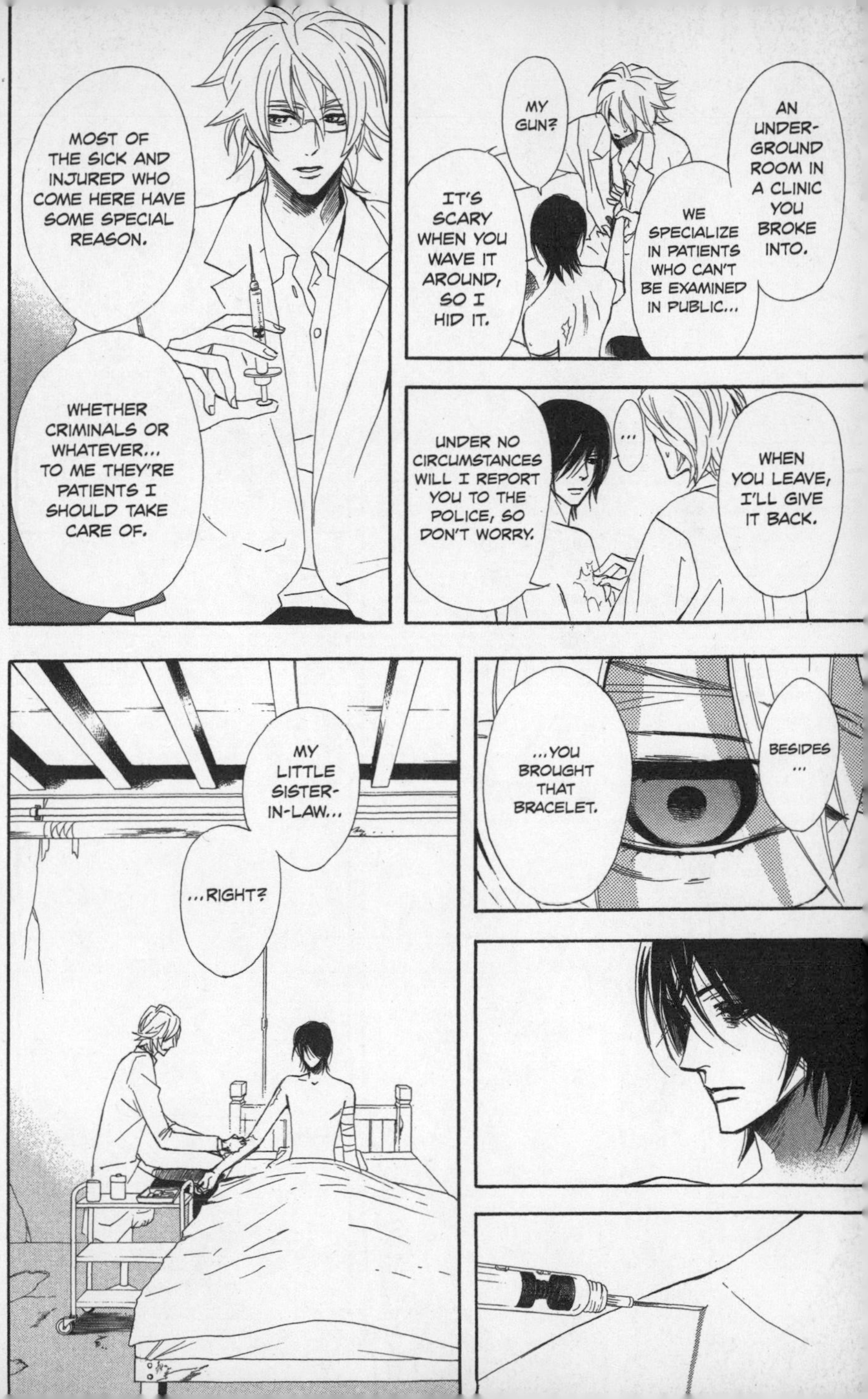
AN UNDER-GROUND ROOM IN A CLINIC YOU BROKE INTO.
WE SPECIALIZE IN PATIENTS WHO CAN'T BE EXAMINED IN PUBLIC...
MY GUN?
IT'S SCARY WHEN YOU WAVE IT AROUND, SO I HID IT.
WHEN YOU LEAVE, I'LL GIVE IT BACK.
...
UNDER NO CIRCUMSTANCES WILL I REPORT YOU TO THE POLICE, SO DON'T WORRY.
MOST OF THE SICK AND INJURED WHO COME HERE HAVE SOME SPECIAL REASON.
WHETHER CRIMINALS OR WHATEVER... TO ME THEY'RE PATIENTS I SHOULD TAKE CARE OF.
BESIDES...
...YOU BROUGHT THAT BRACELET.
MY LITTLE SISTER-IN-LAW...
...RIGHT?

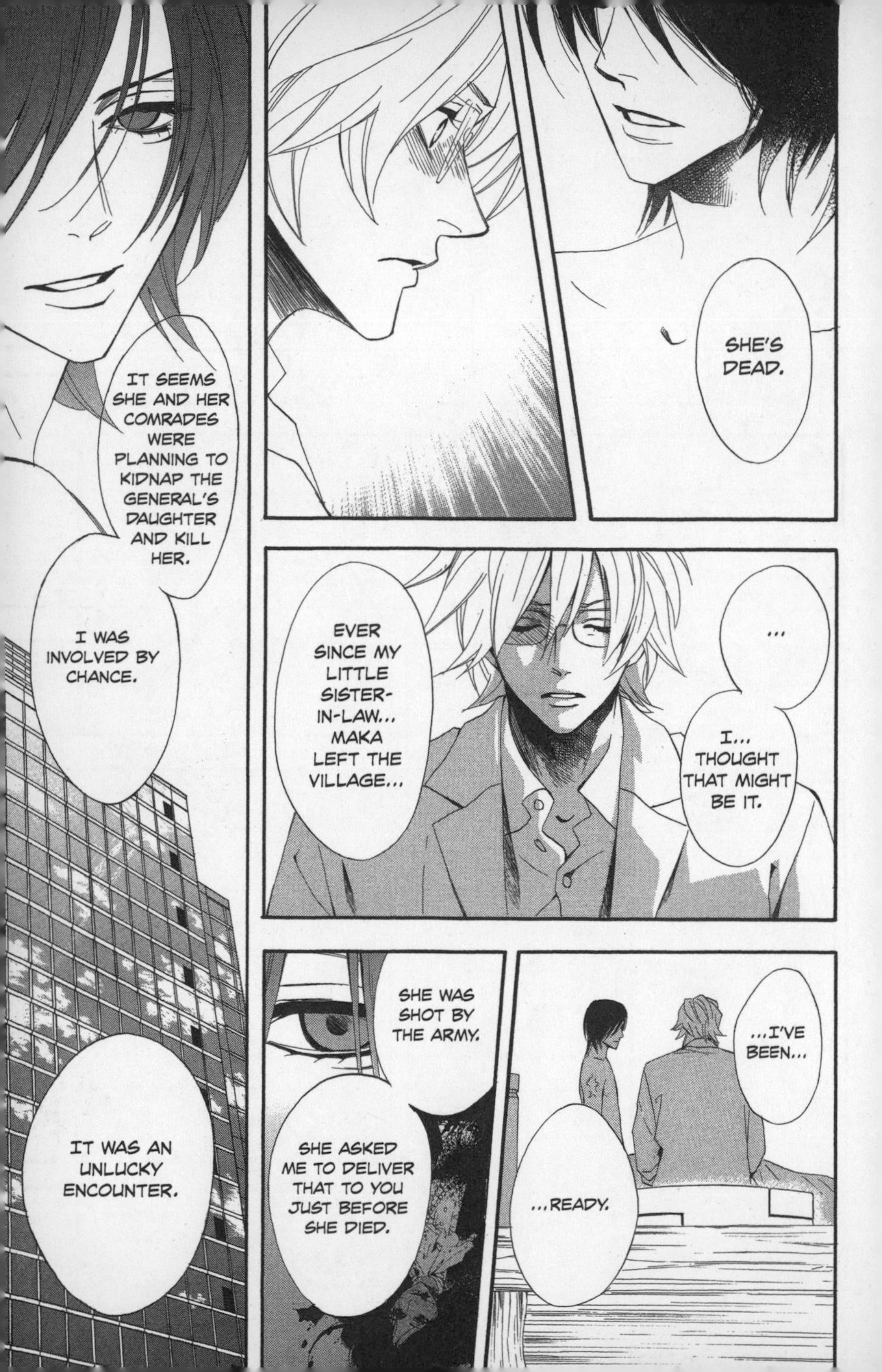
SHE'S DEAD.
...
EVER SINCE MY LITTLE SISTER-IN-LAW... MAKA LEFT THE VILLAGE...
I... THOUGHT THAT MIGHT BE IT.
...I'VE BEEN...
...READY.
SHE WAS SHOT BY THE ARMY.
SHE ASKED ME TO DELIVER THAT TO YOU JUST BEFORE SHE DIED.
IT SEEMS SHE AND HER COMRADES WERE PLANNING TO KIDNAP THE GENERAL'S DAUGHTER AND KILL HER.
I WAS INVOLVED BY CHANCE.
IT WAS AN UNLUCKY ENCOUNTER.

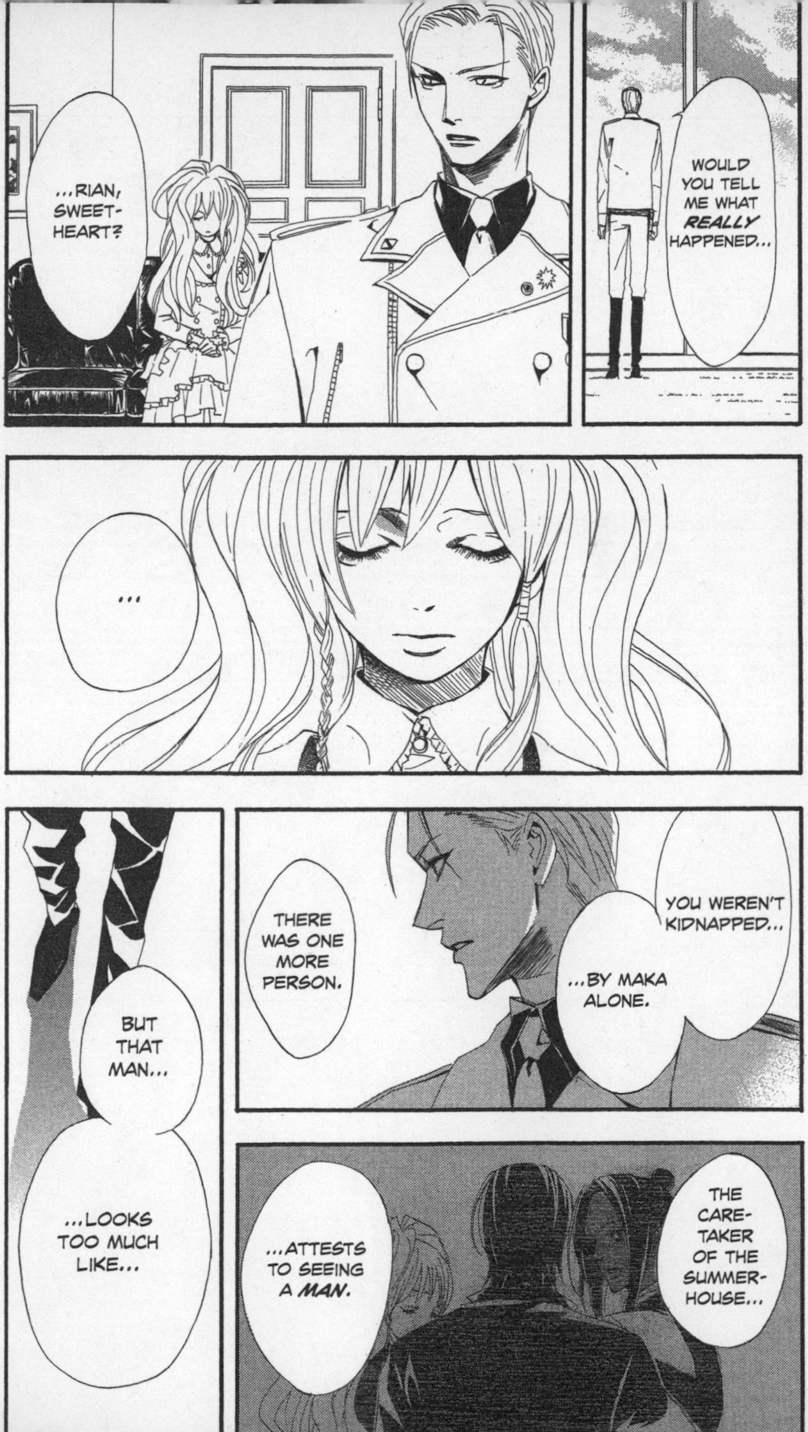
WOULD YOU TELL ME WHAT *REALLY* HAPPENED...
...RIAN, SWEET-HEART?
...
YOU WEREN'T KIDNAPPED...
...BY MAKA ALONE.
THERE WAS ONE MORE PERSON.
THE CARE-TAKER OF THE SUMMER-HOUSE...
...ATTESTS TO SEEING A *MAN*.
BUT THAT MAN...
...LOOKS TOO MUCH LIKE...

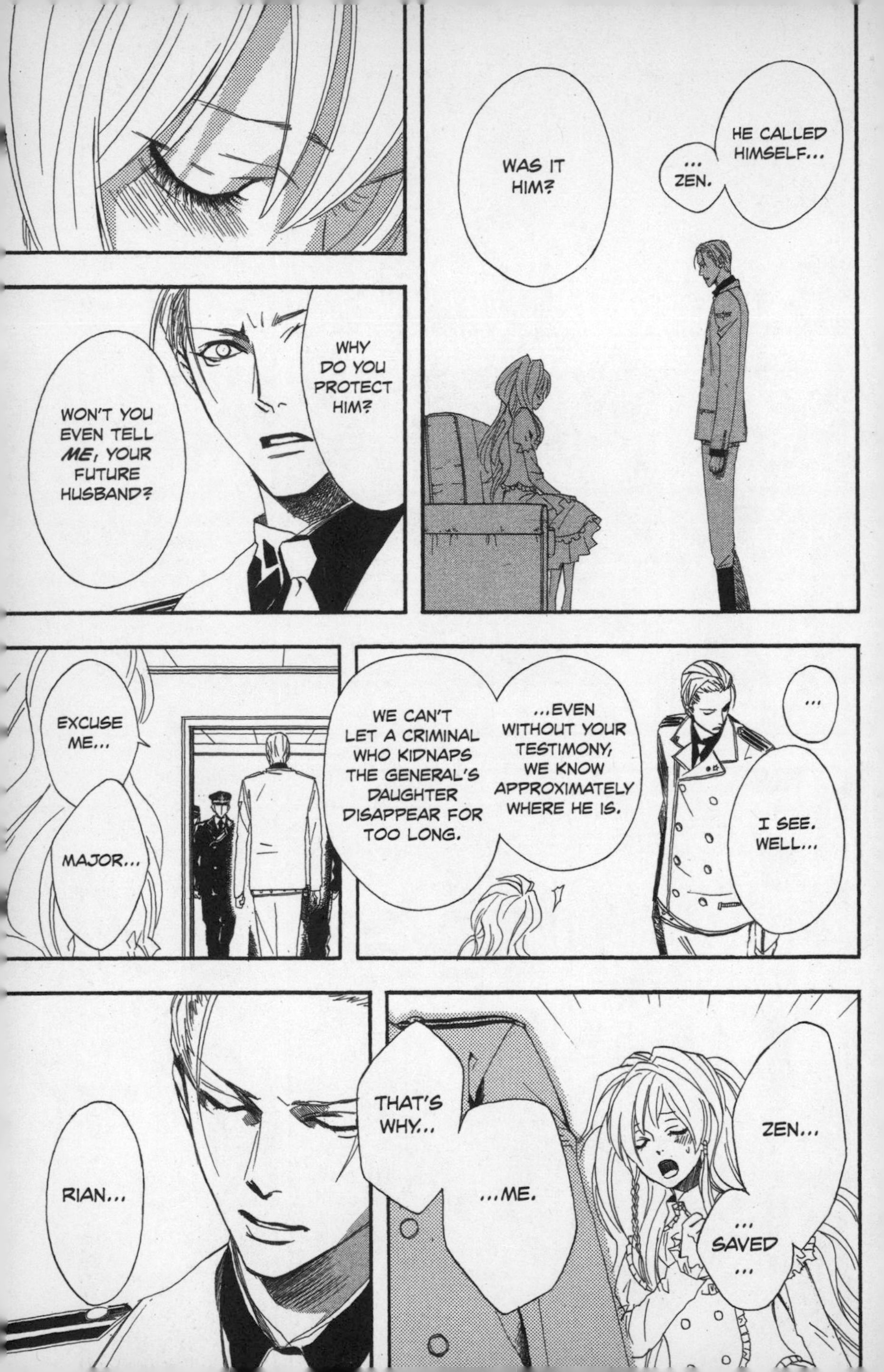
HE CALLED HIMSELF...
...ZEN.
WAS IT HIM?
WHY DO YOU PROTECT HIM?
WON'T YOU EVEN TELL *ME*, YOUR FUTURE HUSBAND?
...
I SEE. WELL...
...EVEN WITHOUT YOUR TESTIMONY, WE KNOW APPROXIMATELY WHERE HE IS.
WE CAN'T LET A CRIMINAL WHO KIDNAPS THE GENERAL'S DAUGHTER DISAPPEAR FOR TOO LONG.
EXCUSE ME...
MAJOR...
ZEN...
...SAVED...
THAT'S WHY...
...ME.
RIAN...

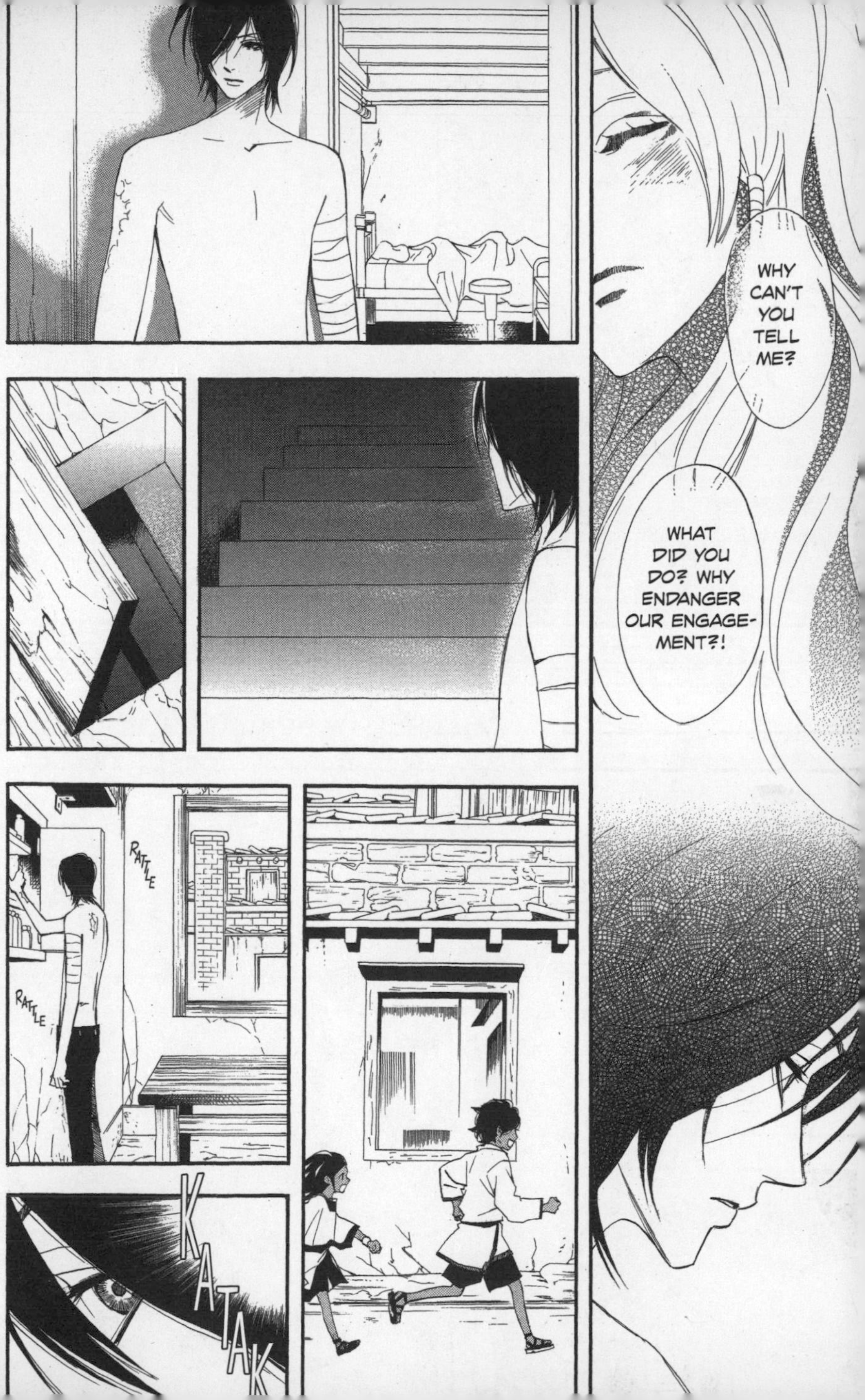
WHY CAN'T YOU TELL ME?
WHAT DID YOU DO? WHY ENDANGER OUR ENGAGE-MENT?!
RATTLE
RATTLE
KATAK

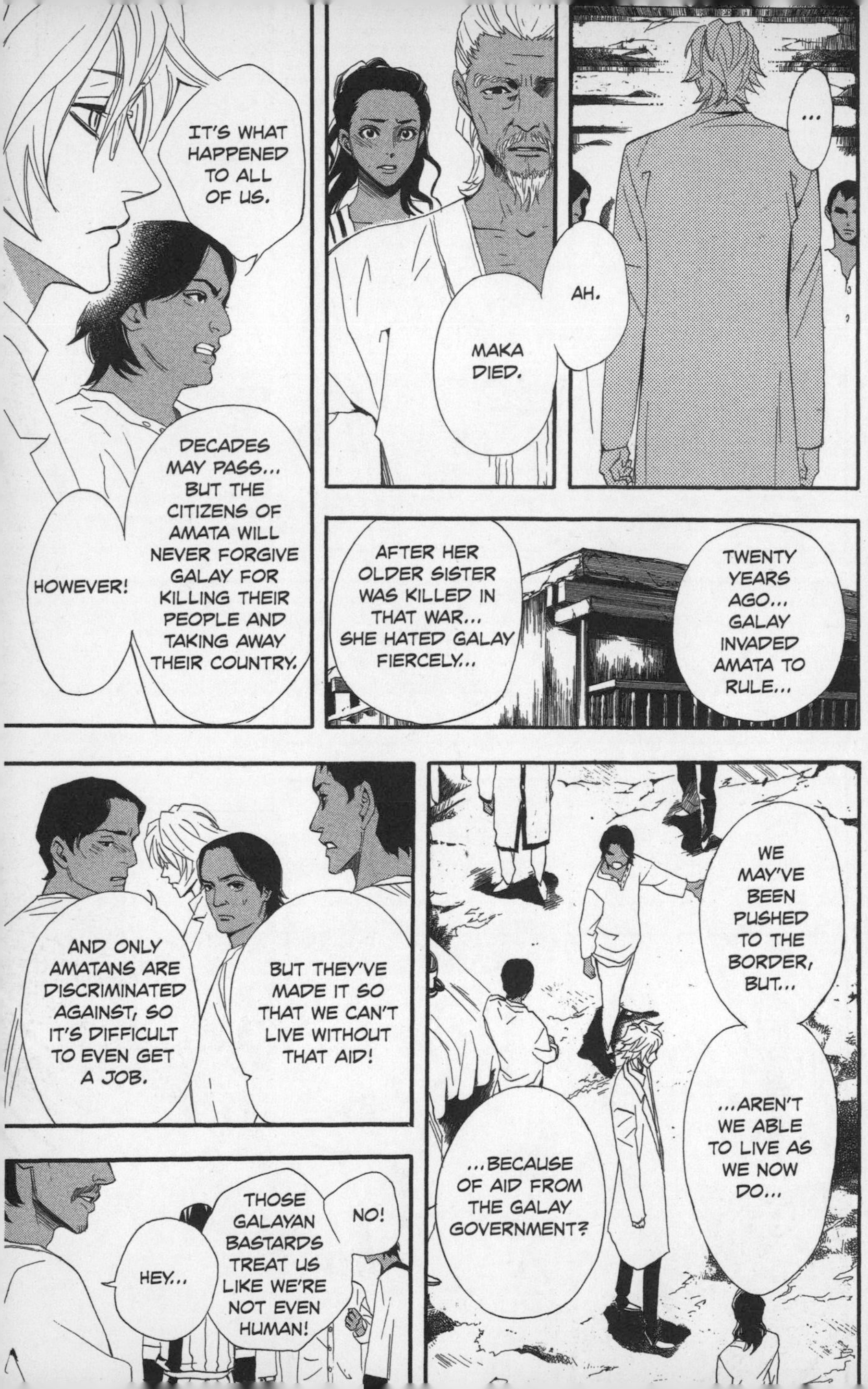
...
AH.
MAKA DIED.
TWENTY YEARS AGO... GALAY INVADED AMATA TO RULE...
AFTER HER OLDER SISTER WAS KILLED IN THAT WAR... SHE HATED GALAY FIERCELY...
IT'S WHAT HAPPENED TO ALL OF US.
DECADES MAY PASS... BUT THE CITIZENS OF AMATA WILL NEVER FORGIVE GALAY FOR KILLING THEIR PEOPLE AND TAKING AWAY THEIR COUNTRY.
HOWEVER!
WE MAY'VE BEEN PUSHED TO THE BORDER, BUT...
...AREN'T WE ABLE TO LIVE AS WE NOW DO...
...BECAUSE OF AID FROM THE GALAY GOVERNMENT?
BUT THEY'VE MADE IT SO THAT WE CAN'T LIVE WITHOUT THAT AID!
AND ONLY AMATANS ARE DISCRIMINATED AGAINST, SO IT'S DIFFICULT TO EVEN GET A JOB.
NO!
THOSE GALAYAN BASTARDS TREAT US LIKE WE'RE NOT EVEN HUMAN!
HEY...

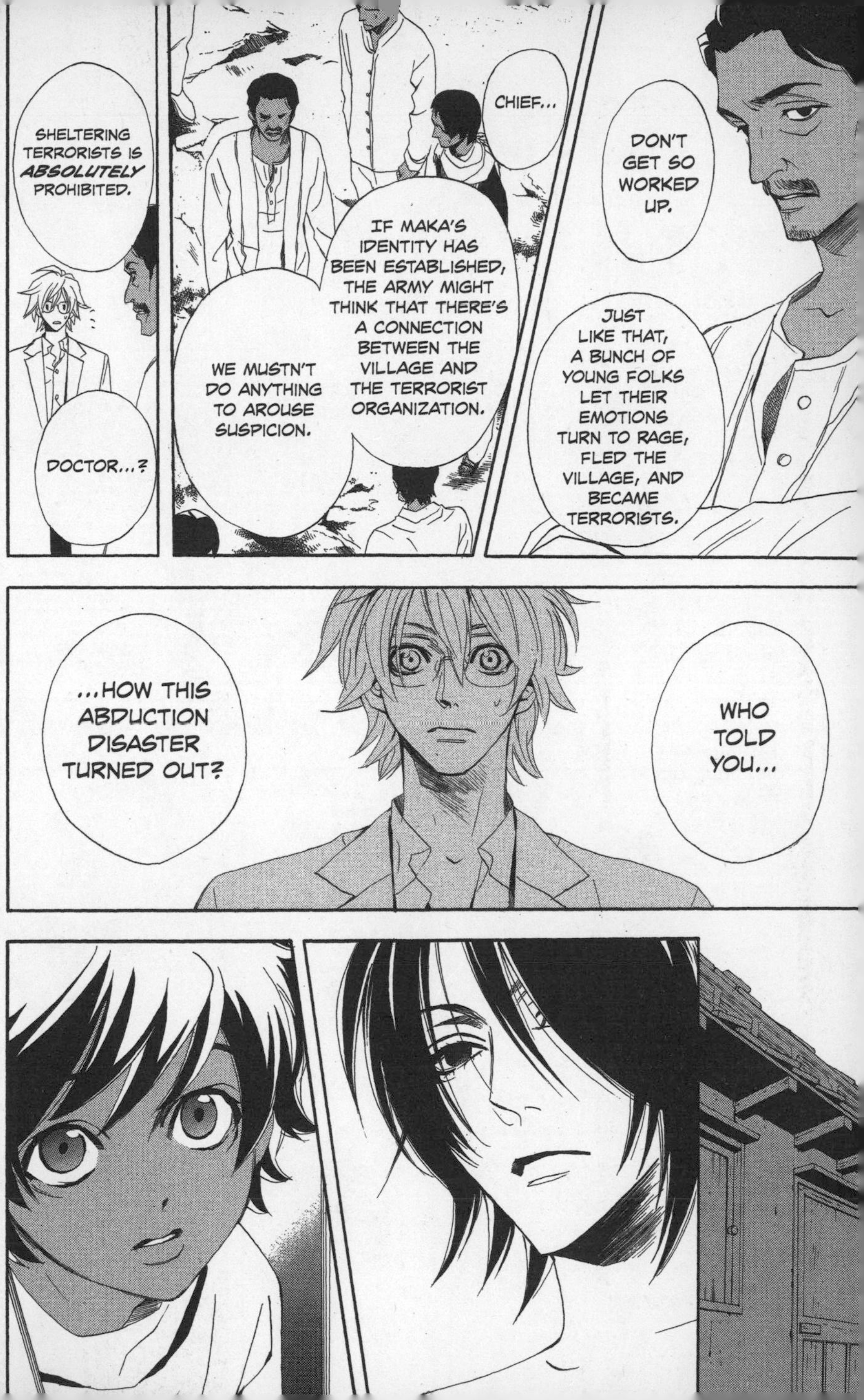
DON'T GET SO WORKED UP.
JUST LIKE THAT, A BUNCH OF YOUNG FOLKS LET THEIR EMOTIONS TURN TO RAGE, FLED THE VILLAGE, AND BECAME TERRORISTS.
CHIEF...
IF MAKA'S IDENTITY HAS BEEN ESTABLISHED, THE ARMY MIGHT THINK THAT THERE'S A CONNECTION BETWEEN THE VILLAGE AND THE TERRORIST ORGANIZATION.
WE MUSTN'T DO ANYTHING TO AROUSE SUSPICION.
SHELTERING TERRORISTS IS *ABSOLUTELY* PROHIBITED.
DOCTOR...?
WHO TOLD YOU...
...HOW THIS ABDUCTION DISASTER TURNED OUT?

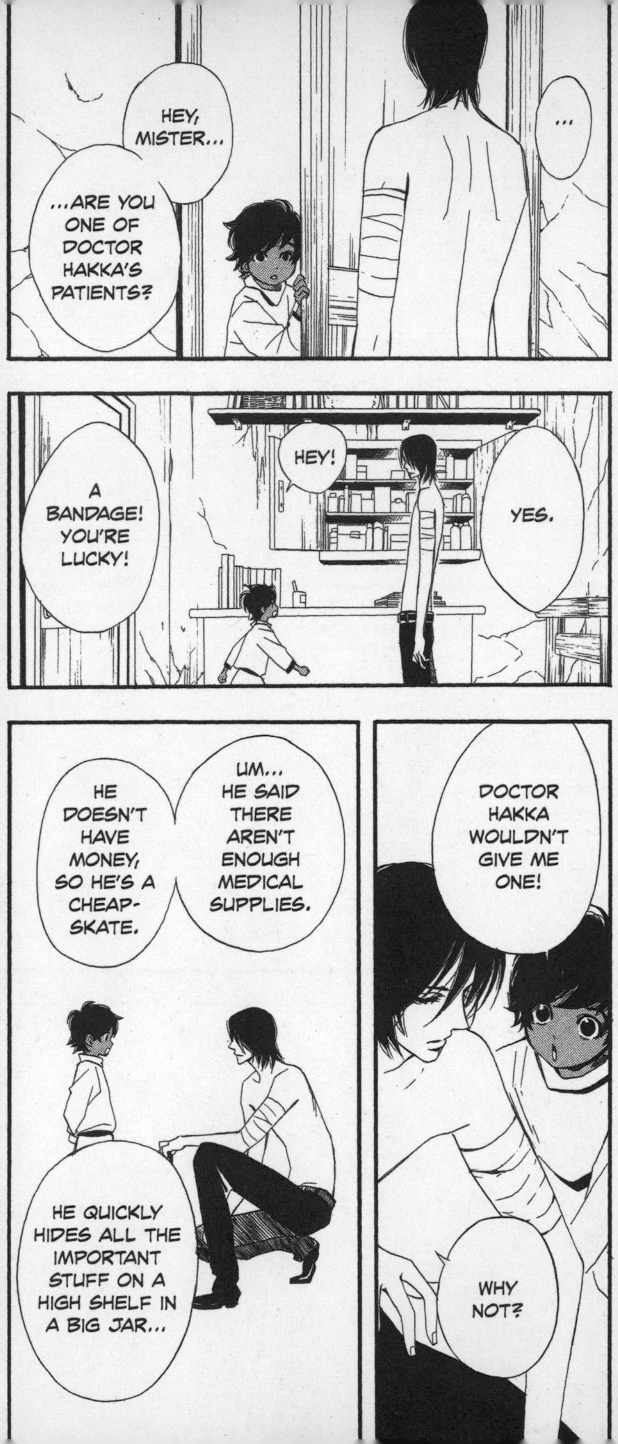
HEY, MISTER...
...ARE YOU ONE OF DOCTOR HAKKA'S PATIENTS?
...
YES.
HEY!
A BANDAGE! YOU'RE LUCKY!
DOCTOR HAKKA WOULDN'T GIVE ME ONE!
WHY NOT?
UM... HE SAID THERE AREN'T ENOUGH MEDICAL SUPPLIES.
HE DOESN'T HAVE MONEY, SO HE'S A CHEAP-SKATE.
HE QUICKLY HIDES ALL THE IMPORTANT STUFF ON A HIGH SHELF IN A BIG JAR...

3

My sincere apologies to all of you who read Chapter 1 and wrote me with hopes for a continuation. And sorry for the confusing story order. I'll try to make sure that nothing like this happens from now on... Of course! I'm also sorry to those of you who got ahold of *Blank Slate* for the first time as a graphic novel. All the sidebars have been filled up with excuses...

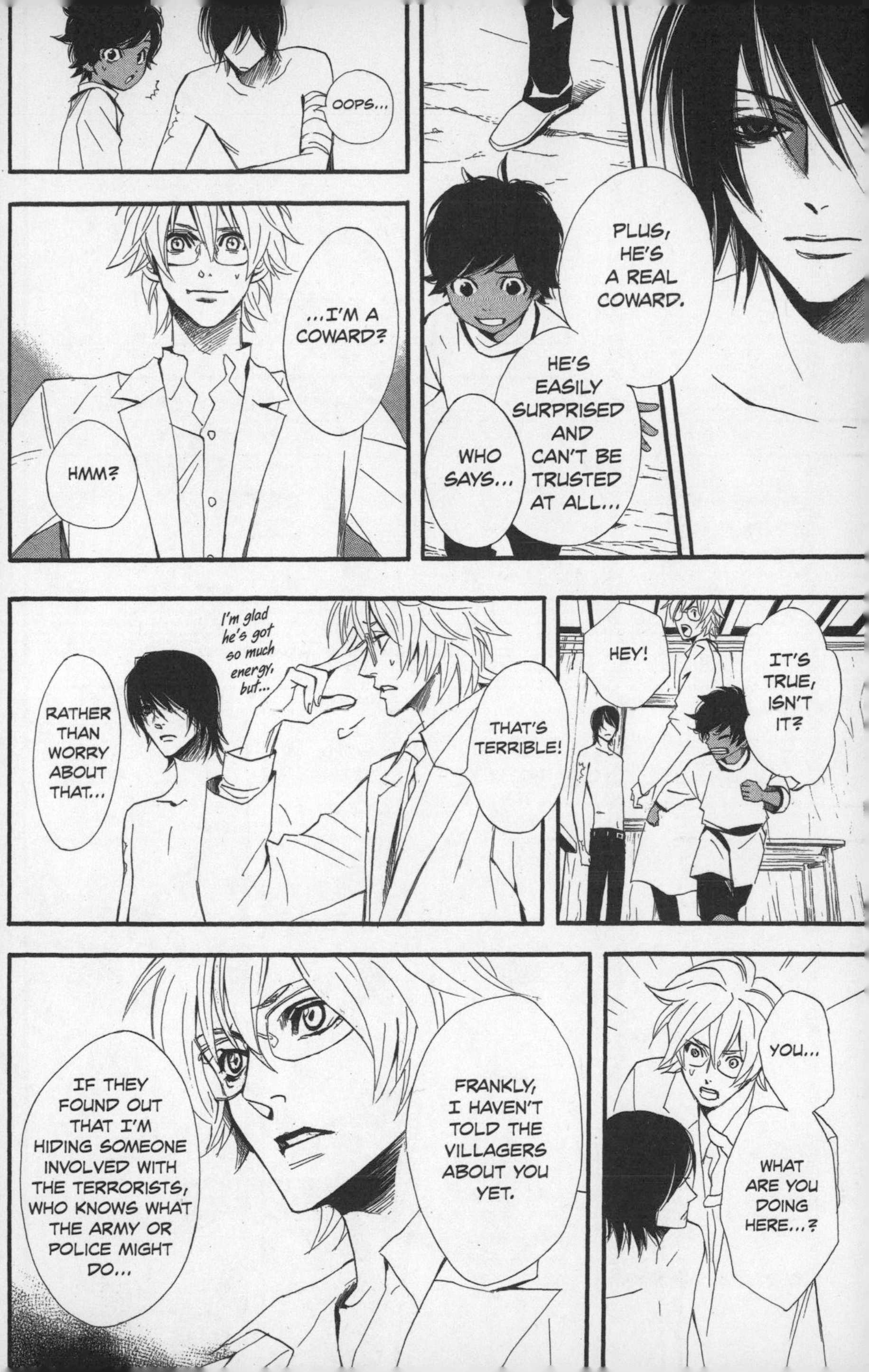
PLUS, HE'S A REAL COWARD.
HE'S EASILY SURPRISED AND CAN'T BE TRUSTED AT ALL...
WHO SAYS...
OOPS...
...I'M A COWARD?
HMM?
IT'S TRUE, ISN'T IT?
HEY!
THAT'S TERRIBLE!
I'm glad he's got so much energy, but...
RATHER THAN WORRY ABOUT THAT...
YOU...
WHAT ARE YOU DOING HERE...?
FRANKLY, I HAVEN'T TOLD THE VILLAGERS ABOUT YOU YET.
IF THEY FOUND OUT THAT I'M HIDING SOMEONE INVOLVED WITH THE TERRORISTS, WHO KNOWS WHAT THE ARMY OR POLICE MIGHT DO...

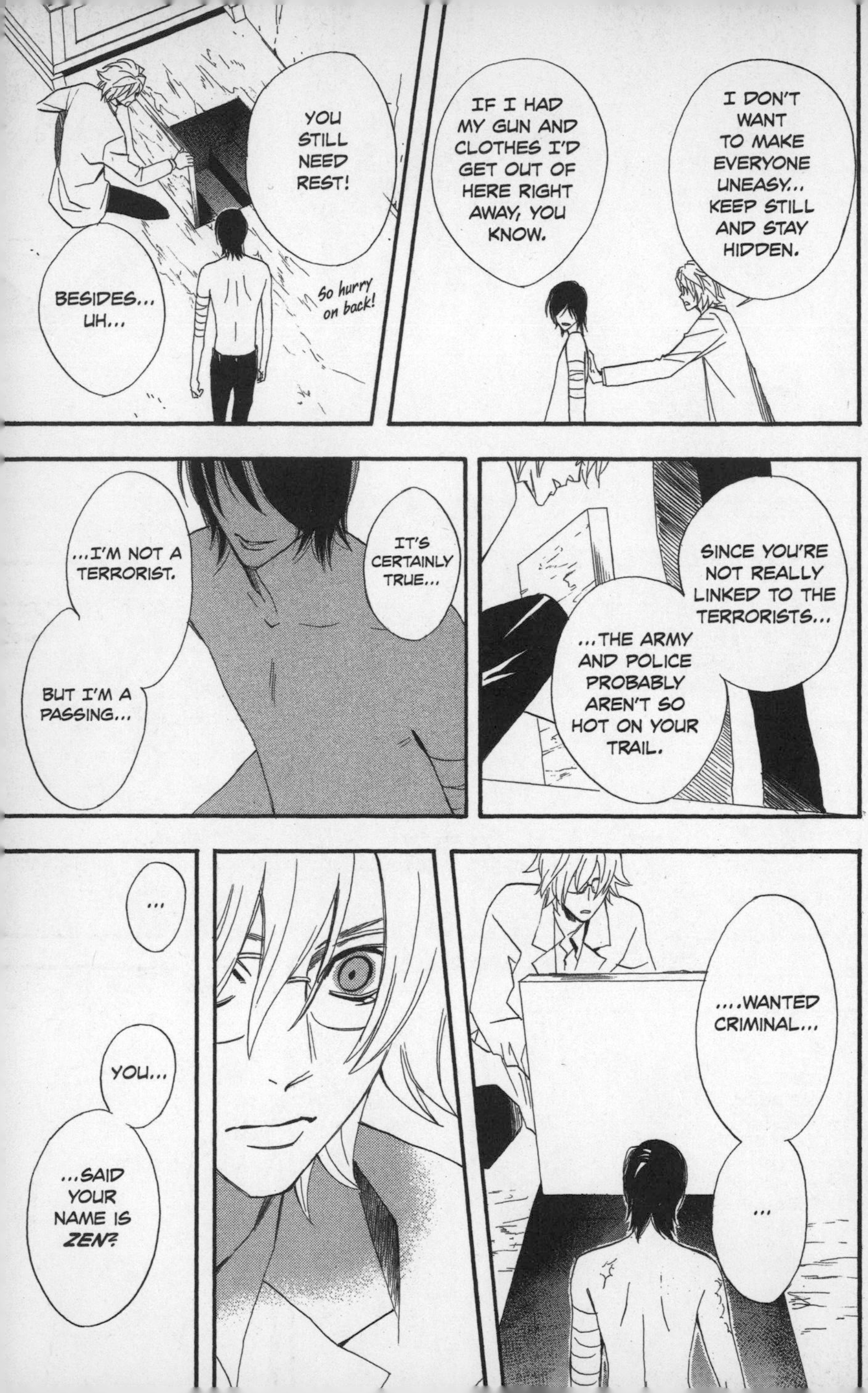
I DON'T WANT TO MAKE EVERYONE UNEASY... KEEP STILL AND STAY HIDDEN.
IF I HAD MY GUN AND CLOTHES I'D GET OUT OF HERE RIGHT AWAY, YOU KNOW.
YOU STILL NEED REST!
So hurry on back!
BESIDES... UH...
SINCE YOU'RE NOT REALLY LINKED TO THE TERRORISTS...
...THE ARMY AND POLICE PROBABLY AREN'T SO HOT ON YOUR TRAIL.
IT'S CERTAINLY TRUE...
...I'M NOT A TERRORIST.
BUT I'M A PASSING...
....WANTED CRIMINAL...
...
...
YOU...
...SAID YOUR NAME IS *ZEN*?

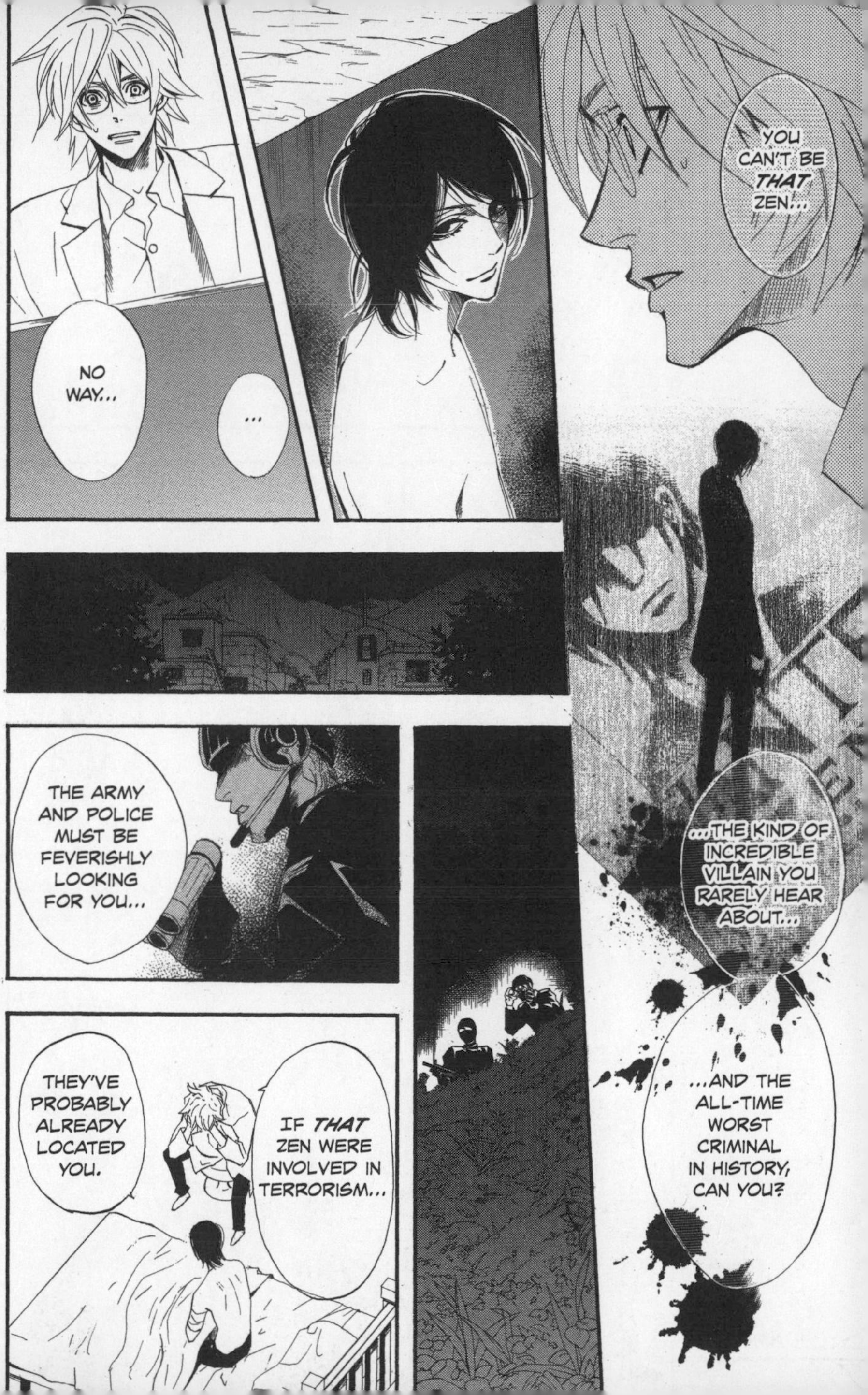
YOU CAN'T BE *THAT* ZEN...
...THE KIND OF INCREDIBLE VILLAIN YOU RARELY HEAR ABOUT...
...AND THE ALL-TIME WORST CRIMINAL IN HISTORY, CAN YOU?
NO WAY...
...
THE ARMY AND POLICE MUST BE FEVERISHLY LOOKING FOR YOU...
IF *THAT* ZEN WERE INVOLVED IN TERRORISM...
THEY'VE PROBABLY ALREADY LOCATED YOU.

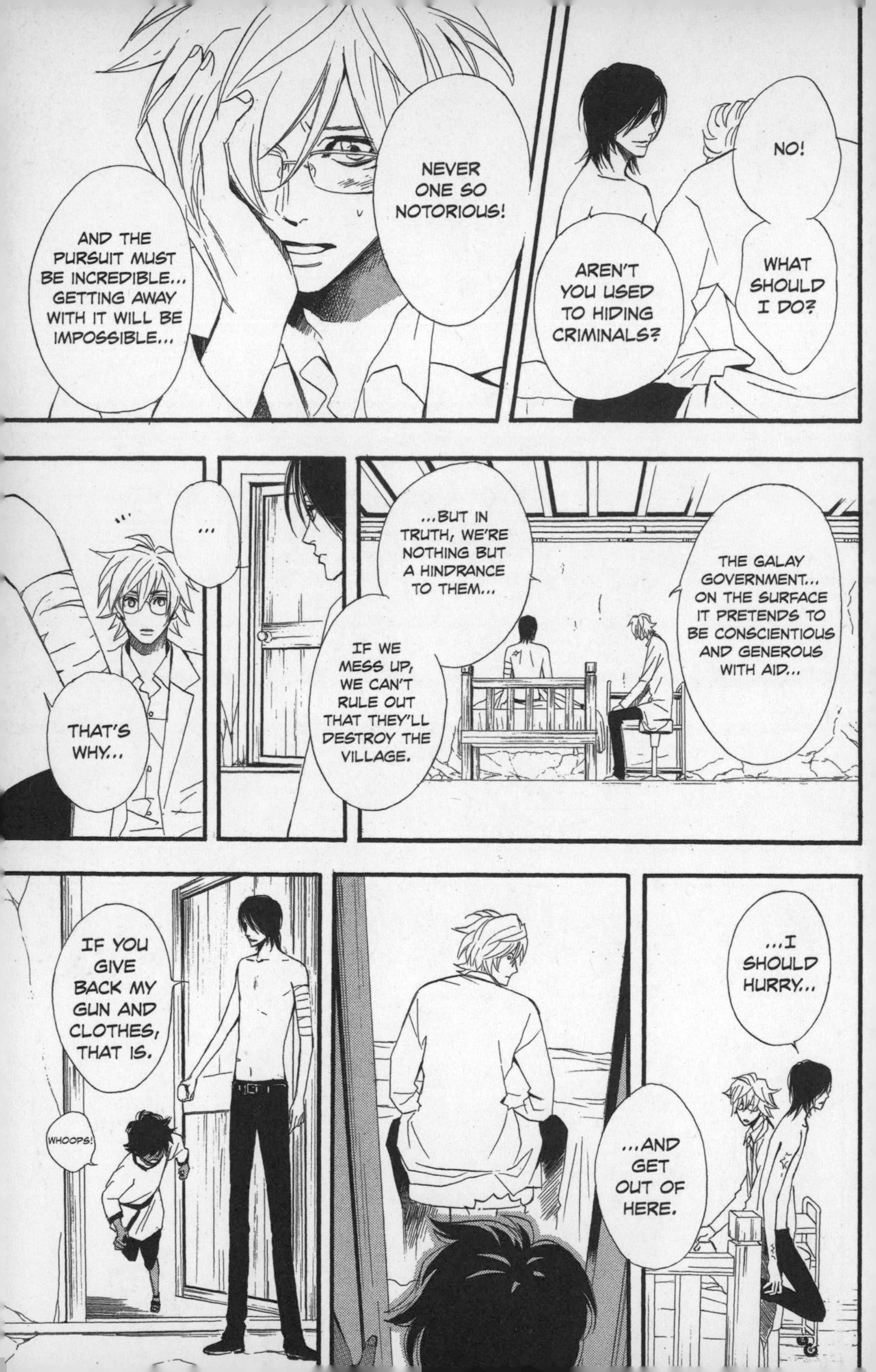
NO!
WHAT SHOULD I DO?
AREN'T YOU USED TO HIDING CRIMINALS?
NEVER ONE SO NOTORIOUS!
AND THE PURSUIT MUST BE INCREDIBLE... GETTING AWAY WITH IT WILL BE IMPOSSIBLE...
THE GALAY GOVERNMENT... ON THE SURFACE IT PRETENDS TO BE CONSCIENTIOUS AND GENEROUS WITH AID...
...BUT IN TRUTH, WE'RE NOTHING BUT A HINDRANCE TO THEM...
IF WE MESS UP, WE CAN'T RULE OUT THAT THEY'LL DESTROY THE VILLAGE.
...
...
THAT'S WHY...
...I SHOULD HURRY...
...AND GET OUT OF HERE.
IF YOU GIVE BACK MY GUN AND CLOTHES, THAT IS.
WHOOPS!

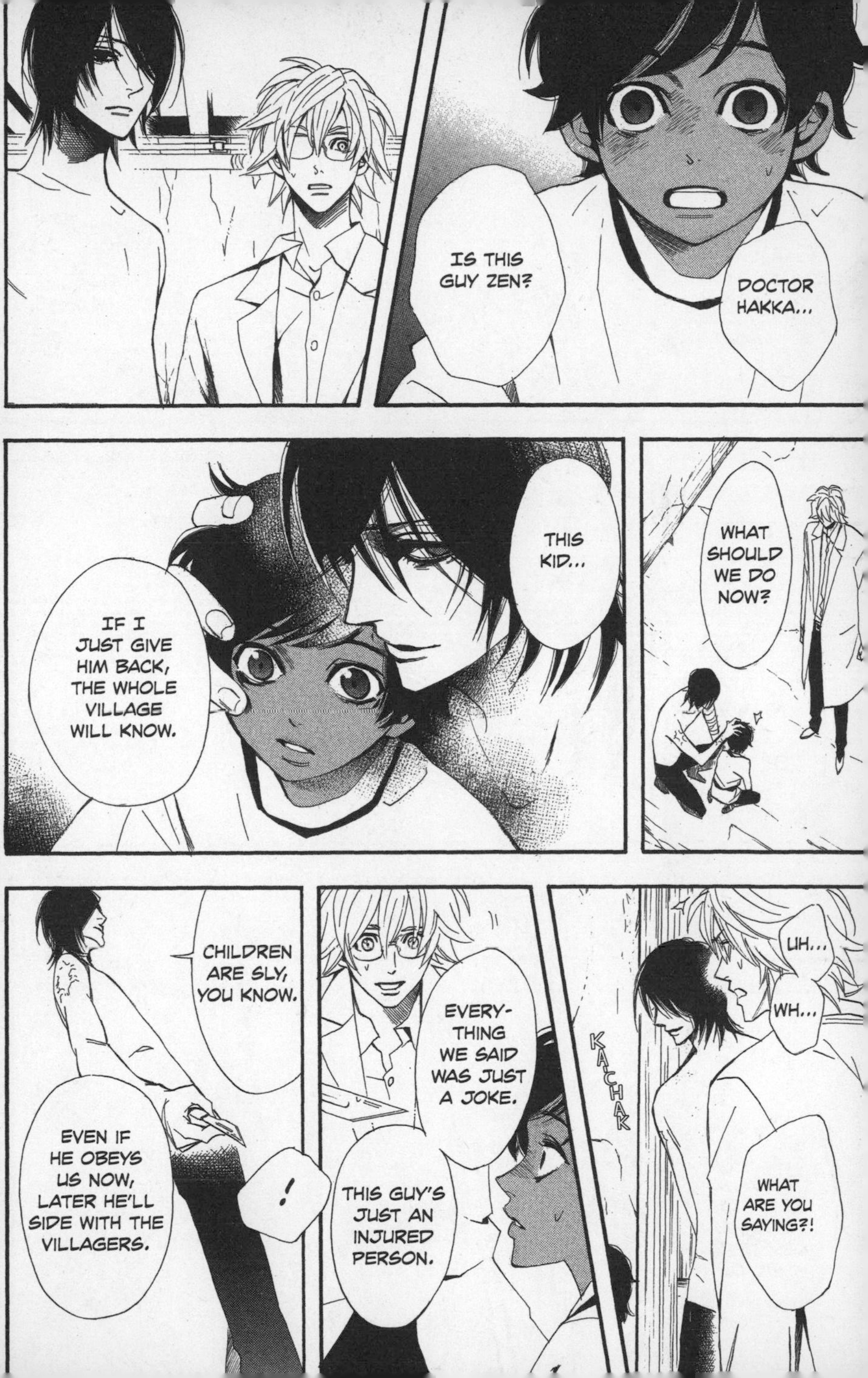
DOCTOR HAKKA...
IS THIS GUY ZEN?
WHAT SHOULD WE DO NOW?
THIS KID...
IF I JUST GIVE HIM BACK, THE WHOLE VILLAGE WILL KNOW.
UH...
WH...
KA-CHAK
WHAT ARE YOU SAYING?!
EVERY-THING WE SAID WAS JUST A JOKE.
THIS GUY'S JUST AN INJURED PERSON.
!
CHILDREN ARE SLY, YOU KNOW.
EVEN IF HE OBEYS US NOW, LATER HE'LL SIDE WITH THE VILLAGERS.

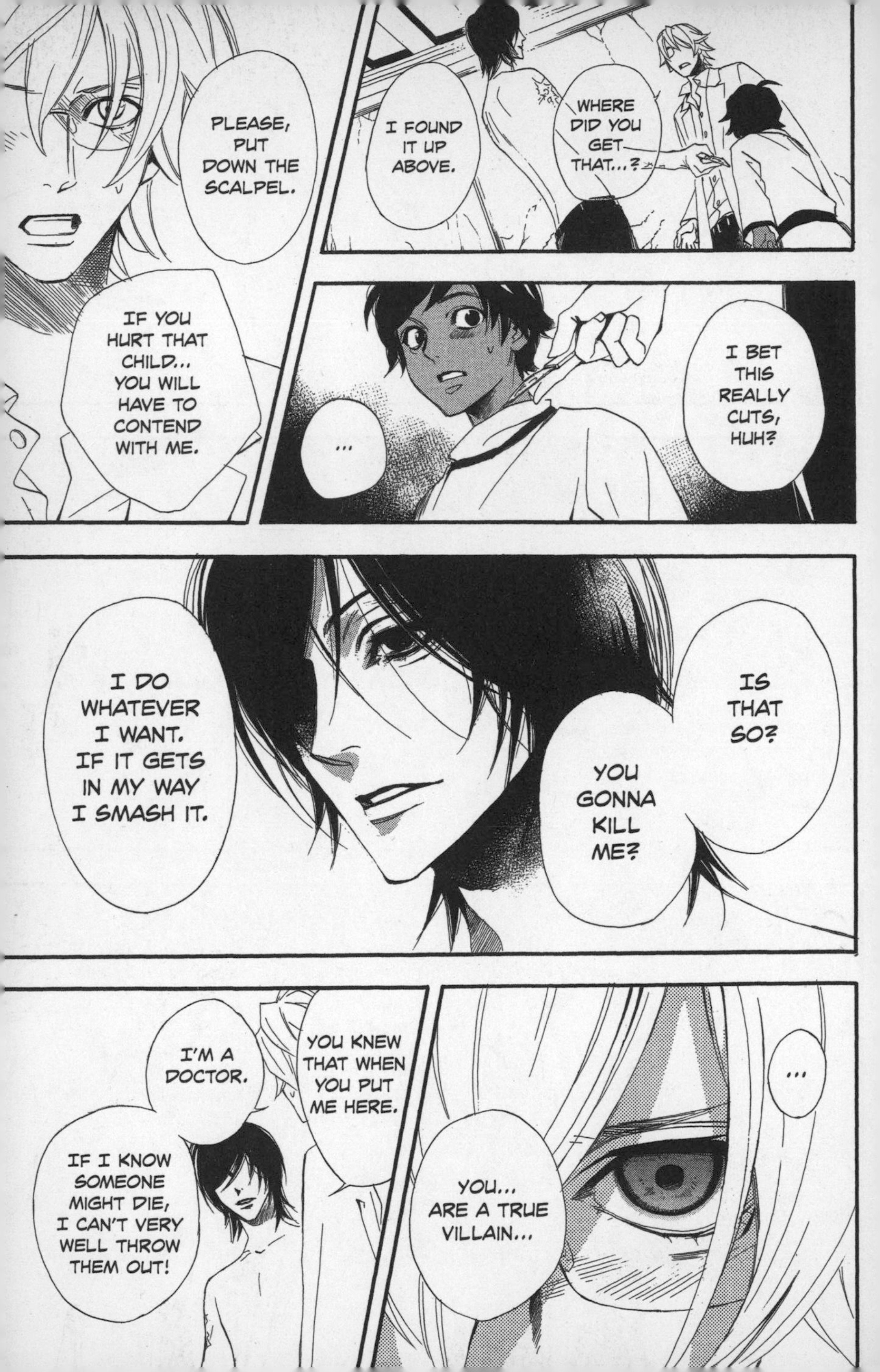
WHERE DID YOU GET THAT...?
I FOUND IT UP ABOVE.
I BET THIS REALLY CUTS, HUH?
...
PLEASE, PUT DOWN THE SCALPEL.
IF YOU HURT THAT CHILD... YOU WILL HAVE TO CONTEND WITH ME.
IS THAT SO?
YOU GONNA KILL ME?
I DO WHATEVER I WANT. IF IT GETS IN MY WAY I SMASH IT.
...
YOU... ARE A TRUE VILLAIN...
YOU KNEW THAT WHEN YOU PUT ME HERE.
I'M A DOCTOR.
IF I KNOW SOMEONE MIGHT DIE, I CAN'T VERY WELL THROW THEM OUT!

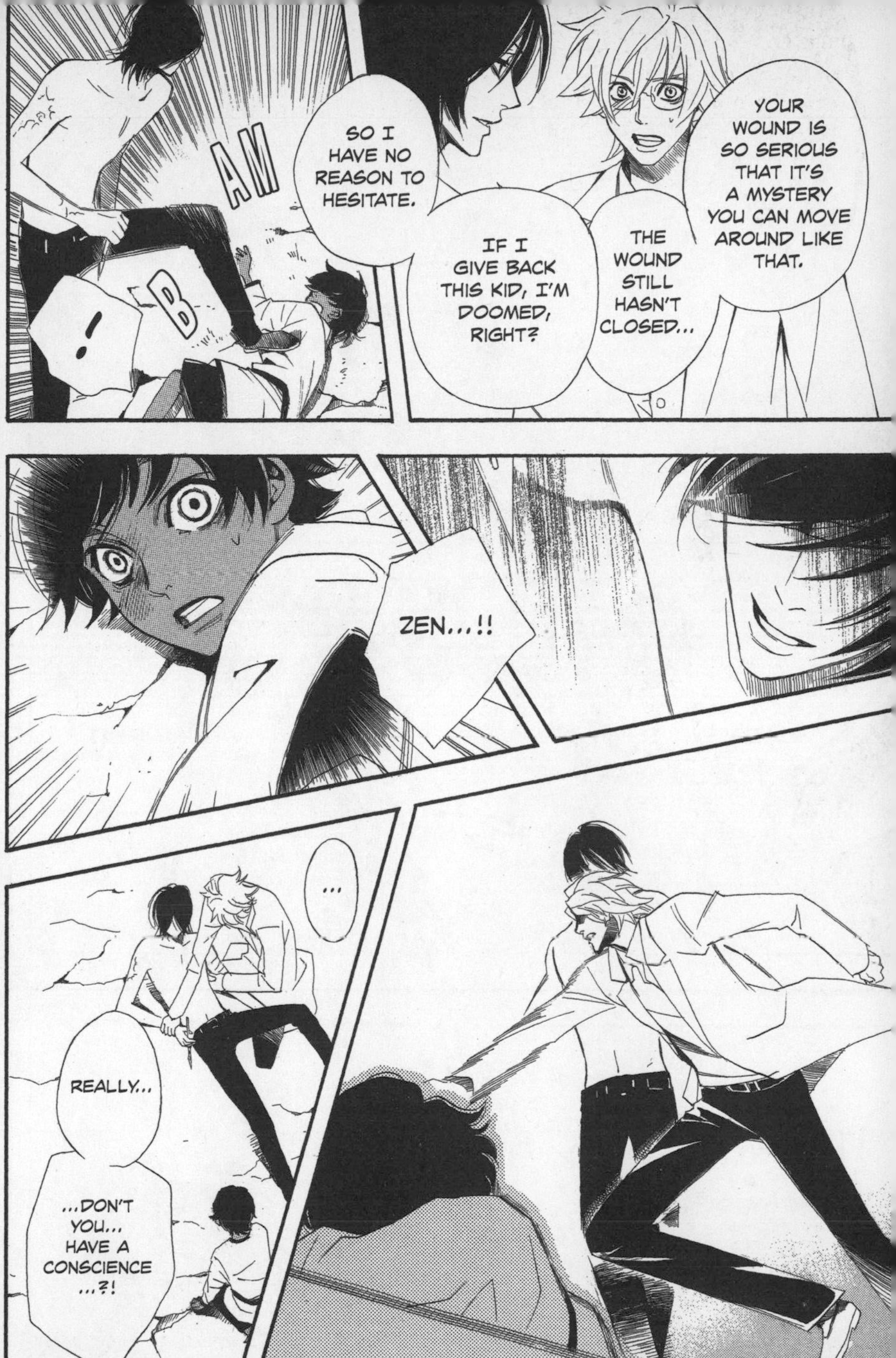
YOUR WOUND IS SO SERIOUS THAT IT'S A MYSTERY YOU CAN MOVE AROUND LIKE THAT.
THE WOUND STILL HASN'T CLOSED...
IF I GIVE BACK THIS KID, I'M DOOMED, RIGHT?
SO I HAVE NO REASON TO HESITATE.
BAM
!
ZEN...!!
...
REALLY...
...DON'T YOU... HAVE A CONSCIENCE ...?!

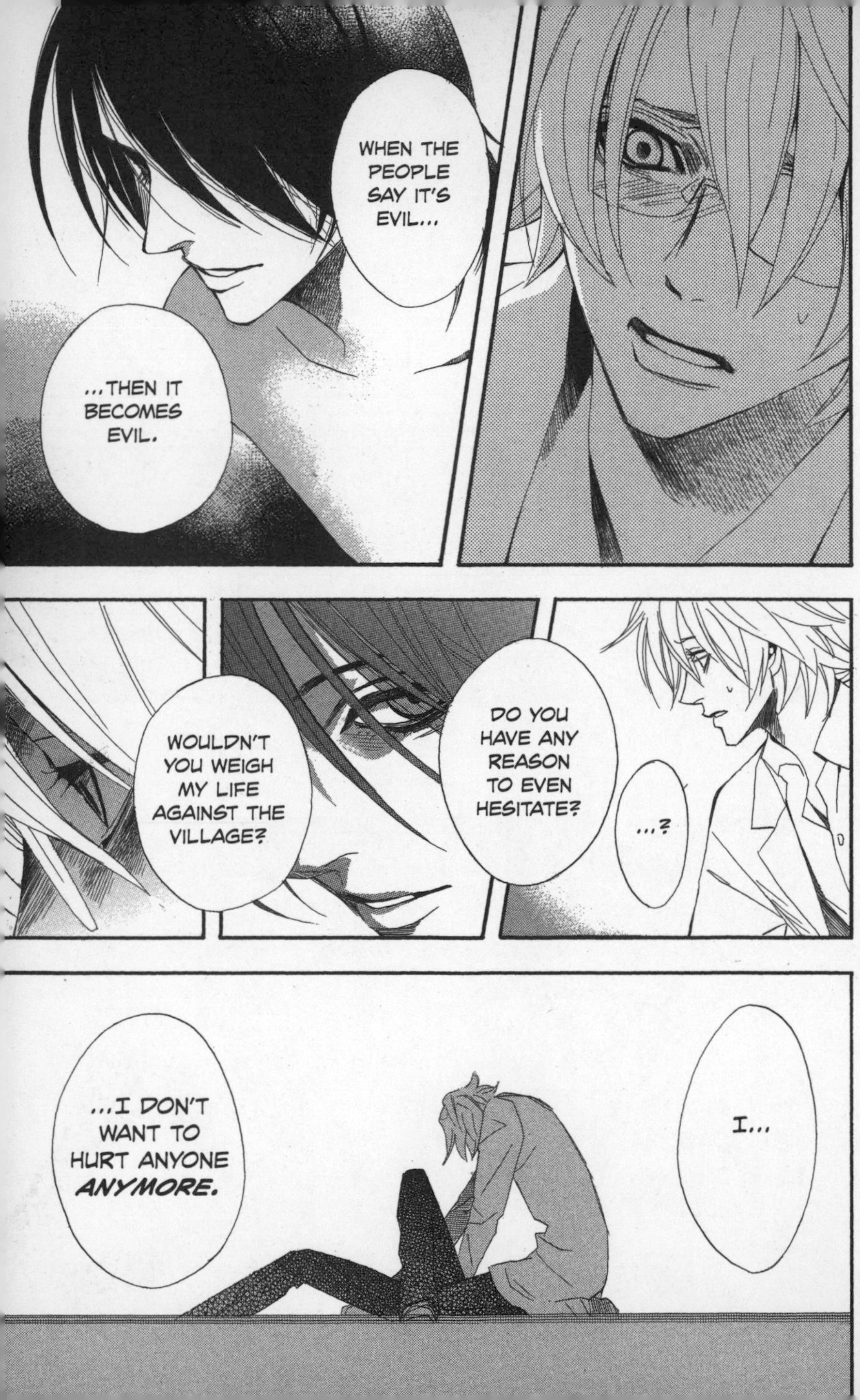
WHEN THE PEOPLE SAY IT'S EVIL...
...THEN IT BECOMES EVIL.
DO YOU HAVE ANY REASON TO EVEN HESITATE?
...?
WOULDN'T YOU WEIGH MY LIFE AGAINST THE VILLAGE?
I...
...I DON'T WANT TO HURT ANYONE *ANYMORE.*

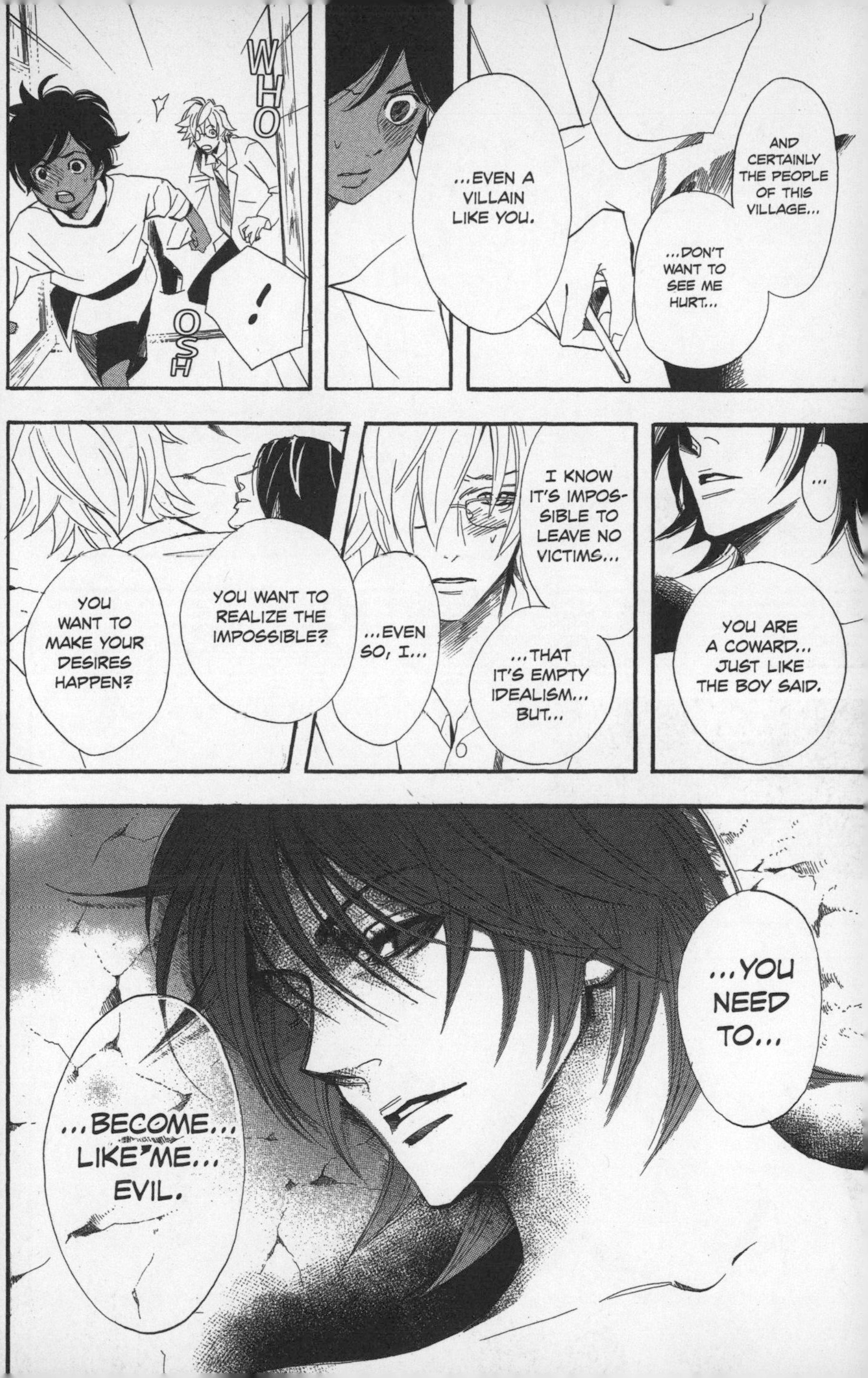
AND CERTAINLY THE PEOPLE OF THIS VILLAGE...
...DON'T WANT TO SEE ME HURT...
...EVEN A VILLAIN LIKE YOU.
WHO
!
OSH
...
YOU ARE A COWARD... JUST LIKE THE BOY SAID.
I KNOW IT'S IMPOSSIBLE TO LEAVE NO VICTIMS...
...THAT IT'S EMPTY IDEALISM... BUT...
...EVEN SO, I...
YOU WANT TO REALIZE THE IMPOSSIBLE?
YOU WANT TO MAKE YOUR DESIRES HAPPEN?
...YOU NEED TO...
...BECOME... LIKE ME... EVIL.

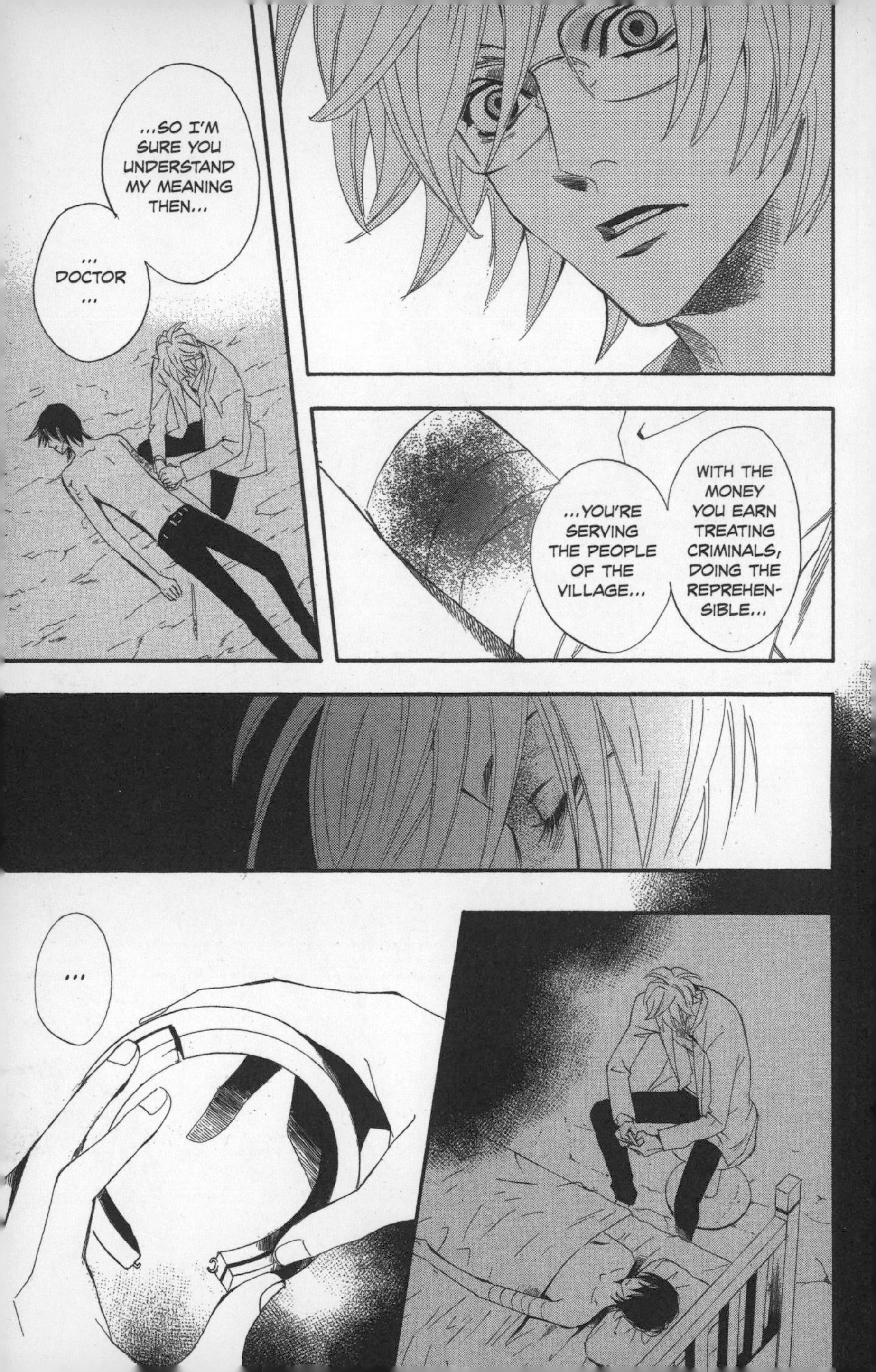
WITH THE MONEY YOU EARN TREATING CRIMINALS, DOING THE REPREHEN-SIBLE...
...YOU'RE SERVING THE PEOPLE OF THE VILLAGE...
...SO I'M SURE YOU UNDERSTAND MY MEANING THEN...
... DOCTOR ...
...

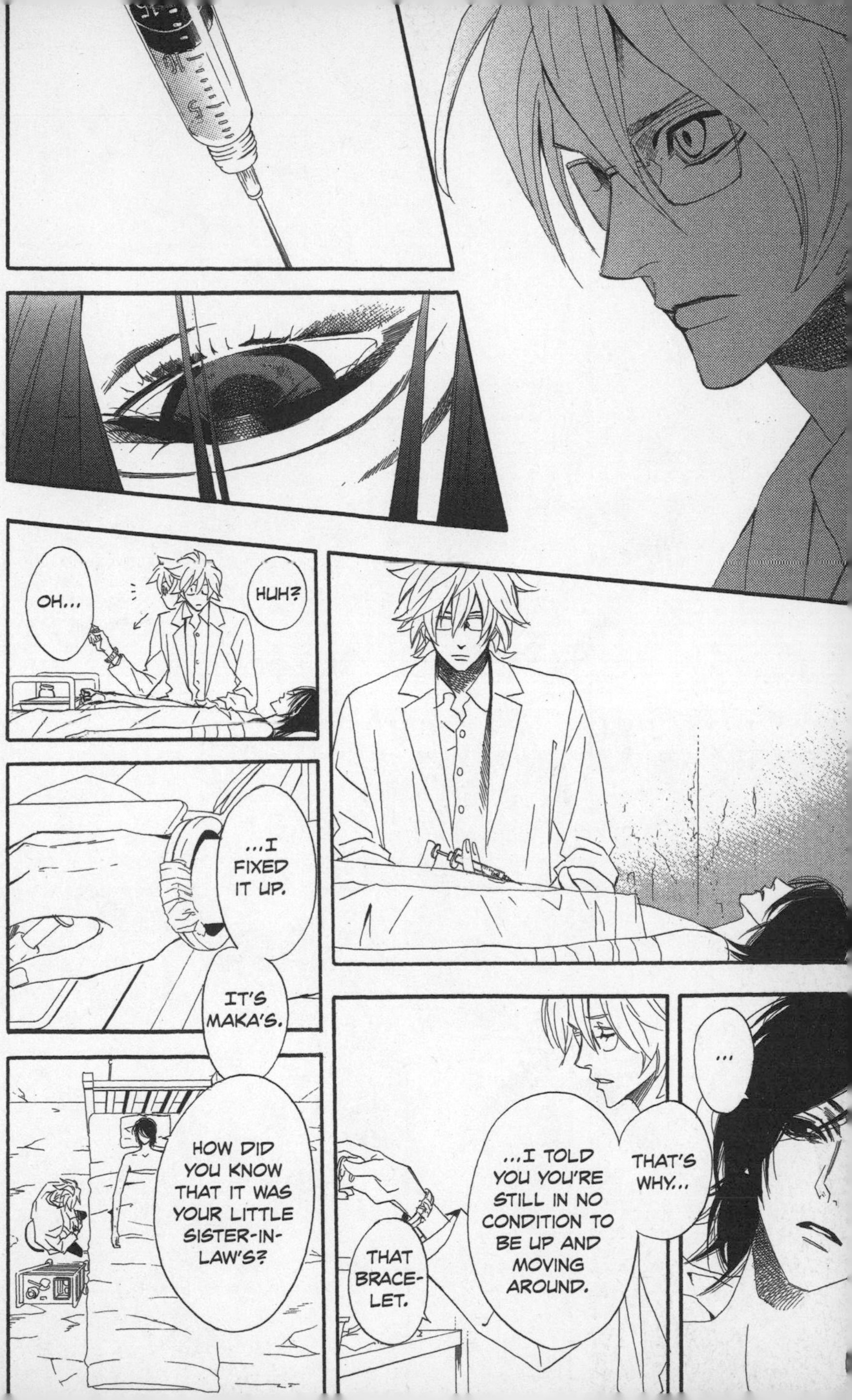
HUH?
OH...
...I FIXED IT UP.
IT'S MAKA'S.
...
THAT'S WHY...
...I TOLD YOU YOU'RE STILL IN NO CONDITION TO BE UP AND MOVING AROUND.
THAT BRACELET.
HOW DID YOU KNOW THAT IT WAS YOUR LITTLE SISTER-IN-LAW'S?

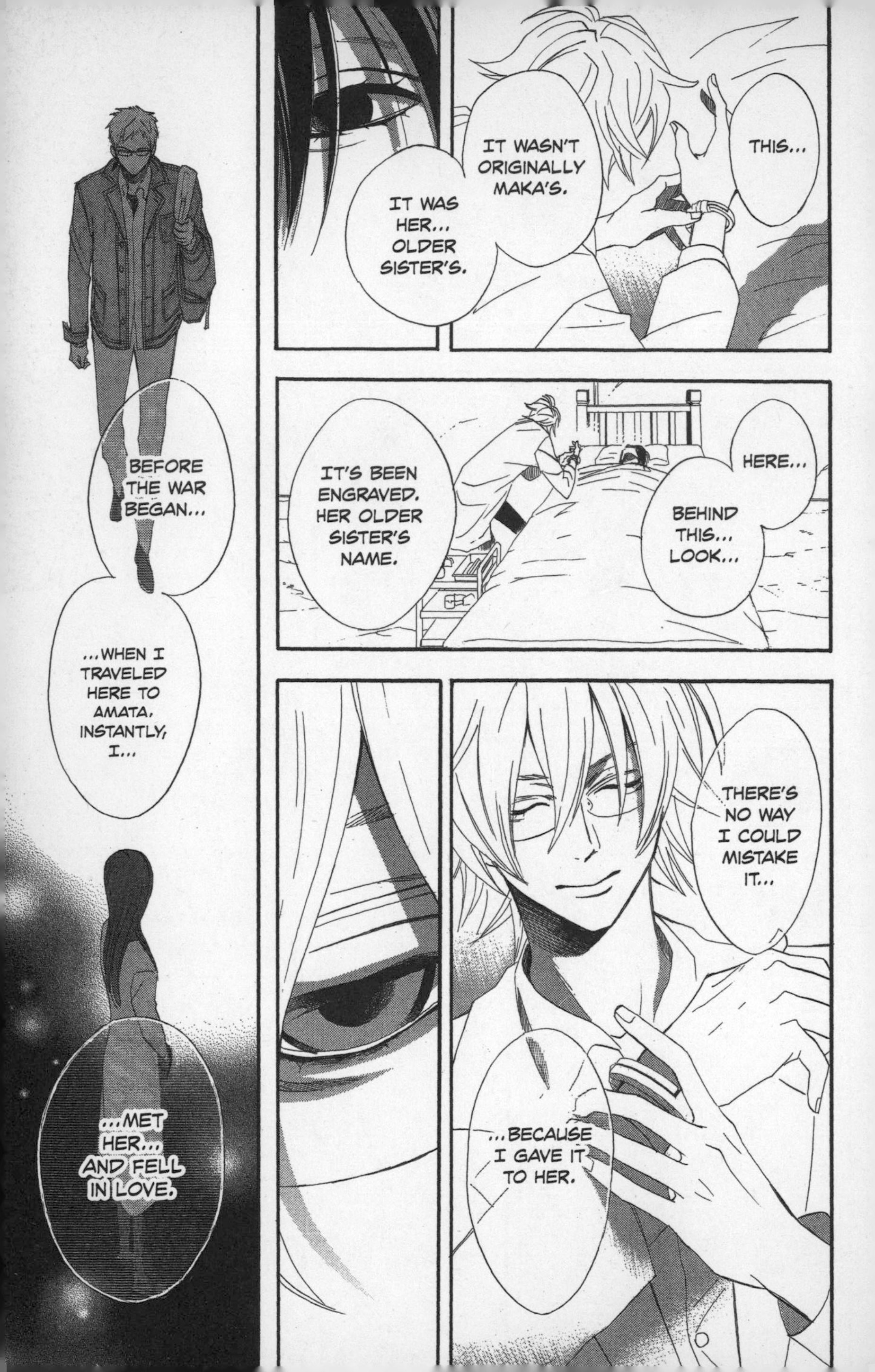
THIS...
IT WASN'T ORIGINALLY MAKA'S.
IT WAS HER... OLDER SISTER'S.
HERE...
BEHIND THIS... LOOK...
IT'S BEEN ENGRAVED. HER OLDER SISTER'S NAME.
THERE'S NO WAY I COULD MISTAKE IT...
...BECAUSE I GAVE IT TO HER.
BEFORE THE WAR BEGAN...
...WHEN I TRAVELED HERE TO AMATA, INSTANTLY, I...
...MET HER... AND FELL IN LOVE.

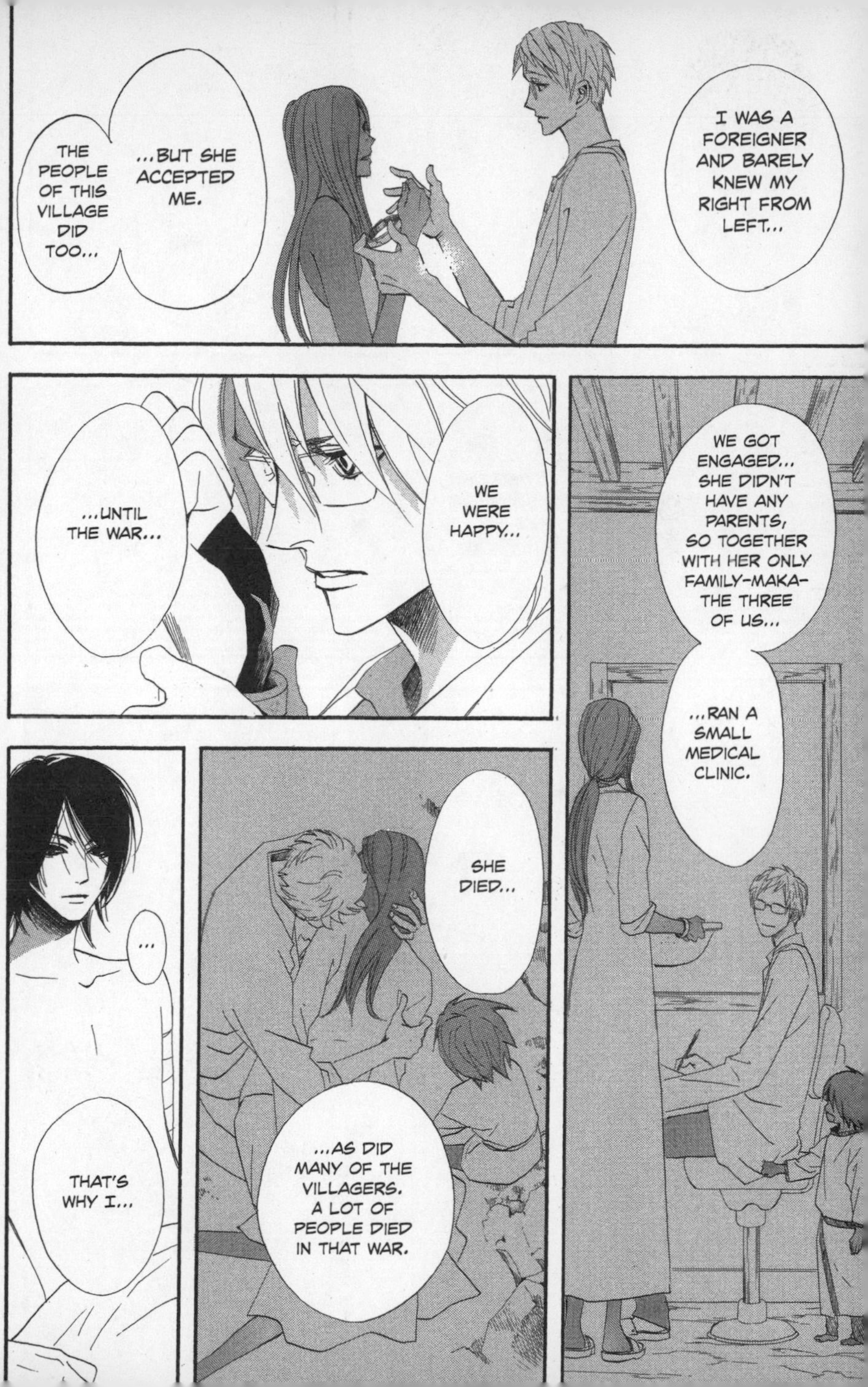
I WAS A FOREIGNER AND BARELY KNEW MY RIGHT FROM LEFT...
...BUT SHE ACCEPTED ME.
THE PEOPLE OF THIS VILLAGE DID TOO...
WE GOT ENGAGED... SHE DIDN'T HAVE ANY PARENTS, SO TOGETHER WITH HER ONLY FAMILY—MAKA—THE THREE OF US...
...RAN A SMALL MEDICAL CLINIC.
WE WERE HAPPY...
...UNTIL THE WAR...
SHE DIED...
...AS DID MANY OF THE VILLAGERS. A LOT OF PEOPLE DIED IN THAT WAR.
...
THAT'S WHY I...

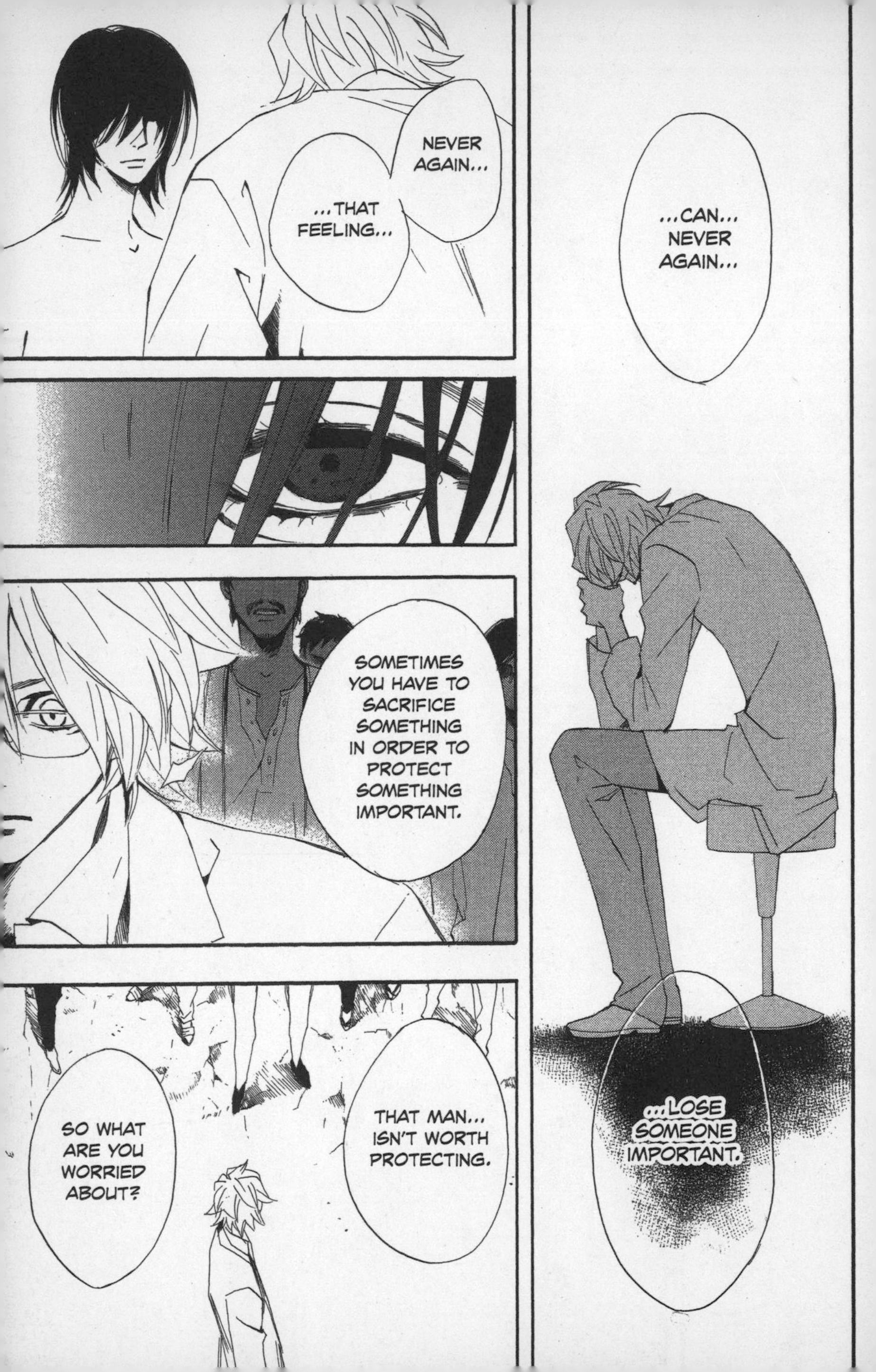
...CAN... NEVER AGAIN...
...LOSE SOMEONE IMPORTANT.
NEVER AGAIN...
...THAT FEELING...
SOMETIMES YOU HAVE TO SACRIFICE SOMETHING IN ORDER TO PROTECT SOMETHING IMPORTANT.
THAT MAN... ISN'T WORTH PROTECTING.
SO WHAT ARE YOU WORRIED ABOUT?

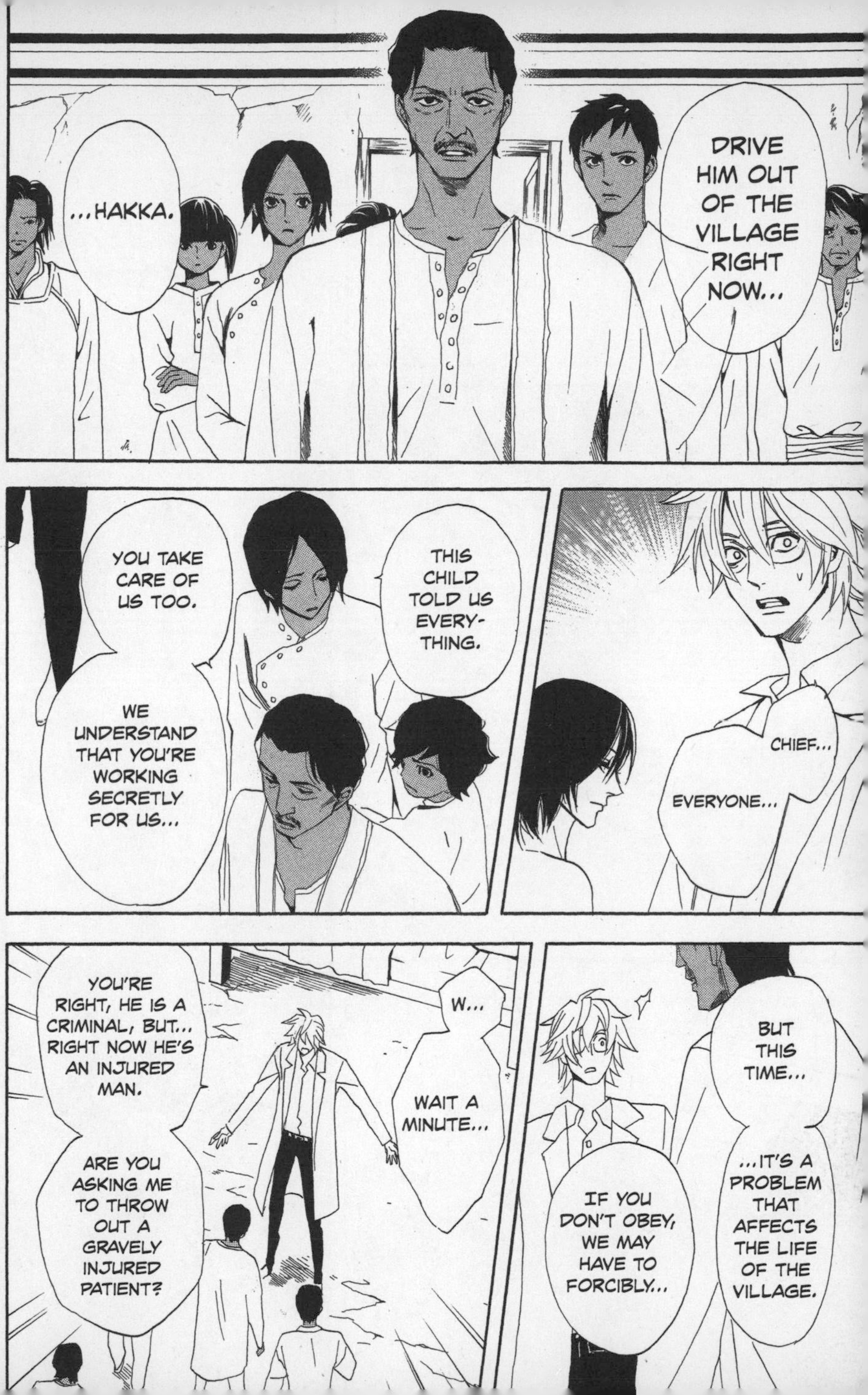
DRIVE HIM OUT OF THE VILLAGE RIGHT NOW...
...HAKKA.
CHIEF...
EVERYONE...
THIS CHILD TOLD US EVERY-THING.
YOU TAKE CARE OF US TOO.
WE UNDERSTAND THAT YOU'RE WORKING SECRETLY FOR US...
BUT THIS TIME...
...IT'S A PROBLEM THAT AFFECTS THE LIFE OF THE VILLAGE.
IF YOU DON'T OBEY, WE MAY HAVE TO FORCIBLY...
W...
WAIT A MINUTE...
YOU'RE RIGHT, HE IS A CRIMINAL, BUT... RIGHT NOW HE'S AN INJURED MAN.
ARE YOU ASKING ME TO THROW OUT A GRAVELY INJURED PATIENT?

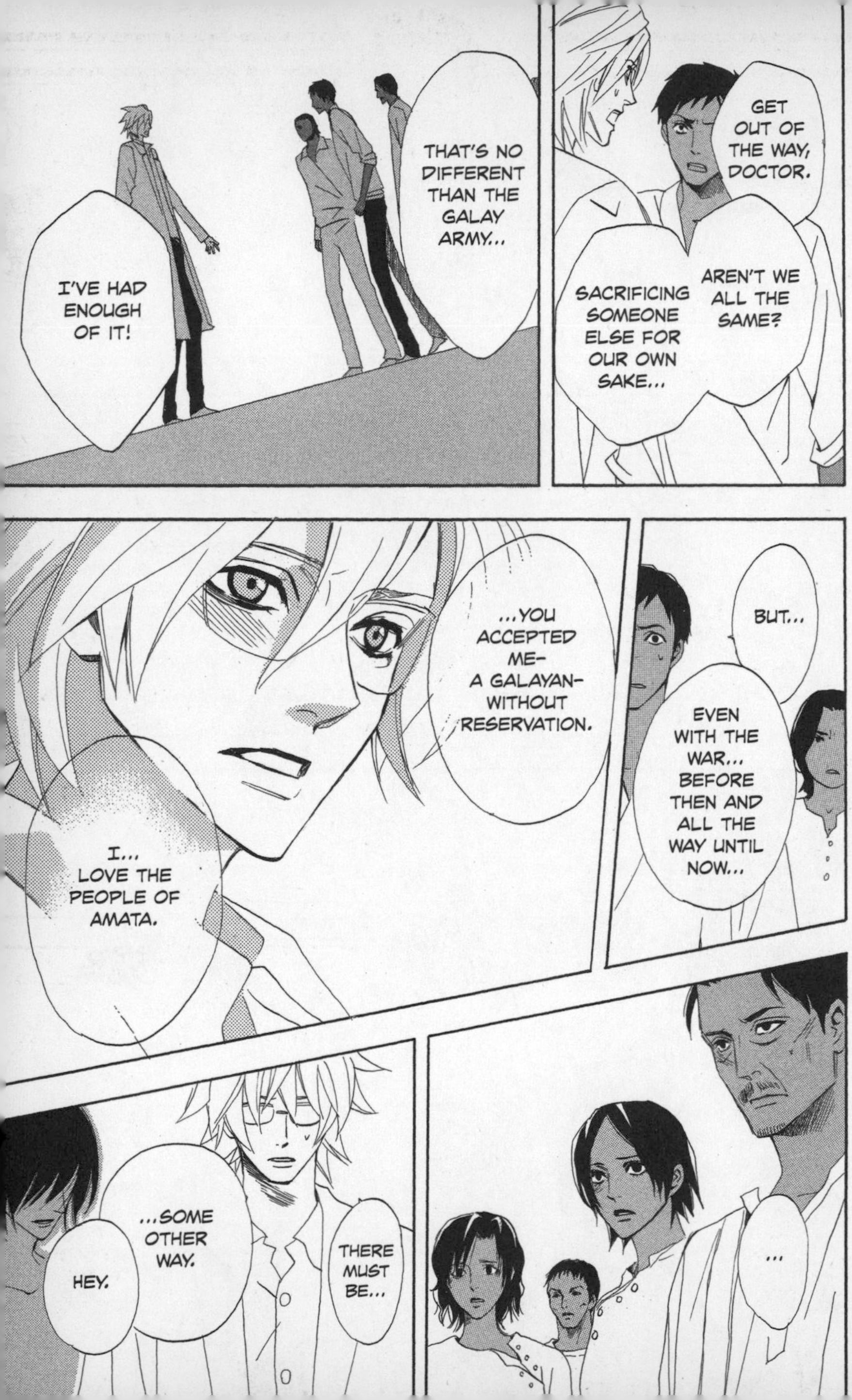
GET OUT OF THE WAY, DOCTOR.
AREN'T WE ALL THE SAME?
SACRIFICING SOMEONE ELSE FOR OUR OWN SAKE...
THAT'S NO DIFFERENT THAN THE GALAY ARMY...
I'VE HAD ENOUGH OF IT!
BUT...
EVEN WITH THE WAR... BEFORE THEN AND ALL THE WAY UNTIL NOW...
...YOU ACCEPTED ME- A GALAYAN- WITHOUT RESERVATION.
I... LOVE THE PEOPLE OF AMATA.
...
THERE MUST BE...
...SOME OTHER WAY.
HEY.

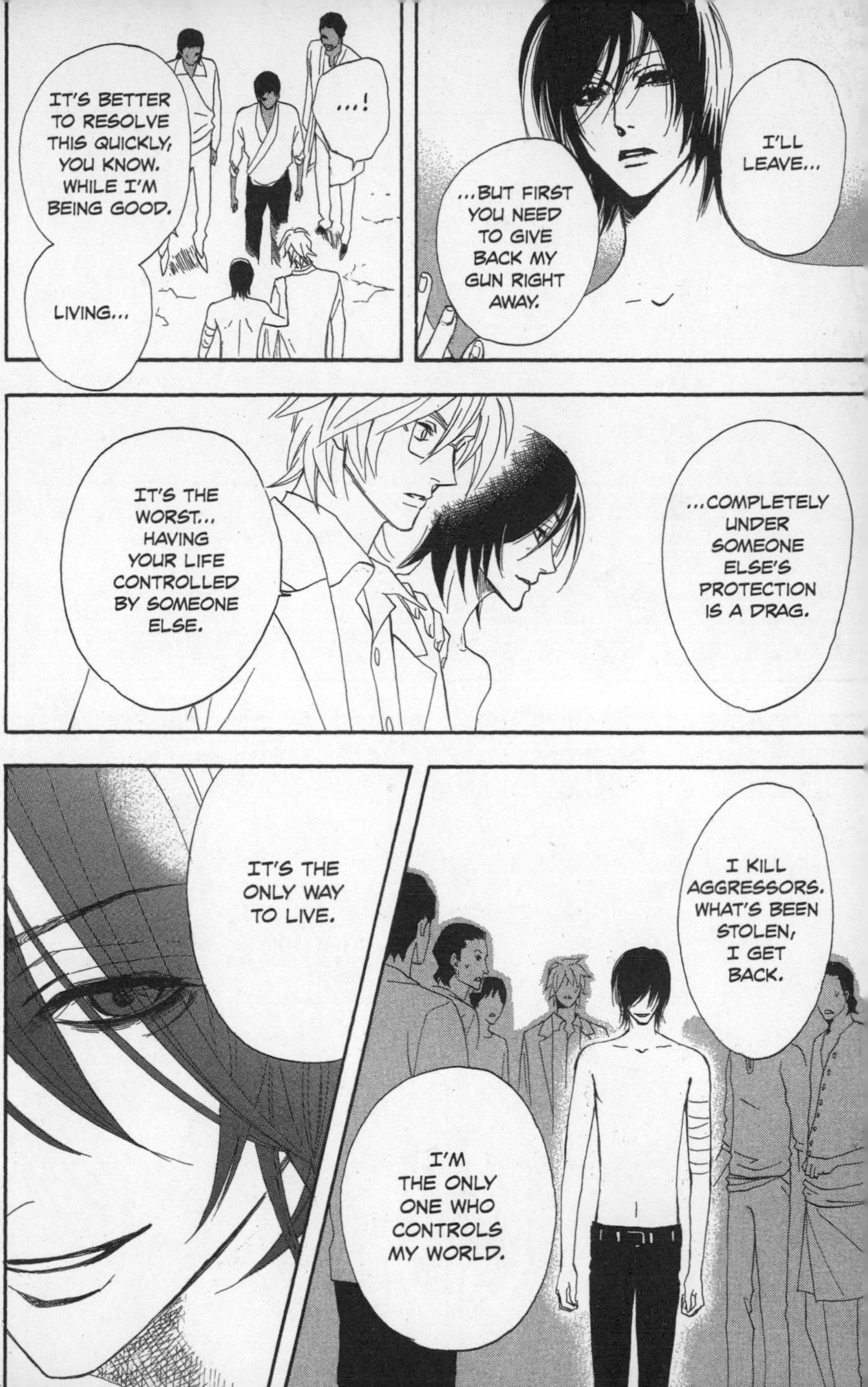
I'LL LEAVE...
...BUT FIRST YOU NEED TO GIVE BACK MY GUN RIGHT AWAY.
...!
IT'S BETTER TO RESOLVE THIS QUICKLY, YOU KNOW. WHILE I'M BEING GOOD.
LIVING...
...COMPLETELY UNDER SOMEONE ELSE'S PROTECTION IS A DRAG.
IT'S THE WORST... HAVING YOUR LIFE CONTROLLED BY SOMEONE ELSE.
I KILL AGGRESSORS. WHAT'S BEEN STOLEN, I GET BACK.
I'M THE ONLY ONE WHO CONTROLS MY WORLD.
IT'S THE ONLY WAY TO LIVE.

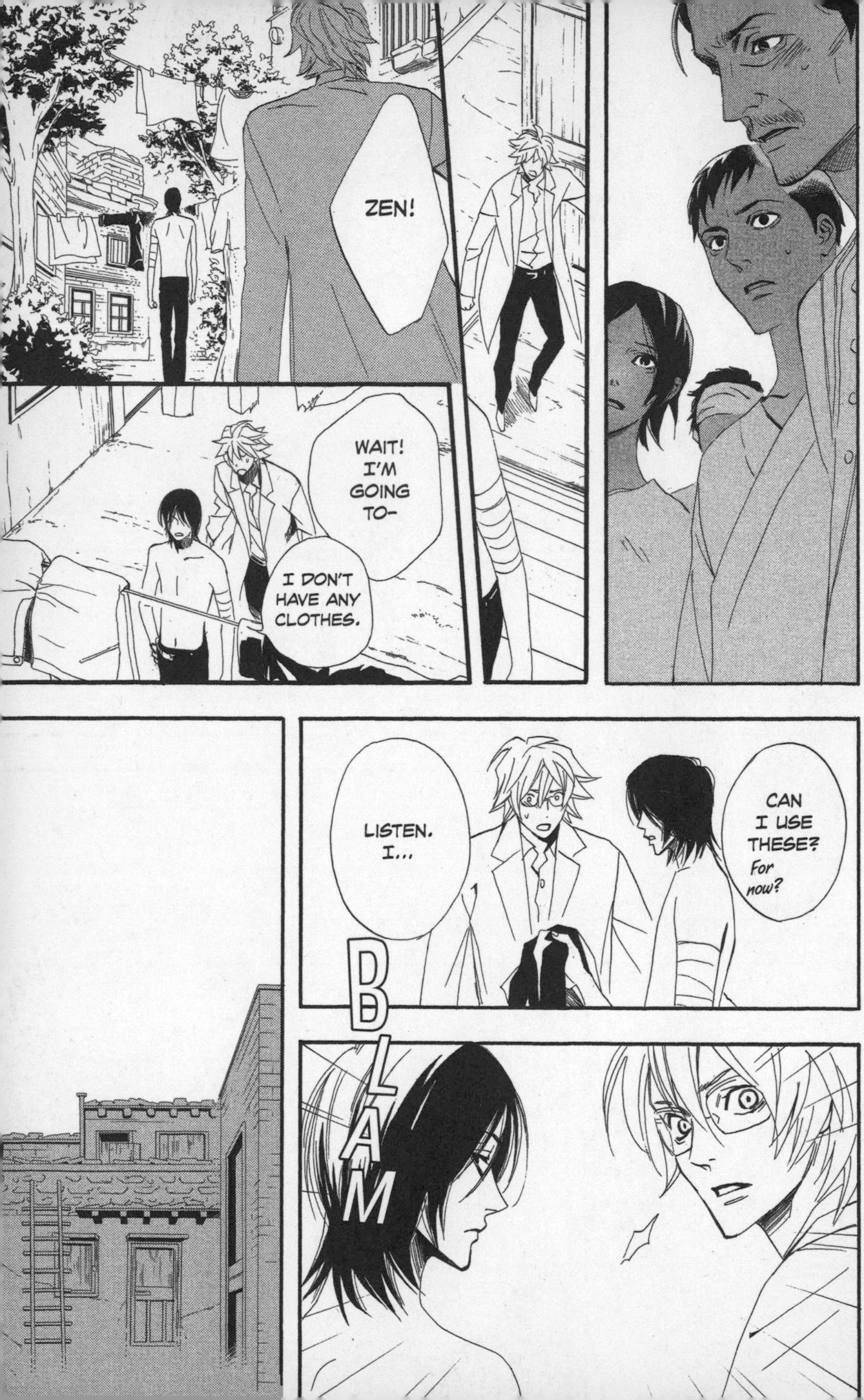
ZEN!
WAIT! I'M GOING TO-
I DON'T HAVE ANY CLOTHES.
CAN I USE THESE? For now?
LISTEN. I...
BLAM

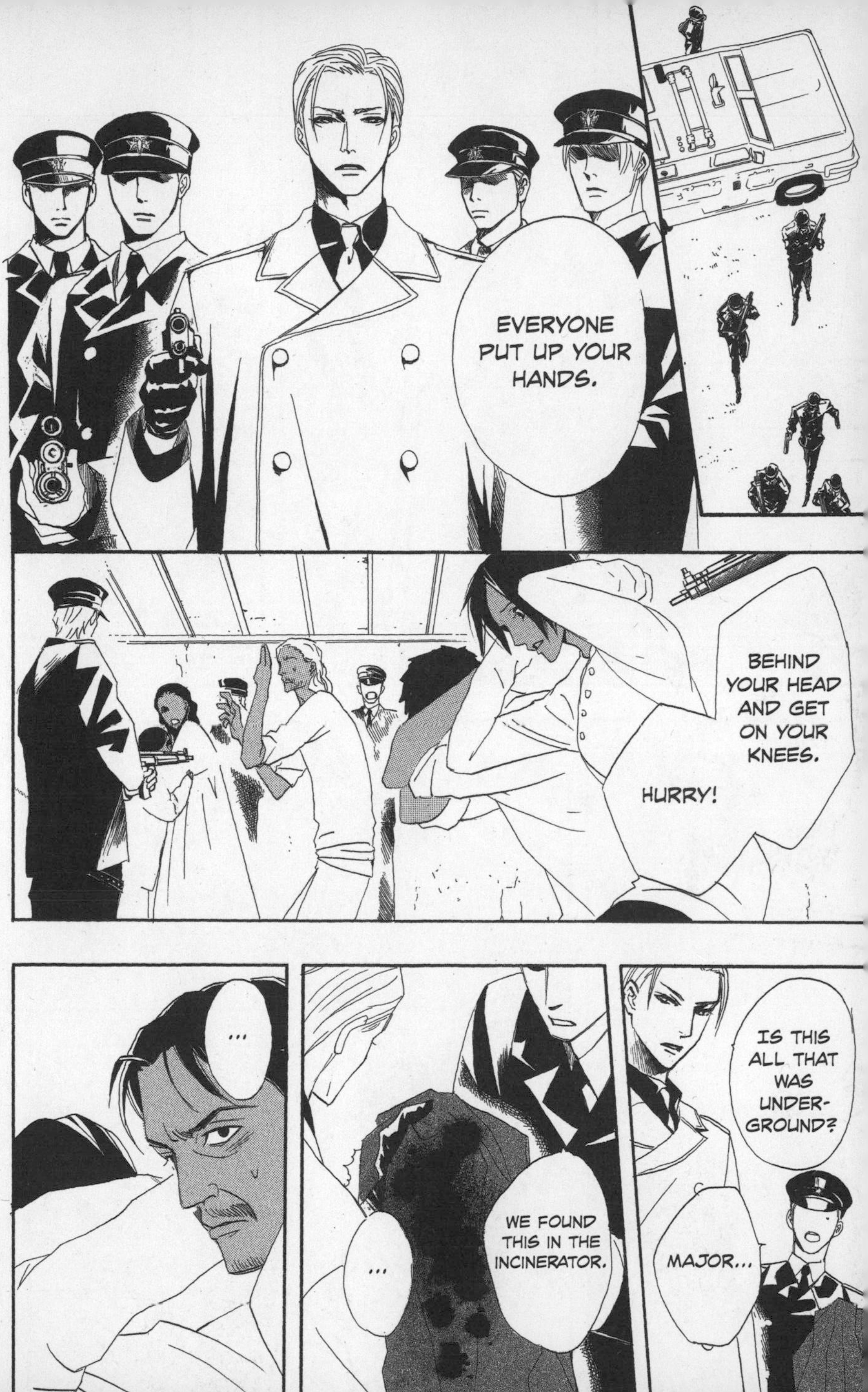
EVERYONE PUT UP YOUR HANDS.
BEHIND YOUR HEAD AND GET ON YOUR KNEES.
HURRY!
IS THIS ALL THAT WAS UNDER-GROUND?
MAJOR...
WE FOUND THIS IN THE INCINERATOR.
...
...

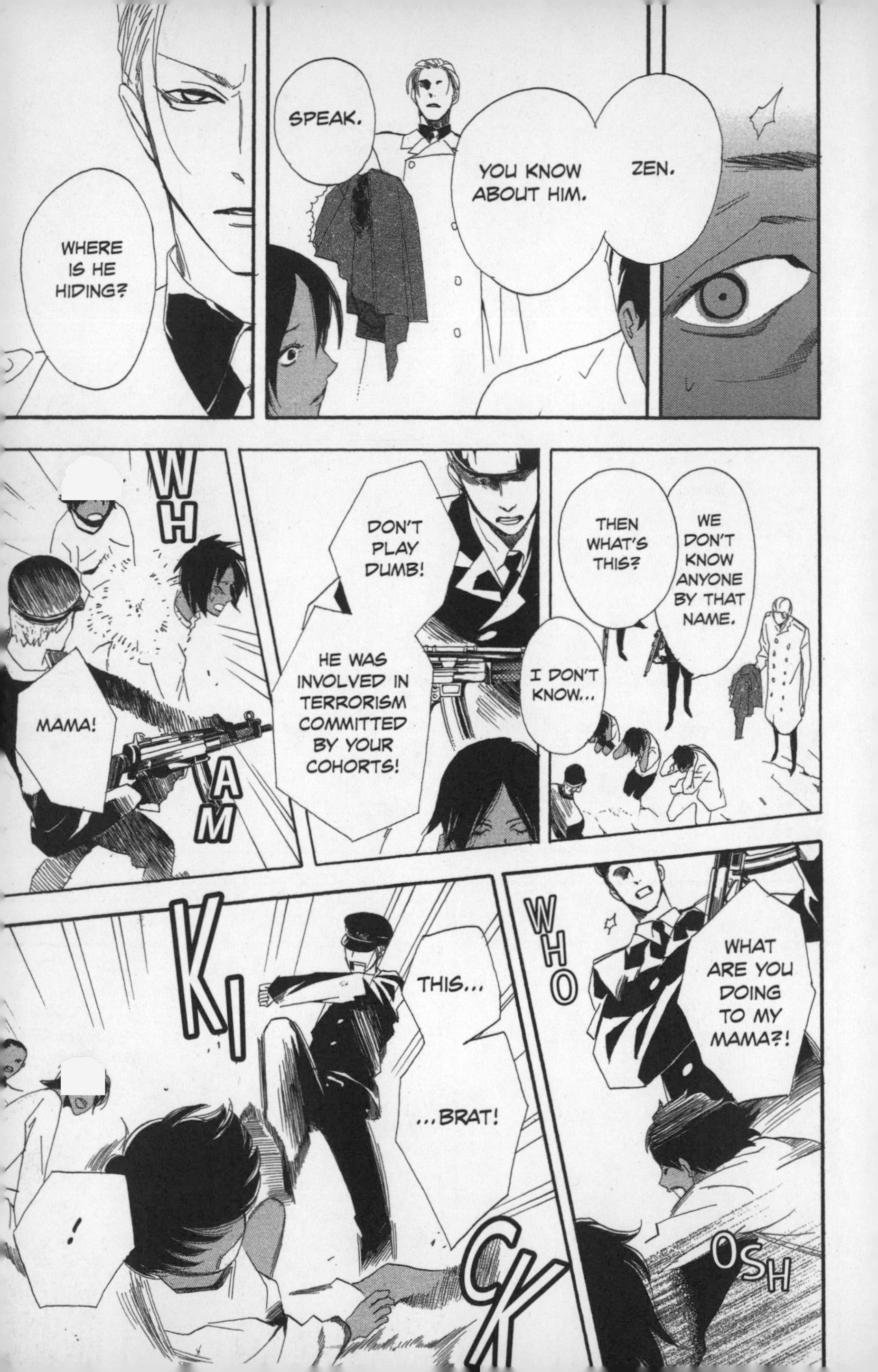
ZEN.
YOU KNOW ABOUT HIM.
SPEAK.
WHERE IS HE HIDING?
WE DON'T KNOW ANYONE BY THAT NAME.
THEN WHAT'S THIS?
I DON'T KNOW...
DON'T PLAY DUMB!
HE WAS INVOLVED IN TERRORISM COMMITTED BY YOUR COHORTS!
WH
AM
MAMA!
WHO
WHAT ARE YOU DOING TO MY MAMA?!
OSH
KI
THIS...
...BRAT!
CK
!

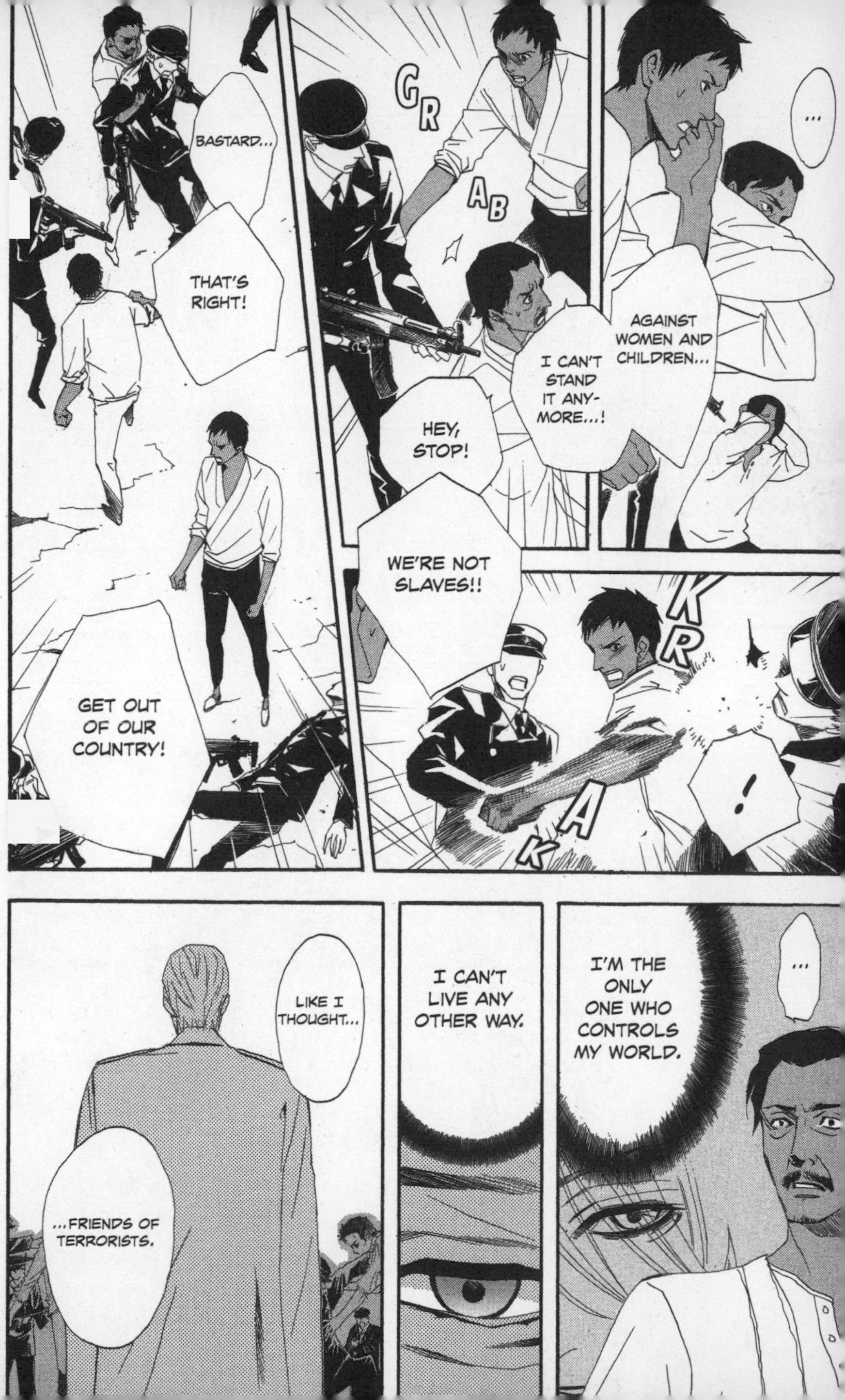
...
AGAINST WOMEN AND CHILDREN...
I CAN'T STAND IT ANYMORE...!
GRAB
HEY, STOP!
WE'RE NOT SLAVES!!
KRAK
!
BASTARD...
THAT'S RIGHT!
GET OUT OF OUR COUNTRY!
...
I'M THE ONLY ONE WHO CONTROLS MY WORLD.
I CAN'T LIVE ANY OTHER WAY.
LIKE I THOUGHT...
...FRIENDS OF TERRORISTS.

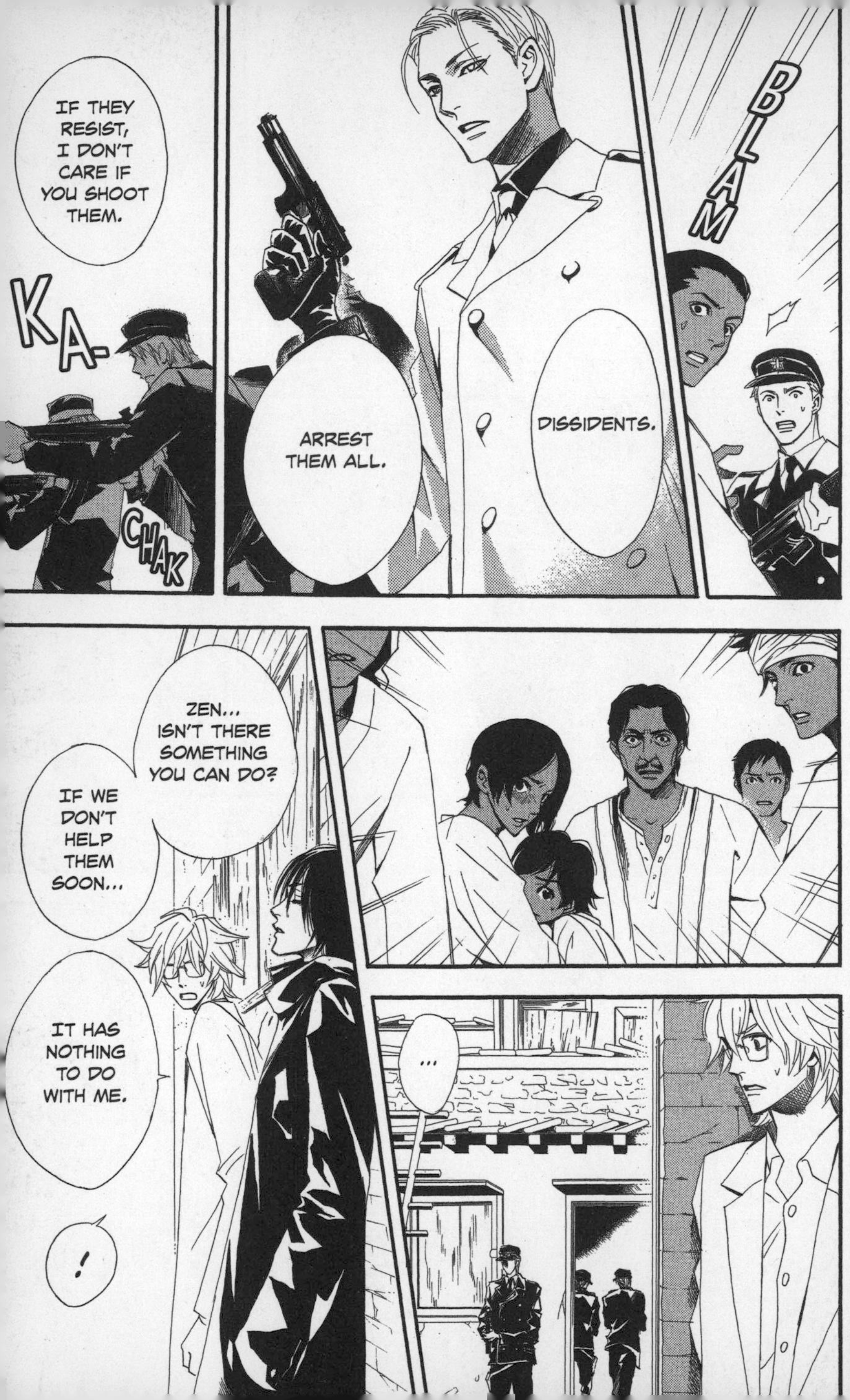
BLAM
DISSIDENTS.
ARREST THEM ALL.
IF THEY RESIST, I DON'T CARE IF YOU SHOOT THEM.
KA-
CHAK
...
ZEN... ISN'T THERE SOMETHING YOU CAN DO?
IF WE DON'T HELP THEM SOON...
IT HAS NOTHING TO DO WITH ME.
!

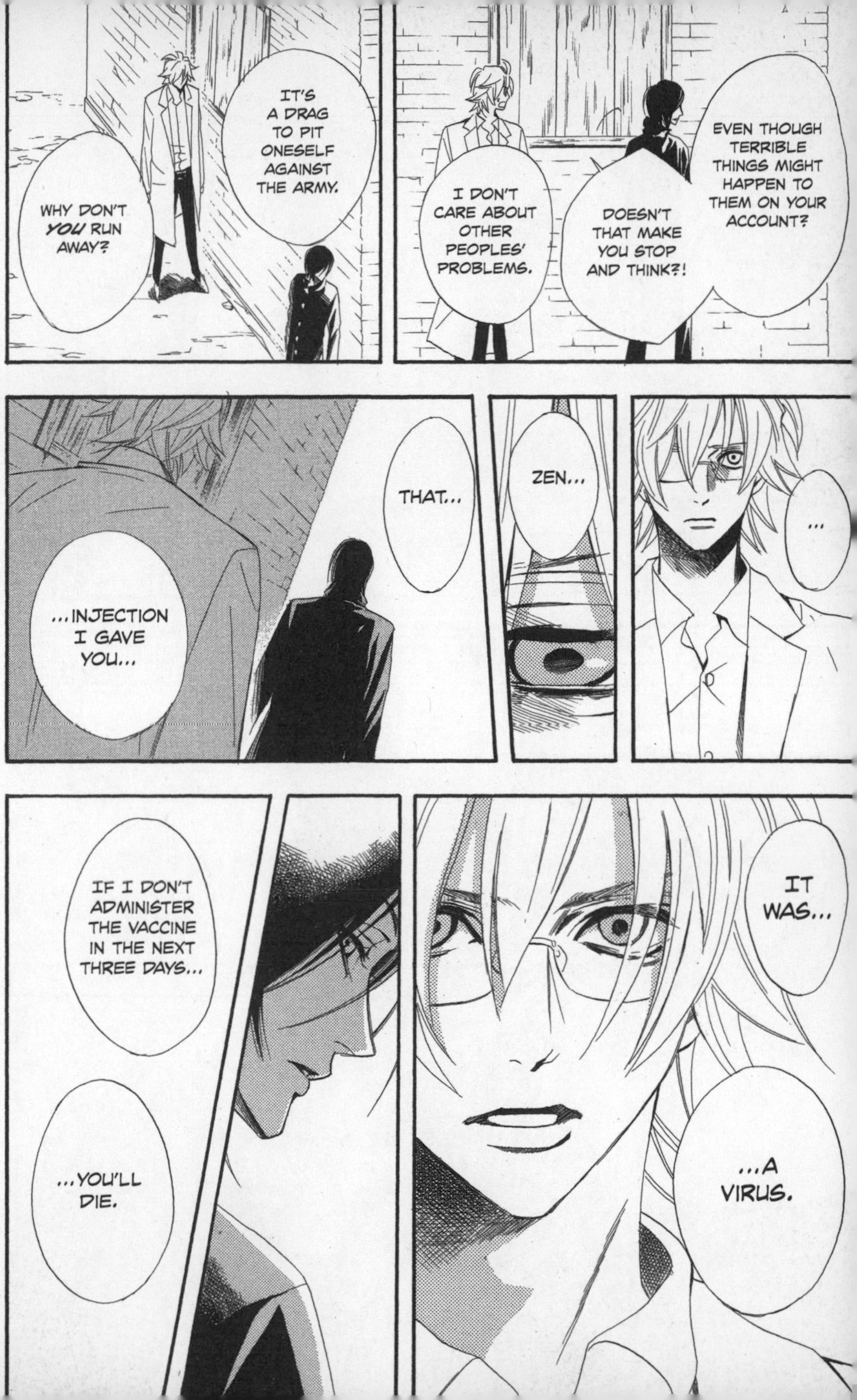
EVEN THOUGH TERRIBLE THINGS MIGHT HAPPEN TO THEM ON YOUR ACCOUNT?
DOESN'T THAT MAKE YOU STOP AND THINK?!
I DON'T CARE ABOUT OTHER PEOPLES' PROBLEMS.
IT'S A DRAG TO PIT ONESELF AGAINST THE ARMY.
WHY DON'T *YOU* RUN AWAY?
...
ZEN...
THAT...
...INJECTION I GAVE YOU...
IT WAS...
...A VIRUS.
IF I DON'T ADMINISTER THE VACCINE IN THE NEXT THREE DAYS...
...YOU'LL DIE.

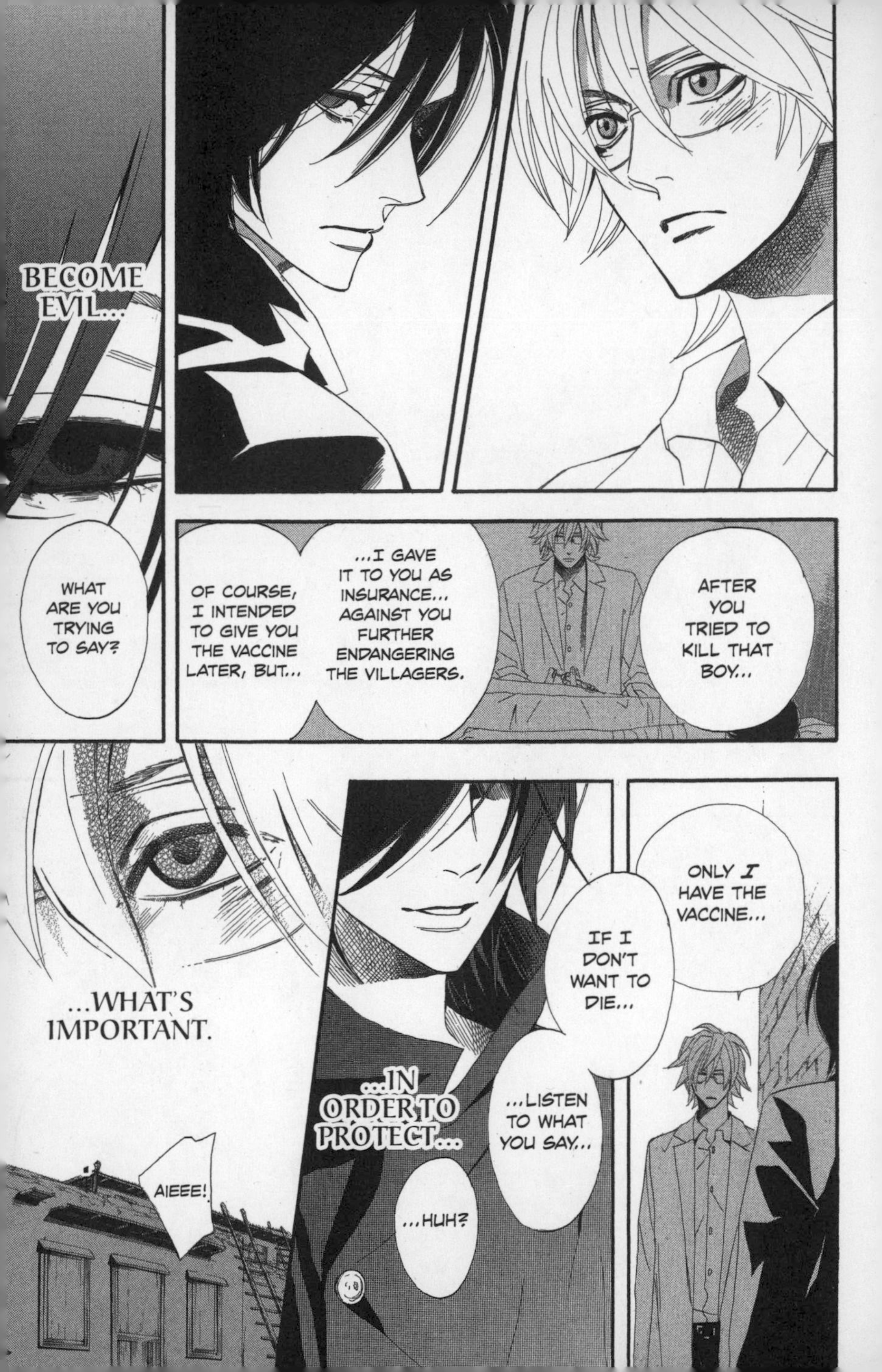
AFTER YOU TRIED TO KILL THAT BOY...
...I GAVE IT TO YOU AS INSURANCE... AGAINST YOU FURTHER ENDANGERING THE VILLAGERS.
OF COURSE, I INTENDED TO GIVE YOU THE VACCINE LATER, BUT...
BECOME EVIL...
WHAT ARE YOU TRYING TO SAY?
ONLY *I* HAVE THE VACCINE...
IF I DON'T WANT TO DIE...
...LISTEN TO WHAT YOU SAY...
...IN ORDER TO PROTECT...
...HUH?
...WHAT'S IMPORTANT.
AIEEE!

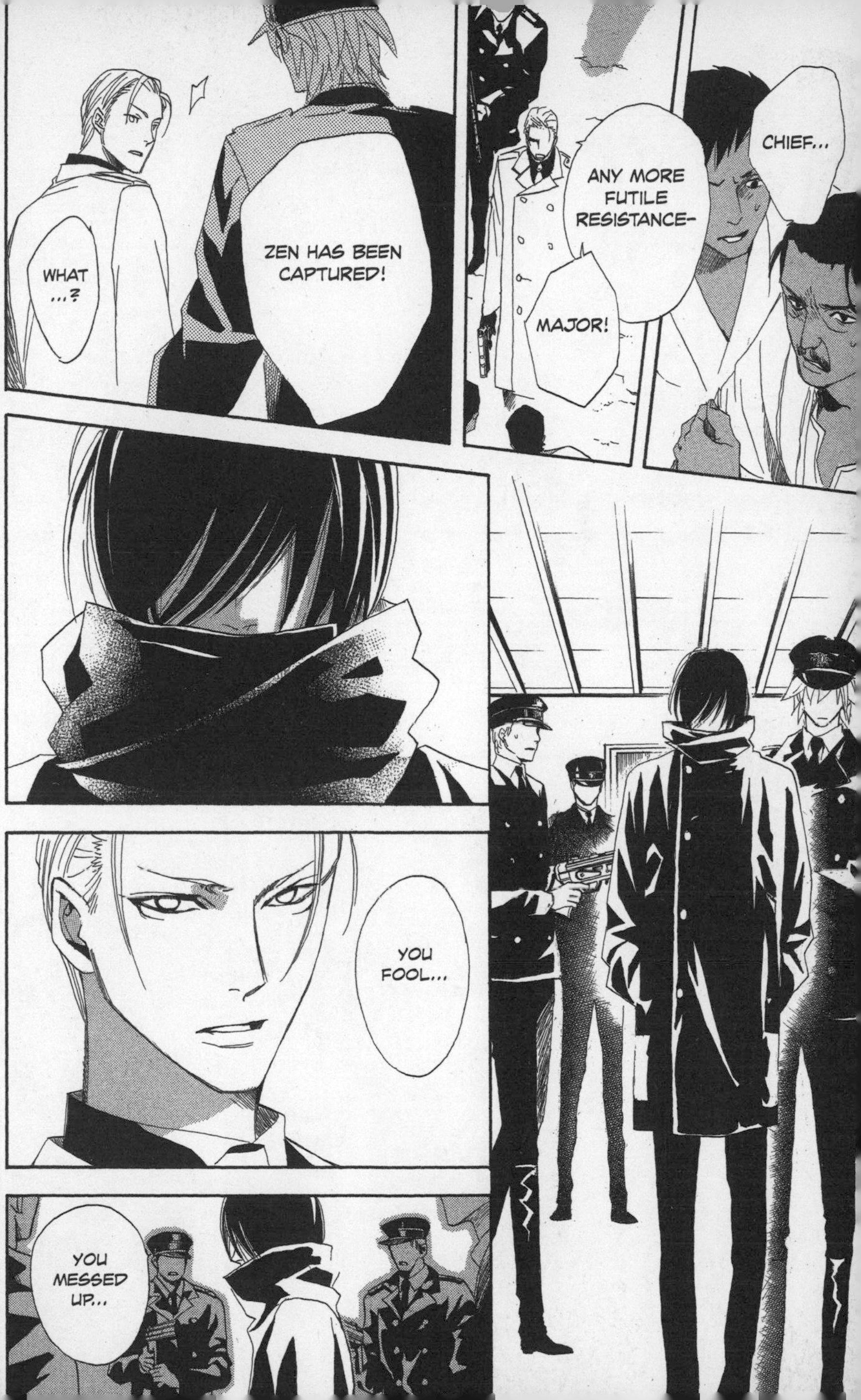
CHIEF...
ANY MORE FUTILE RESISTANCE-
MAJOR!
ZEN HAS BEEN CAPTURED!
WHAT ...?
YOU FOOL...
YOU MESSED UP...

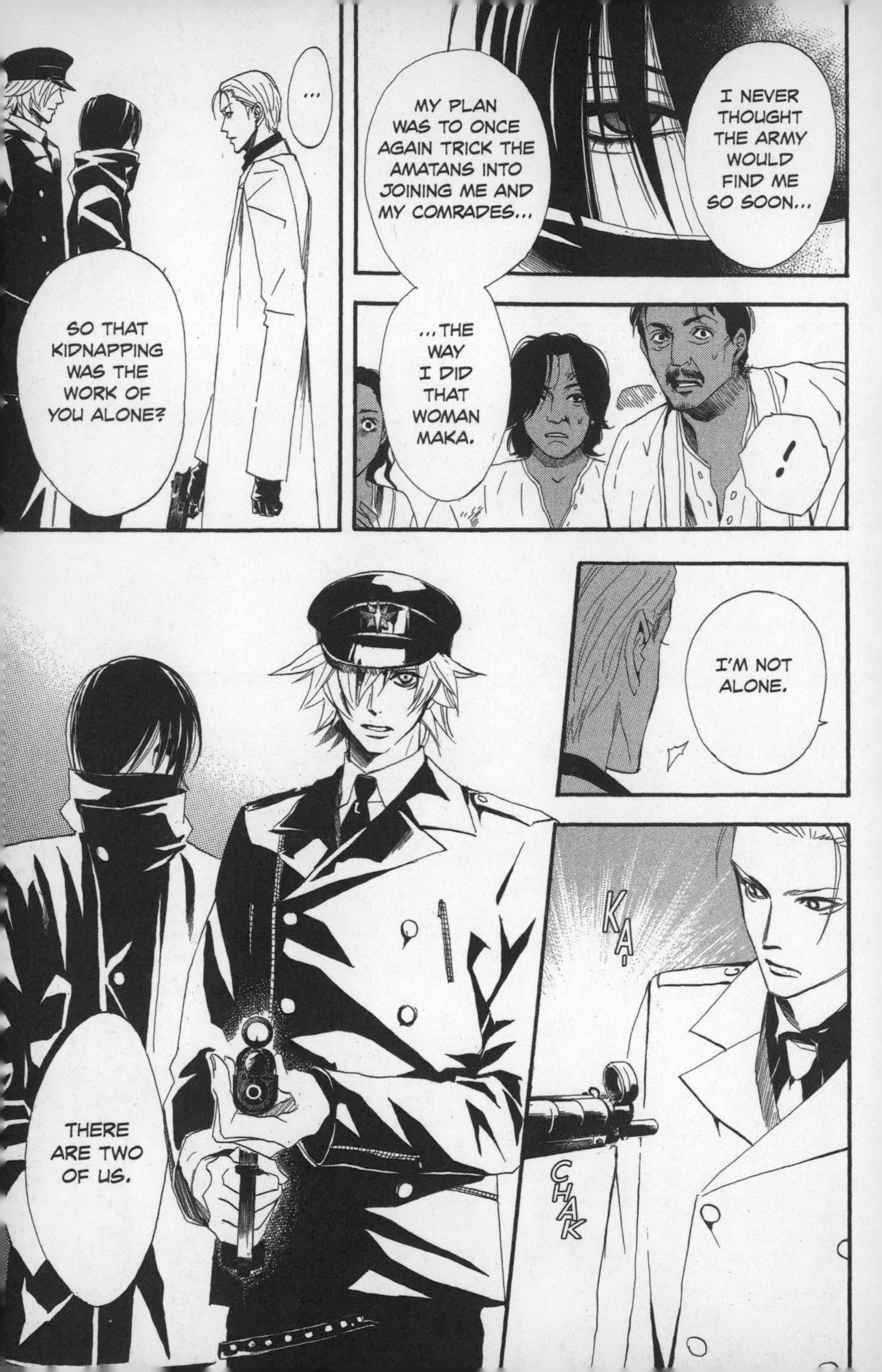
I NEVER THOUGHT THE ARMY WOULD FIND ME SO SOON...
MY PLAN WAS TO ONCE AGAIN TRICK THE AMATANS INTO JOINING ME AND MY COMRADES...
...THE WAY I DID THAT WOMAN MAKA.
!
...
SO THAT KIDNAPPING WAS THE WORK OF YOU ALONE?
I'M NOT ALONE.
KA
CHAK
THERE ARE TWO OF US.

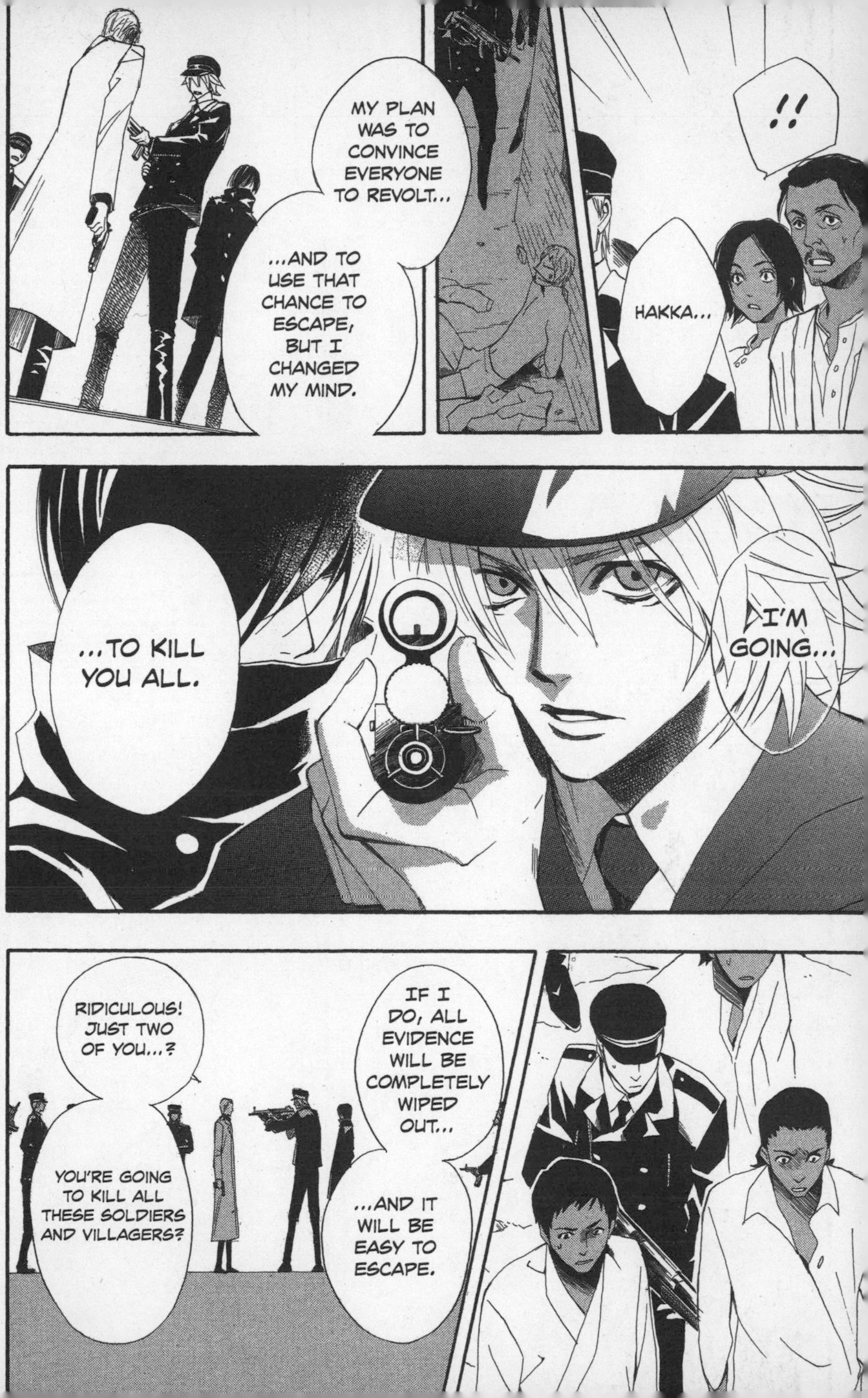
!!
HAKKA...
MY PLAN WAS TO CONVINCE EVERYONE TO REVOLT...
...AND TO USE THAT CHANCE TO ESCAPE, BUT I CHANGED MY MIND.
I'M GOING...
...TO KILL YOU ALL.
RIDICULOUS! JUST TWO OF YOU...?
YOU'RE GOING TO KILL ALL THESE SOLDIERS AND VILLAGERS?
IF I DO, ALL EVIDENCE WILL BE COMPLETELY WIPED OUT...
...AND IT WILL BE EASY TO ESCAPE.

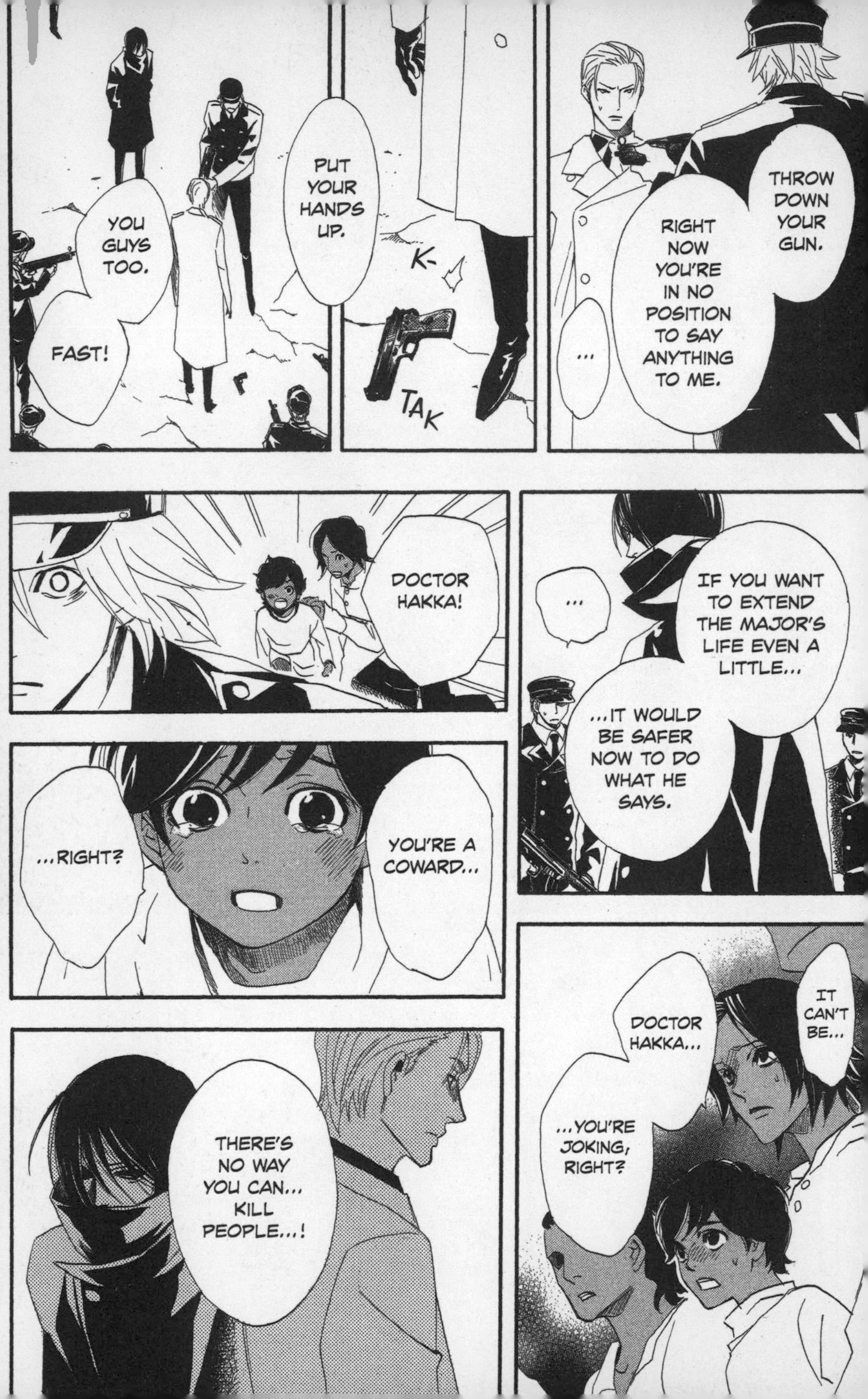
THROW DOWN YOUR GUN.
RIGHT NOW YOU'RE IN NO POSITION TO SAY ANYTHING TO ME.
...
PUT YOUR HANDS UP.
K-
TAK
YOU GUYS TOO.
FAST!
IF YOU WANT TO EXTEND THE MAJOR'S LIFE EVEN A LITTLE...
...IT WOULD BE SAFER NOW TO DO WHAT HE SAYS.
...
DOCTOR HAKKA!
YOU'RE A COWARD...
...RIGHT?
IT CAN'T BE...
DOCTOR HAKKA...
...YOU'RE JOKING, RIGHT?
THERE'S NO WAY YOU CAN... KILL PEOPLE...!

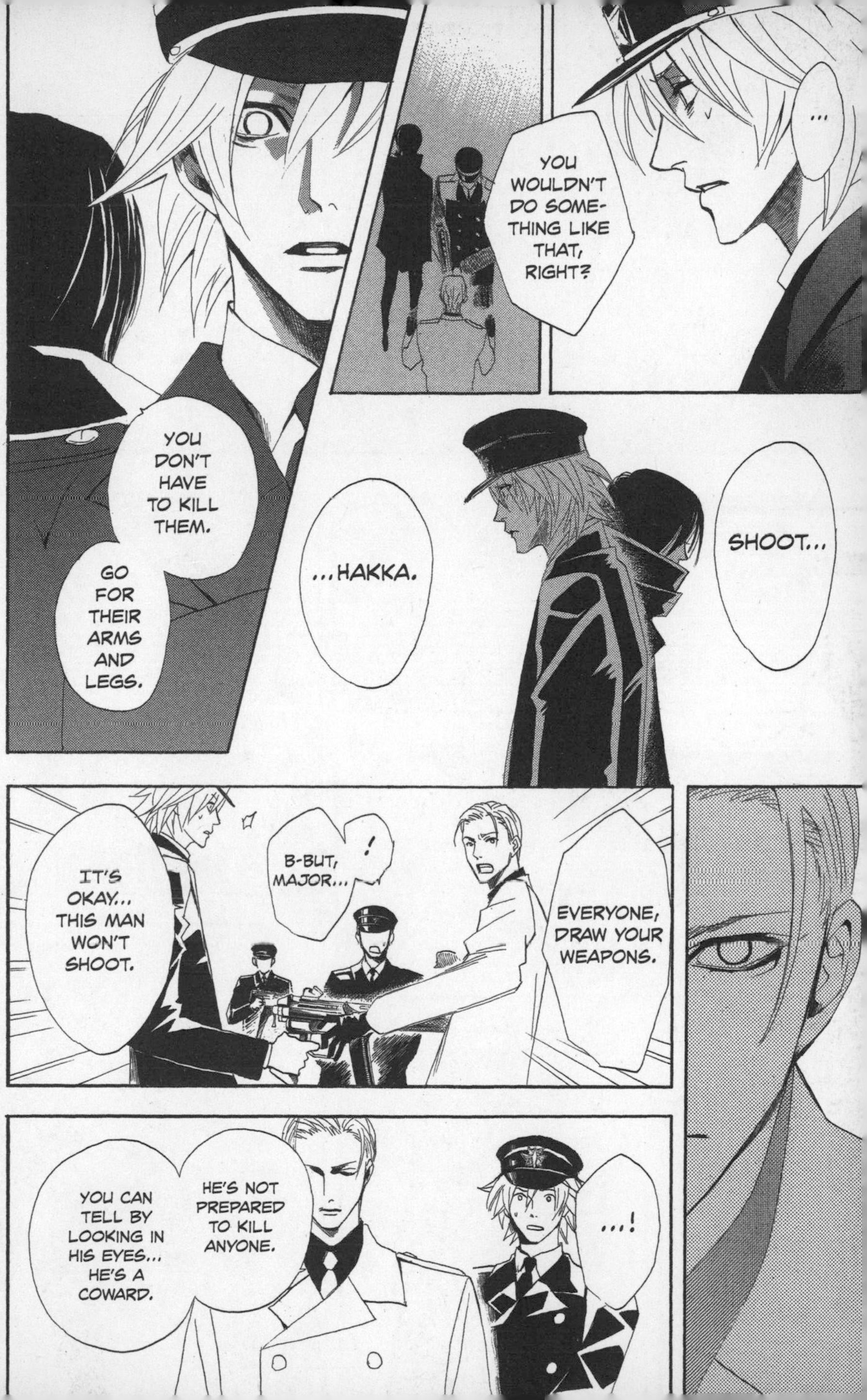
...
YOU WOULDN'T DO SOME-THING LIKE THAT, RIGHT?
SHOOT...
...HAKKA.
YOU DON'T HAVE TO KILL THEM.
GO FOR THEIR ARMS AND LEGS.
EVERYONE, DRAW YOUR WEAPONS.
!
B-BUT, MAJOR...
IT'S OKAY... THIS MAN WON'T SHOOT.
...!
HE'S NOT PREPARED TO KILL ANYONE.
YOU CAN TELL BY LOOKING IN HIS EYES... HE'S A COWARD.

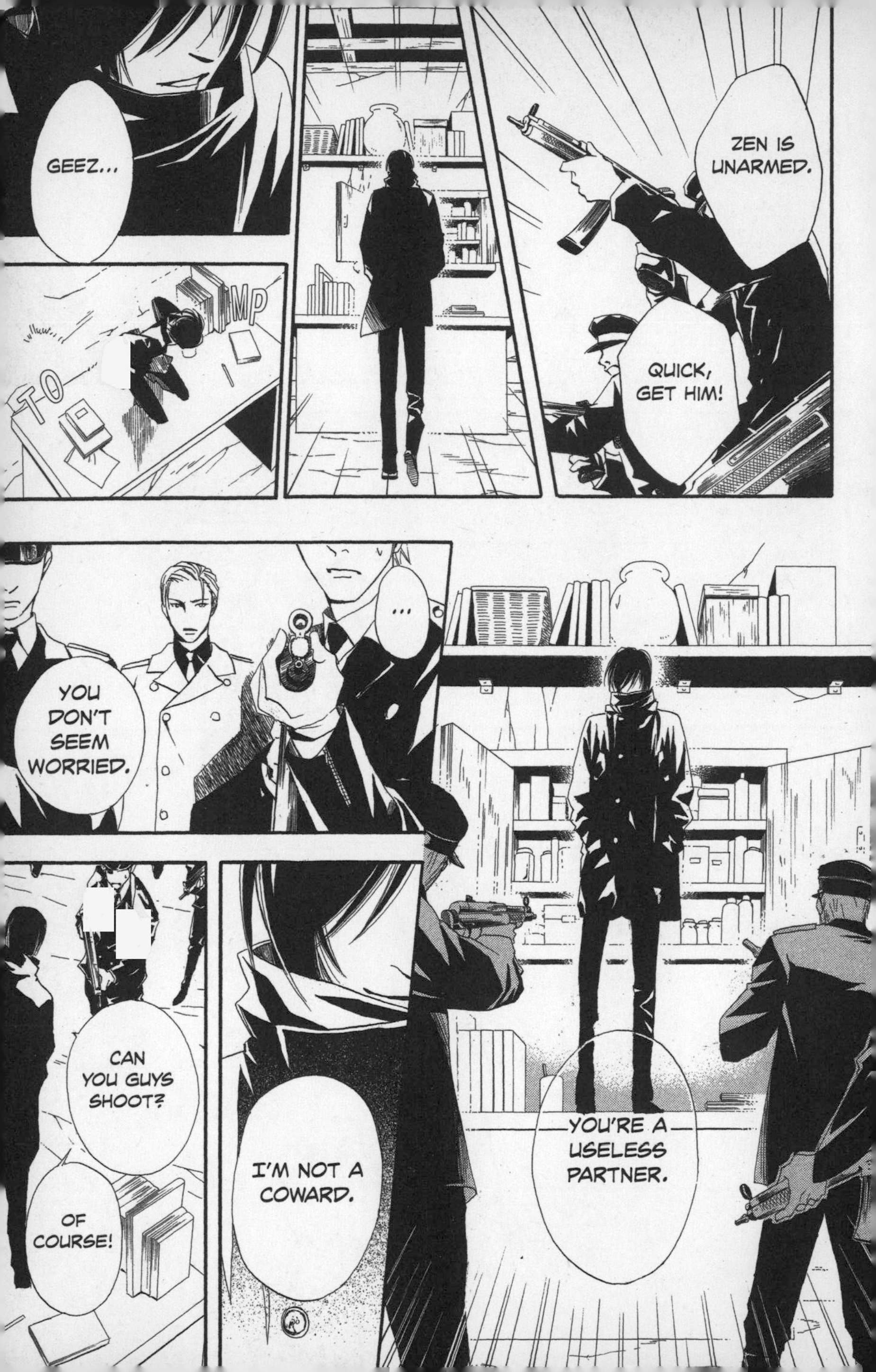
ZEN IS UNARMED.
QUICK, GET HIM!
GEEZ...
YOU'RE A USELESS PARTNER.
...
YOU DON'T SEEM WORRIED.
I'M NOT A COWARD.
CAN YOU GUYS SHOOT?
OF COURSE!

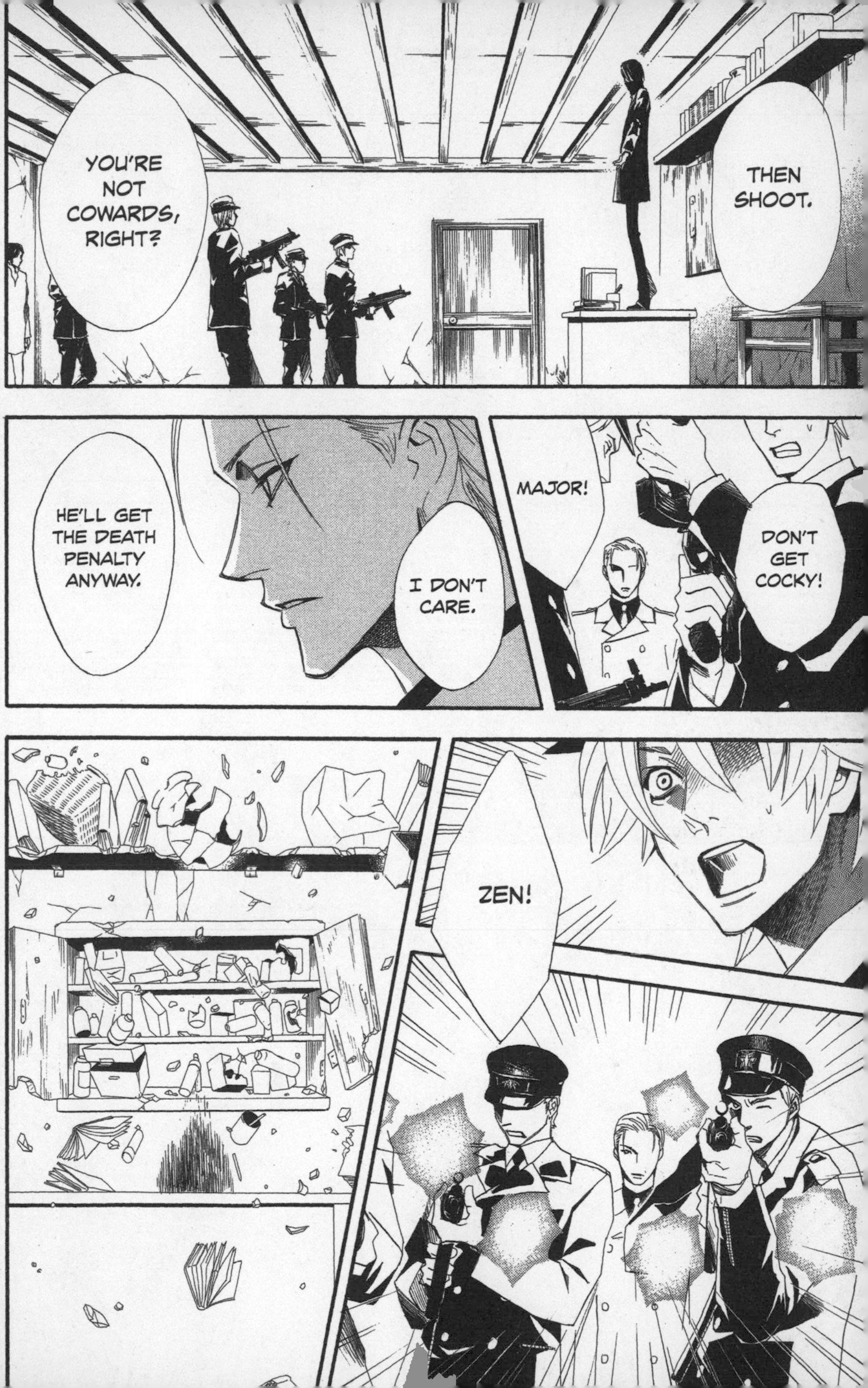
THEN SHOOT.
YOU'RE NOT COWARDS, RIGHT?
MAJOR!
DON'T GET COCKY!
I DON'T CARE.
HE'LL GET THE DEATH PENALTY ANYWAY.
ZEN!

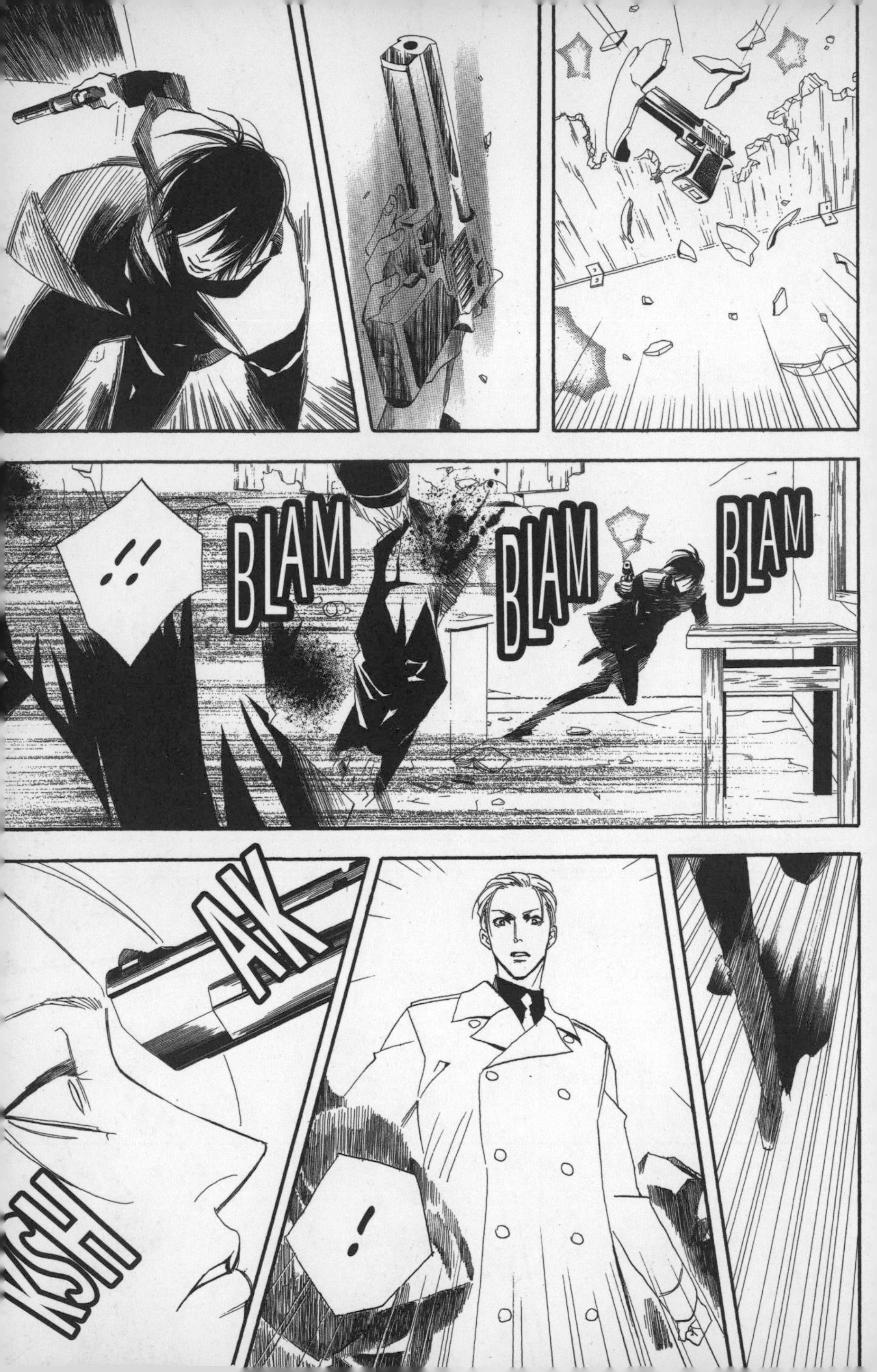
BLAM
BLAM
BLAM
...!!
!
KSH
AK

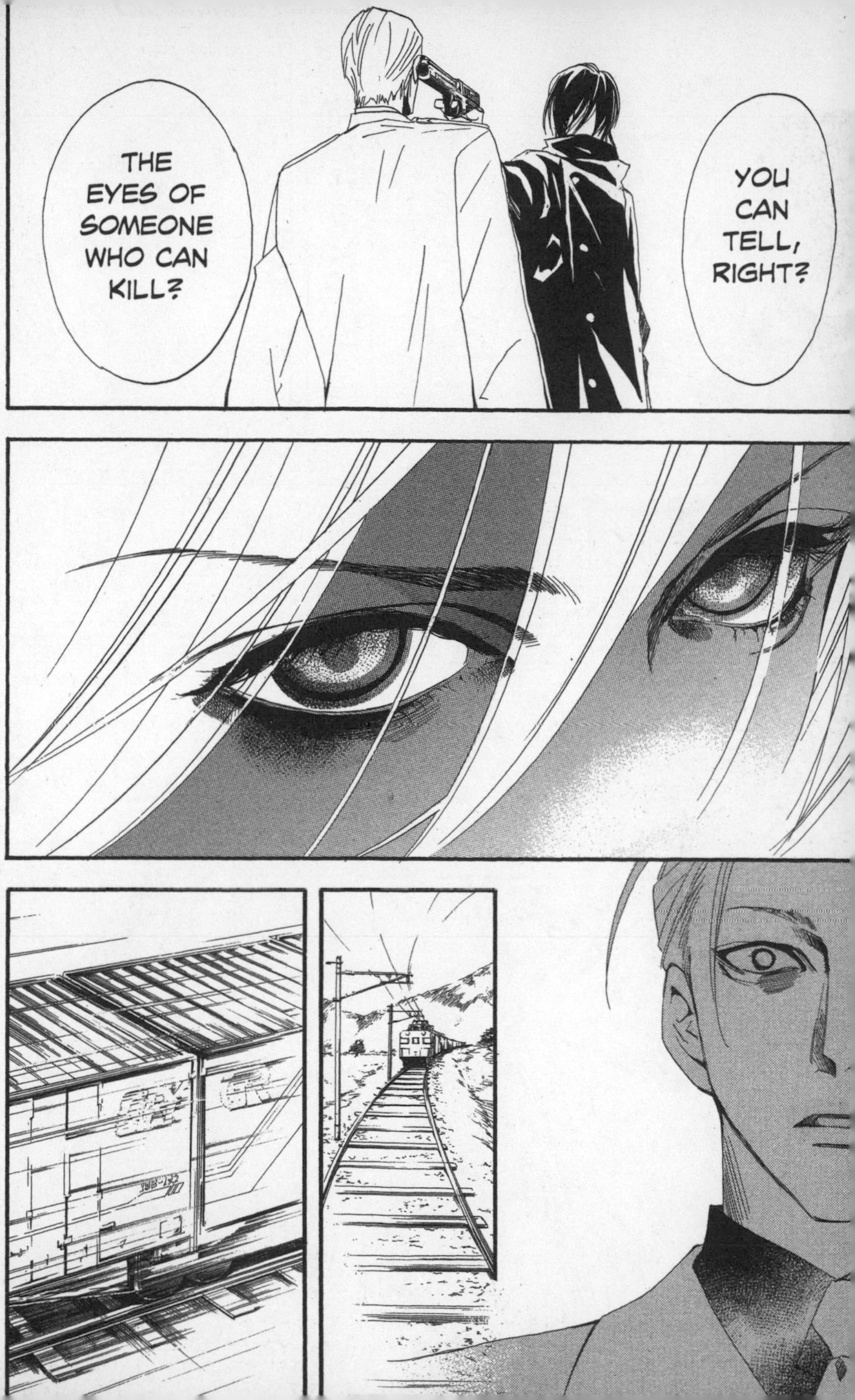
YOU CAN TELL, RIGHT?
THE EYES OF SOMEONE WHO CAN KILL?

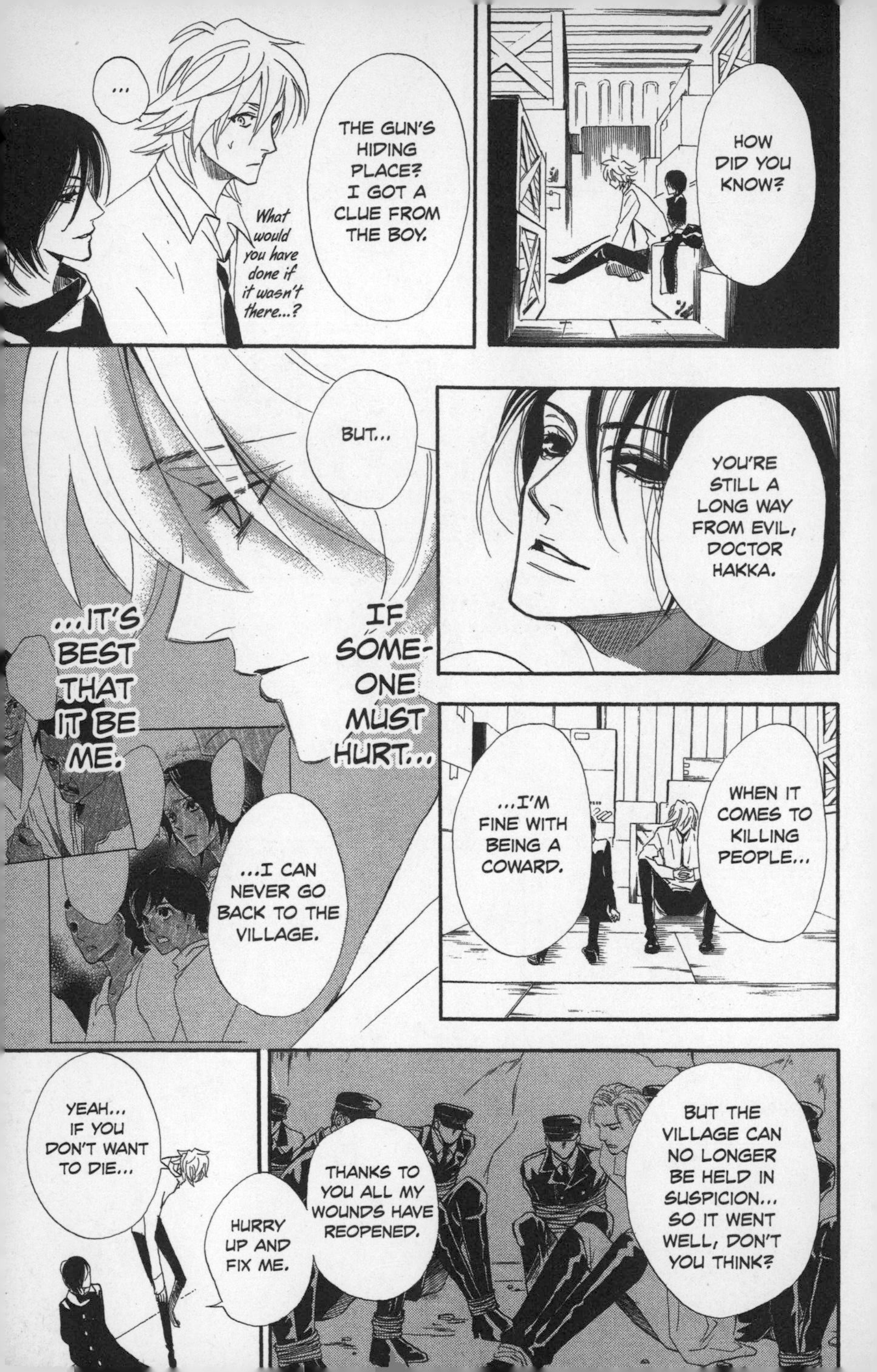
HOW DID YOU KNOW?
THE GUN'S HIDING PLACE? I GOT A CLUE FROM THE BOY.
What would you have done if it wasn't there...?
...
YOU'RE STILL A LONG WAY FROM EVIL, DOCTOR HAKKA.
WHEN IT COMES TO KILLING PEOPLE...
...I'M FINE WITH BEING A COWARD.
BUT...
IF SOME-ONE MUST HURT...
...IT'S BEST THAT IT BE ME.
...I CAN NEVER GO BACK TO THE VILLAGE.
BUT THE VILLAGE CAN NO LONGER BE HELD IN SUSPICION... SO IT WENT WELL, DON'T YOU THINK?
THANKS TO YOU ALL MY WOUNDS HAVE REOPENED.
HURRY UP AND FIX ME.
YEAH... IF YOU DON'T WANT TO DIE...

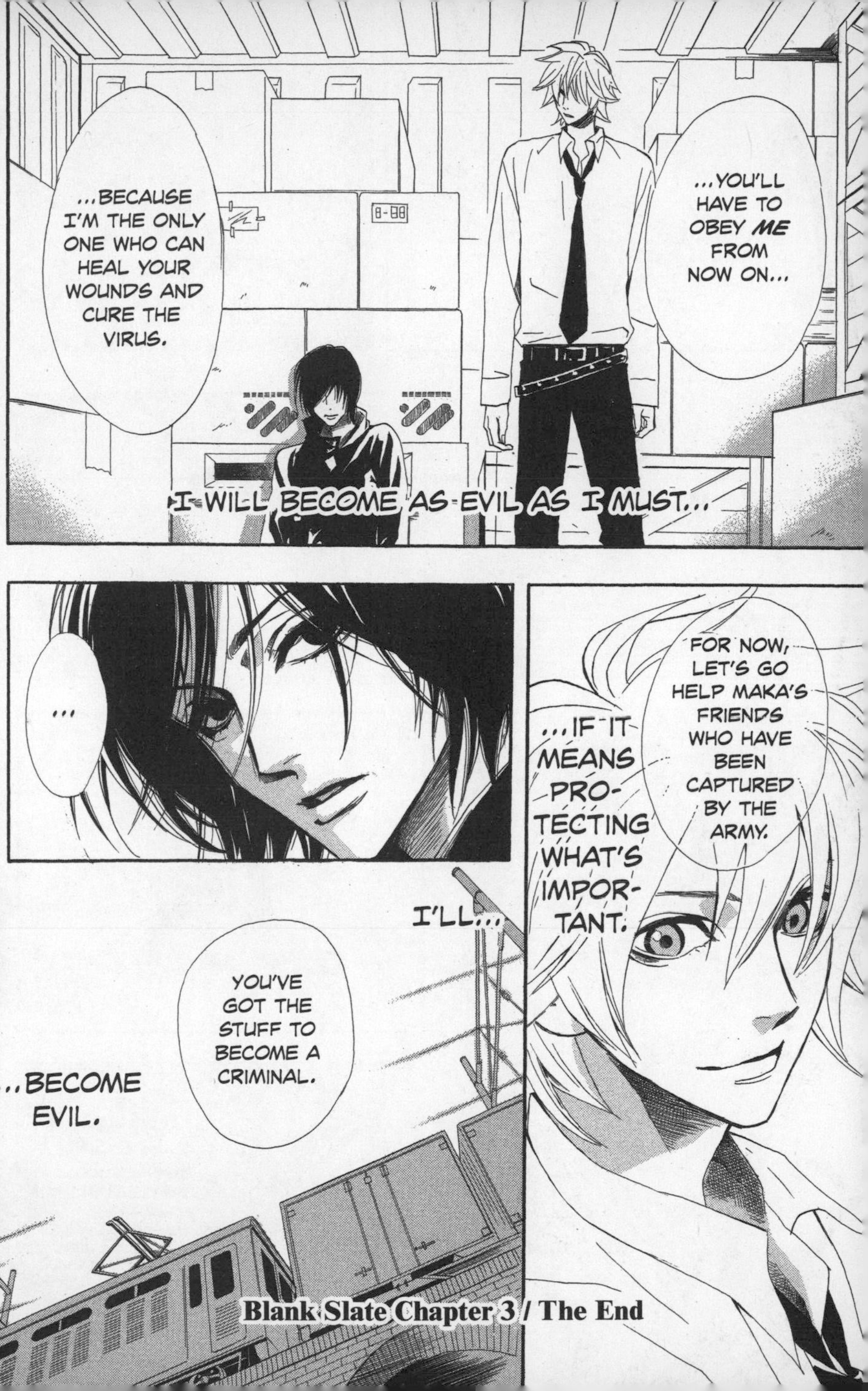
...YOU'LL HAVE TO OBEY *ME* FROM NOW ON...
...BECAUSE I'M THE ONLY ONE WHO CAN HEAL YOUR WOUNDS AND CURE THE VIRUS.
I WILL BECOME AS EVIL AS I MUST...
FOR NOW, LET'S GO HELP MAKA'S FRIENDS WHO HAVE BEEN CAPTURED BY THE ARMY.
...IF IT MEANS PROTECTING WHAT'S IMPORTANT.
...
I'LL...
YOU'VE GOT THE STUFF TO BECOME A CRIMINAL.
...BECOME EVIL.
Blank Slate Chapter 3 / The End

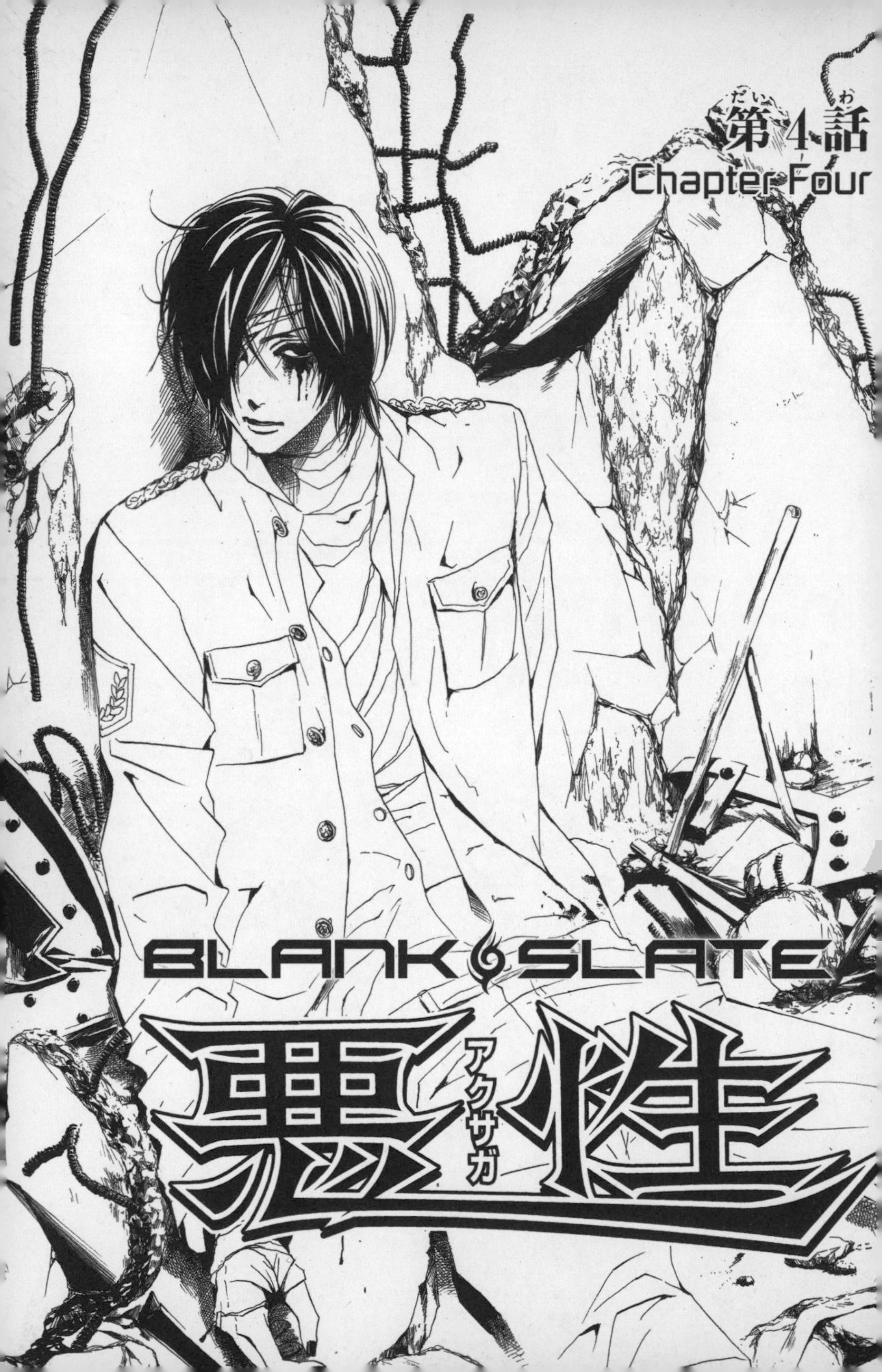
第4話
Chapter Four
BLANK SLATE
悪性
アクサガ

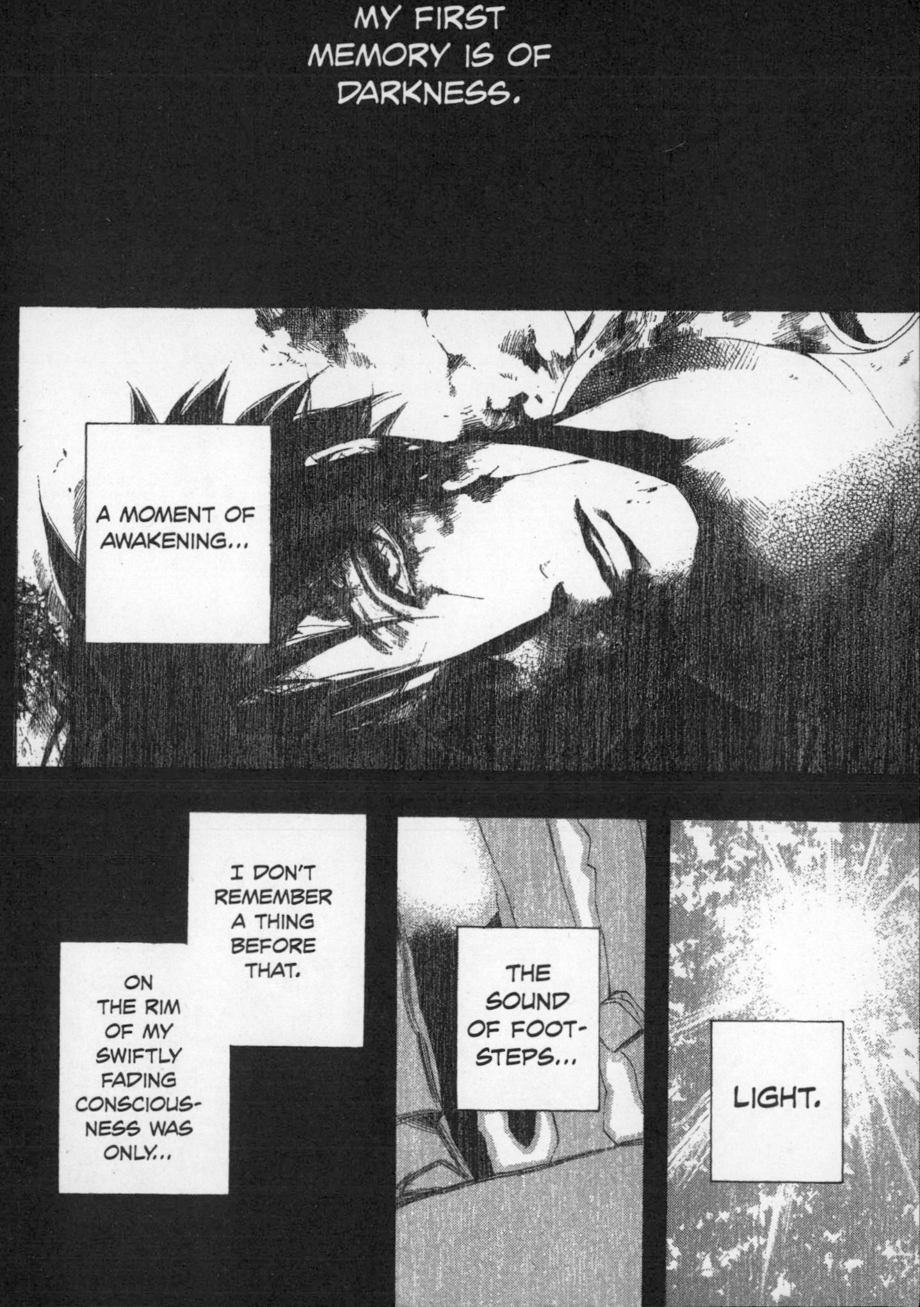
MY FIRST MEMORY IS OF DARKNESS.
A MOMENT OF AWAKENING...
I DON'T REMEMBER A THING BEFORE THAT.
ON THE RIM OF MY SWIFTLY FADING CONSCIOUSNESS WAS ONLY...
THE SOUND OF FOOT-STEPS...
LIGHT.

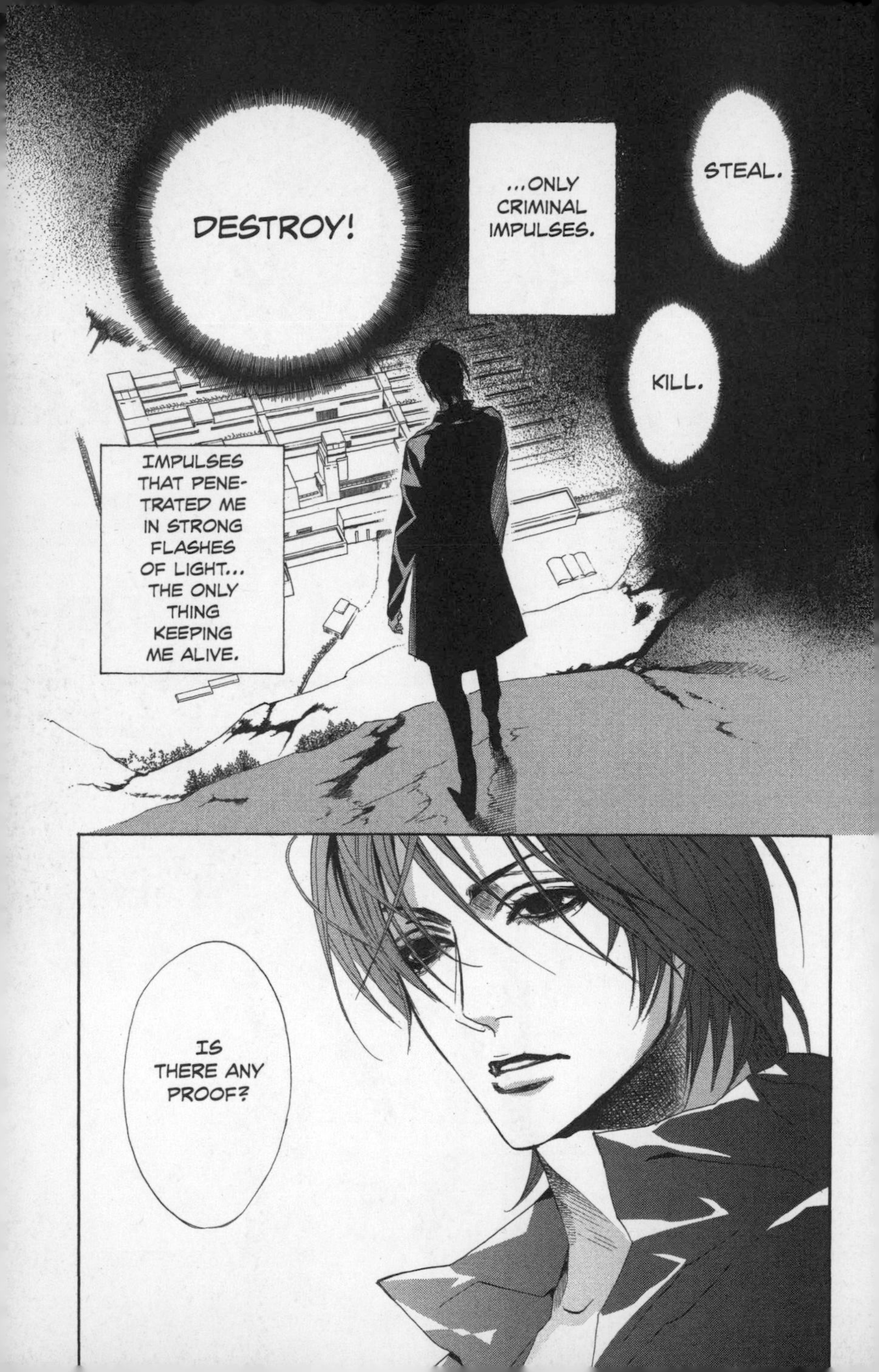
STEAL.
KILL.
...ONLY CRIMINAL IMPULSES.
DESTROY!
IMPULSES THAT PENE-TRATED ME IN STRONG FLASHES OF LIGHT... THE ONLY THING KEEPING ME ALIVE.
IS THERE ANY PROOF?

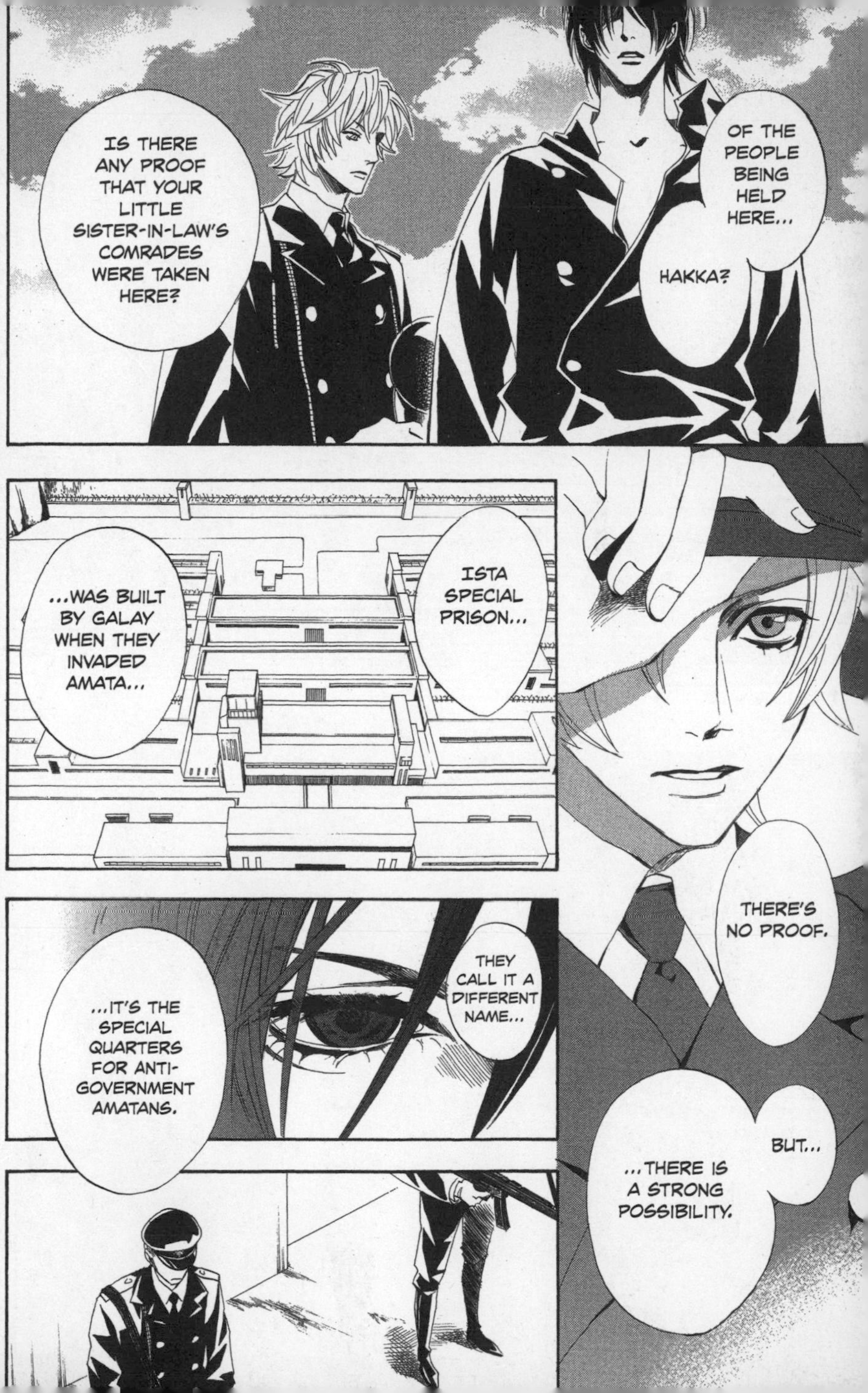
OF THE PEOPLE BEING HELD HERE...
HAKKA?
IS THERE ANY PROOF THAT YOUR LITTLE SISTER-IN-LAW'S COMRADES WERE TAKEN HERE?
THERE'S NO PROOF.
BUT...
...THERE IS A STRONG POSSIBILITY.
ISTA SPECIAL PRISON...
...WAS BUILT BY GALAY WHEN THEY INVADED AMATA...
THEY CALL IT A DIFFERENT NAME...
...IT'S THE SPECIAL QUARTERS FOR ANTI-GOVERNMENT AMATANS.

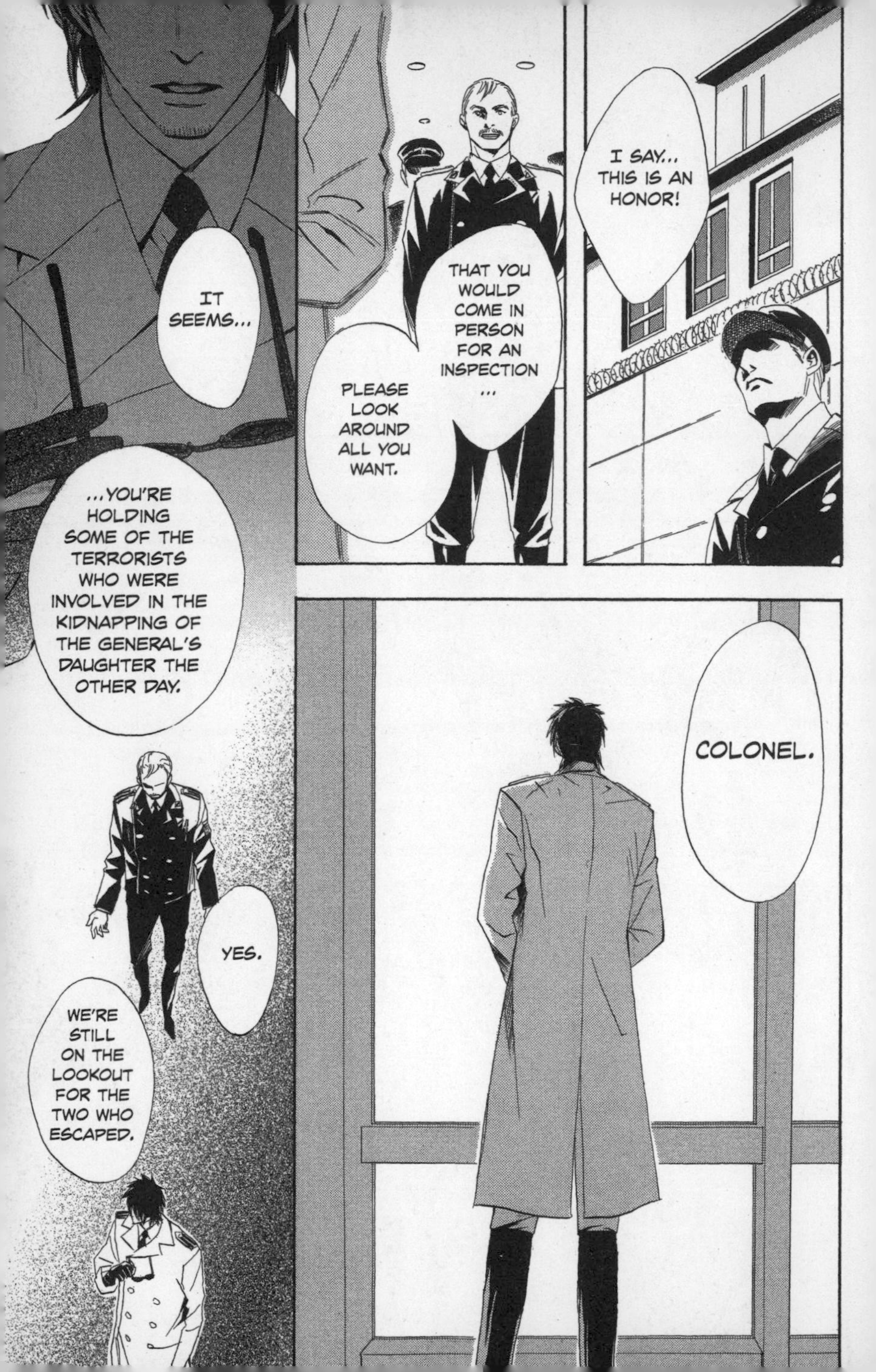
I SAY... THIS IS AN HONOR!
THAT YOU WOULD COME IN PERSON FOR AN INSPECTION ...
PLEASE LOOK AROUND ALL YOU WANT.
COLONEL.
IT SEEMS...
...YOU'RE HOLDING SOME OF THE TERRORISTS WHO WERE INVOLVED IN THE KIDNAPPING OF THE GENERAL'S DAUGHTER THE OTHER DAY.
YES.
WE'RE STILL ON THE LOOKOUT FOR THE TWO WHO ESCAPED.

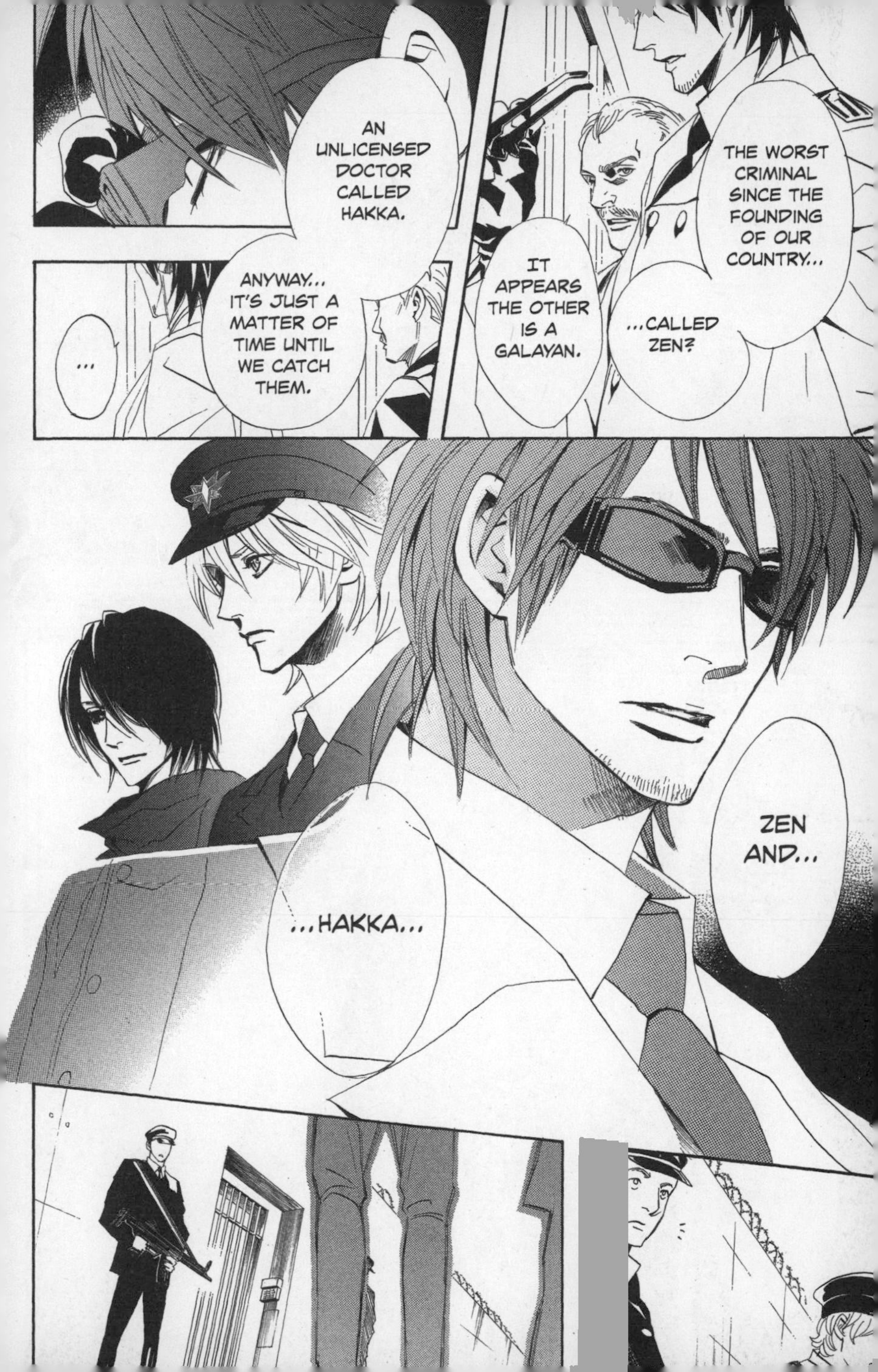
THE WORST CRIMINAL SINCE THE FOUNDING OF OUR COUNTRY...
...CALLED ZEN?
IT APPEARS THE OTHER IS A GALAYAN.
AN UNLICENSED DOCTOR CALLED HAKKA.
ANYWAY... IT'S JUST A MATTER OF TIME UNTIL WE CATCH THEM.
...
ZEN AND...
...HAKKA...

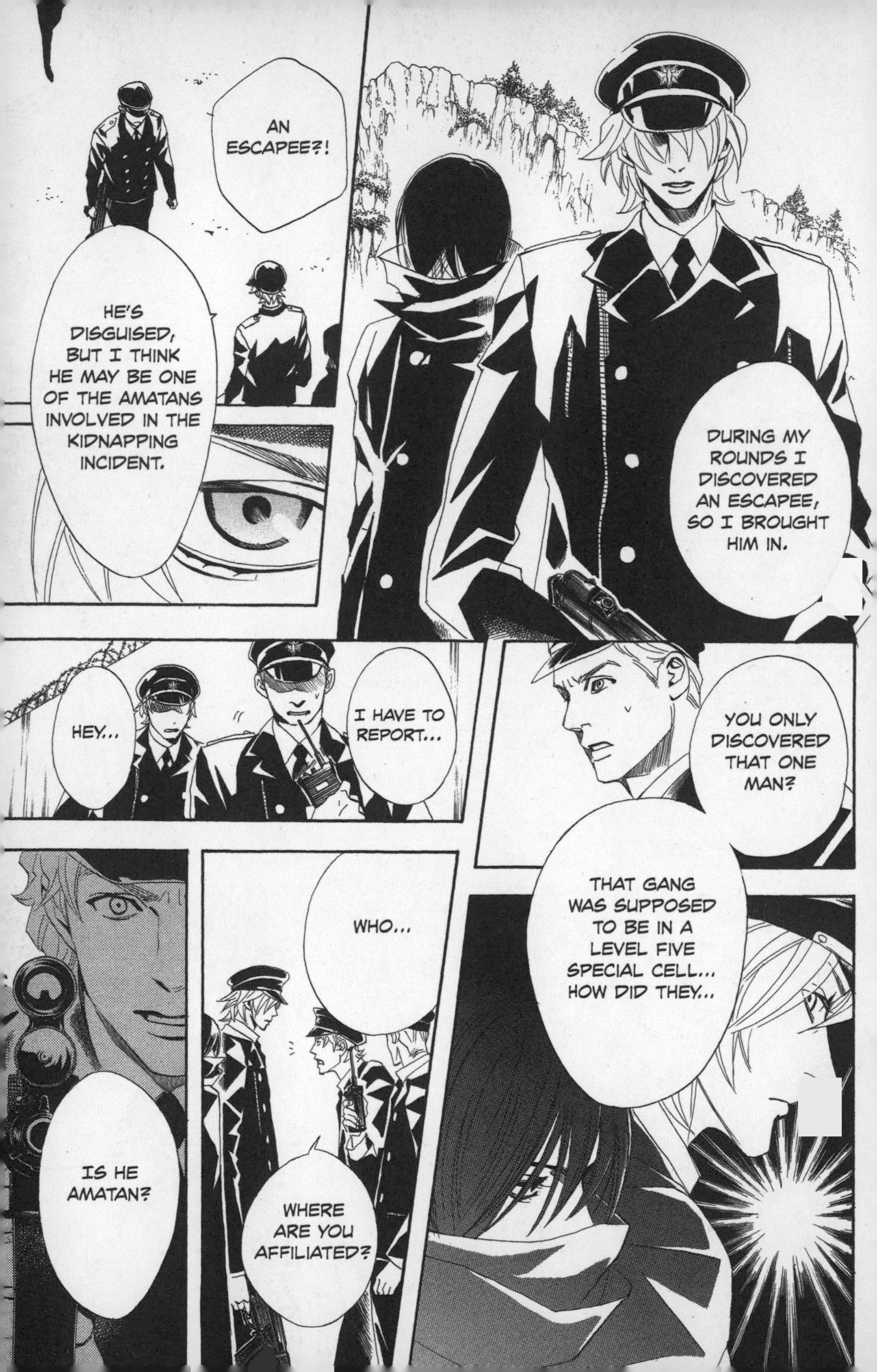
DURING MY ROUNDS I DISCOVERED AN ESCAPEE, SO I BROUGHT HIM IN.
AN ESCAPEE?!
HE'S DISGUISED, BUT I THINK HE MAY BE ONE OF THE AMATANS INVOLVED IN THE KIDNAPPING INCIDENT.
YOU ONLY DISCOVERED THAT ONE MAN?
I HAVE TO REPORT...
HEY...
THAT GANG WAS SUPPOSED TO BE IN A LEVEL FIVE SPECIAL CELL... HOW DID THEY...
WHO...
WHERE ARE YOU AFFILIATED?
IS HE AMATAN?

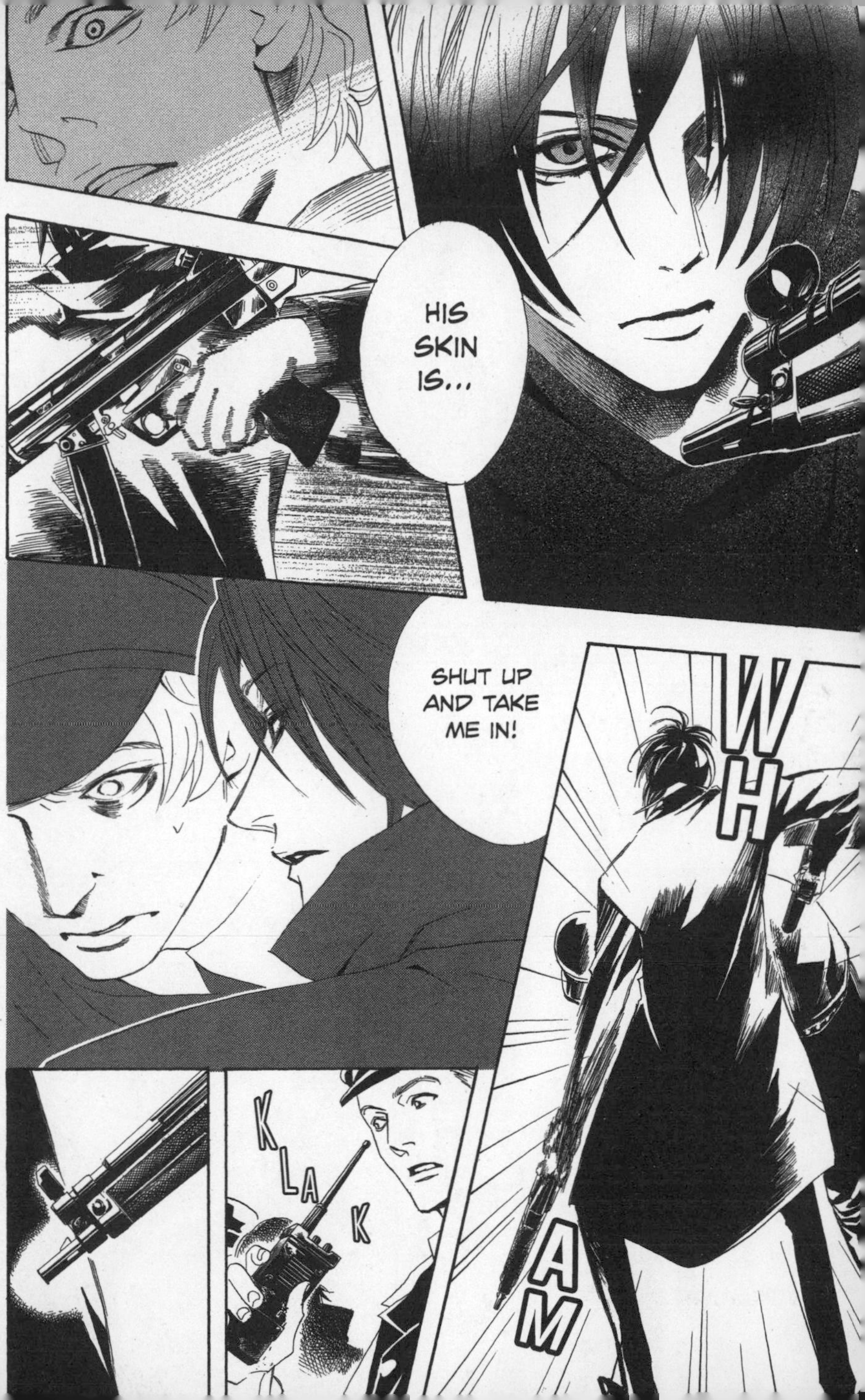
HIS SKIN IS...
WHAM
SHUT UP AND TAKE ME IN!
KLAK

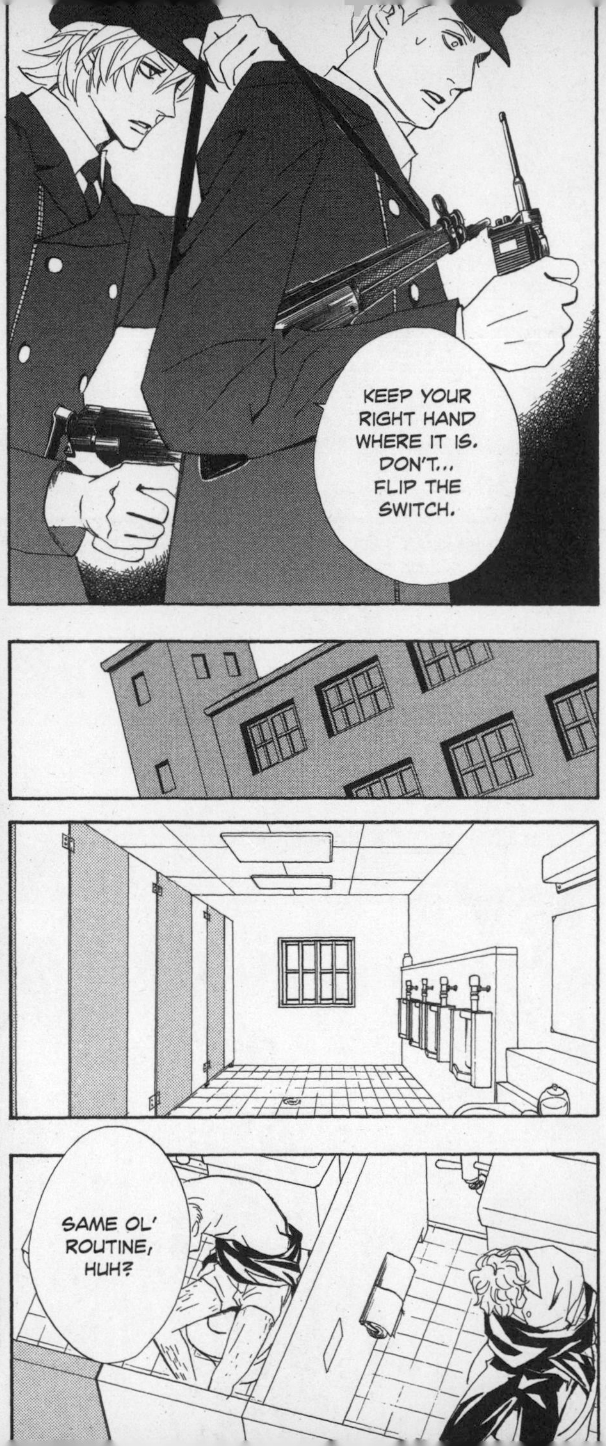
KEEP YOUR RIGHT HAND WHERE IT IS. DON'T... FLIP THE SWITCH.
SAME OL' ROUTINE, HUH?

4

Cooperation in production:

Shimada-san
Kawashima-san
Rabunuma-san
Sayaka-san
Nishizawa-san
Kuwana-san
Abe-san
Tanaka-san
Kaneko-san
Yone-yan

Yurino-san
Sakamoto-san
Suzuki-san

Special Thanks
Rei-san

Thank you for reading. I'll be really happy if we can meet up again in the next volume.

Your thoughts, etc.

Aya Kanno
c/o VIZ Media
P.O. Box 77010
SF, CA 94107

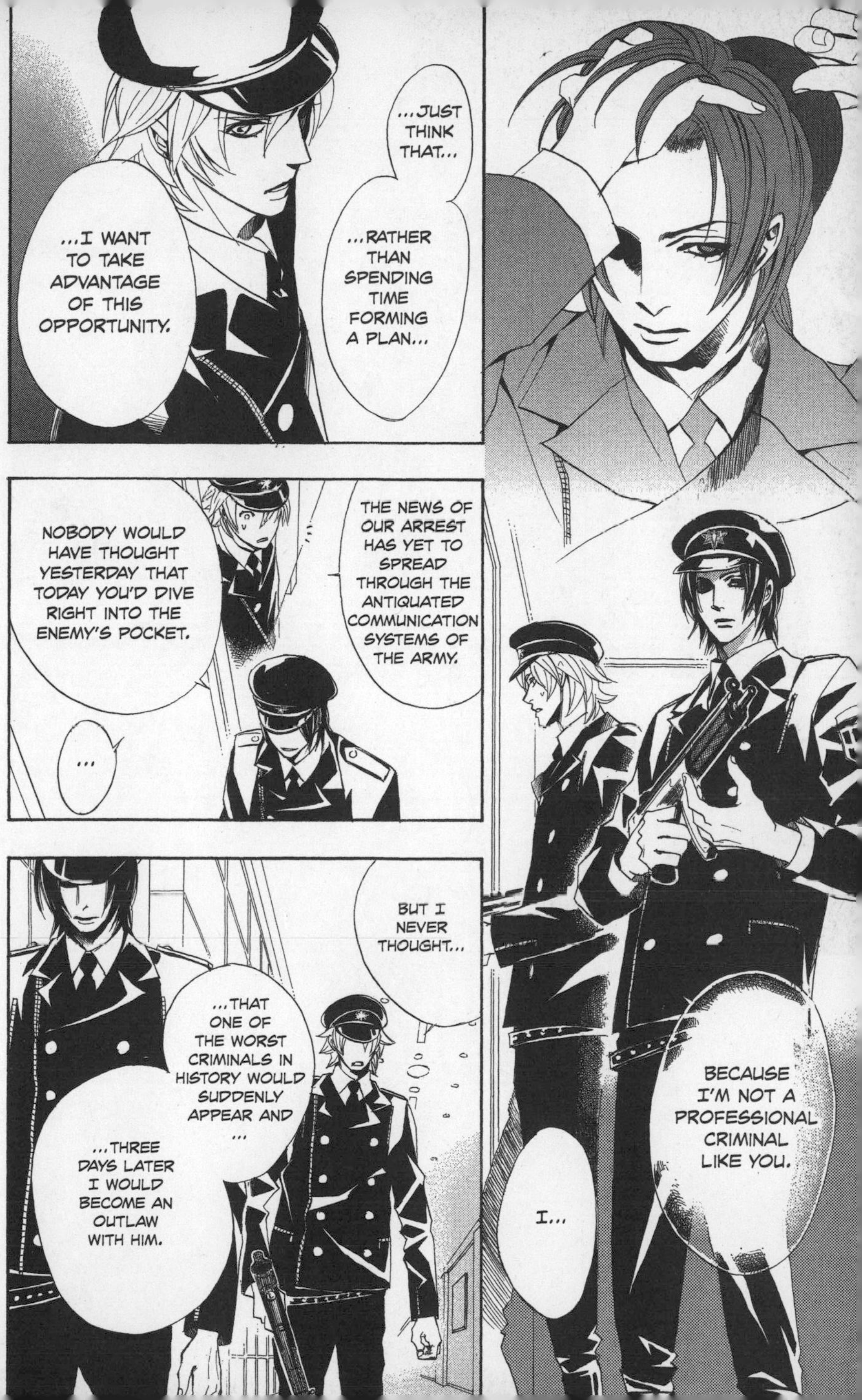
BECAUSE I'M NOT A PROFESSIONAL CRIMINAL LIKE YOU.
I...
...JUST THINK THAT...
...RATHER THAN SPENDING TIME FORMING A PLAN...
...I WANT TO TAKE ADVANTAGE OF THIS OPPORTUNITY.
THE NEWS OF OUR ARREST HAS YET TO SPREAD THROUGH THE ANTIQUATED COMMUNICATION SYSTEMS OF THE ARMY.
NOBODY WOULD HAVE THOUGHT YESTERDAY THAT TODAY YOU'D DIVE RIGHT INTO THE ENEMY'S POCKET.
...
BUT I NEVER THOUGHT...
...THAT ONE OF THE WORST CRIMINALS IN HISTORY WOULD SUDDENLY APPEAR AND ...
...THREE DAYS LATER I WOULD BECOME AN OUTLAW WITH HIM.

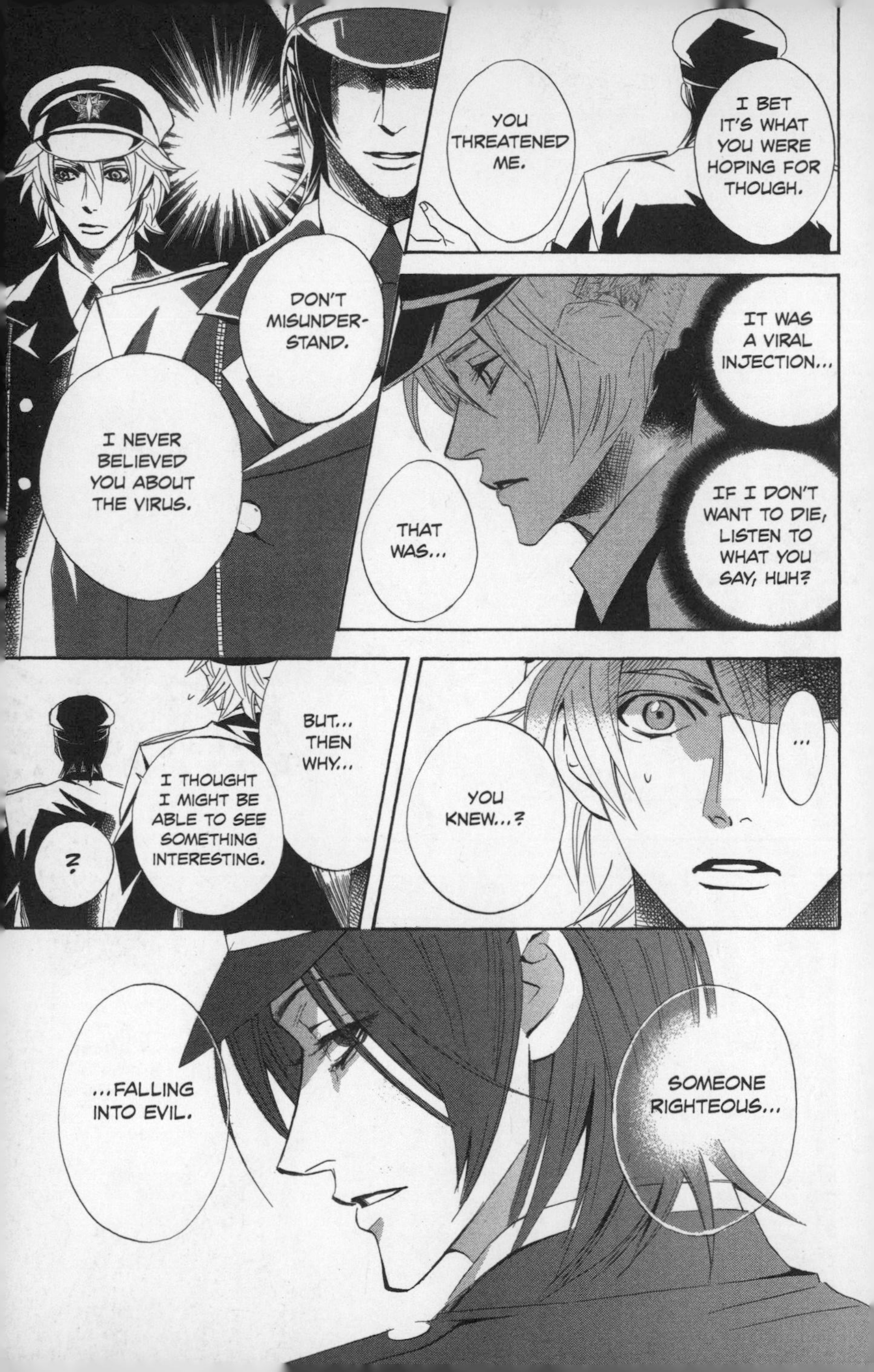
I BET IT'S WHAT YOU WERE HOPING FOR THOUGH.
YOU THREATENED ME.
IT WAS A VIRAL INJECTION...
IF I DON'T WANT TO DIE, LISTEN TO WHAT YOU SAY, HUH?
THAT WAS...
DON'T MISUNDER-STAND.
I NEVER BELIEVED YOU ABOUT THE VIRUS.
...
YOU KNEW...?
BUT... THEN WHY...
I THOUGHT I MIGHT BE ABLE TO SEE SOMETHING INTERESTING.
?
SOMEONE RIGHTEOUS...
...FALLING INTO EVIL.

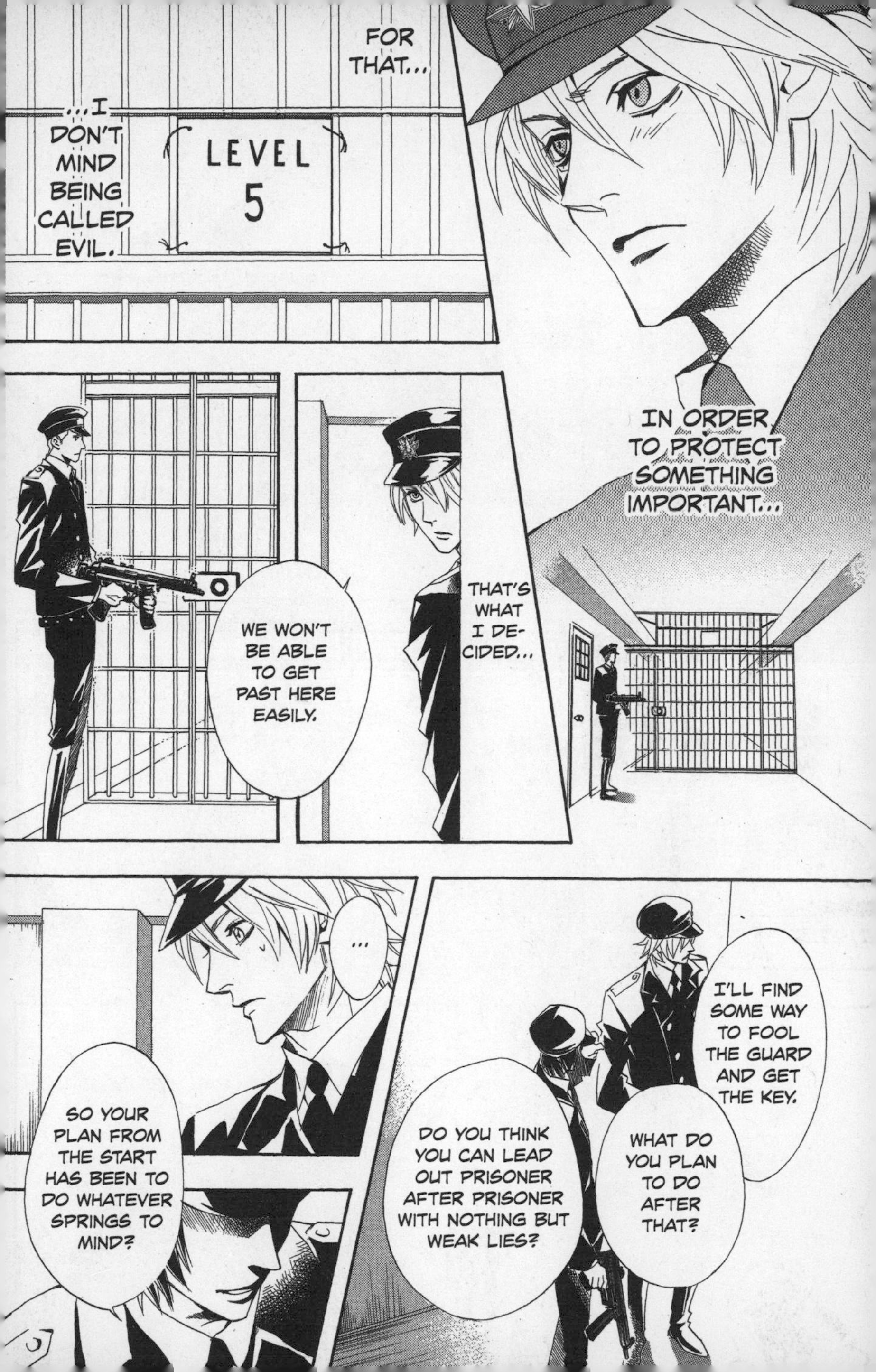
IN ORDER TO PROTECT SOMETHING IMPORTANT...
FOR THAT...
...I DON'T MIND BEING CALLED EVIL.
LEVEL 5
THAT'S WHAT I DE-CIDED...
WE WON'T BE ABLE TO GET PAST HERE EASILY.
I'LL FIND SOME WAY TO FOOL THE GUARD AND GET THE KEY.
WHAT DO YOU PLAN TO DO AFTER THAT?
DO YOU THINK YOU CAN LEAD OUT PRISONER AFTER PRISONER WITH NOTHING BUT WEAK LIES?
...
SO YOUR PLAN FROM THE START HAS BEEN TO DO WHATEVER SPRINGS TO MIND?

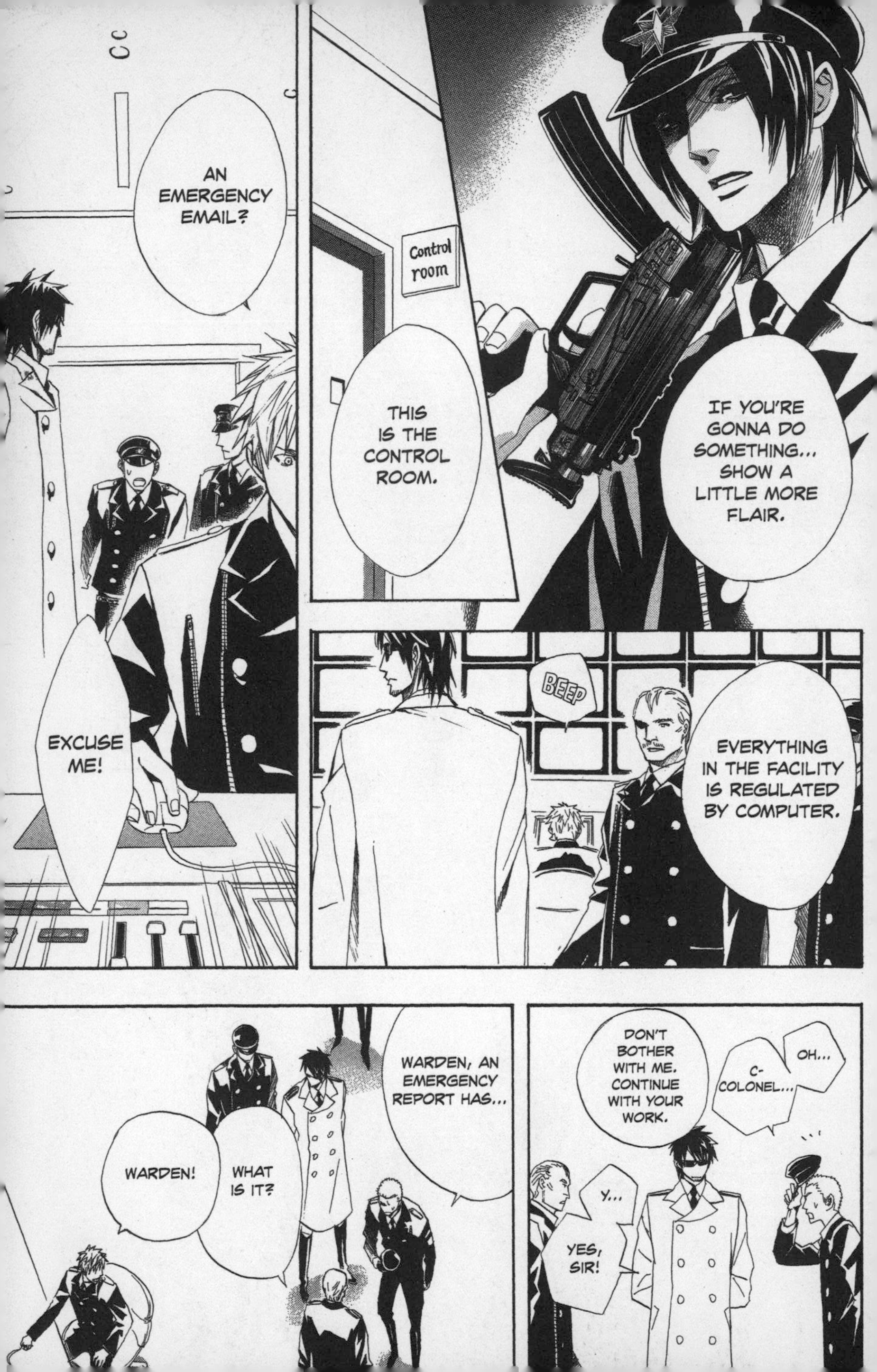
IF YOU'RE GONNA DO SOMETHING... SHOW A LITTLE MORE FLAIR.
Control room
THIS IS THE CONTROL ROOM.
BEEP
EVERYTHING IN THE FACILITY IS REGULATED BY COMPUTER.
AN EMERGENCY EMAIL?
EXCUSE ME!
OH...
C-COLONEL...
DON'T BOTHER WITH ME. CONTINUE WITH YOUR WORK.
Y...
YES, SIR!
WARDEN, AN EMERGENCY REPORT HAS...
WHAT IS IT?
WARDEN!

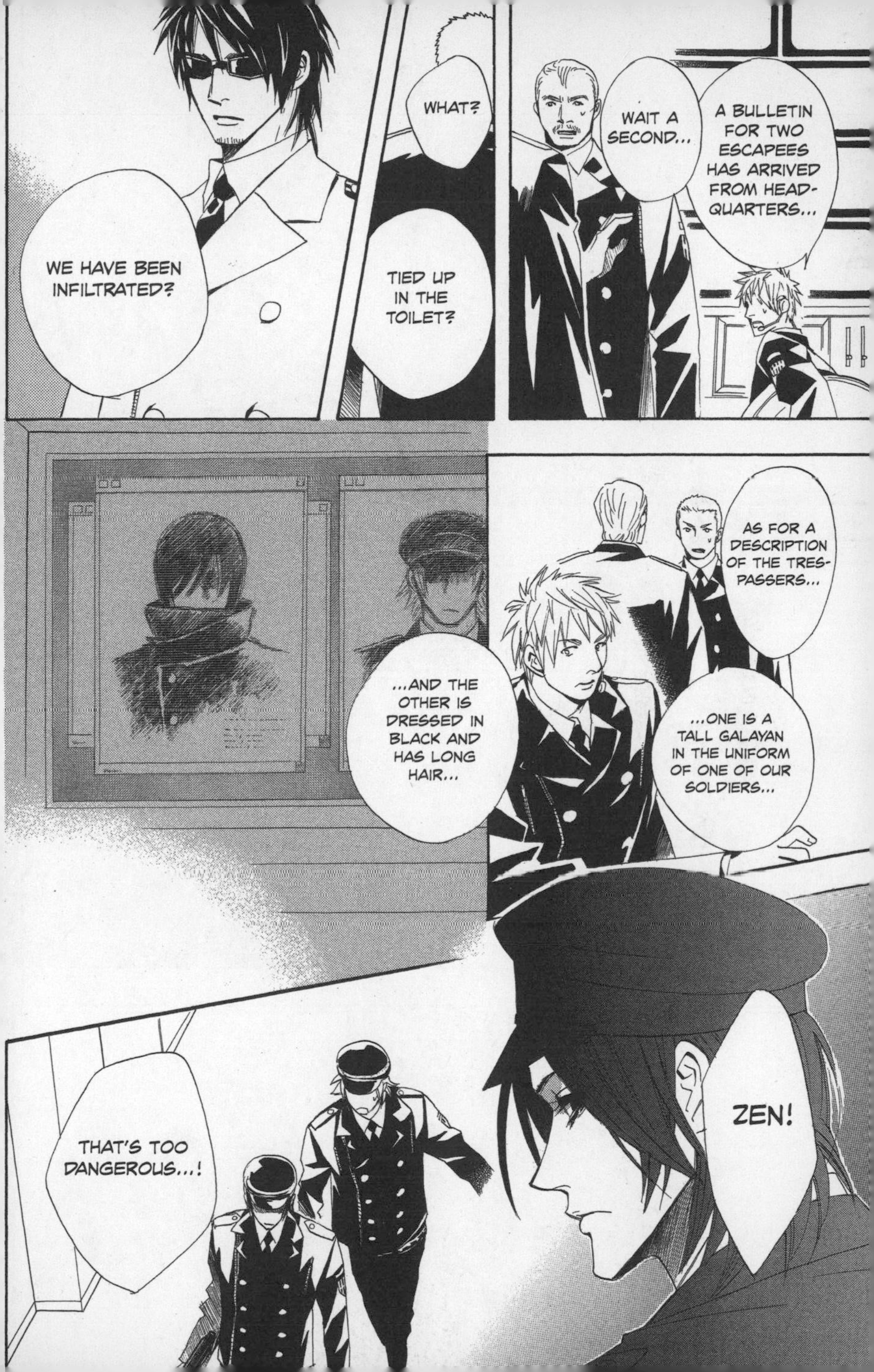
A BULLETIN FOR TWO ESCAPEES HAS ARRIVED FROM HEAD-QUARTERS...
WAIT A SECOND...
WHAT?
TIED UP IN THE TOILET?
WE HAVE BEEN INFILTRATED?
AS FOR A DESCRIPTION OF THE TRES-PASSERS...
...ONE IS A TALL GALAYAN IN THE UNIFORM OF ONE OF OUR SOLDIERS...
...AND THE OTHER IS DRESSED IN BLACK AND HAS LONG HAIR...
ZEN!
THAT'S TOO DANGEROUS...!

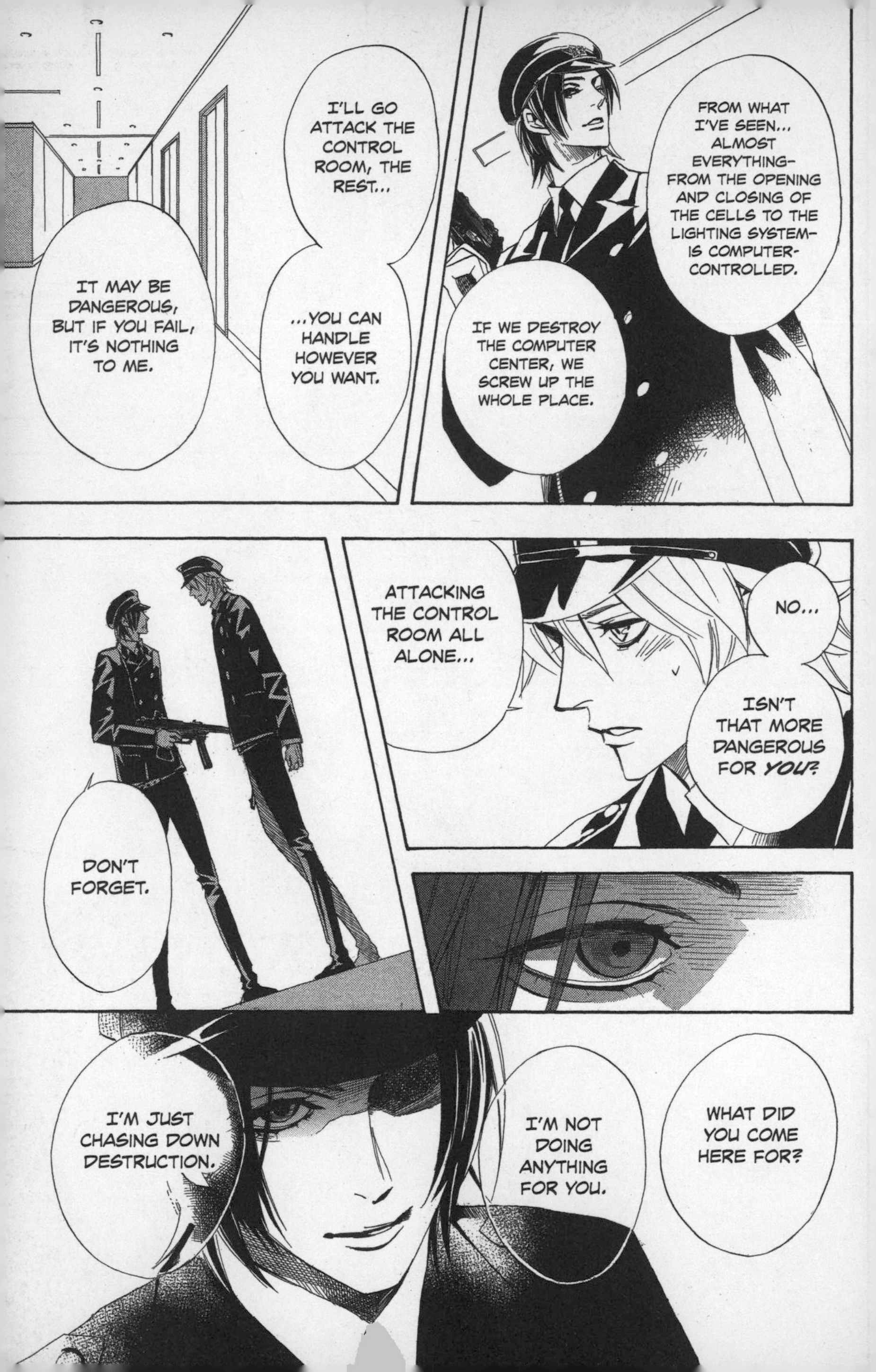
FROM WHAT I'VE SEEN... ALMOST EVERYTHING- FROM THE OPENING AND CLOSING OF THE CELLS TO THE LIGHTING SYSTEM- IS COMPUTER-CONTROLLED.
IF WE DESTROY THE COMPUTER CENTER, WE SCREW UP THE WHOLE PLACE.
I'LL GO ATTACK THE CONTROL ROOM, THE REST...
...YOU CAN HANDLE HOWEVER YOU WANT.
IT MAY BE DANGEROUS, BUT IF YOU FAIL, IT'S NOTHING TO ME.
NO...
ATTACKING THE CONTROL ROOM ALL ALONE...
ISN'T THAT MORE DANGEROUS FOR *YOU*?
DON'T FORGET.
WHAT DID YOU COME HERE FOR?
I'M NOT DOING ANYTHING FOR YOU.
I'M JUST CHASING DOWN DESTRUCTION.

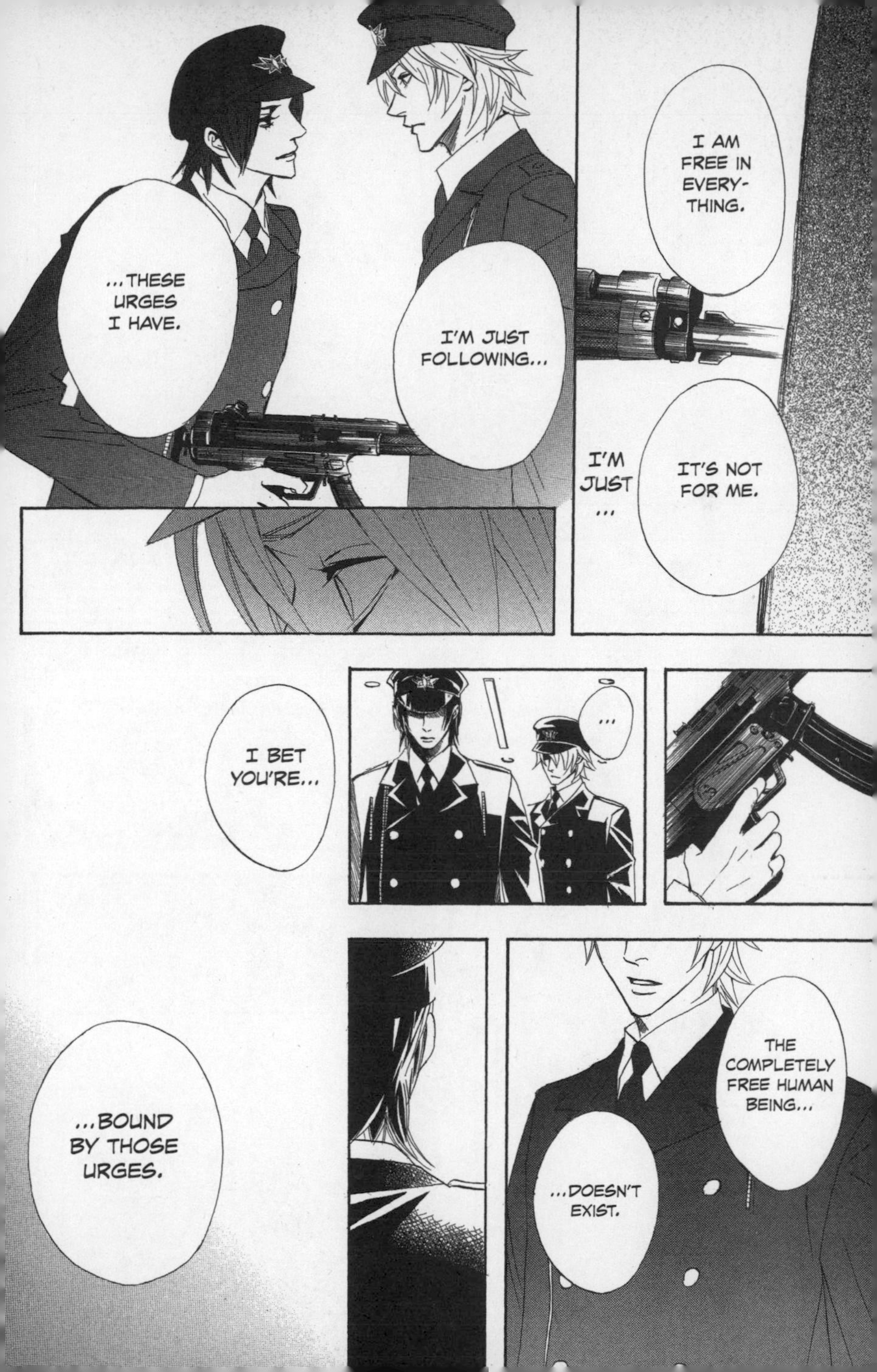
I AM FREE IN EVERY-THING.
IT'S NOT FOR ME.
I'M JUST ...
I'M JUST FOLLOWING...
...THESE URGES I HAVE.
...
I BET YOU'RE...
THE COMPLETELY FREE HUMAN BEING...
...DOESN'T EXIST.
...BOUND BY THOSE URGES.

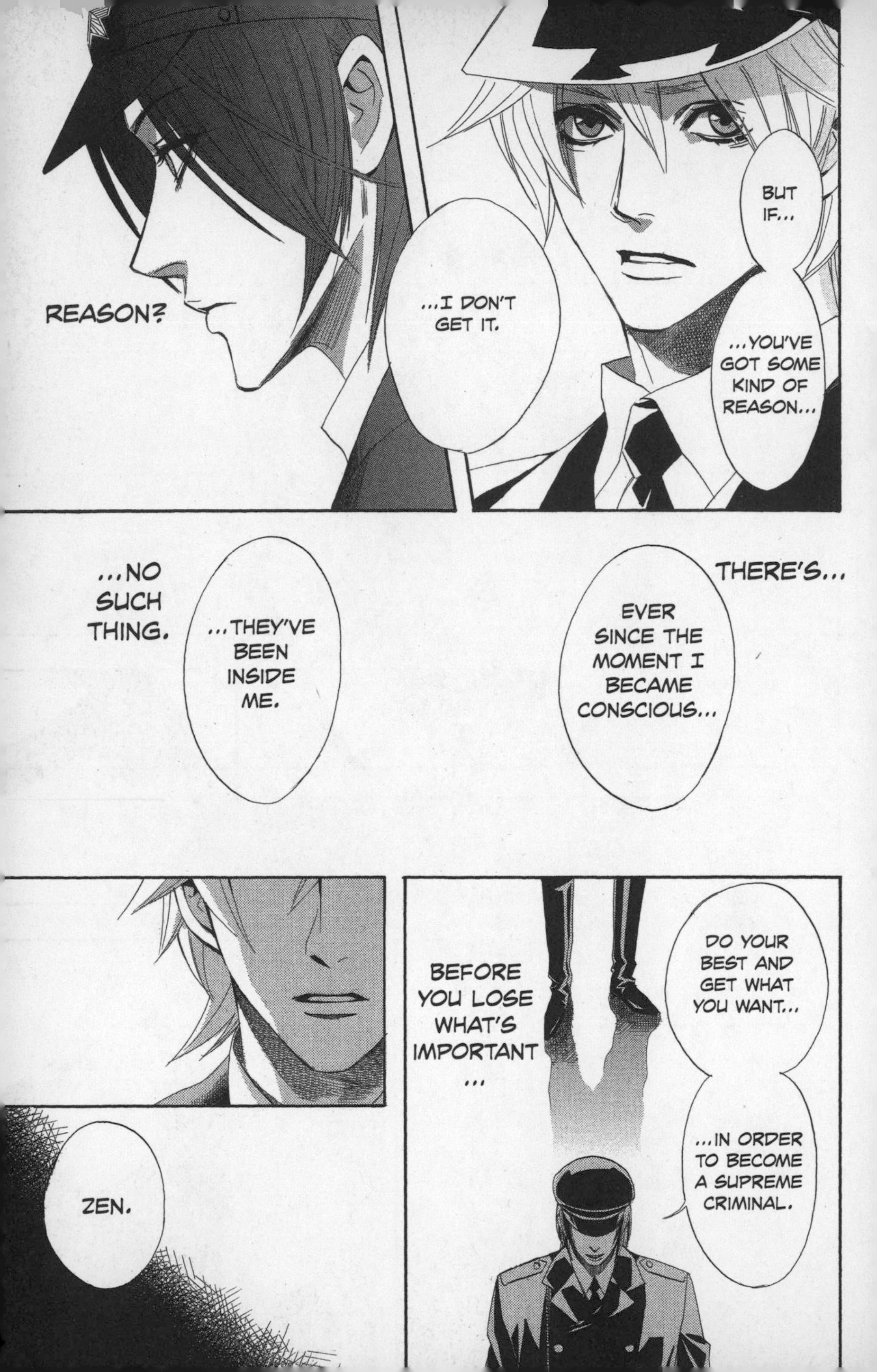
BUT IF...
...YOU'VE GOT SOME KIND OF REASON...
...I DON'T GET IT.
REASON?
THERE'S...
EVER SINCE THE MOMENT I BECAME CONSCIOUS...
...THEY'VE BEEN INSIDE ME.
...NO SUCH THING.
DO YOUR BEST AND GET WHAT YOU WANT...
...IN ORDER TO BECOME A SUPREME CRIMINAL.
BEFORE YOU LOSE WHAT'S IMPORTANT...
ZEN.

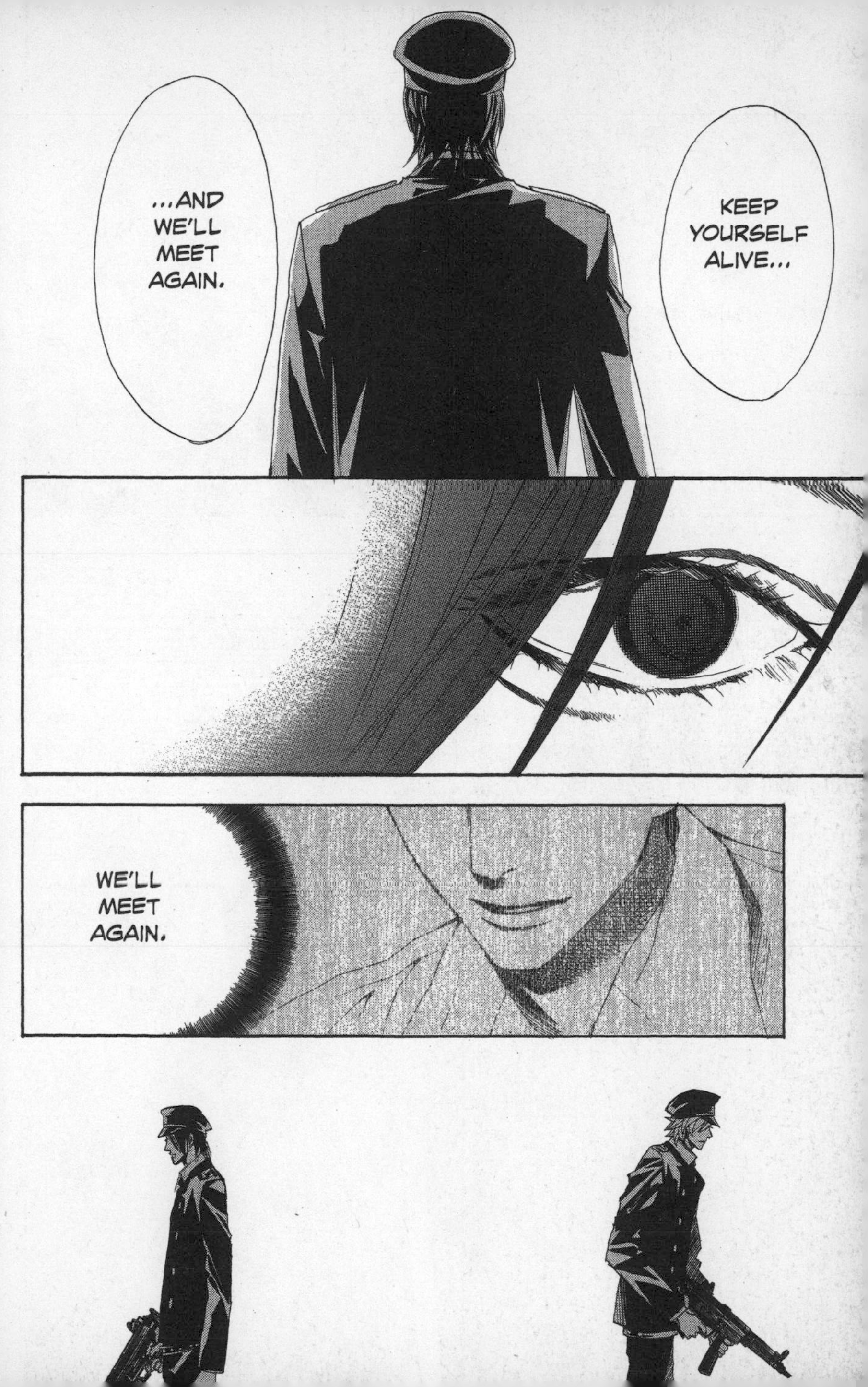
KEEP YOURSELF ALIVE...
...AND WE'LL MEET AGAIN.
WE'LL MEET AGAIN.

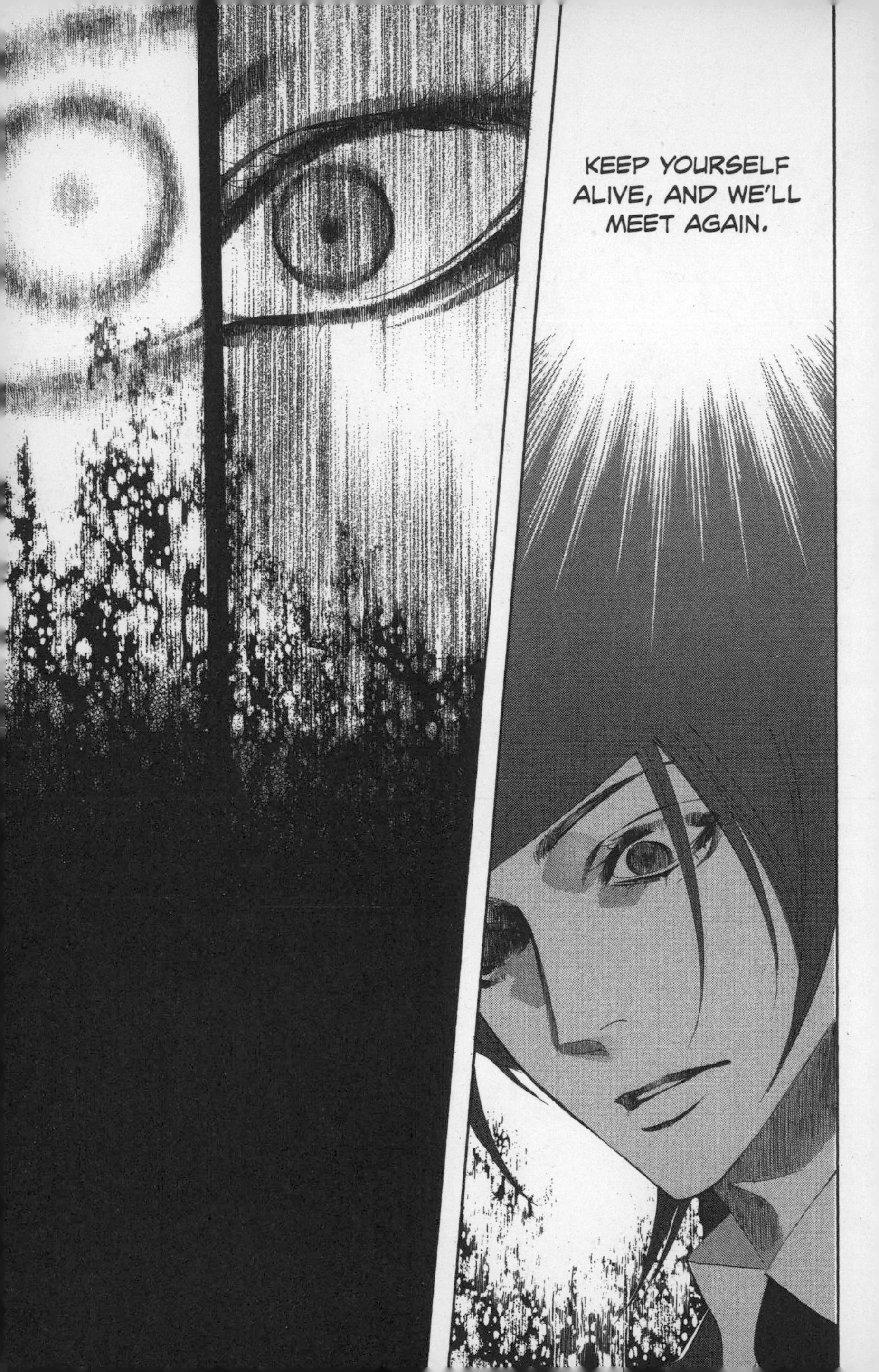
KEEP YOURSELF ALIVE, AND WE'LL MEET AGAIN.

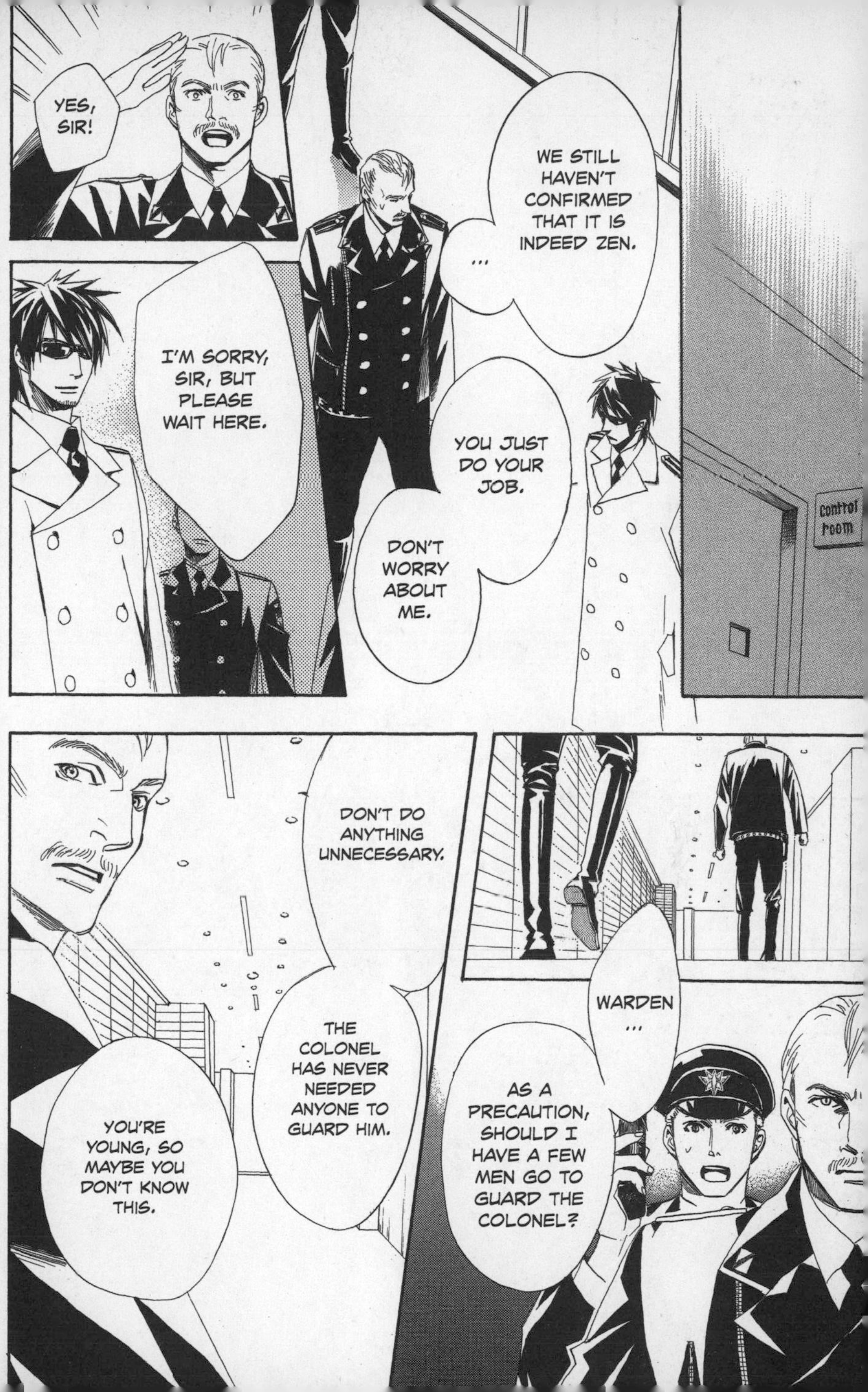
...
WE STILL HAVEN'T CONFIRMED THAT IT IS INDEED ZEN.
YOU JUST DO YOUR JOB.
DON'T WORRY ABOUT ME.
control room
YES, SIR!
I'M SORRY, SIR, BUT PLEASE WAIT HERE.
WARDEN...
AS A PRECAUTION, SHOULD I HAVE A FEW MEN GO TO GUARD THE COLONEL?
DON'T DO ANYTHING UNNECESSARY.
THE COLONEL HAS NEVER NEEDED ANYONE TO GUARD HIM.
YOU'RE YOUNG, SO MAYBE YOU DON'T KNOW THIS.

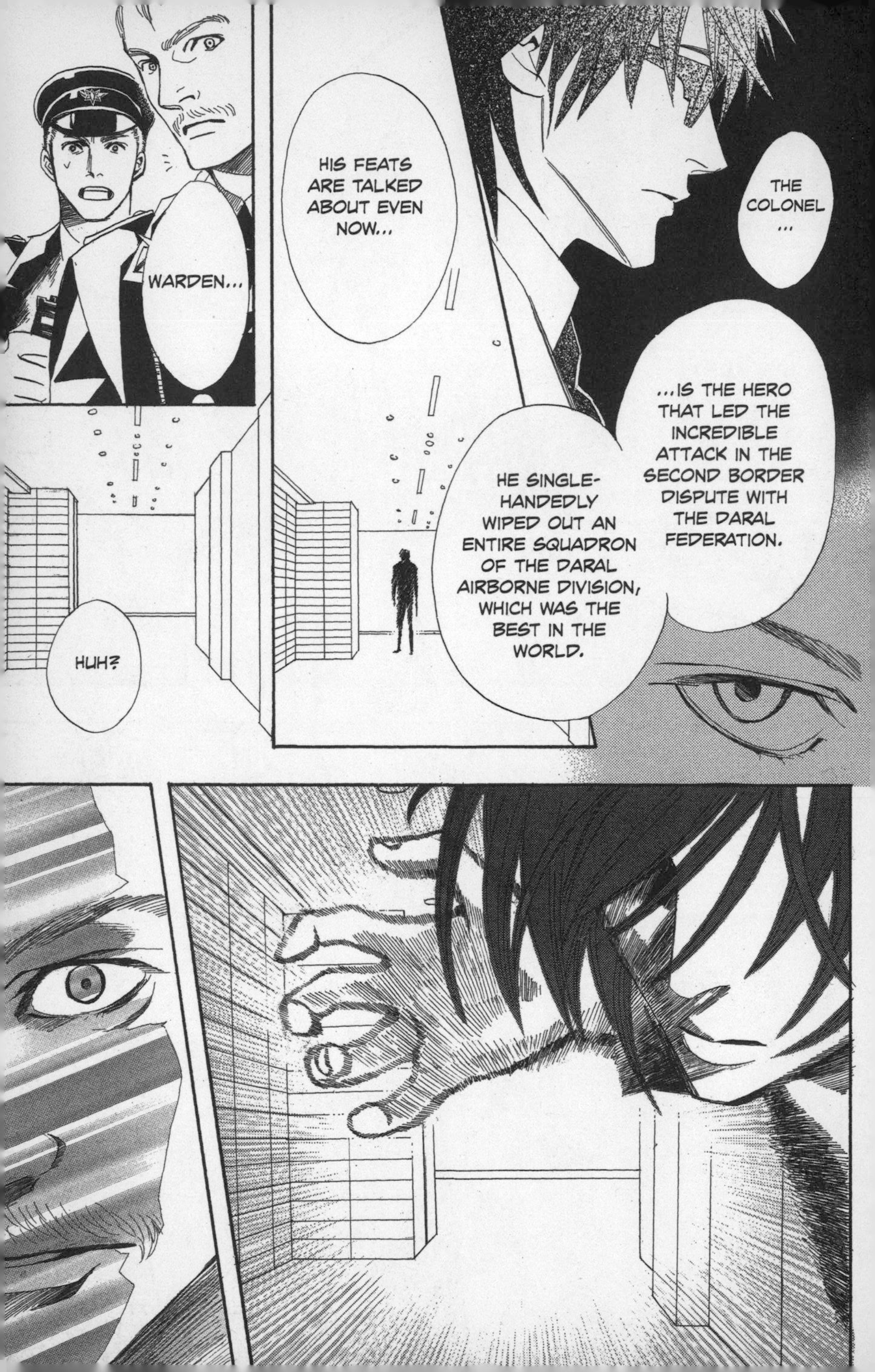
THE COLONEL...
...IS THE HERO THAT LED THE INCREDIBLE ATTACK IN THE SECOND BORDER DISPUTE WITH THE DARAL FEDERATION.
HE SINGLE-HANDEDLY WIPED OUT AN ENTIRE SQUADRON OF THE DARAL AIRBORNE DIVISION, WHICH WAS THE BEST IN THE WORLD.
HIS FEATS ARE TALKED ABOUT EVEN NOW...
WARDEN...
HUH?

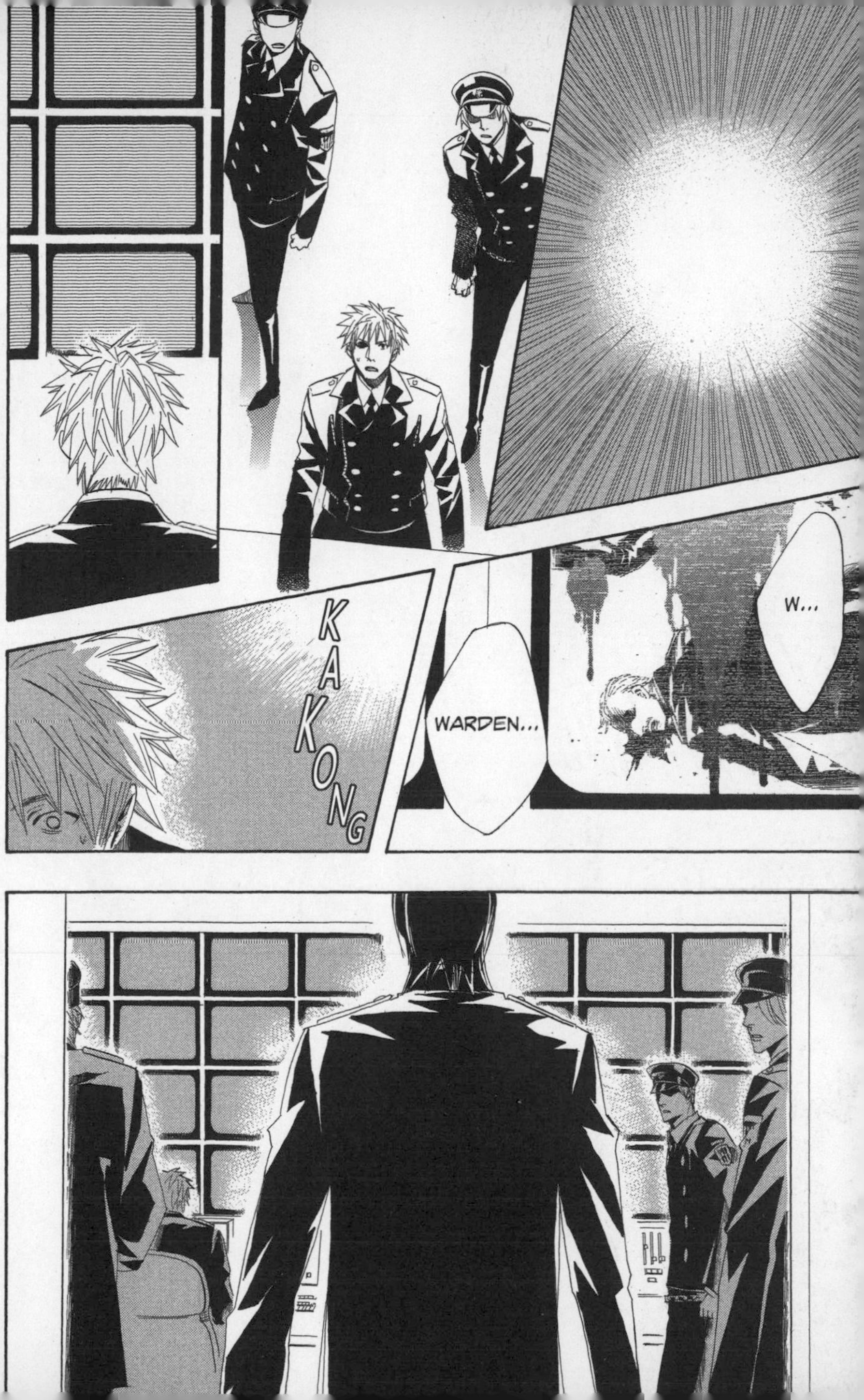
W...
WARDEN...
KAKONG

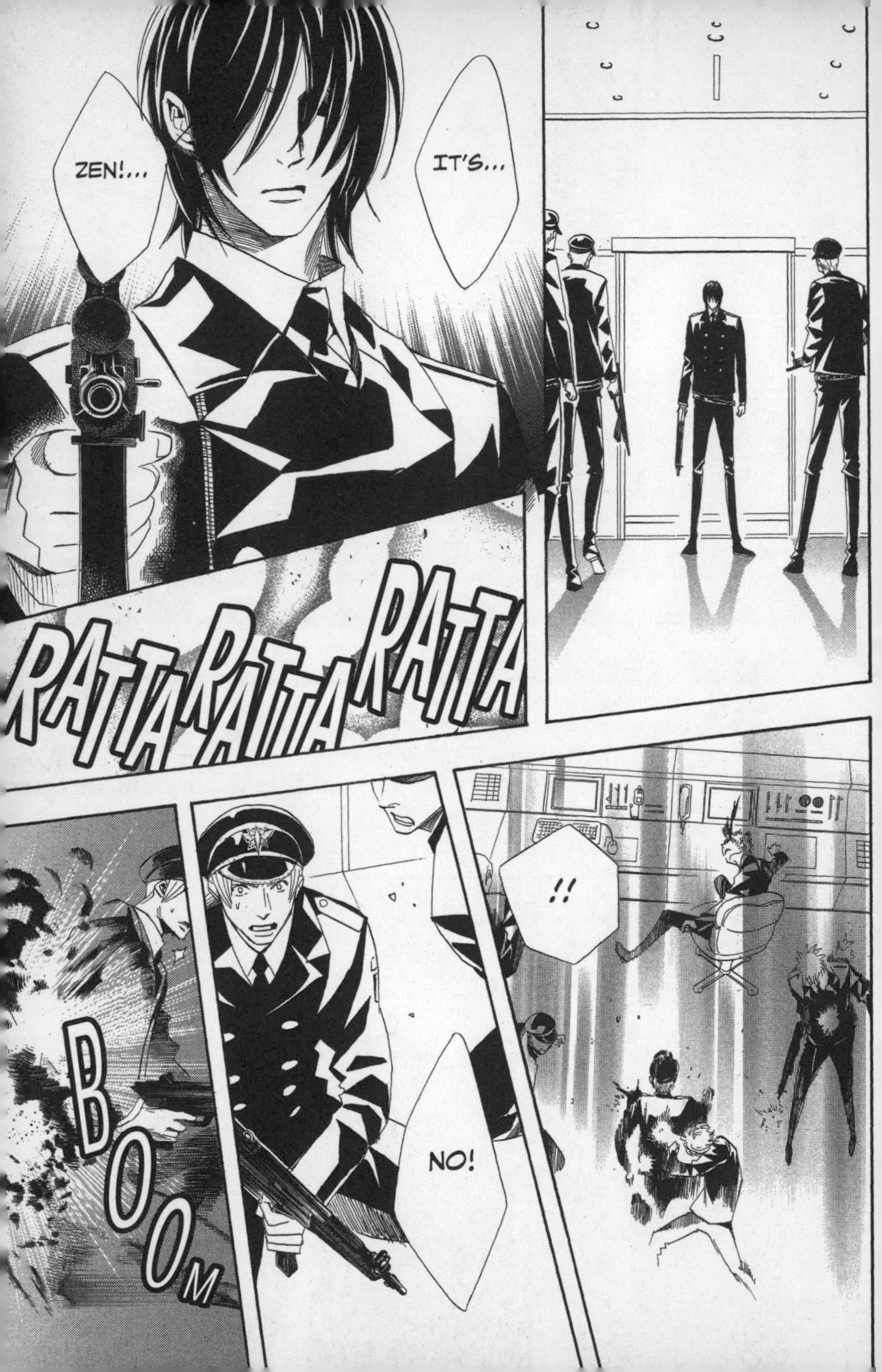
IT'S...
ZEN!...
RATTA
RATTA
RATTA
!!
NO!
BOOOM

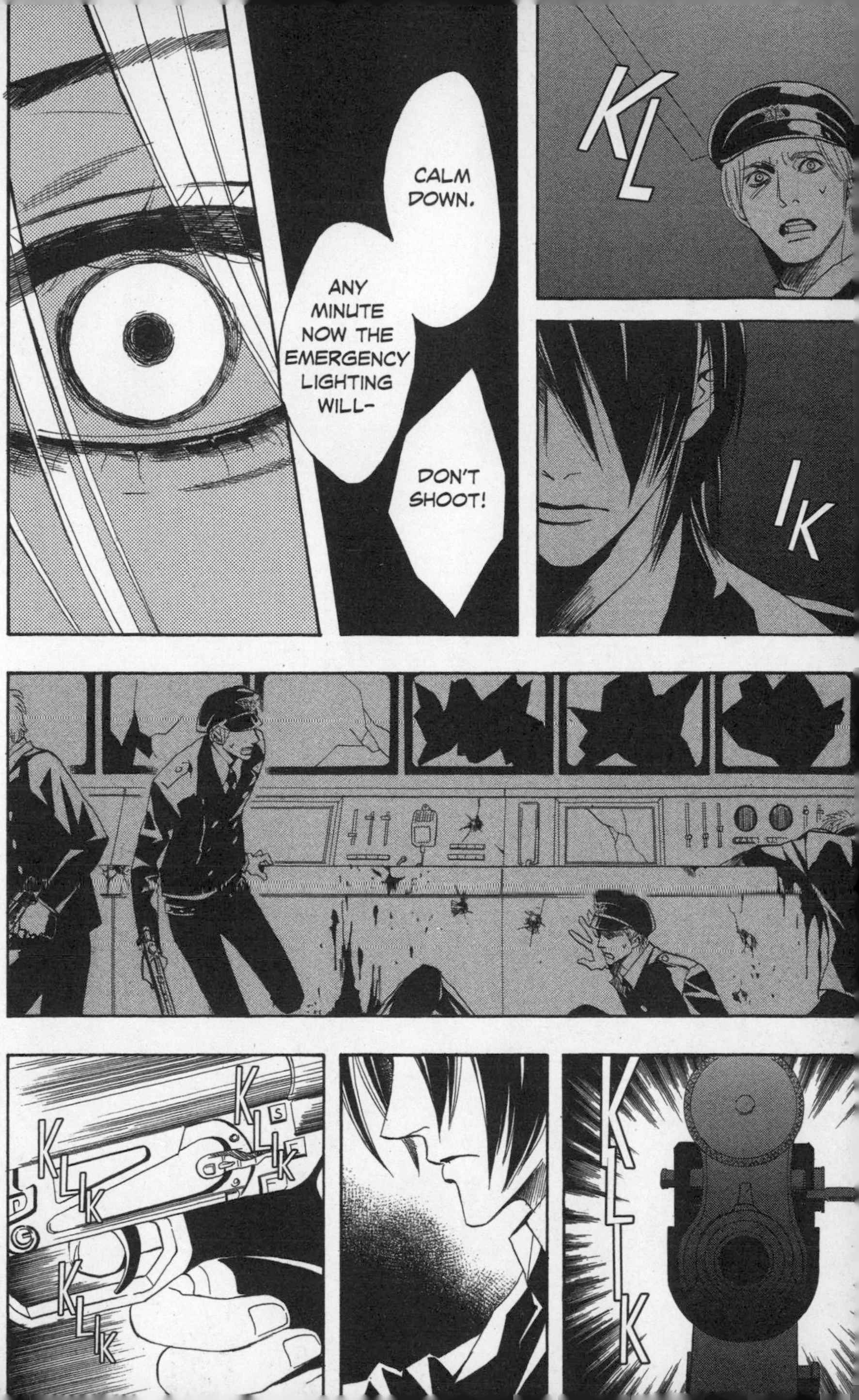
KL
IK
CALM DOWN.
ANY MINUTE NOW THE EMERGENCY LIGHTING WILL-
DON'T SHOOT!
KLLIK
KLIK
KLIK
KLIK

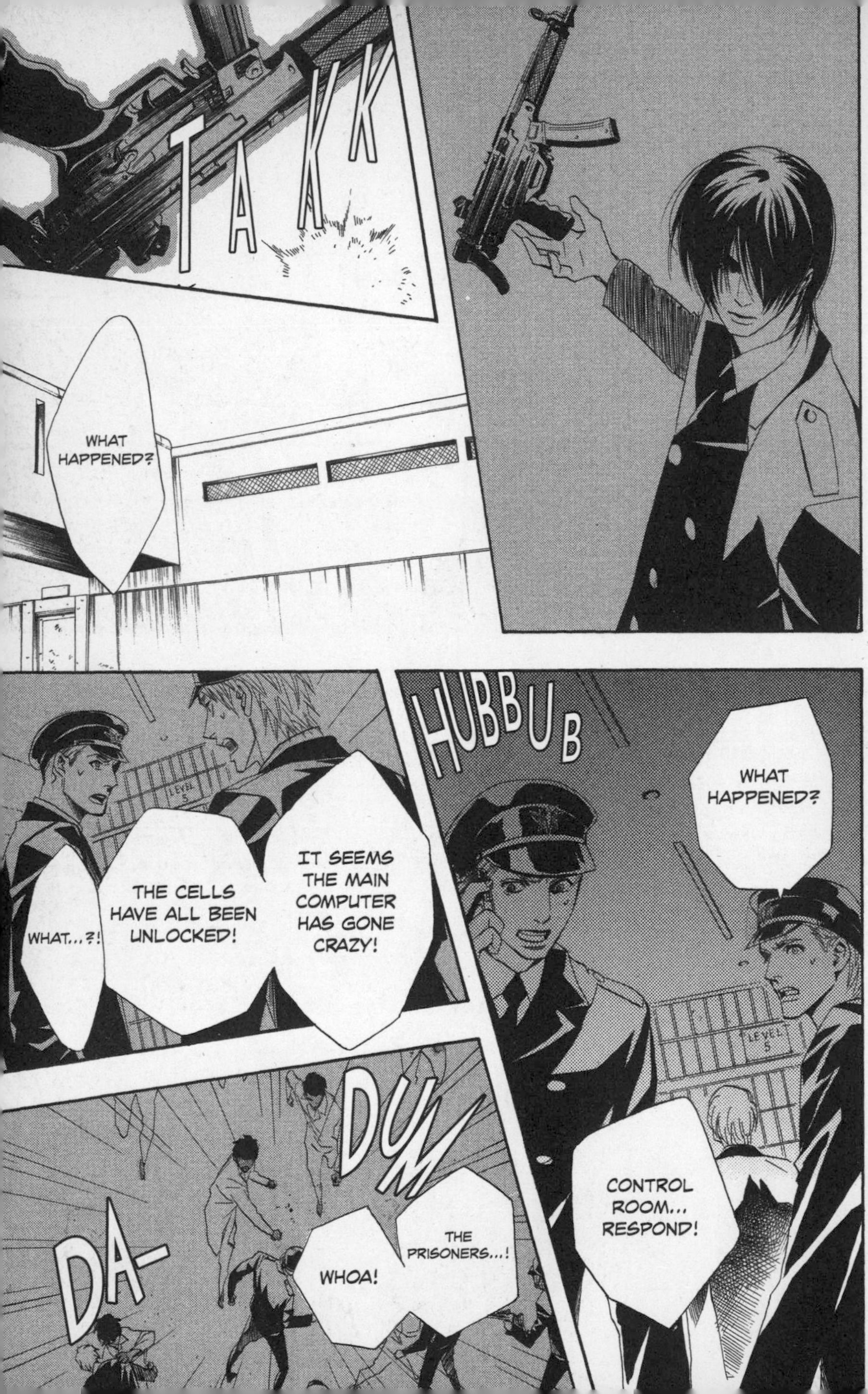
TAKK
WHAT HAPPENED?
HUBBUB
WHAT HAPPENED?
CONTROL ROOM... RESPOND!
IT SEEMS THE MAIN COMPUTER HAS GONE CRAZY!
THE CELLS HAVE ALL BEEN UNLOCKED!
WHAT...?!
DUM
THE PRISONERS...!
WHOA!
DA-

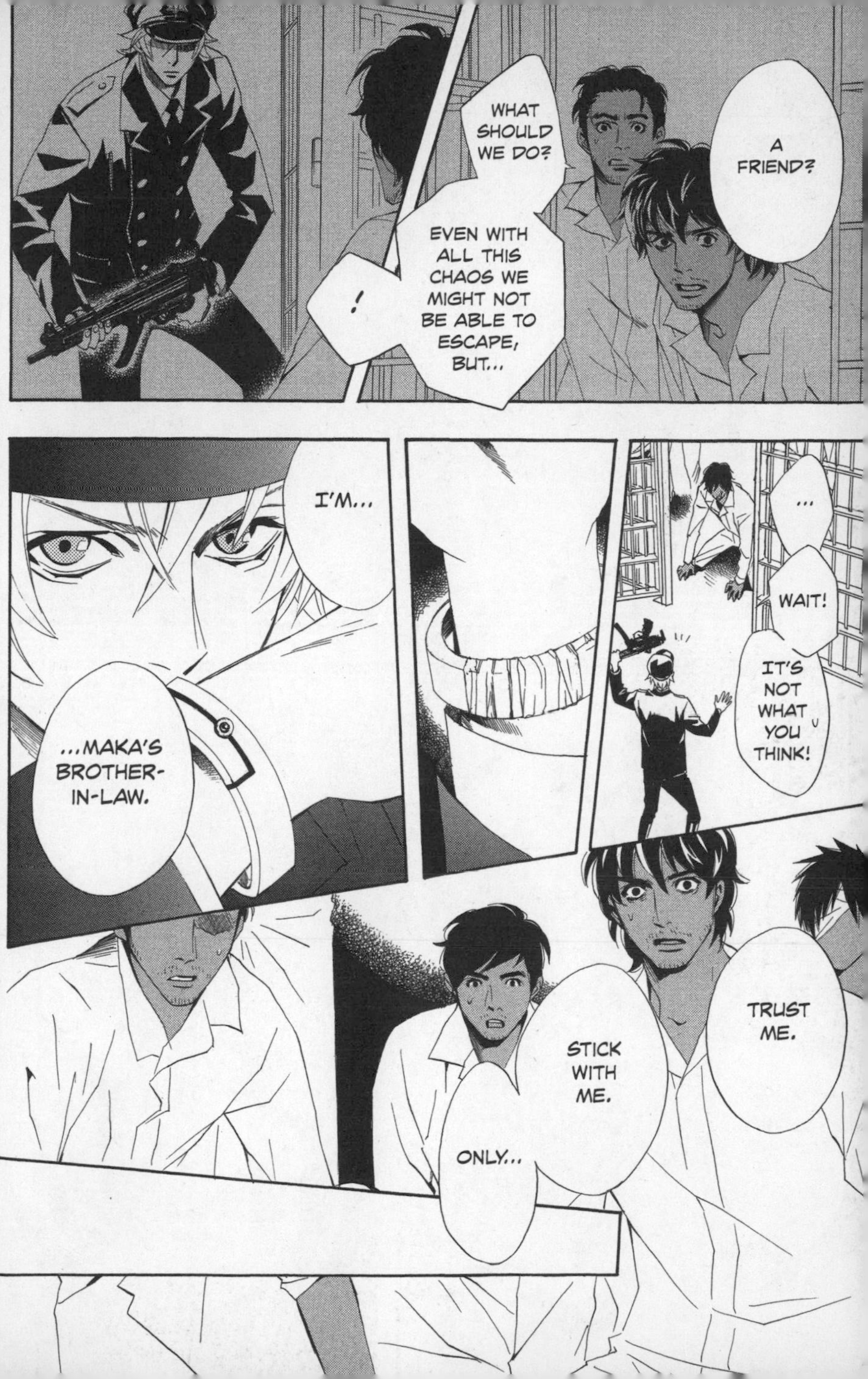
A FRIEND?
WHAT SHOULD WE DO?
EVEN WITH ALL THIS CHAOS WE MIGHT NOT BE ABLE TO ESCAPE, BUT...
!
...
WAIT!
IT'S NOT WHAT YOU THINK!
I'M...
...MAKA'S BROTHER-IN-LAW.
TRUST ME.
STICK WITH ME.
ONLY...

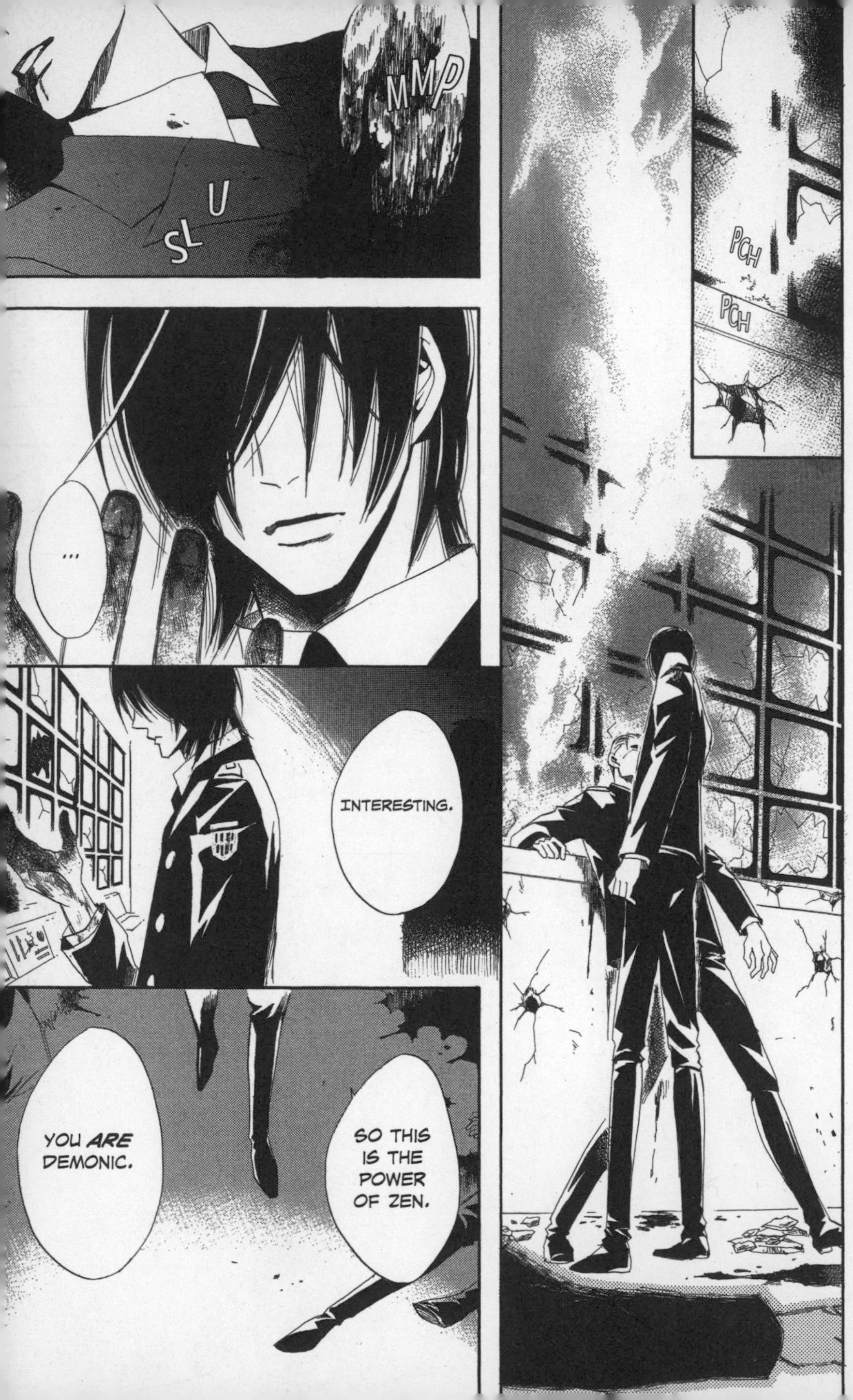
PCH
PCH
MMP
SLU
...
INTERESTING.
SO THIS IS THE POWER OF ZEN.
YOU *ARE* DEMONIC.

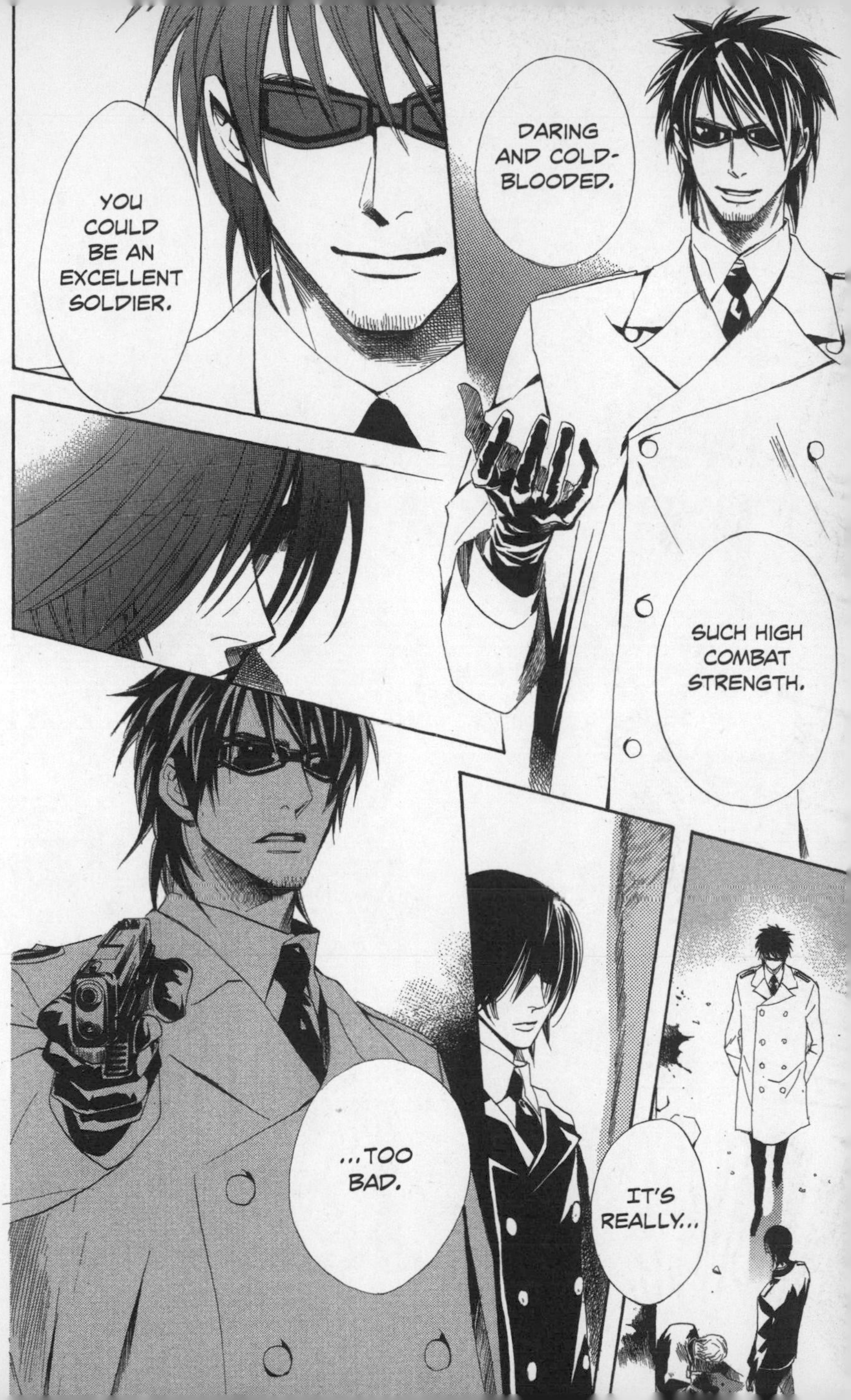
DARING AND COLD-BLOODED.
SUCH HIGH COMBAT STRENGTH.
YOU COULD BE AN EXCELLENT SOLDIER.
IT'S REALLY...
...TOO BAD.

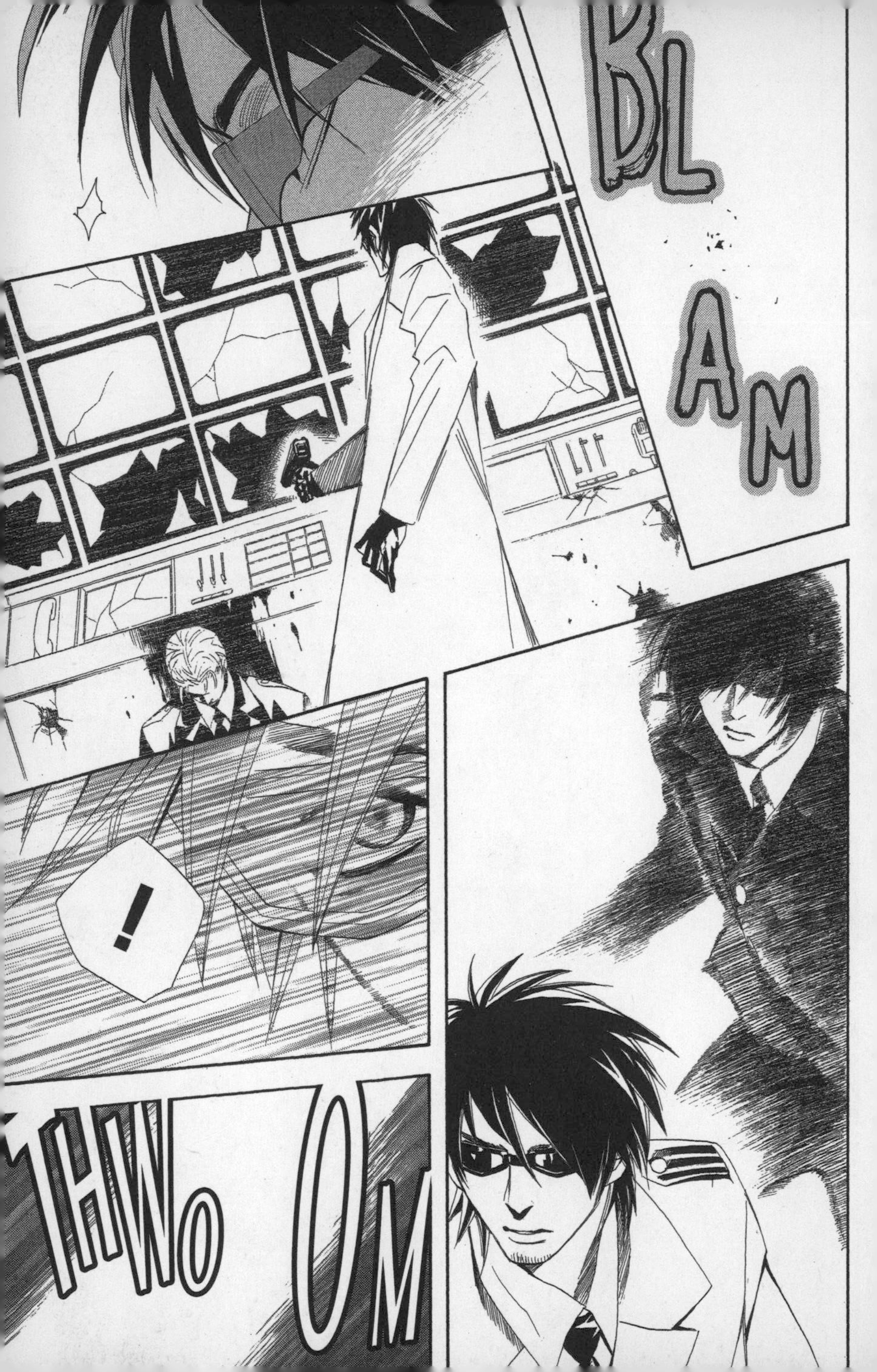
BLAM
!
THWOOM

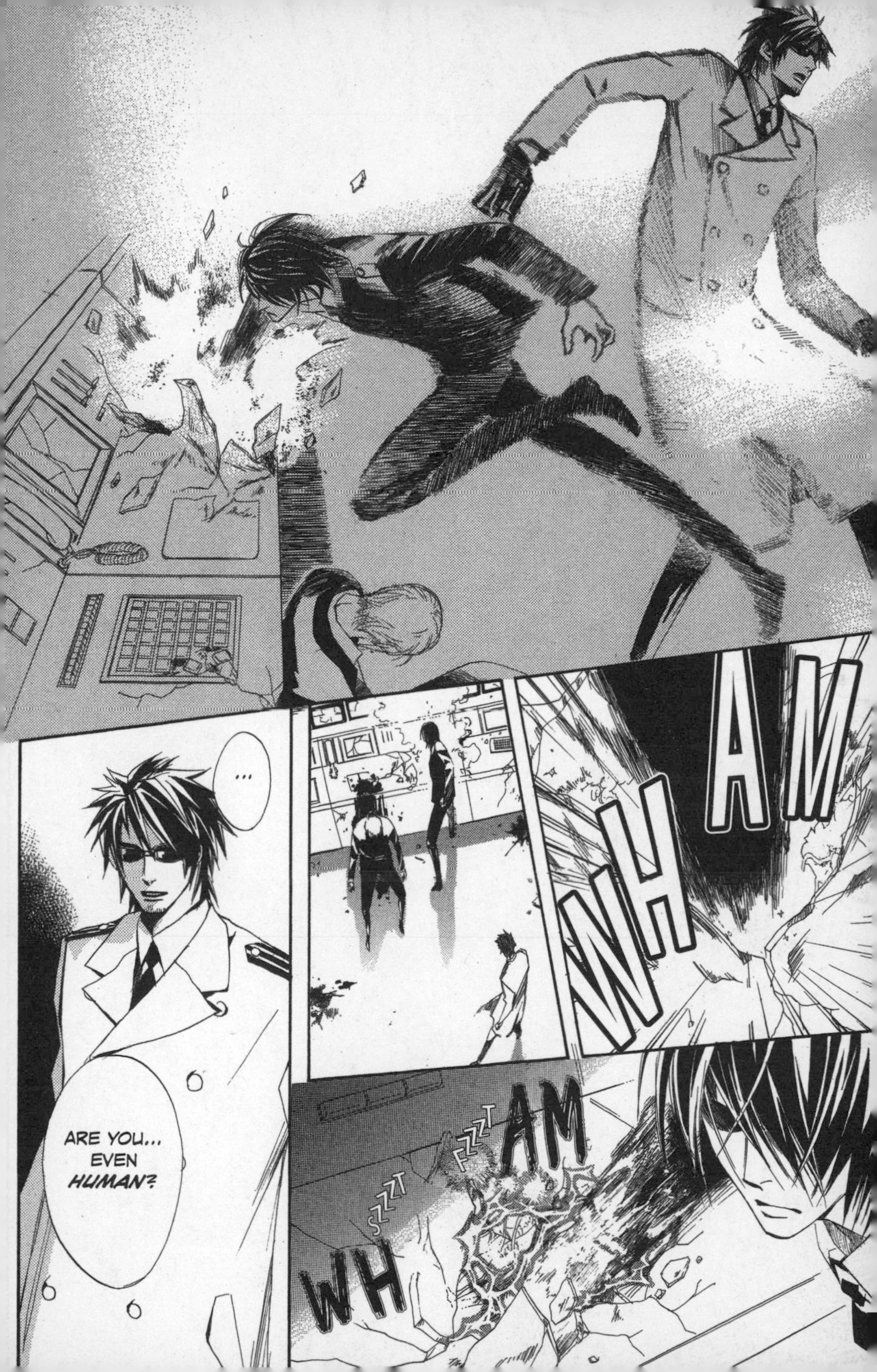
WHAM
WHAM
FZZZT
SZZZT
...
ARE YOU... EVEN *HUMAN*?

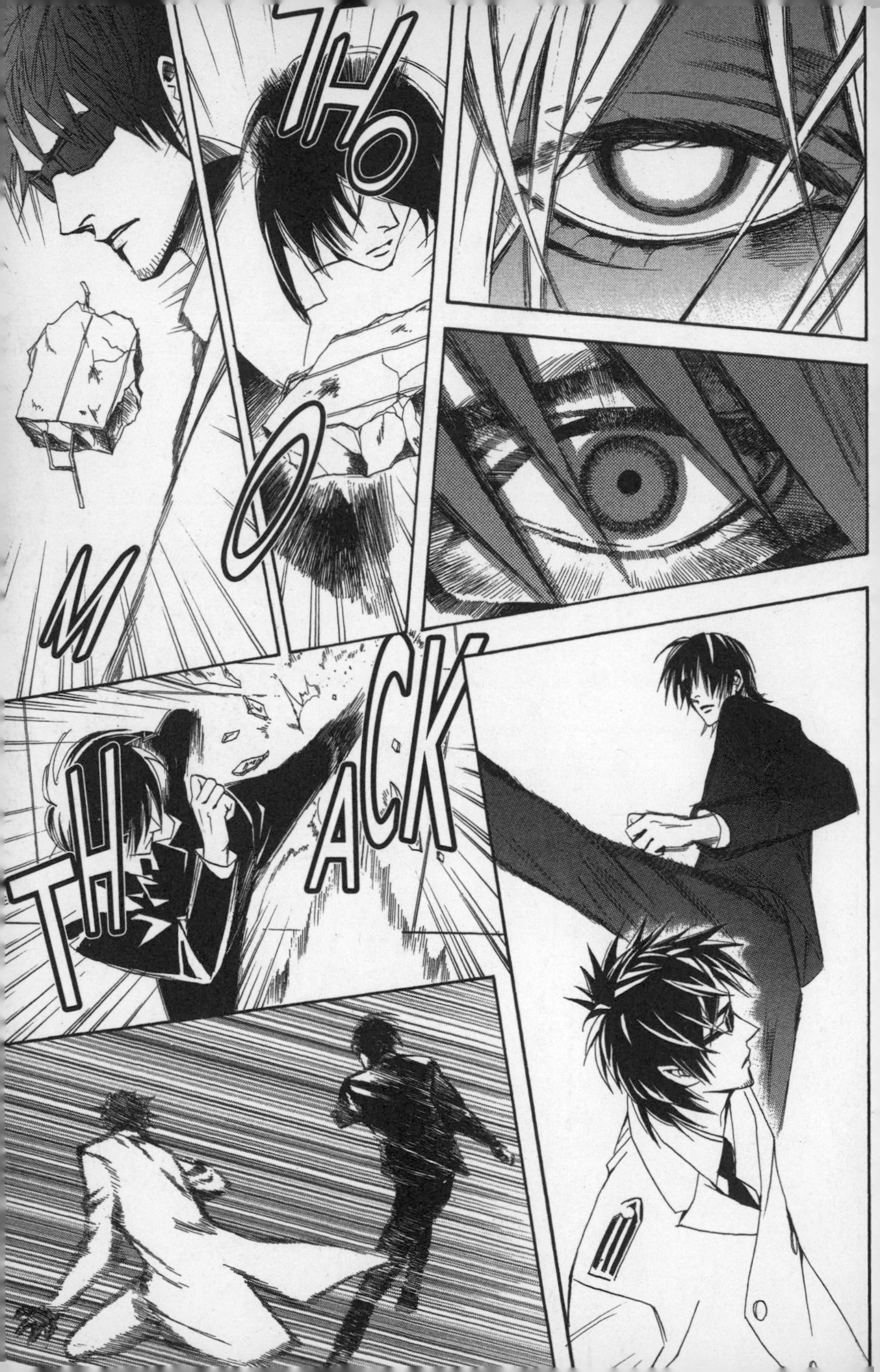
THOOM
THACK

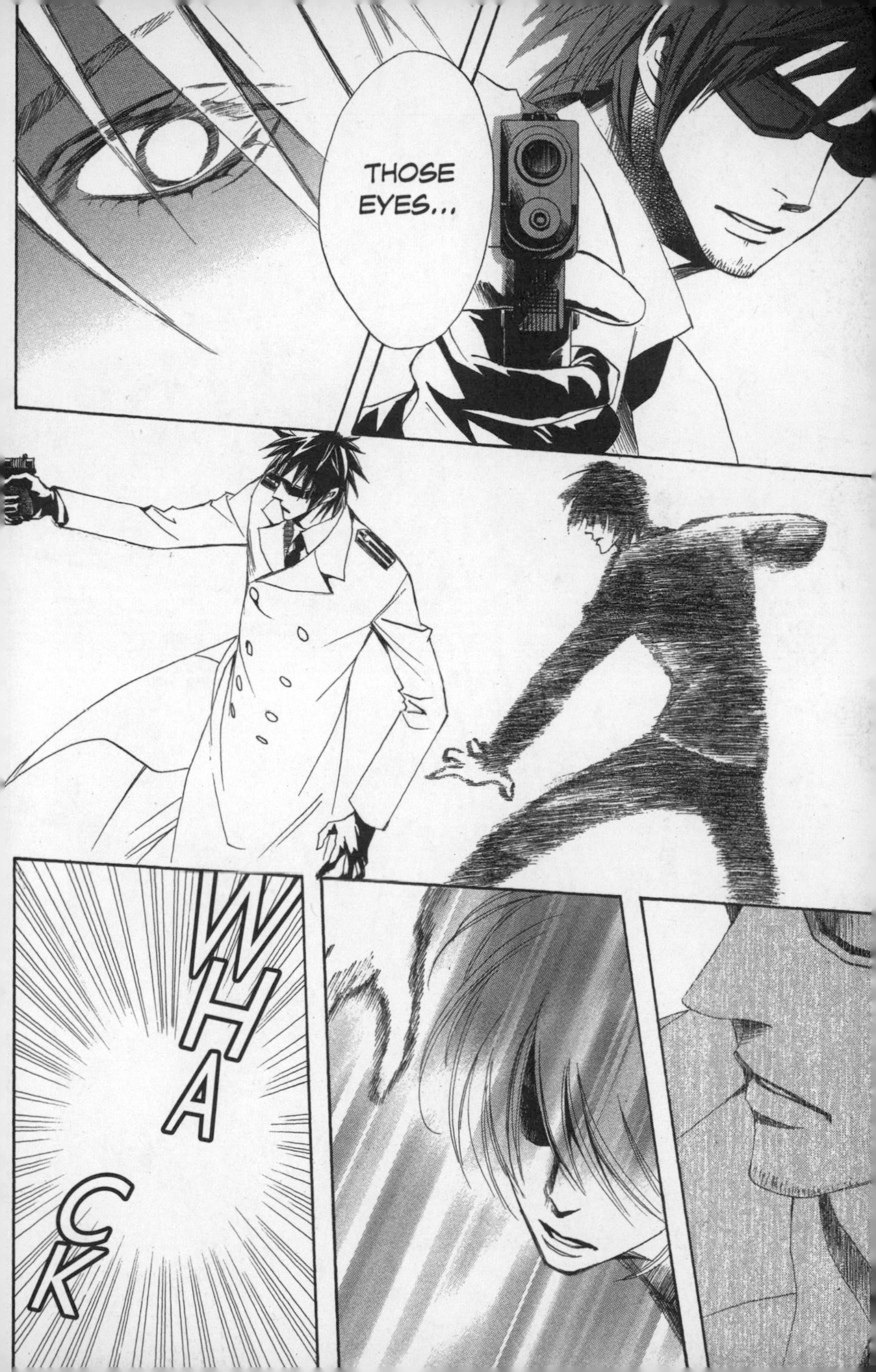
THOSE EYES...
WHACK

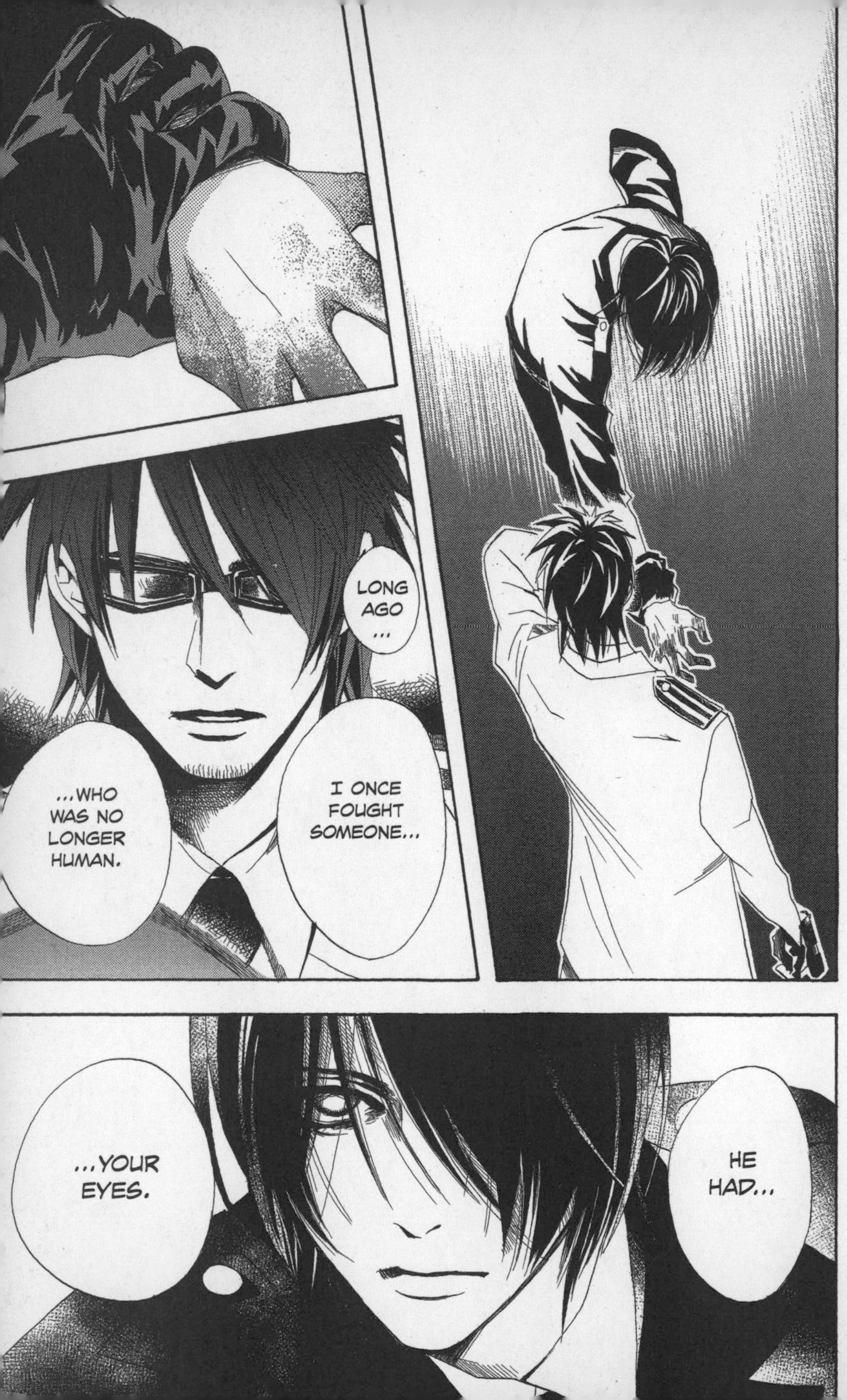
LONG AGO ...
I ONCE FOUGHT SOMEONE...
...WHO WAS NO LONGER HUMAN.
HE HAD...
...YOUR EYES.

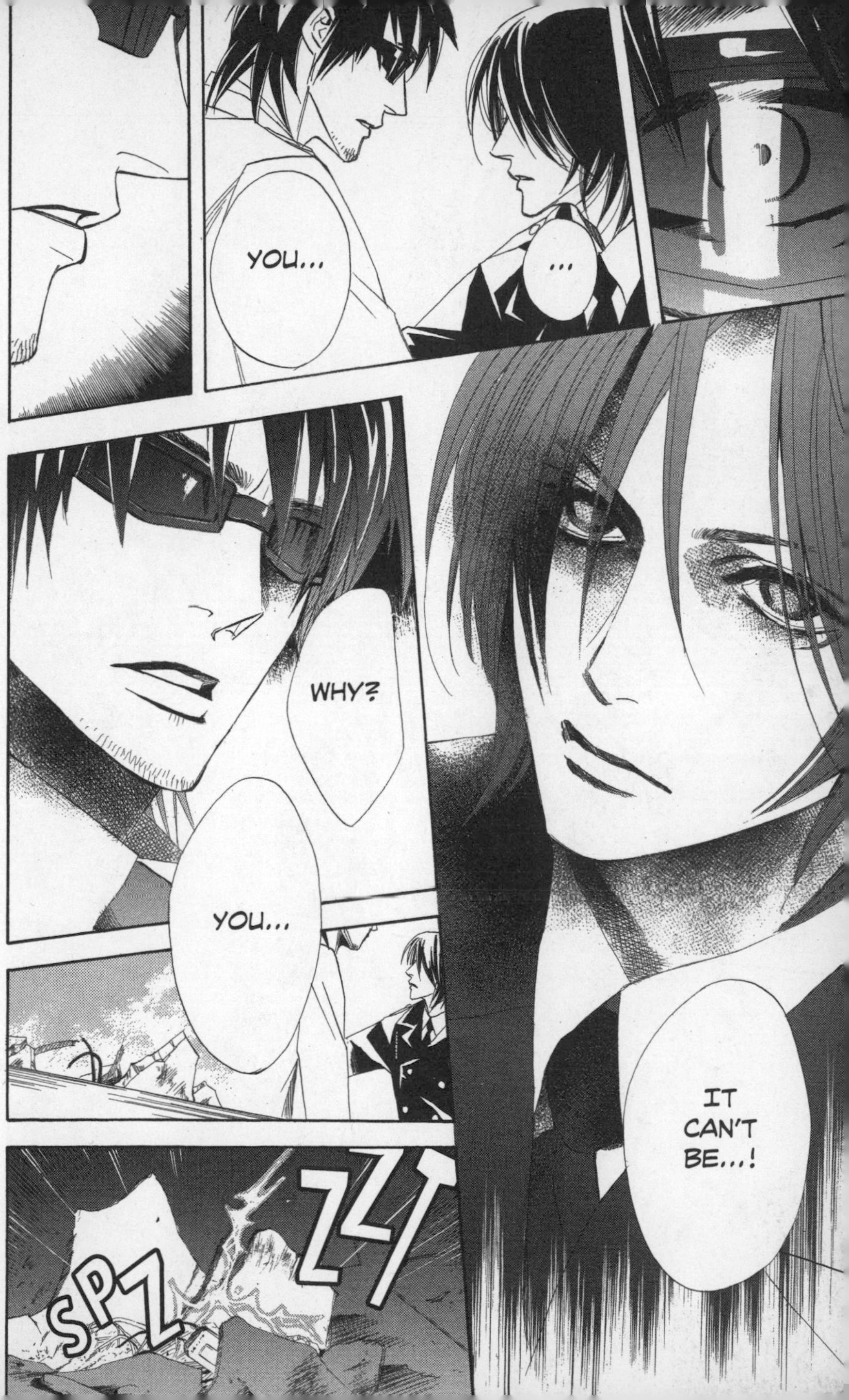
...
YOU...
IT CAN'T BE...!
WHY?
YOU...
ZZT
SPZ

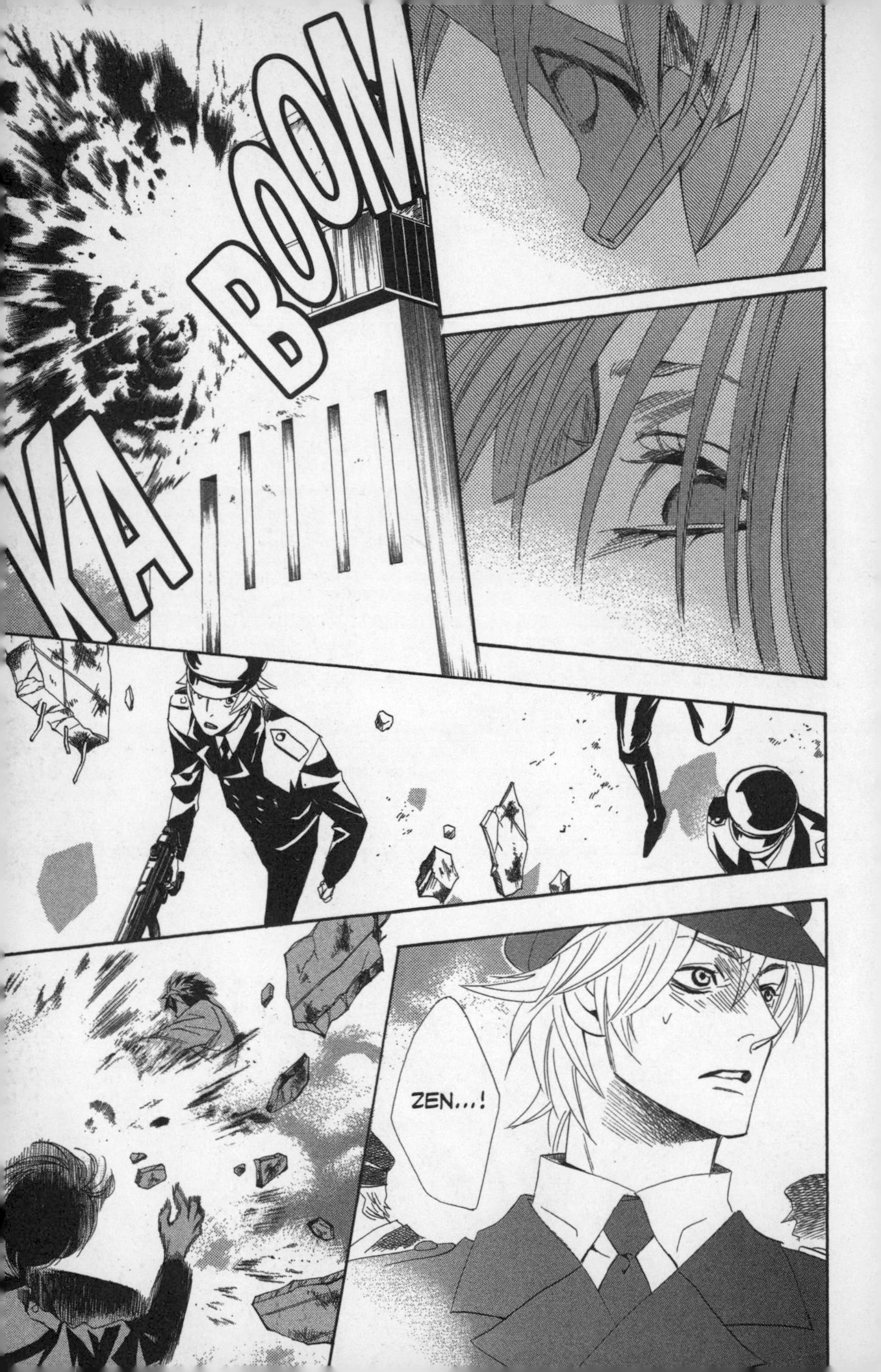
KA BOOM
ZEN...!

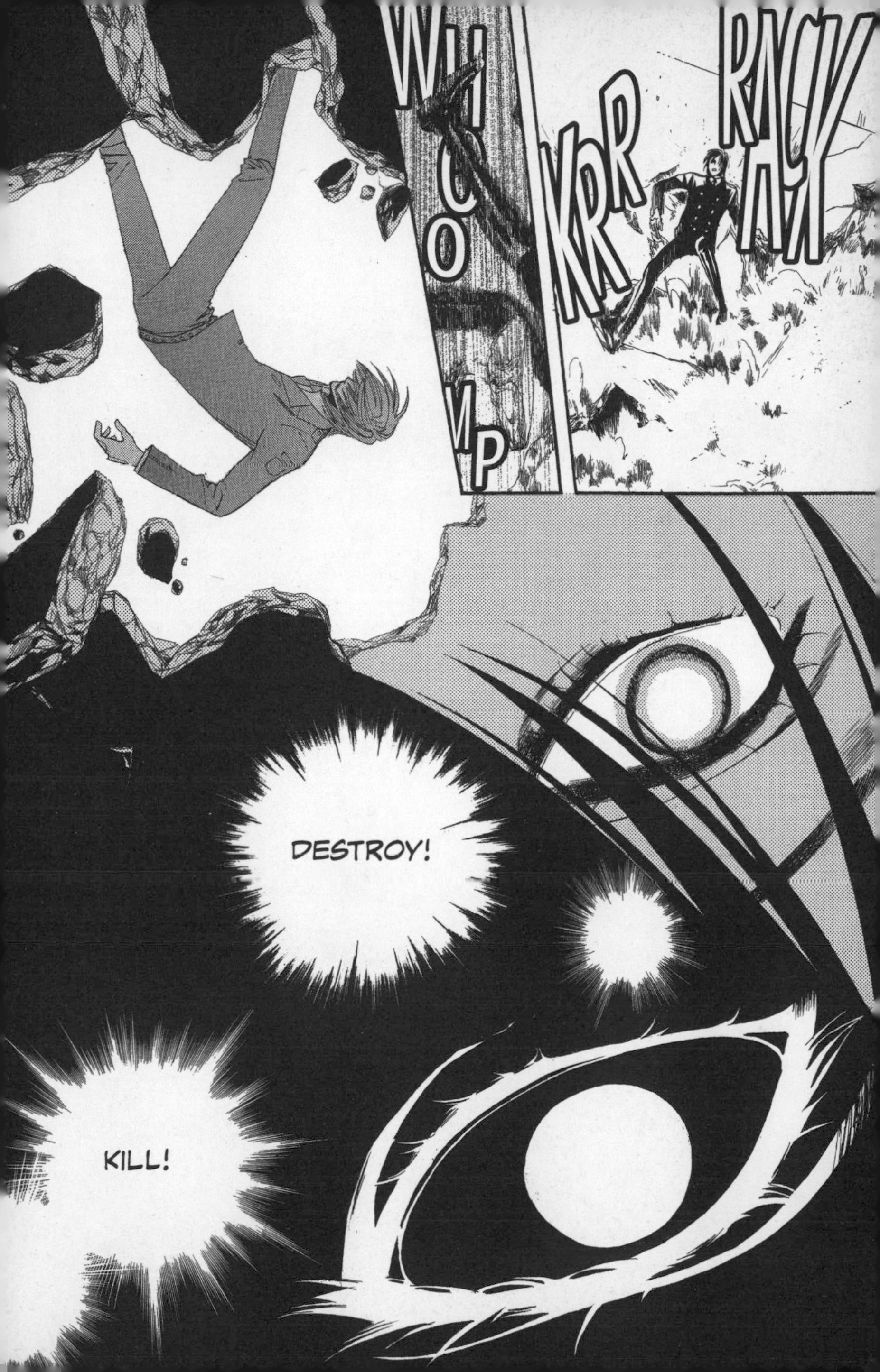
KRR
RACK
RACK
WHOOMP
DESTROY!
KILL!

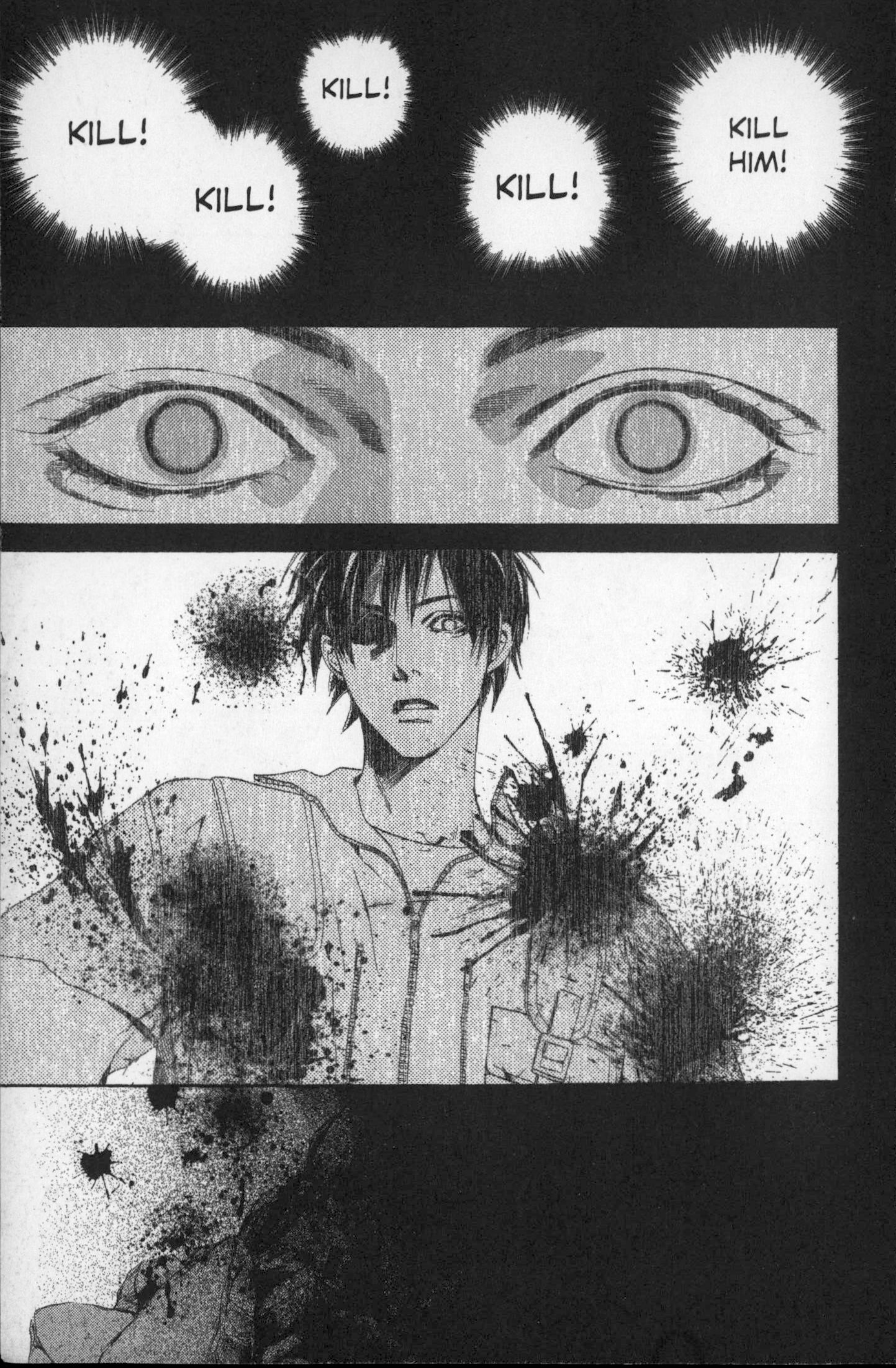
KILL HIM!
KILL!
KILL!
KILL!
KILL!

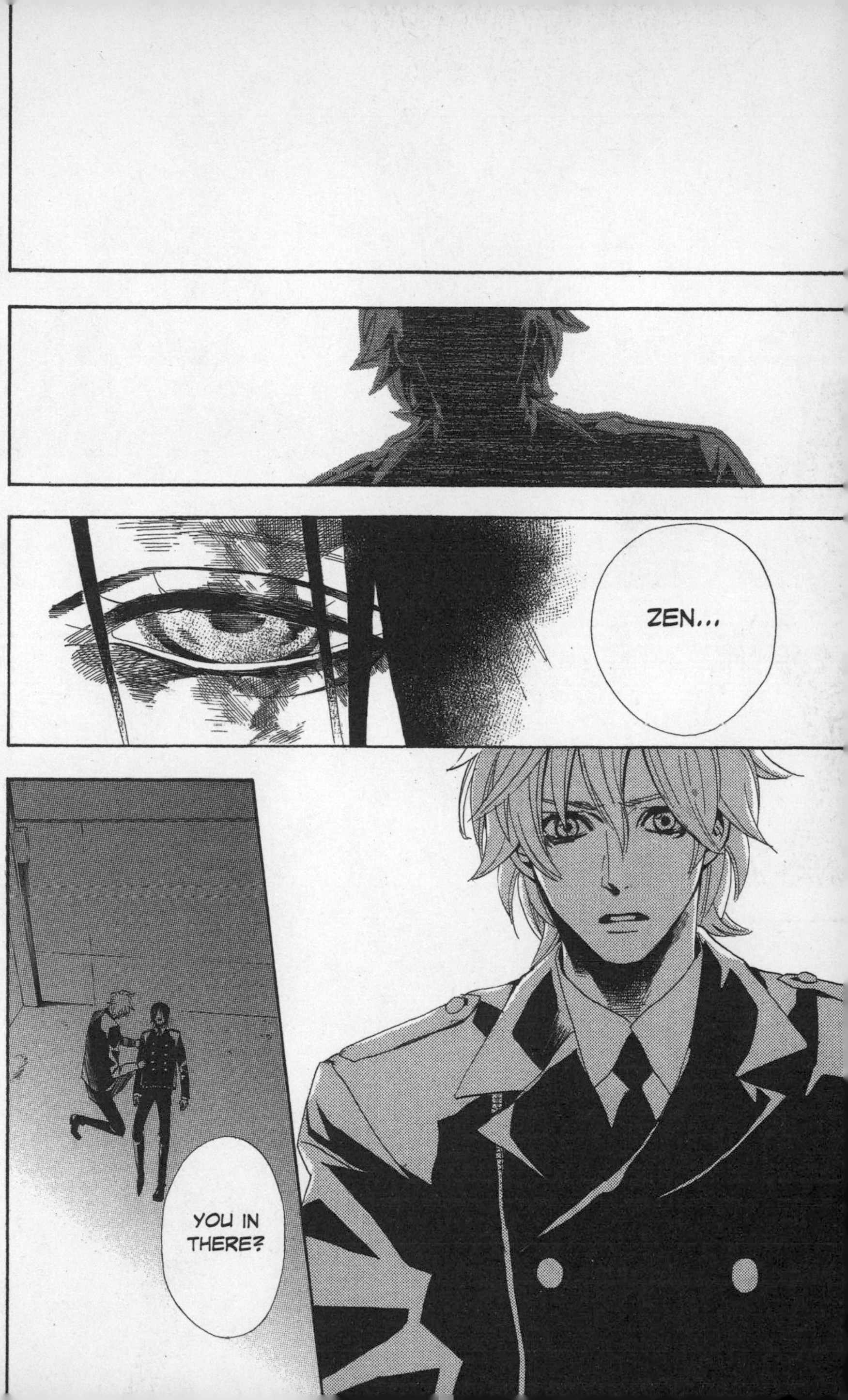
ZEN...
YOU IN THERE?

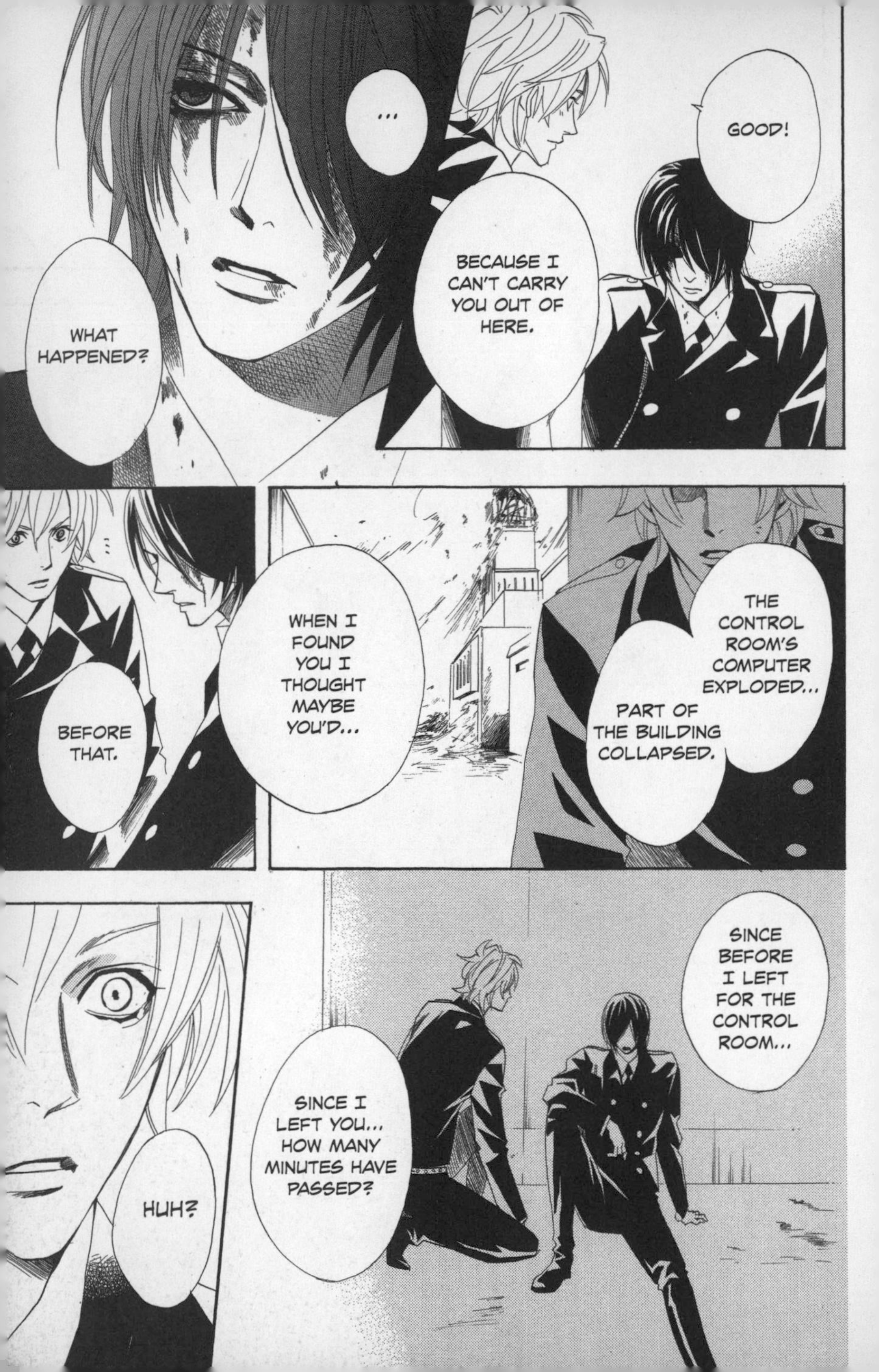
GOOD!
BECAUSE I CAN'T CARRY YOU OUT OF HERE.
...
WHAT HAPPENED?
THE CONTROL ROOM'S COMPUTER EXPLODED...
PART OF THE BUILDING COLLAPSED.
WHEN I FOUND YOU I THOUGHT MAYBE YOU'D...
BEFORE THAT.
SINCE BEFORE I LEFT FOR THE CONTROL ROOM...
SINCE I LEFT YOU... HOW MANY MINUTES HAVE PASSED?
HUH?

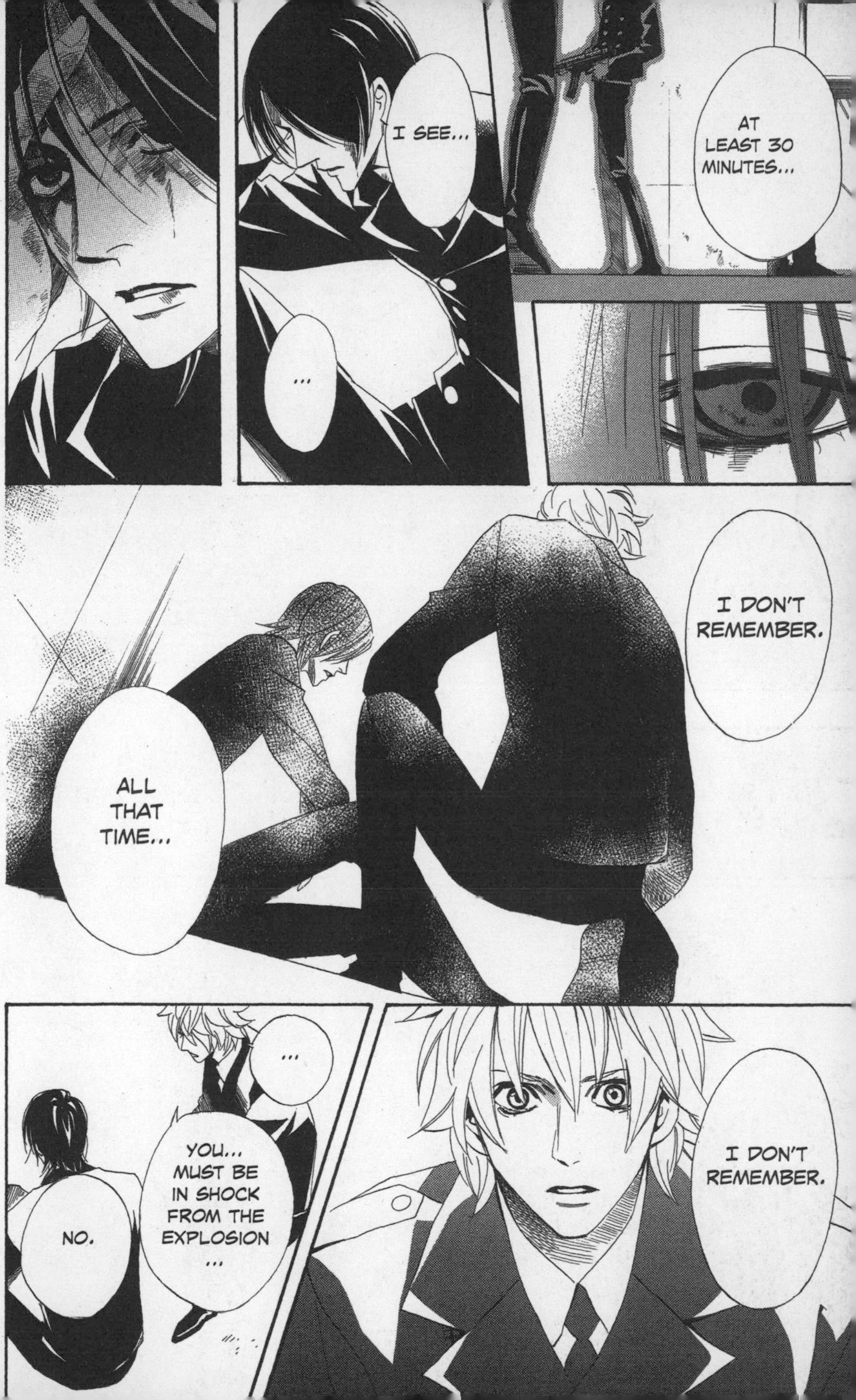
AT LEAST 30 MINUTES...
I SEE...
...
I DON'T REMEMBER.
ALL THAT TIME...
I DON'T REMEMBER.
...
YOU... MUST BE IN SHOCK FROM THE EXPLOSION ...
NO.

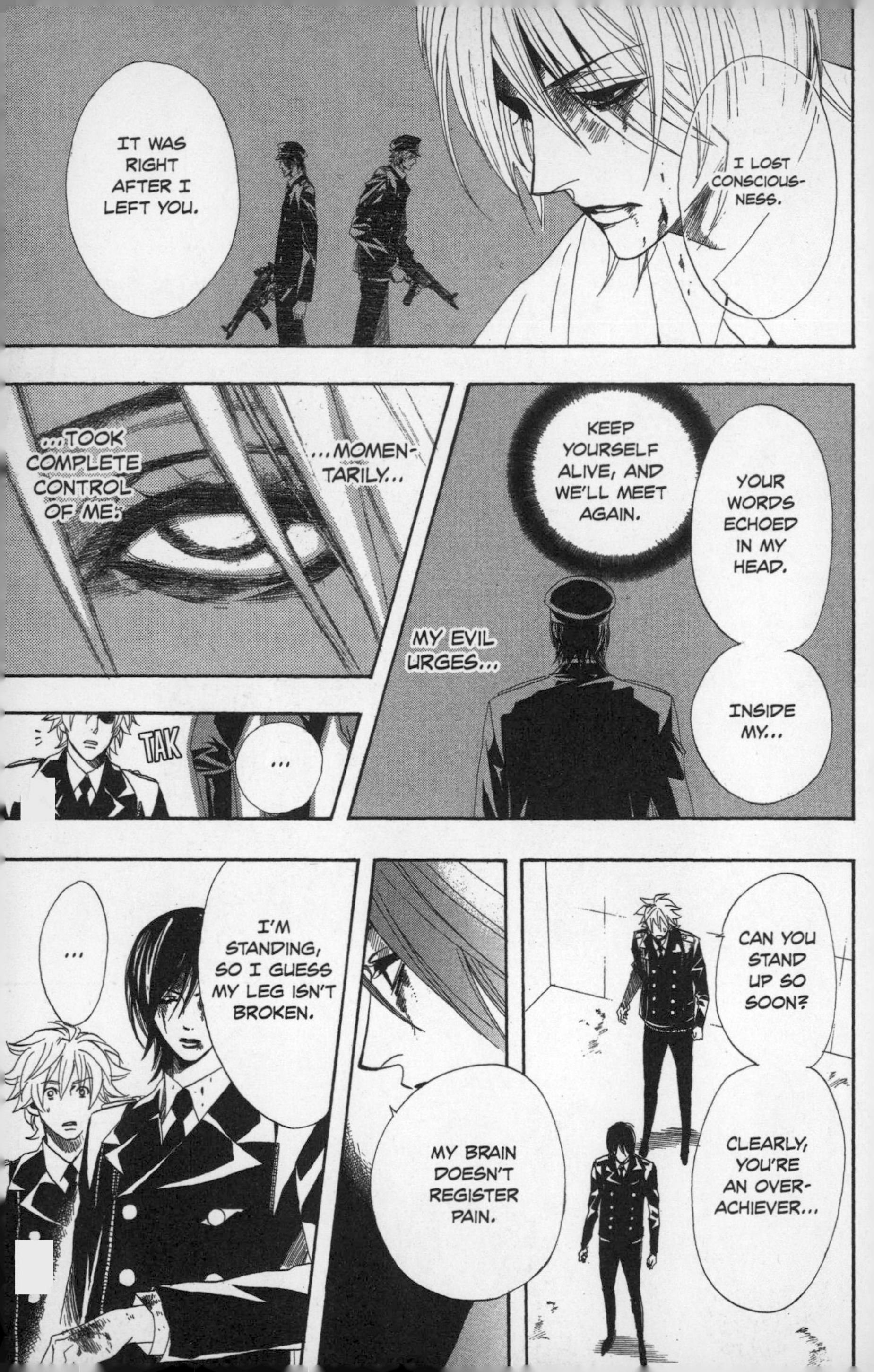
I LOST CONSCIOUS-NESS.
IT WAS RIGHT AFTER I LEFT YOU.
YOUR WORDS ECHOED IN MY HEAD.
INSIDE MY...
KEEP YOURSELF ALIVE, AND WE'LL MEET AGAIN.
MY EVIL URGES...
...MOMEN-TARILY...
...TOOK COMPLETE CONTROL OF ME.
TAK
...
CAN YOU STAND UP SO SOON?
CLEARLY, YOU'RE AN OVER-ACHIEVER...
MY BRAIN DOESN'T REGISTER PAIN.
I'M STANDING, SO I GUESS MY LEG ISN'T BROKEN.
...

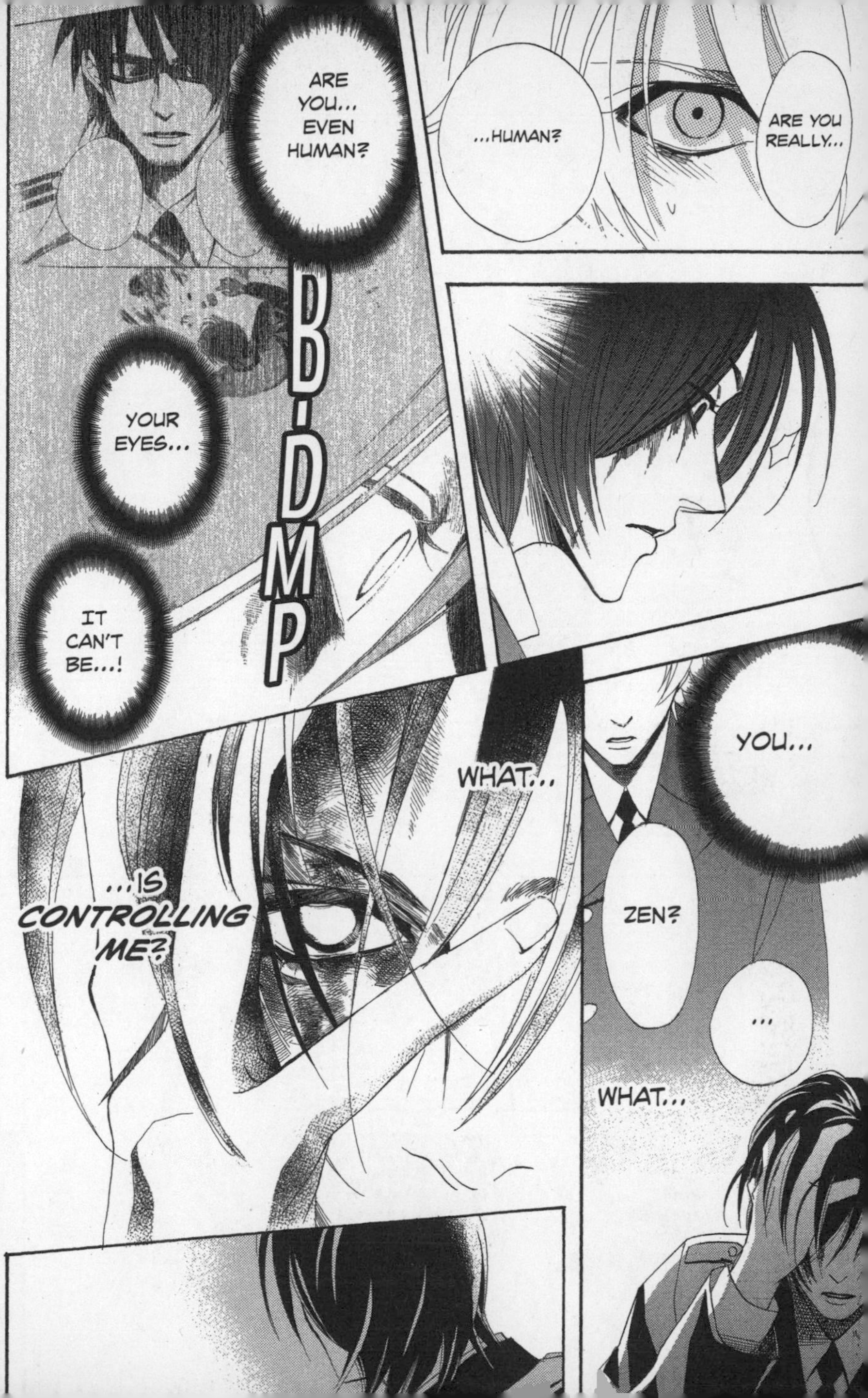
ARE YOU REALLY...
...HUMAN?
ARE YOU... EVEN HUMAN?
B-DMP
YOUR EYES...
IT CAN'T BE...!
YOU...
ZEN?
...
WHAT...
WHAT...
...IS CONTROLLING ME?

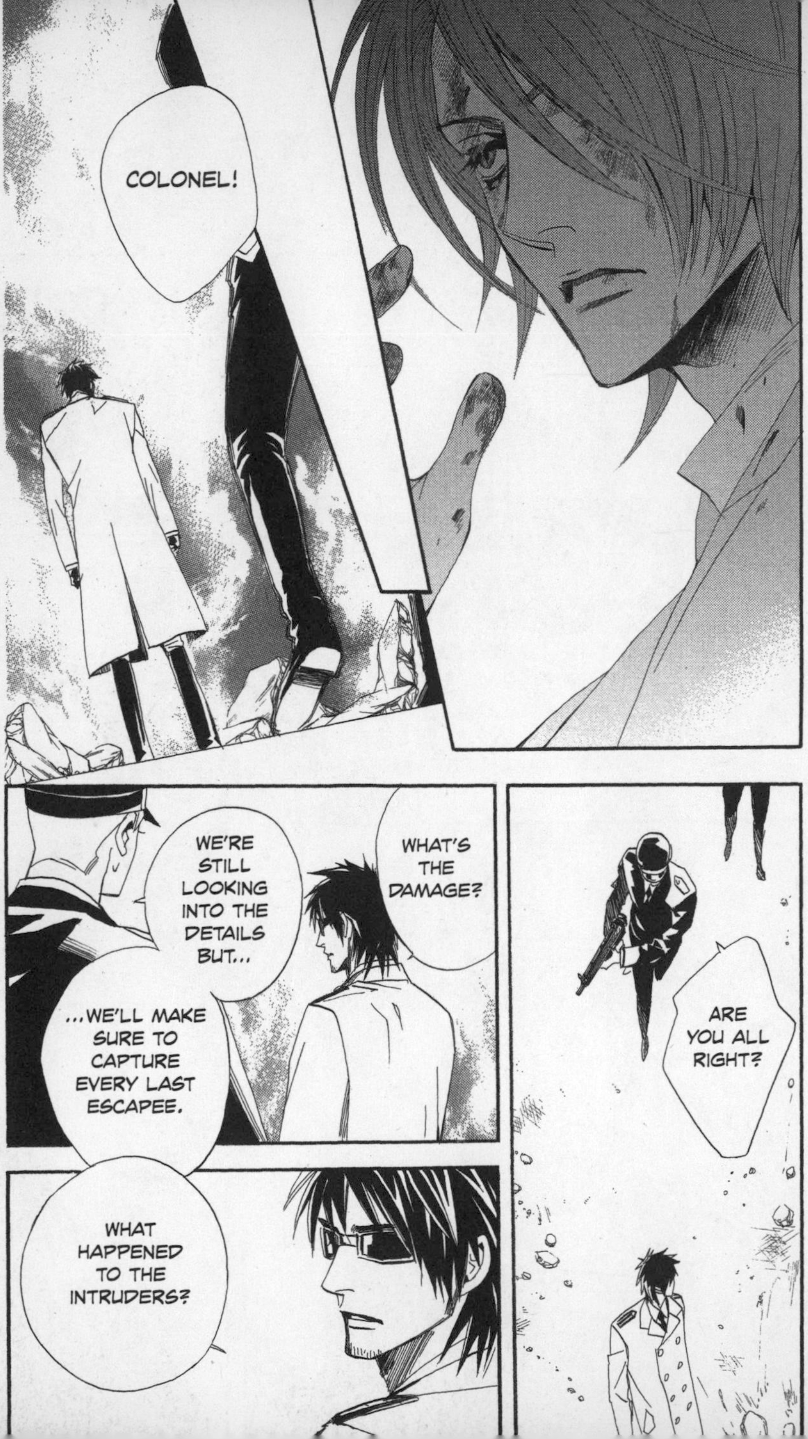
COLONEL!
ARE YOU ALL RIGHT?
WHAT'S THE DAMAGE?
WE'RE STILL LOOKING INTO THE DETAILS BUT...
...WE'LL MAKE SURE TO CAPTURE EVERY LAST ESCAPEE.
WHAT HAPPENED TO THE INTRUDERS?

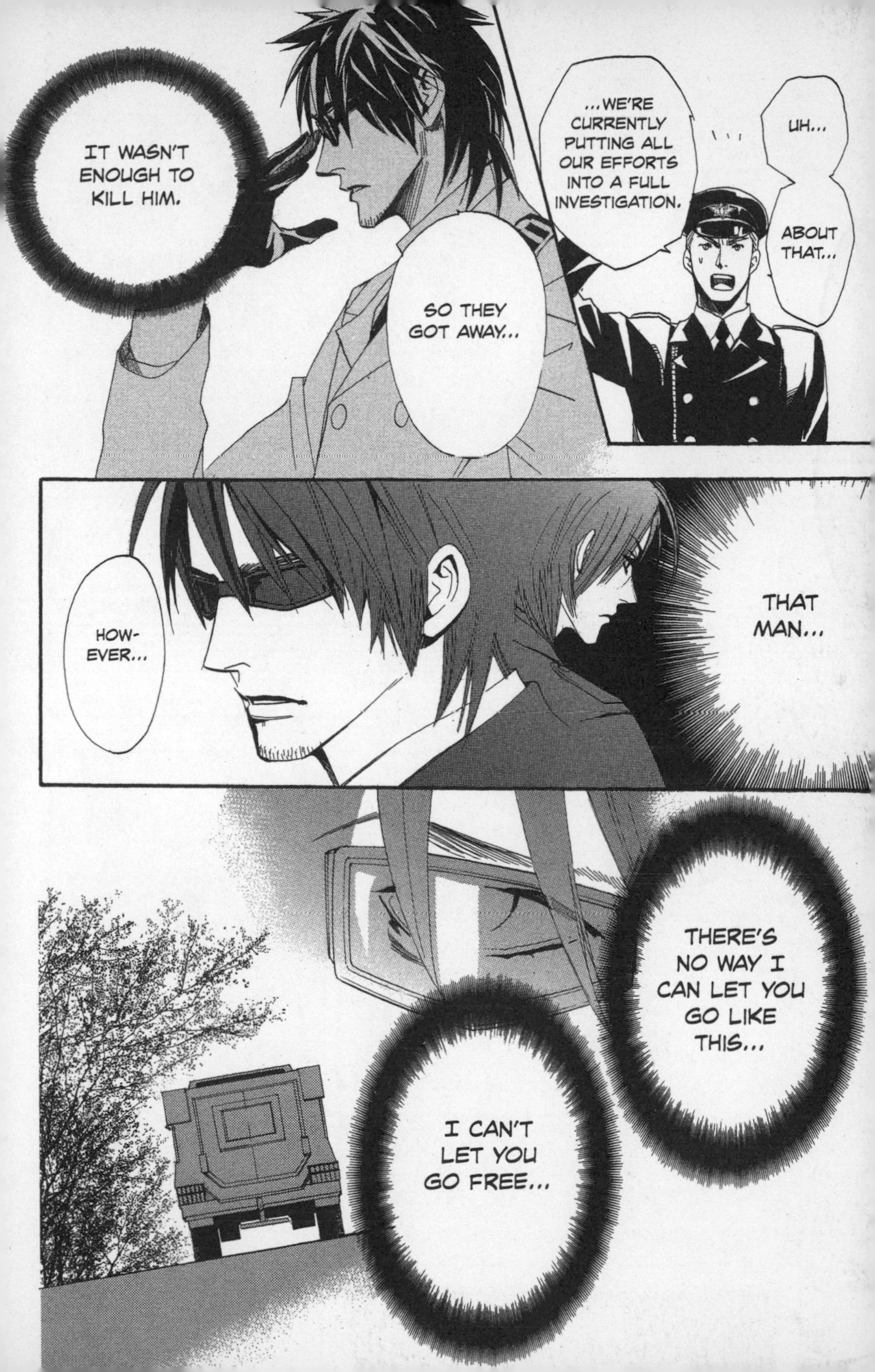
UH... ABOUT THAT...
...WE'RE CURRENTLY PUTTING ALL OUR EFFORTS INTO A FULL INVESTIGATION.
SO THEY GOT AWAY...
IT WASN'T ENOUGH TO KILL HIM.
THAT MAN...
HOW-EVER...
THERE'S NO WAY I CAN LET YOU GO LIKE THIS...
I CAN'T LET YOU GO FREE...

HM?

RATTLE

RATTLE

RATTLE

STOP. STOP.

...

AN INSPECTION?

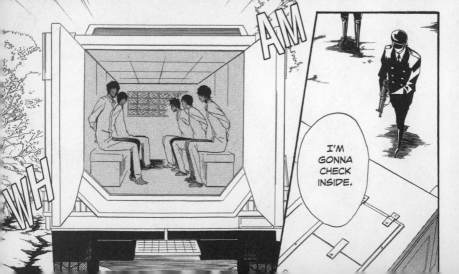

WH

AM

I'M GONNA CHECK INSIDE.

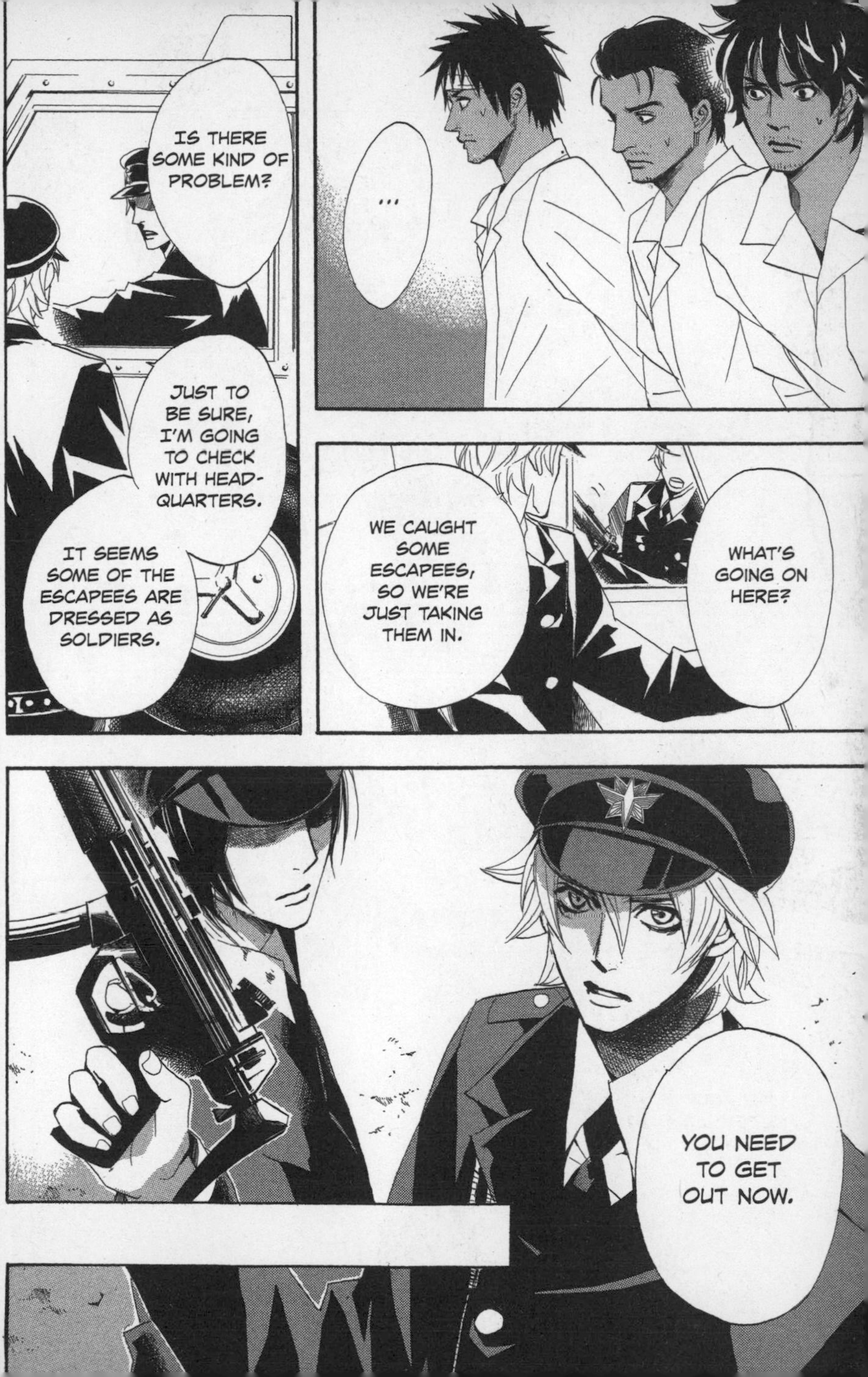
...
WHAT'S GOING ON HERE?
WE CAUGHT SOME ESCAPEES, SO WE'RE JUST TAKING THEM IN.
IS THERE SOME KIND OF PROBLEM?
JUST TO BE SURE, I'M GOING TO CHECK WITH HEAD-QUARTERS.
IT SEEMS SOME OF THE ESCAPEES ARE DRESSED AS SOLDIERS.
YOU NEED TO GET OUT NOW.

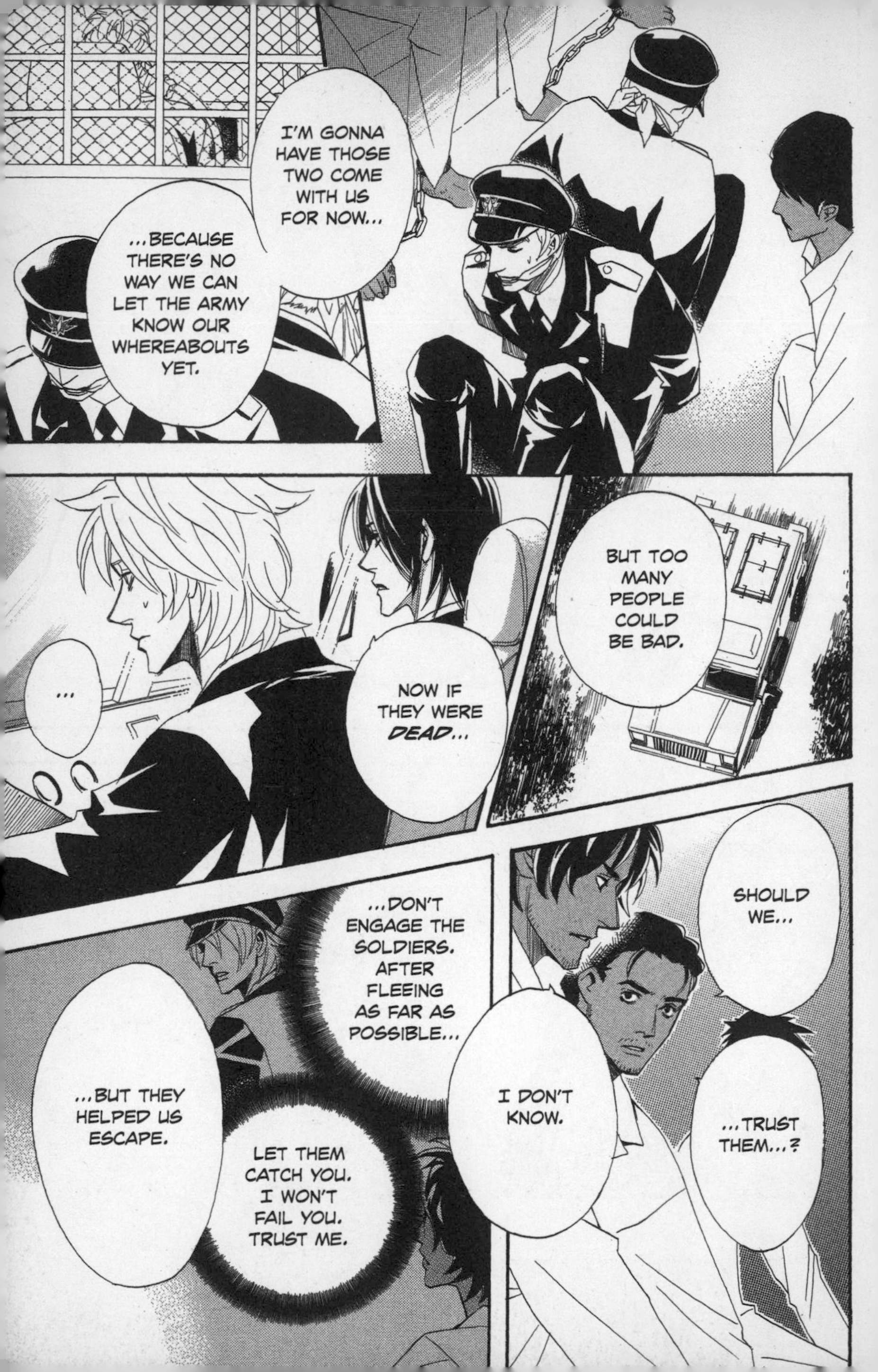
I'M GONNA HAVE THOSE TWO COME WITH US FOR NOW...
...BECAUSE THERE'S NO WAY WE CAN LET THE ARMY KNOW OUR WHEREABOUTS YET.
BUT TOO MANY PEOPLE COULD BE BAD.
NOW IF THEY WERE *DEAD*...
...
SHOULD WE...
...TRUST THEM...?
I DON'T KNOW.
...DON'T ENGAGE THE SOLDIERS. AFTER FLEEING AS FAR AS POSSIBLE...
LET THEM CATCH YOU. I WON'T FAIL YOU. TRUST ME.
...BUT THEY HELPED US ESCAPE.

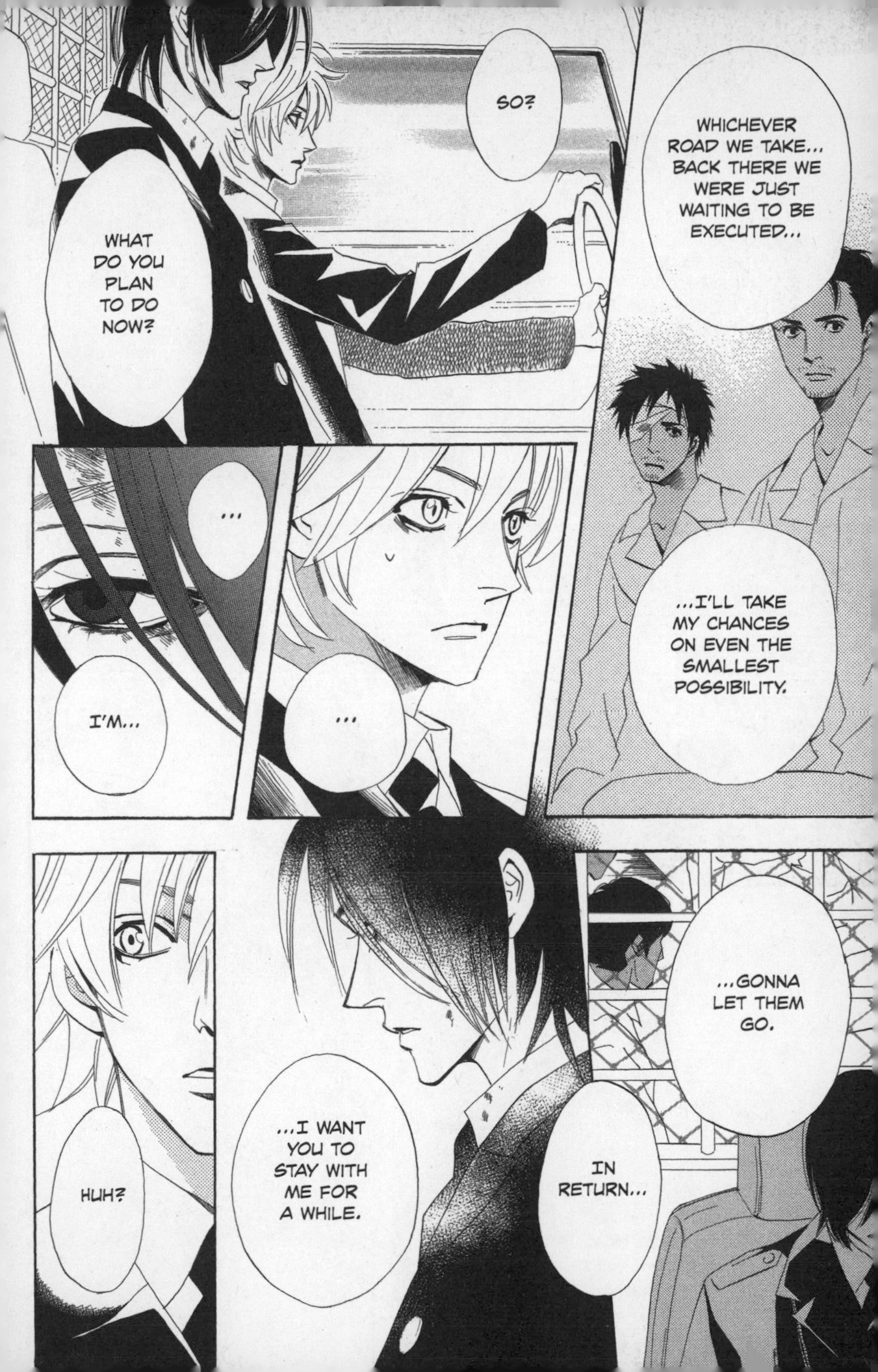
WHICHEVER ROAD WE TAKE... BACK THERE WE WERE JUST WAITING TO BE EXECUTED...
...I'LL TAKE MY CHANCES ON EVEN THE SMALLEST POSSIBILITY.
SO?
WHAT DO YOU PLAN TO DO NOW?
...
...
I'M...
...GONNA LET THEM GO.
IN RETURN...
...I WANT YOU TO STAY WITH ME FOR A WHILE.
HUH?

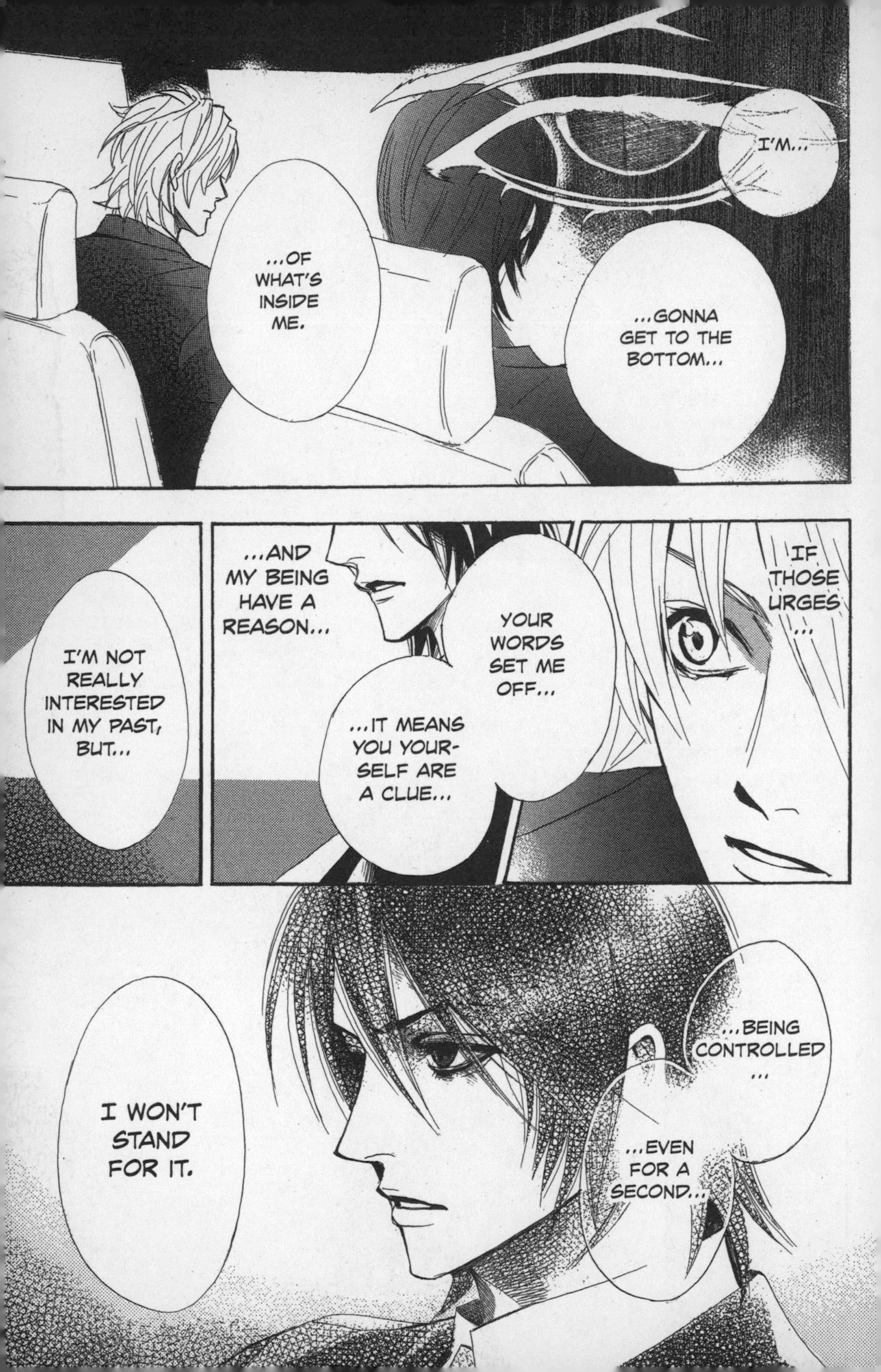
I'M...
...GONNA GET TO THE BOTTOM...
...OF WHAT'S INSIDE ME.
IF THOSE URGES...
YOUR WORDS SET ME OFF...
...AND MY BEING HAVE A REASON...
...IT MEANS YOU YOUR-SELF ARE A CLUE...
I'M NOT REALLY INTERESTED IN MY PAST, BUT...
...BEING CONTROLLED...
...EVEN FOR A SECOND...
I WON'T STAND FOR IT.

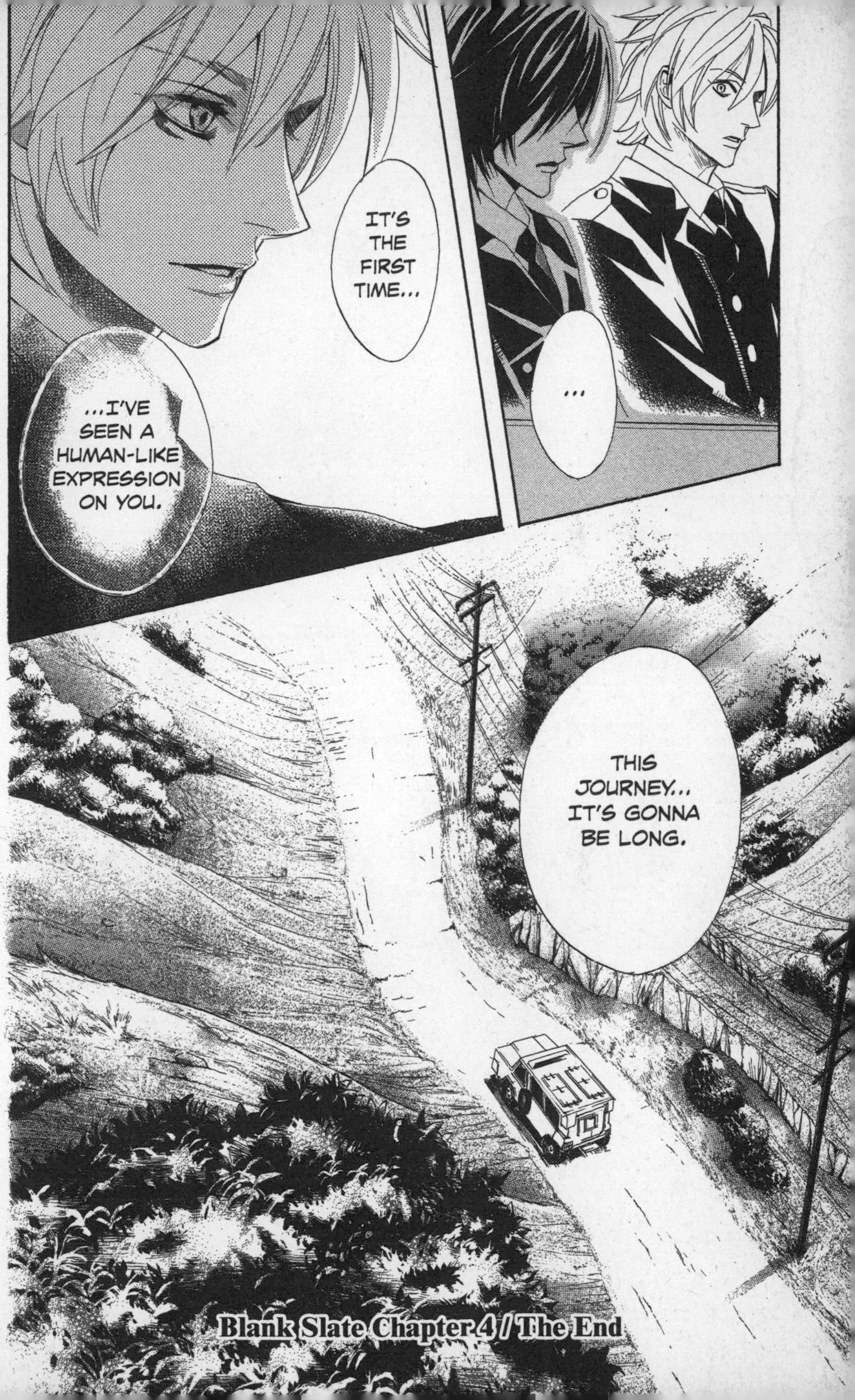
...
IT'S THE FIRST TIME...
...I'VE SEEN A HUMAN-LIKE EXPRESSION ON YOU.
THIS JOURNEY... IT'S GONNA BE LONG.
Blank Slate Chapter 4 / The End

Aya Kanno was born in Tokyo, Japan. She is the creator of *Soul Rescue*, which has been published in the United States, and her latest work, *Otomen*, is currently being serialized in Japan's *BetsuHana* magazine. *Blank Slate* was also originally published as *Akusaga* in Japan in *BetsuHana*.

BLANK SLATE, VOL. 1
The Shojo Beat Manga Edition

Story and Art by AYA KANNO

Translation/John Werry, HC Language Solutions, Inc.
English Adaptation/Carla Sinclair
Touch-up Art & Lettering/James Gaubatz
Design/Sam Elzway
Editor/Joel Enos

Editor in Chief, Books/Alvin Lu
Editor in Chief, Magazines/Marc Weidenbaum
VP of Publishing Licensing/Rika Inouye
VP of Sales/Gonzalo Ferreyra
Sr. VP of Marketing/Liza Coppola
Publisher/Hyoe Narita

Printed in Canada

Published by VIZ Media, LLC
P.O. Box 77010
San Francisco, CA 94107

Shojo Beat Manga Edition
10 9 8 7 6 5 4 3 2 1
First printing, October 2008

store.viz.com

www.viz.com